LXX-Isaiah as Translation and Interpretation

Supplements to the

Journal for the Study of Judaism

Editors

John J. Collins
The Divinity School, Yale University

Associate Editors

Florentino García Martínez
Qumran Institute, University of Groningen

Hindy Najman
Department of Near and Middle Eastern Civilizations
University of Toronto

Advisory Board

J. DUHAIME — A. HILHORST — P.W. VAN DER HORST

A. KLOSTERGAARD PETERSEN — M.A. KNIBB

J.T.A.G.M. VAN RUITEN — J. SIEVERS — G. STEMBERGER

E.J.C. TIGCHELAAR — J. TROMP

VOLUME 124

LXX-Isaiah as Translation and Interpretation

The Strategies of the Translator of the Septuagint of Isaiah

By

Ronald L. Troxel

BRILL

LEIDEN • BOSTON
2008

This book is printed on acid-free paper.

Library of Congress Cataloging-in-Publication Data

A C.I.P. record for this book is available from the Library of Congress

ISSN 1384-2161
ISBN 978 90 04 15394 3

© Copyright 2008 by Koninklijke Brill NV, Leiden, The Netherlands.
Koninklijke Brill NV incorporates the imprints Brill, Hotei Publishing,
IDC Publishers, Martinus Nijhoff Publishers and VSP.

PRINTED IN THE NETHERLANDS

For Jacki

CONTENTS

PREFACE

I might well have chosen as the subtitle for this book, "A Prolegomenon to Understanding the Translator of LXX-Isaiah,"[1] inasmuch as this monograph lays the foundation for a new view of the translator's work. However, with due apologies to Wellhausen, "prolegomenon" does not seem well suited for the title of a book the author wishes read. It reeks of preliminary steps that spur prospective readers to look elsewhere for a tome that gets to the heart of the matter.

This book gets to the heart of the matter, and I certainly want it read. The sketch of the translator of Isaiah promoted by many scholars over the past fifty years (that he deliberately infused his translation with the beliefs and issues of his day) is, I argue, based on undisciplined associations between unique phraseology in the book and significant events known from the second century B.C.E. In order to reevaluate this portrayal, however, we must consider how translation was conceived in the Hellenistic era, how ancient scholars (especially those in the Alexandrian Museum) studied and used revered texts, and how to determine if a distinctive Greek locution is based on a reading in the translator's *Vorlage* at variance with the one in the MT, or even whether we have sufficient evidence to draw a conclusion in every case. Only after we answer these fundamental questions will we have parameters within which to evaluate the translator's work.

Accordingly, the first two chapters will explore the study and writing of literature in the translator's Alexandrian milieu. After surveying the scholarship that stands behind the prevailing view that the Isaiah translator was captivated with "contemporizing" or "actualizing" the book of Isaiah as he rendered it into Greek, chapter one addresses the study and production of literature in the Museum of Alexandria. Chapter two seeks to situate the Jewish community in Alexandria, illuminate

---

[1] I am aware that the phrase "LXX-Isaiah" might well be regarded a barbarism, since "LXX" properly refers to the translation of the Torah executed in the early third century B.C.E., whereas subsequent translations of other "biblical" books simply imitated the style of the LXX. Nevertheless, I will use "LXX-Isaiah" as shorthand for this translation, given the longstanding and widespread custom of referring to all translations of works handed down with the Pentateuch as "the Septuagint." Similarly, I will use "LXX-Pentateuch," despite its redundancy.

how that community viewed the work of scholars in the Museum, and describe the practice of translation in the Hellenistic world.

After chapter three articulates an approach to reconstructing the translator's *Vorlage* in light of one's perception of his *Übersetzungsweise*, while simultaneously testing and refining that perception, chapter four assesses how the translator worked on the linguistic plane, beginning with an inquiry into how extensively Greek word order and syntax follow the Hebrew of his *Vorlage*. That exploration will also entail measuring to what degree the translator inserted (or omitted) conjunctions and particles or even reformulated clauses to create smoother syntax for his Greek-reading audience. The remainder of chapter four investigates his lexical choices, including Greek lexemes he employed frequently and for a variety of Hebrew words, on some occasions without apparent justification from his *Vorlage*.

Chapter five extends evaluation of the translator's *Übersetzungsweise* to the area of contextual interpretation, exploring his pattern of borrowings from elsewhere in the sacred literature of his community to interpret verses in Isaiah. It is in this discussion that the question of "contemporization"—in particular, *Erfüllungsinterpretation*—is taken up again, probing the origins of this notion in Seeligmann's work of the 1940's and subjecting subsequent use of that hypothesis to critical evaluation.

Chapter six probes two facets of the translation that should indicate whether the translator deliberately "contemporized" Isaiah's oracles. On the one hand, given that those who argue that he engaged in *Erfüllungsinterpretation* assume that he was an enthusiast of eschatology, we would expect eschatological terminology and ideology to permeate the translation. Concomitantly, we would expect that a translator who wished to "contemporize" Isaiah's prophecies would render ancient place names with toponyms current in his own day in order to permit his readers (and hearers) to identify the geography of Isaiah with the world they knew. The inquiries of chapter six disappoint both of those expectations.

Chapter seven explores motifs commonly identified as topoi through which the translator revealed the era in which he lived: the redescription of Israel's oppressors in Isaiah's oracles in terms of Seleucid rulers, particularly Antiochus IV Epiphanes, and the suppression of study and practice of Torah during Jerusalem's Hellenistic crisis of the early second century B.C.E. Examination of the relevant passages undermines these perceptions.

Using scattered and sometimes brief passages throughout the book to disconfirm the prevailing notion of deliberate "contemporization" is, however, insufficient to develop the observations about the translator's grammatical and contextual interpretations outlined in chapters four and five into a description of the translator's *Übersetzungsweise*. As a prelude to summarizing his approach to translation, chapter eight explores Isaiah 28 as a test case for an alternative description of the translator's approach to his task. Even though that sample chapter does not exhibit all the interpretative tacks described in chapters four and five, it provides evidence of how the translator proceeded within a large literary unit. In that light, and in light of observations drawn throughout the book, chapter nine offers a sketch of the translator as interpreter.

Study of LXX-Isaiah (or the Septuagint generally) was not what I had in mind when, in the fall of 1983, I began graduate study in the Department of Hebrew and Semitic Studies at the University of Wisconsin–Madison. And yet, that fall did not pass before my mentor (and now colleague), Michael V. Fox, introduced me to the perplexities of LXX-Isaiah. In fact, it was he who suggested the topic of my dissertation on the "Eschatology of the Septuagint of Isaiah." While I can no longer agree with salient tenets of that study, based as it was on the assumption that the Isaiah translator used the prophet's oracles as a cipher for the events of his own day, nevertheless Michael gave me the impetus for study of this topic and has continually encouraged me to continue this facet of my research. For his support I am, as always, profoundly grateful.

I have also benefited from interaction and discussions of the Septuagint (Isaiah, in particular) with colleagues and students. I am especially grateful for the cordial discussions and debates with Arie van der Kooij, as well as the enthusiasm for this project shared by Ross Wagner, who read early drafts of key chapters. Equally generous in providing feedback were Andy Teeter, of Notre Dame, and John J. Collins, editor of this series. Their observations and criticisms improved the manuscript at many points, although undoubtedly I have left enough faults for readers and reviewers to criticize. Hopefully what survives those tests will advance our understanding of this curious translation.

My greatest debt is owed to my family, whose ability to keep me grounded in real meanings in life makes my delight in this topic more of a fascination than an obsession. My sons, Ben and Bryan, have shown remarkable patience with a father whom they most frequently see engrossed in either reading or writing. Nevertheless, working on this project at home over two summers and on weekends during two academic years has kept me around these two fine young men, much to my delight and benefit.

By far my greatest debt and gratitude are due to my wife, Jacki, who has shown more support for my devotion to ancient languages and texts than I have a right to expect. My respect for her as a teacher, researcher, and writer has deepened over the years. Her influence on this book, while not traceable in retroversions or discussions of the translator's interpretative devices, is nonetheless palpable to me. Only a scholar's spouse knows what it is like to try to engage their mate in conversation when he or she is preoccupied by the latest leg of their argument. But also, only a scholar knows how much his or her mate has contributed to the character of their work. I dedicate this book to her with love and appreciation.

Ronald L. Troxel
May, 2007

ACKNOWLEDGEMENTS

I wish to thank Mary Lou Daniel, Professor Emerita of the Department of Spanish and Portuguese at the University of Wisconsin-Madison, for translating for my use two articles written in Catalan:

Raurell, Frederic. "«Archontes» en la interpretació midràshica d'Is-LXX." *RevCT* 1 (1976) 315–74.
———. "La «Doxa» com a Participació en la Vida Escatológica." *RevCT* 7 (1982) 57–89.

I am also grateful to the following editors and publishers for allowing me to use material that appeared originally in their journals and books.

The material on Isa 7:14–16 in chapters four and five was originally published as "Isaiah 7,14–16 through the Eyes of the Septuagint," *ETL* 79 (2003) 1–22.

Discussion of the phrase ἐν (ταῖς) ἐσχάταις ἡμέραις in LXX-Isaiah (chapter six) appeared in an earlier form as "Ἔσχατος and Eschatology in LXX-Isa," *BIOSCS* 25 (1992) 18–27.

The overview of the translator's handling of toponyms in chapter six appeared as "What's in a Name? Contemporization and the Rendering of Toponyms in LXX-Isa," in *Seeking Out the Wisdom of the Ancients*, edited by Ronald L Troxel, Kelvin Friebel and Dennis Magary (Winona Lake: Eisenbrauns, 2005) 327–44.

The discussion of "fiscal oppression" in chapter seven is excerpted and revised from my article, "Economic Plunder as a Leitmotif in LXX-Isaiah," *Bib* 83 (2002) 375–91.

ABBREVIATIONS

AB	The Anchor Bible
ABD	*The Anchor Bible Dictionary*
AJT	*American Journal of Theology*
AncW	*The Ancient World*
ASTI	*Annual of the Swedish Theological Institute*
ATR	*Australasian Theological Review*
BDAG	W. Bauer, F. W. Danker, W. F. Arndt, and F. W. Gingrich. *A Greek-English Lexicon of the New Testament and Other Early Christian Literature.* Third edition. Chicago: University of Chicago Press, 2000.
Bib	*Biblica*
BIOSCS	*Bulletin of the International Organization for Septuagint and Cognate Studies*
BO	*Bibliotheca orientalis*
CBQ	*Catholic Biblical Quarterly*
DJD	Discoveries in the Judaean Desert
DSD	*Dead Sea Discoveries*
DSS	Dead Sea Scrolls. Unless otherwise noted, citations are from Martínez, Florentino García, and Eibert J. C. Tigchelaar. *The Dead Sea Scrolls: Study Edition.* 2 vols. Grand Rapids: Wm. B. Eerdmans, 1997–1998.
ETL	*Ephemerides theologicae lovanienses*
GRBS	*Greek, Roman, and Byzantine Studies*
HTR	*Harvard Theological Review*
HUCA	*Hebrew Union College Annual*
ICC	International Critical Commentary
JBL	*Journal of Biblical Literature*
JEA	*Journal of Egyptian Archaeology*
JNES	*Journal of Near Eastern Studies*
JNSL	*Journal of Northwest Semitic Languages*
JSJ	*Journal for the Study of Judaism in the Persian, Hellenistic, and Roman Periods*
JSJSup	Supplements to the Journal for the Study of Judaism in the Persian, Hellenistic, and Roman Periods
JSOTSup	Journal for the Study of the Old Testament: Supplement Series
JTS	*Journal of Theological Studies*
KB	Koehler, Ludwig, Walter Baumgartner, and Johann Jakob Stamm. *The Hebrew and Aramaic Lexicon of the Old Testament.* 5 vols. Leiden: E. J. Brill, 1994–2000.
LSJ	Liddell, H. G., R. Scott, H. S. Jones. *A Greek-English Lexicon.* Ninth ed. with revised supplement. Oxford: Oxford University Press, 1996.
LXX	The "Septuagint," referring solely to works translated into Greek from Hebrew.
ms/mss	manuscript/manuscripts
MT	The Masoretic text as embodied in Leningrad Codex B19a, as reproduced in *Biblia Hebraica Stuttgartensia* (without vowels and *maqqeph*).
OG	Old Greek
OL	Old Latin
OtSt	*Oudtestamentische Studiën*
Payne-Smith	Payne-Smith, J. *A Compendious Syriac Dictionary.* Oxford: Clarendon Press, 1903.
RevCT	*Revista Catalana de Teologia*

RevQ	*Revue de Qumran*
S	The Peshiṭta. For Isaiah, citations are from Brock, S. P. *Isaiah. The Old Testament in Syriac*, part III, fascicle 1. Leiden: Brill, 1993.
SBLSP	*Society of Biblical Literature Seminar Papers*
SP	Samaritan Pentateuch
ST	*Studia theologica*
StPatr	Studia patristica
T	Targum. All citations are from Sperber, Alexander. *The Bible in Aramaic*. Three volumes. Leiden: Brill, 2004.
TWNT	*Theologische Wörterbuch zum Neuen Testament*
V	Vulgate. All citations are fromFischer, Bonifatio, et al. *Biblia Sacra Iuxta Vulgatam Versionem*. Two volumes. Stuttgart: Deutsche Bibelgesellschaft, 1983.
VT	*Vetus Testamentum*
VTSup	Supplements to Vetus Testamentum
ZAW	*Zeitschrift für die alttestamentliche Wissenschaft*
Ziegler, *Isaias*	Ziegler, Joseph. *Isaias*. Göttingen: Vandenhoeck and Ruprecht, 1983.

[ ] in verse references designates versification in Hebrew when different from the LXX.

|| separates Greek and Hebrew equivalents.

CHAPTER ONE

THE TRANSLATOR OF ISAIAH

A significant question for study of the Septuagint translation of Isaiah is, who was the translator?[1] Obviously, this is not a quest for a name but for an image of what kind of translator he was, how he approached his task. As Aejmelaeus observes, our estimation of how the translators "worked, what they aimed at, what was their attitude towards the text, what they were or were not capable of doing, etc." determines our view of their "translation style,"[2] on which rest our judgments about what their *Vorlage* read in specific cases. Such estimations typically arise from a dialectic between our assumptions of how we would proceed and evidence of how a translator went about rendering his *Vorlage* into Greek. Even if our image of the translator of Isaiah is disciplined, to some extent, by previous research into how he rendered his *Vorlage*,[3] we need a more precise way of answering the question of who he was by identifying, insofar as possible, "to which milieu or circles in ancient Judaism [the translator] belonged."[4]

A person of the ancient world capable of translating a text from Hebrew into Greek would have belonged to a relatively small circle, since the need to translate the text attests a widespread unfamiliarity with Hebrew. However, even granting that translators would have belonged to a small circle of educated people, we cannot assume that

---

[1] Arie van der Kooij posed this question for the Septuagint as a whole in his "Perspectives on the Study of the Septuagint: Who are the Translators?" in *Perspectives in the Study of the Old Testament and Early Judaism*, ed. Florentino García Martínez and Edward Noort (Leiden: Brill, 1998).

[2] Anneli Aejmelaeus, "Translation Technique and the Intention of the Translator," in *VII Congress of the International Organization for Septuagint and Cognate Studies* (Atlanta: Scholars Press, 1991) 24. She follows Soisalon-Soininen in rejecting the term "translation technique" (ibid., 35 n. 2). Cf. Barr's call for an "attempt to discover the method by which translators read Hebrew texts and decided on a rendering" (James Barr, "Common Sense and Biblical Language," *Bib* 49 [1968] 379).

[3] I share Seeligmann's conclusion that the "fundamental set-up" of the translation was the product of a single translator (I. L. Seeligmann, *The Septuagint Version of Isaiah* [Leuven: Brill, 1948] 42), although I also accept Hurwitz's argument that chapters 36–39 are to be attributed to a different translator (Marshall S. Hurwitz, "The Septuagint of Isaiah 36–39 in Relation to that of 1–35, 40–66," *HUCA* 28 [1957] 75–83).

[4] Van der Kooij, "Who are the Translators?" 217.

all translators fit one mold. Since the translations of Septuagintal books vary in their relationship to their *Vorlagen*, we must construct the translator's "profile" for each book. Naturally, the more literally a book is translated, the less we are able to say anything distinctive about its translator, since he rendered his *Vorlage* into Greek with little interference from his own ideas.

The Septuagint of Isaiah, however, offers a unique opportunity to construct a "professional profile" for its translator. As Ziegler observed, while other LXX books leave "die Person des Übers. völlig in den Hintergrund," LXX-Isaiah "ein ganz eigenartiges, individuelles Gepräge trägt."[5] Accordingly, "um das Verhältnis der Js-LXX zum MT recht zu würdigen, muß zunächst die ganze Persönlichkeit des Übers. vor uns erstehen."[6] By "Persönlichkeit" Ziegler has in mind the translator's idiosyncratic approach that conveys a palpability of the person that, while not permitting access to his psychology, offers an opportunity to gauge something of how he undertook his task.[7] It is the peculiar way that this translator works—investing Isaiah's oracles with meanings that cannot always be justified linguistically from his source text—that urges the question of who he was. It is not enough to call him a translator, because he seems to have gone beyond simply offering a translation.

Arie van der Kooij locates the LXX translators "in circles where the text of these 'biblical' books was read and studied, that is in *scribal* circles."[8] Of course, this begs the question of precisely in what sense translators were scribes, since "scribe" typically denotes copyists and editors rather than translators, while those authors of works who identify themselves as scribes to one degree or another (e.g., Ben Sira and the evangelist of the Gospel of Matthew)[9] exhibit different models of scribal

---

[5] Joseph Ziegler, *Untersuchungen zur Septuaginta des Buches Isaias* (Münster: Aschendorffschen Verlagsbuchhandlung, 1934) 7.

[6] Ibid.

[7] On the problems of circular reasoning this presents, see Anneli Aejmelaeus, "What Can We Know about the Hebrew *Vorlage* of the Septuagint?" *ZAW* 99 (1987) 58–89.

[8] Van der Kooij, "Who are the Translators?" 219, italics his. He identifies the translator as "ein Schriftgelehrter" as early as his *Die alten Textzeugen des Jesajabuches* (Orbis Biblicus et Orientalis 35; Göttingen: Vandenhoeck und Ruprecht, 1981) 63. For a more recent and fuller discussion of what he means by this, see his *The Oracle of Tyre: The Septuagint of Isaiah 23 as Version and Vision* (Leiden: Brill, 1998) 112–23.

[9] For the discussions of these "scribal" authors, see P. C. Beentjes, "Scripture and Scribe: Ben Sira 38:34c–39:11," in *Unless Some One Guide Me*, ed. J. W. Dyk (Maastricht: Shaker, 2001); Jan Liesen, *Full of Praise: An Exegetical Study of Sir 3,12–35* (JSJSup 64; Leiden: Brill, 2000); Krister Stendahl, *The School of St. Matthew*, 2nd ed. (Philadelphia: Fortress Press, 1968; reprint, Sigler Press, 1991); and David E. Orton, *The Understanding Scribe: Matthew and the Apocalyptic Ideal* (London and New York: T&T Clark, 1989).

authorship. Moreover, the Isaiah translator's interpretation of his *Vorlage* cannot be considered apart from the question of how he went about the task of translation, a unique type of literary project.

Van der Kooij's inference that the translator was a scribe relies especially on 33:18, where ספר is rendered by οἱ γραμματικοί, the only occurrence of this term in the LXX. Elsewhere, LXX-Isaiah employs γραμματεύς for ספר,[10] which is also the most common equivalence throughout the LXX (45x). This anomaly suggests to van der Kooij that the translator identified himself as a γραμματικός, rather than a simple γραμματεύς, since "als γραμματικός galt im damaligen Alexandrien jemand, der philologischen Fragen nachging, und sich vor allem mit Etymologie, dem Lesen und Interpretieren von Literatur, allem voran poetischen Texten, beschäftige."[11]

Most important, for van der Kooij, is that the translator's understanding of his role as a γραμματικός entailed understanding himself as an interpreter of prophecy, construed not merely as words spoken by a figure of the past but as forecasts that applied to the translator's day. For van der Kooij, the translator took on the mantle of a scholar tutoring the reader of an ancient text,[12] interpreting prophecies in the mode of *Erfüllungsinterpretation*, after the manner of the scribe extolled in Sir 39:1.[13] Accordingly, one must explore

> whether [a] passage does not only constitute, as a translation, a transformation from the linguistic point of view, but also a transformation in the sense of a reinterpretation of the temporal application of an ancient prophecy....did the translator aim at producing a version of an ancient prophecy which would make sense as an oracle at his time?[14]

In advocating this image of the Isaiah translator, van der Kooij propounds a conception of him that has become commonplace over the past half century. Jennifer Dines accurately epitomizes the prevailing view that this translator "rendered a text closely resembling the MT, but with considerable freedom," investing it with "some historical updating

---

[10] Most notably, γραμματεύς is the translation equivalent for הסופר in 36:3, 22 and 37:2.

[11] Van der Kooij, *Die alten Textzeugen*, 63.

[12] Arie van der Kooij, "The Old Greek of Isaiah in Relation to the Qumran Texts of Isaiah: Some General Comments," in *Septuagint, Scrolls and Cognate Writings*, ed. George J. Brook and Barnabas Lindars (Septuagint and Cognate Studies 33; Atlanta: Scholars Press, 1992) 208.

[13] Van der Kooij, *Die alten Textzeugen*, 62.

[14] Van der Kooij, *The Oracle of Tyre*, 18 (cf. 96).

in places, presumably to show the translator's own generation that the prophecies apply to them."[15] Behind this summary lies a substantial body of research.[16]

"Contemporizing" Interpretation

The categorization of LXX-Isaiah among the "freer" translations in the LXX has been staked out against earlier estimations. Scholz took the position that "der Verfasser folgt im Wesentlichen seinem Originale von Wort zu Wort."[17] Although he allowed that in some passages "eine solche Verschiendenheit vorliegt, dass sich fast nicht mehr feststellen lässt, was das Ursprüngliche gewesen sein möchte,"[18] he confidently asserted that "dem Uebersetzer lag ein Exemplar für sein Unternehmen vor,...das alle Verschiedenheiten, die uns seine Arbeit vorführt, bis auf jene, welche ihrer Natur nach Sache des Uebersetezers sein müssen, bereits enthielt."[19]

1902 saw the publication of three studies that hewed to Scholz's thesis with varying nuances. Swete's judgment that the translator's willingness to sacrifice Greek idiom so as to render his *Vorlage* accurately left "entire sentences...unintelligible" assumes a very literal manner of translation.[20] Ernst Liebmann, in exploring chapters 24–27, maintained that one can depend on the LXX to reflect its *Vorlage* "bezüglich der Wortstellung, der Person beim Verbum und mit der nötigen Einschränkung auch bezüglich der Zusätze."[21] However, in a subsequent issue of the same journal that published Liebmann's article, Alfred Zillesen examined passages in Isaiah 40–66 where "die Bereicherungen und Abweichungen

---

[15] Jennifer M. Dines, *The Septuagint*, (Understanding the Bible and its World; London and New York: T & T Clark, 2004) 22.

[16] I will review only studies that make observations about the translation, bypassing articles devoted to particular pericopae. My goal is to provide a picture of the trends in research that led to the consensus Dines summarizes.

[17] Anton Scholz, *Die alexandrinische Übersetzung des Buches Jesaias* (Würzburg: L. Woerl, 1880) 14.

[18] Ibid. He included in his lists a collection of examples he labeled, "Bis zur Unerkennbarkeit des Ursprünglichen verschiedener Text" (ibid., 44–45).

[19] Ibid., 21.

[20] Henry B. Swete, *An Introduction to the Old Testament in Greek* (New York: KTAV, 1968; reprint, 1902 edition) 324. Swete concludes that "the Psalms and more especially the book of Isaiah shew obvious signs of incompetence" (ibid., 316).

[21] Ernst Liebmann, "Der Text zu Jesaja 24–27," *ZAW* 22 (1902) 45.

des G lediglich auf Beeinflussung durch Parallelstellen beruhen," so that "in diesen Fällen G kaum zur Correctur des hebräischen Textes herangezogen werden darf."[22] In such instances one must reckon with the translator contributing to the translation's differences with the MT.

Similarly, two years later, Richard Ottley concluded that Scholz's lists of differences with the MT, although valuable in their own right, actually pointed towards the translator's *Vorlage* "very closely resembling the M.T."[23] In contrast to Liebmann, Ottley inferred from his study of Scholz's lists that agreement between the OG and the MT in matters of "number, person, and case, insertion or omission of pronouns and particles, exchange of pronouns and nouns, and instances where the letters ' and ן are concerned....is not to be expected in the Book of Isaiah."[24] In his view, differences with the MT are due primarily to misreading, an illegible *Vorlage*, or an inadequate knowledge of Hebrew,[25] and he concluded that the translator rather frequently lost his way or resorted to guessing, in such a manner that "the root-ideas of the words are retained, but their grammatical functions are ignored."[26] He judged the translator's deliberate expansions of the text to be limited to the insertion of "a word or two...to complete the supposed sense, or define it," while at other times "a misreading of the Hebrew is developed further."[27] Like Zillessen, Ottley noted that occasionally "words...were inserted from other chapters, when the memory of something similar prompted the writer," who was also sometimes influenced by "a reminiscence of other [biblical] books."[28]

In 1927 Franz Wutz introduced his hypothesis that the Septuagintal translators worked from a Greek transcription of a text much like the MT, and deviations from it are attributable to misreading by the translators.[29] However, Johann Fischer disputed Wutz's "transcription theory," arguing that the LXX's *Vorlage* was composed in Aramaic and that divergences

---

[22] Alfred Zillessen, "Bermerkungen zur alexandrinischen Übersetzung des Jesaja (c. 40–66)," *ZAW* 22 (1902) 240.

[23] Richard R. Ottley, *The Book of Isaiah According to the Septuagint*, 2 vols. (Cambridge: Cambridge University, 1904–06) 1:51.

[24] Ibid., 1:49.

[25] Ibid., 1:50.

[26] Ibid.

[27] Ibid., 1:46.

[28] Ibid., 1:47.

[29] Franz Wutz, *Die Transkriptionen von der Septuaginta bis zu Hieronymus* (Texte und Untersuchungen zur vormasoretischen Grammatik des Hebräischen; Stuttgart: W. Kohlhammer, 1927).

from it were not due to misreading, but rather the translator "mit seinem Texte ziemlich frei verfahren ist."[30] Indeed, the translator's goal
"ist vorzüglich daraufgerichtet, den Sinn zum Ausdruck zu bringen,"
for which he resorted to reformulation when faced with difficulties.[31] In
such cases, as Ottley had concluded, the translator conformed details
of person, number, and suffixes to the context.[32]

In 1934, LXX-Isaiah's character was evaluated still more rigorously
by Joseph Ziegler. He agreed with those who rejected the image of a
translator slavishly following his *Vorlage*, conceding that "dieser [Über-
setzer] hat eine ausgesprochene Neigung zu erklären and zu para-
phrasieren."[33] However, he challenged the assumption that differences
were the translator's own creations, asserting that "bereits in seiner
Vorlage können ganz gut manche Varianten und erklärende Glossen
gestanden haben, die er für seine Wiedergabe benützt hat."[34] Pointing
particularly to the Hebrew fragments of Ben Sira (especially codex B),
where "zahlreiche Varianten und erklärende Glossen stehen," including references to parallel biblical passages, Ziegler contended that this
"läßt die Möglichkeit von glossierten hebr. Hss als LXX-Vorlagen nicht
unwahrscheinlich erscheinen."[35] Accordingly, while Ziegler devoted
space to the minuses and pluses of LXX-Isaiah (pp. 31–45 and 46–55,
respectively), as well as a chapter on "die Bilder und Vergleiche in
der Js- LXX" (pp. 80–102), the heart of his study was an exposition
of connections between distinctive renderings in LXX-Isaiah and other
scriptural passages (pp. 103–33), as well as evidence of "gegenseitige
Beeinflussung sinnverwandter Stellen in der Js-LXX" (pp. 134–74).
Accordingly, for Ziegler LXX-Isaiah constitutes a witness to a *written*
tradition of interpretation of the book of Isaiah via comparison with
other scriptural passages.[36]

When Seeligmann's study of LXX-Isaiah appeared in 1948—revisit-
ing all the fundamental questions about the transmission of the text,

---

[30] Johann Fischer, *In welcher Schrift lag das Buch Isaias den LXX vor?* (Giessen: Alfred Töpelmann, 1930) 8.
[31] Ibid., 8–9.
[32] Ibid., 9.
[33] Ziegler, *Untersuchungen*, 4.
[34] Ibid.
[35] Ibid., 4–5.
[36] Additionally, Ziegler's catalog of terminology that betrays the translation's "alexandrinisch-ägyptische Hintergrund" (ibid., 175–212) is of great importance for consideration of what we mean by the translator "contemporizing" Isaiah as he renders it into Greek.

the number of translators involved, and the translator's technique—he also acknowledged the influence on the translator from other scriptural passages, although he justifiably criticized Ziegler as "too generous in assuming glossae and quotations...which the translator had before him."[37] He also cited evidence that the translator was familiar with the Greek translations of biblical books outside the Torah.[38]

However, Seeligmann expanded the question of perceptible influences on the translation of Isaiah to include traditions from the translator's religious community. Besides literal translations of passages from the Torah, there are also allusions to scriptural passages that have more the character of *reminiscences*,[39] suggesting that the translator stood under "the influence of the traditional exegesis of the Synagogue and of the Pentateuch."[40] Moreover, his renderings draw on the common "religious terminology in Hellenistic Jewry,"[41] including liturgical formulations.[42] So much, in Seeligmann's view, does the translator's work breathe "the atmosphere of the synagogue and religious teaching in Alexandria"[43] that he devotes his final chapter to "The Translation as a Document of Jewish-Alexandrian Theology." Even though earlier Seeligmann spoke of the translator's "inclination to an independent interpretation of the text,"[44] it becomes clear in his final chapter that he did not consider that an *idiosyncratic* interpretation, but one guided by the beliefs of his community.[45]

---

[37] Seeligmann, *Septuagint Version*, 7.

[38] Ibid., 70–76. Seeligmann recognizes the unevenness in the translation that led both Gray (George Buchanan Gray, "The Greek Version of Isaiah, Is It the Work of a Single Translator?" *JTS* 12 [1911] 20–31) and Baumgärtel (Friedrich Baumgärtel, "Die Septuaginta zu Jesaja das Werk zweier Übersetzer," in *Beiträge zur Entstehungsgeschichte der Septuaginta*, ed. Johannes Hermann and Friedrich Baumgärtel [Berlin: W. Kohlhammer, 1923]) to posit that lxx-Isaiah was produced by multiple translators, but concludes that "the great majority of such inconsistencies...must be imputed to the translator's unconstrained and carefree working method" (ibid., 41), coupled with the recognition of "a unity of, at any rate, the foundational set-up of the translation" (ibid., 42).

[39] Ibid., 47–48.

[40] Ibid., 49.

[41] Ibid., 44.

[42] Ibid., 101–03.

[43] Ibid., 47.

[44] Ibid., 56. Compare his earlier statement that while the translation "evinces [a]...marked influence from the surrounding cultural atmosphere," it also represents "the author's personal views" (ibid., 4). Similarly, he later surmises that "the translator...must have woven his own suggestions and images into his interpretation" (ibid., 58).

[45] Notice especially Seeligmann's observation at the outset of the chapter, that "in order...to be in a position to express a definite opinion on the full significance of the

In accord with this, although the translator's knowledge of Hebrew was "a product of theoretical study rather than of living experience,"[46] he drew on Greek equivalents for Hebrew words in translations of other biblical works, his knowledge of Aramaic, as well as the application of various strains of "etymological theory among Hellenistic Jewry" or some other "widespread lexicological or exegetical tradition."[47] Once again, in Seeligmann's estimation, the translator's Alexandrian Jewish community, in whose traditions he was steeped, was the most significant influence on his work.

Seeligmann found the clearest window on the translator's Alexandrian milieu in indications that "this translation...repeatedly reflects contemporaneous history."[48] It is in this connection that he first employs the term "contemporize" in his monograph on LXX-Isaiah:[49]

> Those places where the paraphrase of the text contains allusions to events happening in the more or less immediate neighbourhood of the translator's place of residence give one a surprising image of the translator's notion that the period in which he lived was to be time for the fulfillment of ancient prophecies, and of his efforts to *contemporize* the old biblical text and revive it by inspiriting it with the religious conceptions of a new age.[50]

This statement is remarkable for how it shifts the focus in the study of LXX-Isaiah. No longer is the primary concern the recovery of the Hebrew *Vorlage* but the discernment of the translator's ideas, purposes, and milieu. In particular, his contemporizations of Isaiah's oracles enable us "to take the difference between the original and the translation as a basis for an attempt to reconstrue the complex of theological ideas behind the translation."[51]

Equally noteworthy is Seeligmann's juxtaposition of the translator's belief that his day "was to be time for the fulfillment of ancient prophecies" and his efforts to "contemporize the old biblical text and revive it

---

terms chosen by the translator, we cannot confine ourselves exclusively to the Isaiah text, as for the interpretation of this text we shall be compelled occasionally to make use of other writings in the Jewish-Alexandrian literature" (ibid., 96). Whatever distinctive contributions the translator made must be understood as partially due to his Jewish-Alexandrian milieu.

    [46] Ibid., 49.
    [47] Ibid., 50–51.
    [48] Ibid., 4.
    [49] For his use of the term prior to that monograph, see below, chapter 6.
    [50] Seeligmann, *Septuagint Version*, 4.
    [51] Ibid.

by inspiriting it with the religious conceptions of a new age."[52] Aligning Isaiah's oracles with events that "fulfill" them, on the one hand, and "reviving...the *old* biblical text" by infusing it with contemporary notions, on the other, are distinct activities, inasmuch as the first seeks to infuse the *present* with significance by reading it in light of the text, while the second seeks to infuse the *text* with relevance by importing names and locutions familiar to his readers in place of names and phrases unfamiliar to them. For the sake of clarity, I will call the first of these activities "mantological exegesis,"[53] while the replacement of ancient names or expressions with ones current in the translator's day I will term "modernization."[54]

Despite Seeligmann's distinction between these two phenomena in the opening pages of his book, he effectively fuses them in discussing examples, so that mantological exegesis and modernization are equally classed as "contemporization." For example, his first forays into identifying "contemporization" lead him to explore toponyms, which he considers "eminently suited to giving one an impression of the translator's mental and spiritual horizon,"[55] inasmuch as they reveal "his habit...of contemporizing and anachronizing his interpretations...his conscious or unconscious tendency to rediscover, in the text he was translating, the world of his own period."[56] His equation of "contemporizing" and "anachronizing" accords with his prior description of the translator infusing his text with "conceptions of a new age." However, his comments on the toponyms of 9:12(11) seems to shade into mantological exegesis:

אֲרָם מִקֶּדֶם   Συρίαν ἀφ' ἡλίου ἀνατολῶν
וּפְלִשְׁתִּים מֵאָחוֹר   καὶ τοὺς Ἕλληνας ἀφ' ἡλίου δυσμῶν
וַיֹּאכְלוּ אֶת־יִשְׂרָאֵל   τοὺς κατεσθίοντας τὸν Ισραηλ

Seeligmann comments that here "we are directly and unmistakably transported into the historical atmosphere of Palestine in Hellenistic times," since the translator seems to reflect "the hostility of the Greek cities on the west coast towards the Jewish population of Palestine," with Συρία designating the Seleucid realm.[57] This is no longer simply

---

[52] Ibid.
[53] This phrase comes from Michael Fishbane, *Biblical Interpretation in Ancient Israel* (Oxford: Clarendon Press, 1985), especially pp. 443–46.
[54] Arie van der Kooij uses similar terms in his *Die alten Textzeugen*, 33.
[55] Seeligmann, *Septuagint Version*, 76.
[56] Ibid., 79.
[57] Ibid., 81.

an "anachronistic" identification of toponyms with contemporary geography; it is a matter of fitting Isaiah's oracles to the events and circumstances of his day.

Seeligmann's description of the translator "contemporizing" the toponyms of 9:11 is paralleled by his assertion that "the figure of the great king...as the mighty one threatening Israel, was transmuted in the translation into a Hellenistic ruler of the translator's own period."[58] He asserts that this is a matter of "attributing to the text *contemporaneous* application, i.e. to show that the ancient Word also refers to the period of those who later endeavour to interpret it."[59] There can be no mistaking that "contemporization" has come to embrace both the translator's "unconscious tendency to rediscover...the world of his own period" and exegesis motivated by belief that "the period in which he lived was to be time for the fulfillment of ancient prophecies."

The influence of Seeligmann's formulation of this is palpable in J. C. M. das Neves's 1973 study that uses Isaiah 24 as the matrix for discussing themes and motifs throughout the translation.[60] He asserts more stridently than Seeligmann that "le TM est le texte original, tandis que la LXX d'Isaïe est une interpretation théologique de l'original Hébreu."[61] While Seeligmann allowed that the work reflects a mixture of the translator's "conscious or unconscious tendency" to contemporize the text,[62] das Neves stresses the translator's *deliberate* interpretation of the book in light of his beliefs and circumstances, inasmuch as the translator's hermeneutical impulse impelled him to use any paleographic ambiguity or surface association "à fin de preciser et de mettre de l'ordre dans sa pensée."[63] In contrast to Seeligmann, who considered the translator poorly acquainted with Hebrew and emphasized the influence of a tradition of interpretation, das Neves esteems the translator "bien au courant de l'hébreu," so that differences with the MT are not a matter "d'erreurs inconscientes, mais plutôt d'un

---

[58] Ibid., 82.
[59] Ibid.
[60] J. C. M. das Neves, *A Teologia da Tradução Grega dos Setenta no Livro de Isaías* (Lisbon: Universidade Católica Portuguesa, 1973). While das Neves's study takes chapter 24 as its focus, he cites passages from throughout LXX-Isaiah to illustrate his conclusions about the translation of chapter 24, thus offering a comprehensive portrayal of the translator's style of rendering and his ideology.
[61] Ibid., 294.
[62] Seeligmann, *Septuagint Version*, 79.
[63] Das Neves, *A Teologia*, 282.

travail repensé et prévu d'avance dans une méthodologie qu'il fallait suivre et qui avait pour but l'exposition de leur pensée théologique à la lumière de la Bible."[64]

Accordingly, in epitomizing the translation,[65] das Neves writes, "bref, dans la LXX d'Isaïe, nous n'avons pas une version, mais plutôt une «interpretation» où l'on utilize la méthode des «relectures», autrement dit, la méthode d'une nouvelle lecture, pas encore contenue dans l'original, et la méthode de l'«actualization» prophétique."[66] It is not an "unconscious tendency" that drives the translator, but deliberate identification of prophecies fulfilled in his day. In fact, das Neves compares the translator's method particularly to the "método exegético da comunidade de Qumrân,"[67] although he ultimately locates the translator's work within the broader stream of early Jewish exegesis: "O Alexandrino segue o mesmo método de «actualização» de Qumrân, da Mishna, dos Midrashim, dos Targumim, inclusivamente, do N. T., tendo por caracterisa apresentar o original hebraico segundo as necessidades religiosas do seu tempo."[68]

Das Neves identifies the "necessidades religiosas do seu tempo" as the Hellenistic crisis in Jerusalem of the early second century B.C.E., alleging evidence of a clear picture of the distress of the pious commoners at the hands of an impious class:

> C'est, bien sûr sa *mentalité religieuse* qui amène le traducteur à s'exprimer de la sorte. Cette mentalité est dépendante des facteurs historiques et

---

[64] Ibid. Das Neves cites with approval Coste's assertion that to content oneself with identifying paleographic errors or confusion that led to the translator's choice of equivalents is merely "reconstruire le mecanisme d'une erreur…mais cela ne suffit pas à nous expliquer plenement un acte de traduction qui plonge ses raciness dans le subconscient et la personnalité du traducteur" (J. Coste, "La première expérience de traduction biblique: la Septante," *Maison Dieu* 14 (1958) 79, quoted by das Neves, *A Teologia*, 24). It is but a short step from here to das Neves's inference that the translator's ideology so thoroughly determined his reading of his *Vorlage* that the accidents of Hebrew morphology and paleography were of no consequence for him.

[65] Das Neves presents his conclusions in Portuguese (pp. 265–80), followed by a French translation (pp. 281–97).

[66] Das Neves, *A Teologia*, 283. Das Neves refers to the translator's discovery of events of his day forecast in Isaiah as "actualização" (ibid., 22). In his view, "une mentalité *d'actualisation* éffleure tout le temps à travers le texte" (ibid., 285, italics his); "contemporization" is not a periodic reflex of the translator, as with Seeligmann, but permeates the translation.

[67] Ibid., 26. He devotes pp. 26–38 to a survey of Qumran's exegetical techniques (referring also to the mantological exegesis of the book of Daniel) in preparation for studying LXX-Isaiah.

[68] Ibid., 42–43.

des methods littéraires de l'exégèse biblique de l'époque. Les facteurs
historiques conduisent Israël, en tant que nation, et au point de vue
religieux, aux deux factions, qui, comme on le sait bien, finiront avec la
révolte des Maccabées. C'est là un point clair de la version G d'Isaïe. Il
nous montre l'existence des deux classes par devant la toile de fond qu'est
l'«actualization» historique. Et il n'est pas étonnant que la faction fidèle
à Yahweh et à la Loi vive dans l'attente de la redemption.[69]

Not surprisingly, then, das Neves agrees with Seelgimann that the
translator saw himself, and the pious with whom he sided, as living
in the time of prophecy's fulfillment, although he gives this scenario
starker expression. Because these prophecies "se rapportent aux derniers
temps," in the translator's view "les temps eschatologiques commencent dès maintenant,"[70] so that the deliverance expected by the pious
constitutes "la redemption messianique-eschatologique."[71]

The early 1980's saw three works that further developed Seeligmann's
perception of the translator's approach to Isaiah. First, Robert Hanhart
endorsed Seeligmann's perception that "die vorgegebnen Zeugnisse des
hebräischen Originals von den zeitgeschictelichen Voraussetzungen
der Übersetzer her interpretiert und an den Geschehnisse aktualisert
werden, die den Zeugen dieser Zeit als Analogon der Geschehnisse
ihrer Heilstradition erscheinen."[72] Calling for resumption of the path
Seeligmann established, Hanhart defined "actualization" as the use of
Heilstradition in such a way that the translator deliberately caused its
contemporary relevance to resonate for the reader.[73] However, such
actualizations are "meist mehr erfühlbaren als erweisbaren" and "der
Zeit der Entstehung des Originals fremd, der Zeit der Entstehung der
Übersetzung aber nahe sind."[74]

Hanhart applied his description of "actualization" to an assessment
of Isa 9:1(8:23)–7(6), in which he drew special attention to divergences

---

[69] Ibid., 284, italics his.

[70] Ibid., 283. Das Neves regards the translator as clearly having thrown his lot in
with the pious, referred to as "the remnant" (ibid., 286–87).

[71] Ibid., 288.

[72] Robert Hanhart, "Die Septuaginta als Interpretation und Aktualisierung," in
The Bible and the Ancient World: Isaac Leo Seeligmann Volume, ed. Alexander Rofé and Yair
Zakovitch, vol. 3, non-Hebrew Section (Jerusalem: E. Rubinstein's Publishing, 1983)
331.

[73] Ibid., 339 n. 18.

[74] Ibid.

from the MT in 9:2(1), which he deemed decisive for understanding the translator's construal of the passage:[75]

העם ההלכים בחשך	ὁ λαὸς ὁ πορευόμενος ἐν σκότει
ראו אור גדול	ἴδετε φῶς μέγα
ישבי בארץ	οἱ κατοικοῦντες ἐν χώρᾳ
צלמות אור נגה עליהם	καὶ σκιᾷ θανάτου φῶς λάμψει ἐφ' ὑμᾶς

The translation of ראו (ראָה in the MT) by the imperative ἴδετε, clarifies the LXX's command to "the territory of Zebulon and the land Naphtali" in 9:1(8:23):

הראשון הקל	τοῦτο πρῶτον ποίει ταχὺ ποίει
וארצה זבלון וארצה נפתלי	χώρα Ζαβουλων ἡ γῆ Νεφθαλιμ
והאחרון הכביד	
דרך הים	ὁδὸν θαλάσσης
	καὶ οἱ λοιποὶ οἱ τὴν παραλίαν κατοικοῦντες
עבר הירדן	καὶ πέραν τοῦ Ιορδάνου
גליל הגוים	Γαλιλαία τῶν ἐθνῶν τὰ μέρη τῆς Ιουδαίας

Hanhart correctly concluded that "eine textliche Grundlage für die Umdeutung des hebräischen Textes kann nur in der...Äquivalenz zwischen τάχυ ποίει und als Imperative verstandenem הקל in der Bedeutung 'schnell, eilen' und im adverbialen Verständnis des Ausdrucks הראשון...in der Bedeutung 'zuerst' gesehen werden."[76] The summons to do τοῦτο can only be understood as anticipating the command ἴδετε φῶς μέγα in 9:1(8:23), so that the LXX demarcates between the time of disaster in the earlier verses of chapter 8 and the time of salvation in 8:22–9:7(6).[77]

Furthermore, observed Hanhart, in v. 3(2) the translator made a distinction, unsupported by the Hebrew, between an event already accomplished and one yet anticipated:[78]

הרבית הגוי לא הגדלת השמחה	τὸ πλεῖστον τοῦ λαοῦ ὃ κατήγαγες ἐν εὐφροσύνῃ σου
שמחו לפניך	καὶ εὐφρανθήσονται ἐνώπιόν σου
כשמחת בקציר	ὡς οἱ εὐφραινόμενοι ἐν ἀμήτῳ
כאשר יגילו בחלקם שלל	καὶ ὃν τρόπον οἱ διαιρούμενοι σκῦλα

---

[75] Ibid., 336.
[76] Ibid., 333.
[77] Ibid., 337.
[78] Ibid., 334.

Not only are these people the Kyrios has brought down but, according to v. 4(3), their joy will arise from his liberation of them from oppression:

כָּא כֹל סְאוֹן סֹאֵן בְּרַעַשׁ	διότι ἀφαιρεθήσεται ὁ ζυγὸς ὁ ἐπ' αὐτῶν κείμενος
וְאַת מַטֵּה שִׁכְמוֹ	καὶ ἡ ῥάβδος ἡ ἐπὶ τοῦ τραχήλου αὐτῶν
שֵׁבֶט הַנֹּגֵשׂ בּוֹ הַחִתֹּתָ	τὴν γὰρ ῥάβδον τῶν ἀπαιτούντων διεσκέδασεν κύριος
כְּיוֹם מִדְיָן	ὡς τῇ ἡμέρᾳ τῇ ἐπὶ Μαδιαμ

Thus, the translator transposed the comparison of an already accomplished deliverance with one in the *Heilstradition* into a bridge "zwischen der verheissenen Befreiung und dem errinnerten Heilsgeschehen von Gideons Sieg über die Midianiter," in which he found "das Zeichen der kommenden endgültigen Befreiung" and on which grounds "die alte jesajanische Verheissung aktualisiert."[79]

Seeking to identify the accomplished events the translator had in mind, as well as what the announcement of deliverance in 9:1(8:23)–7(6) portends, Hanhart concluded that

> hier vom Übersetzer in einer Gestalt, die der Überlieferung des 1. und 2. Makkabäerbuches nahe steht, die makkabäischen Heerzüge nach er Wiederweihung des geschändeten Heiligtums am 14. Dezember des Jahres 164 v. Chr. und dem fast gleichzeitigen Tod des Antiochos Epiphanes anvisiert sind und ihm als Zeichen erscheinen, die den Tag der Befreiung ankündigen.[80]

The deliverance anticipated is that begun with the purification of the temple, when the brothers of Judas began conquering territory in Galilee, in the Transjordan, and in Judah itself.[81]

This example demonstrates, claimed Hanhart, that actualizations have special "Beweiskraft" when the translator renders his *Vorlage* not simply "in freier Übersetzung der als solche noch erkennbaren Vorlage sondern in einer vom Original her überhaupt nicht erklärbaren Aussage."[82] The translator's distinction between past action and promised deliverance in v. 4(3) urges "den Schluss auf traditiongeschichtliche, nicht auf literarische Abhängigkeit."[83]

---

[79] Ibid., 337–38.
[80] Ibid., 339.
[81] Ibid., 341.
[82] Ibid.
[83] Ibid., 339–40 n. 18.

At the same time Hanhart composed his summons to resume Seeligmann's agenda, two monographs took up that task. Jean Koenig's 1982 assessment of the translator's hermeneutic accords with das Neves' description of the translator, even though he seems to have been unfamiliar with das Neves' work.[84] Just as das Neves insisted that the translator's method involved a flexible construal of the features of Hebrew grammar, Koenig shunned explaining the translator's renderings by paleographic details and borrowings from other scripture passages, both of which he disparaged as "empiricism." Such empiricism, he argued, fails to perceive that the translator adopted a *method* of interpretation and serves "à annuler l'interprète grec et, par consequent, aussi le facteur culturel qui pourrait l'avoir guidé."[85] The patterns of borrowings Ziegler identified inevitably lead to a recognition that "la repetition de faits aussi caractéristiques a toutes les chances de s'expliquer par l'application d'une méthode spécifique de traitement textual."[86] Koenig designated this "une herméneutique analogique," embodied in "participation des écrits les uns aux autres" and "participation des mots à des valeurs extracontextuelles, livrées par les homonymies, les homographies et tous le types de resemblances formelles discernables."[87] This recognition obviates empirical explanation, since it does not operate linearly but analogically. Moreover, only occasionally are the translator's interpretations to be explained as failure to comprehend his Hebrew *Vorlage*:

> En effet le niveau de connaissance des texts et donc de la langue, requis par l'usage des emprunts exclut des incompréhensions fréquentes, et implique, par conséquent, que les changements ont été généralement determines par d'autres motifs, d'ordre ideologique et plus spécialement religieux.[88]

Accordingly, Koenig focused on the translator as exegete.

Also part of this analogical method, were "certaines divergences of G...qui permettent de conclure à une utilization oraculaire du passage,"

---

[84] Jean Koenig, *L'Herméneutique analogique du Judaïsme antique* (VTSup 33; Leiden: Brill, 1982).

[85] Ibid., 7.

[86] Ibid., 9. Needless to say, Koenig gives no berth to Ziegler's theory of borrowings deriving from a glossator's marginal notes, repudiating the hypothesis as the height of empiricism (ibid., 11–12).

[87] Ibid., 35.

[88] Ibid., 32.

whether used to speak of contemporary events or the future.[89] Whereas
Seeligmann could use "contemporization" for incidental reflections
of the translator's milieu, for Koenig, contemporization is equivalent
to "une utilization oraculaire du passage."[90] Indeed, such "utilization
oraculaire" rests on a method that made them *capables d'imposer leur
autorité à l'égal du texte hébreu considéré dans son sens obvie.*"[91]

His insistence on this is especially evident in his discussion of Isa
8:11–16, in which (like Seeligmann) he finds the translator deriving from
Isaiah's oracle a condemnation of the "antilégalistes" of his own day,
under the recognition that "le passage d'Is avait *un valeur oraculaire.*"[92]
His oracular interpretation derives legitimacy solely from "une méthode
accréditée, capable de s'imposer aux 2 partis en présence et de garantir
l'exégèse retenue par G, non pas forcément comme la seule valable,
mais…comme un sense émanant avec d'autres d'un texte inépuisable."[93]
Ironically, then, Koenig's insistence on oracular interpretation, based
on *analogical* associations, hews to a type of empiricism by insisting
that the translator had to be able to validate his exegesis by using an
authoritative method of treating textual realia.

Although Koenig explored the exegetical methods employed by the
later rabbis, on the grounds that such methods must have had roots
at least as early the exegesis found in the OG,[94] the primary parallel
he adduced were the texts from Qumran. Indeed, it is for that reason
that Koenig devoted the second half of his book to the use of "une
herméneutique analogique" in 1QIsa[a].[95] Like das Neves, Koenig

---

[89] Ibid., 44. Koenig finds this phenomenon so pervasive in LXX-Isaiah that he judges
it to be "l'une des manifestations qui illustrent un grand courant de speculation oraculaire sur les Écrits traditionnels d'Israël" (ibid., 45).

[90] In fact, he chastises Seeligmann for failing to perceive in the translator's rendering of 9:10–11(9–10), admittedly produced in light of Genesis eleven's story of the
tower, an allusion to the Samaritan community. He laments that, for Seeligmann,
"l'adaptateur grec, loin d'appliquer le message prophétique à des circonstances contemporaines…serait remonté dans un lointain passé," with the result that this passage
"aurait été «historicisé»" (ibid., 100). Accordingly, he accuses Seeligmann of reducing
the translator to "un amateur d'antiquités bibliques" (ibid., 101 n. 30).

[91] Ibid., 47, italics his. In Koenig's view, recognizing this method is crucial, since
"une actualization des paroles d'Isaïe obtenue au prix de modifications uniquement
inspirées par le spectacle de l'actualité eût été, en un mot, la perte pure et simple du
principe oraculaire lui-même" (ibid., 46).

[92] Ibid., 121, italics his.

[93] Ibid., 123.

[94] Ibid., 48.

[95] Ibid., 28 et passim.

regarded biblical interpretation undertaken at Qumran as the closest analogue to LXX-Isaiah.

Despite the similarities between Koenig and das Neves, the scholar Koenig identified as his predecessor was not das Neves, but Alfred Zillessen. By introducing the subject of scriptural borrowings in LXX-Isaiah, Zillessen broke with the doctrine that "chaque expression de G...avait pour origine une expression hébraïque correspondante."[96] Zillessen simply failed to perceive "clairement toute la portée méthodologique,"[97] with the result that he treated the translator as a mere channel, "comme si le passage analogue avait «pénétré» dans l'autre par l'effet d'un véritable automatisme textual qui supprimerait l'initiative de l'adaptateur."[98]

Arie van der Kooij criticized Koenig's assessment of the Isaiah translator, drawing on principles he had expounded in his *Die alten Textzeugen*, published the year before Koenig's work appeared.[99] In van der Kooij's view, Koenig's "analogical method" failed to assess how the translator interpreted his *Vorlage* grammatically and syntactically, gave no account for the coherence of a passage as a literary unit and its relationship to related passages in LXX-Isaiah, and did not apply an accurate and careful assessment of Hellenistic history and culture to the question of how and to what degree the translator "actualized" a passage.[100]

In keeping with this, van der Kooij's own work, from *Die alten Textzeugen des Jesajabuches* to the present, has emphasized the literary, linguistic, and historical contexts of the translator's renderings. He has challenged Seeligmann's caution against expecting "logical connexions in any chapter or part of a chapter in our Septuagint text," so that we should expect, instead, to find "historical allusions or expressions of the translator's own views and ideas" only in "isolated, free renderings."[101] By contrast, van der Kooij asks whether "free" translations of passages "im Licht wörtlich übersetzter Teile anderswo in der Buchrolle Jesaja" did not attest a unity to the translation,[102] even as Ziegler had

---

[96] Ibid., 4.
[97] Ibid., 5.
[98] Ibid., 7.
[99] Arie van der Kooij, "Accident or Method? On 'Analogical' Interpretation in the Old Greek of Isa and in 1QIs^a," review of *L' Herméneutique Analogique du Judaïsme Antique*, BO 43 (1986) 366–76.
[100] Ibid., 368–70.
[101] Seeligmann, *Septuagint Version*, 41.
[102] Arie van der Kooij, "Die Septuaginta Jesajas als Dokument Jüdischer Exegese,"

suggested: "Der Js-Übers. scheint überhaupt sein Buch sehr gut dem Inhalte nach im Gedächtnis gehabt zu haben; denn es begegnen viele Wiedergaben, die sich nur auf Grund der Exegese nach sinnverwandten Stellen erklären lassen."[103] Throughout his researches, van der Kooij has maintained that the translator's views are discoverable only by analyzing the literary structure of passages.[104]

Although the interpretation of passages as literary units is fundamental for van der Kooij, more important for this chapter is the way he has developed Seeligmann's observations about contemporization. Van der Kooij has distinguished between "freie Übersetzungen, die im Licht von anderen Texten innherhalb oder auch ausserhalb von Jesaja durchsichtig werden" and those "die eine aktualisierende Tendenz zeigen,"[105] thus reinstating Seeligmann's recognition that not all exegesis in LXX-Isaiah is mantological.

However, alongside this van der Kooij introduced a distinction between the translator's "Modernisiergungen und Aktualisierungen von Namen von Städten, Ländern und Völkern" and what he called "Erfüllungsinterpretationen"[106] as a discrete exegetical ploy. For van der Kooij, such a "marked tendency toward contemporization by means of fulfillment-interpretation of the old oracles of the prophet Isaiah" provides "an important key not only for explaining differences between the Hebrew and the Greek text of Isaiah, but also for a better understanding of the Greek itself."[107] Indeed, this characterization of the translator's method is, according to van der Kooij, the prime way LXX-Isaiah is to be comprehended: as a *genre* of interpretation in which Isaiah has been translated so as to make sense "as 'prophecy' at the time of the translator."[108] Accordingly, "der Autor der LXX Jes war

---

in *Übersetzung und Deutung: Fs. Alexander Hulst*, ed. Dominique Barthélemy (Nijkerk: Uitgeverij G. F. Callenback, 1977) 93.

[103] Ziegler, *Untersuchungen*, 135.

[104] Van der Kooij, *Die alten Textzeugen*, 33.

[105] Van der Kooij, "Die Septuaginta Jesajas als Dokument Jüdischer Exegese," 91.

[106] Idem, *Die alten Textzeugen*, 33. He attributes the phrase, "fulfillment-interpretation" to Geza Vermes, "Bible and Midrash. Early O.T. Exegesis," in *Cambridge History of the Bible*, ed. S. L. Greenslade, vol. 3 (Cambridge: Cambridge University Press, 1970) 225 (van der Kooij, "Die Septuaginta Jesajas als Dokument Jüdischer Exegese," 101 n. 8).

[107] Arie van der Kooij, "A Short Commentary on Some Verses of the Old Greek of Isaiah 23," *BIOSCS* 15 (1982) 36.

[108] Idem, "Isaiah in the Septuagint," in *Writing and Reading the Scroll of Isaiah*, vol. 2 (VTSupp 70; Leiden: Brill, 1997) 516. In context, these words form part of a query

vom Glauben getragen, die entschedende Periode (vgl. τὰ ἔσχατα) der Geschichte sei angebrochen."[109]

As noted earlier in this chapter, van der Kooij has contended, on the basis of γραμματικός in 33:18, that the translator viewed himself in the role of "ein Schriftgelehrter." In particular, the translator is comparable to the author of Daniel and, above all, to the interpreters of texts at Qumran, like whom he considered himself inspired to interpret the ancient oracles as presaging events of his own day.[110] Accordingly, the fundamental assumption of the *Schriftgeleherter* who translated Isaiah into Greek was "daß Ereignisse zur Zeit des Übersetzers vom Propheten Jesaja vorausgesagt worden waren, und daß also die Zeit der Umdeutung vorliegt."[111]

Thus, while van der Kooij has revived Seeligmann's initial recognition that "fulfillment-interpretation" is merely one type of "contemporization" found in LXX-Isaiah, he (like Seeligmann, das Neves, and Koenig) has seen this form of interpretation so constitutive of the warp-and-woof of the translation as to become the lens through which the translator's exegesis is best apprehended. And like his predecessors (especially das Neves and Koenig), van der Kooij has found strong similarities between the actualizing interpretation among the members of the Qumran community and the translator of Isaiah.

Van der Kooij's elaboration of Seeligmann over the past two decades has created the aura of this perception of the translator's *Übersetzungsweise* as settled scholarship. However, there are salient questions to be raised about both this general description and the particular passages on which it rests. Before doing so, however, it is important to notice an alternative to this view of the translator, one that attends to his translation of סֹפֵר by οἱ γραμματικοί in 33:18.

---

as to whether LXX-Isaiah fits this description. However, it is clear from the remainder of the article and, in fact, the whole of van der Kooij's work, that he considers this an apt description.

[109] Idem, *Die alten Textzeugen*, 64.

[110] Ibid.

[111] Idem, "Zur Theologie des Jesajabuches in der Septuaginta," in *Theologische Probleme der Septuaginta und der hellenistischen Hermeneutik*, ed. Henning Graf Reventlow (Gütersloh: Christian Kaiser, 1997) 16.

The translator as an Alexandrian

In describing the translator as a scribe interested in *Erfüllungsinterpre-tation*, van der Kooij compares him to the scribes that produced the *pesharim*. However, this association with a type of literature found only in *eretz Israel* raises the question in what the sense the translator was an Alexandrian.[112]

Van der Kooij moves from the inference that the rendering of ספר by οἱ γραμματικοί in 33:18 indicates that the translator regarded himself a γραμματικός, to an equation of him with a ספר of the sort that composed the *pesharim*. However, there is good reason to question that set of equations. In the first place, it is not clear that the translator's use of γραμματικοί in 33:18 implies anything about his self-understanding.

33:18	לבך יהגה אימה	ἡ ψυχὴ ὑμῶν μελετήσει φόβον
	איה ספר איה שקל	ποῦ εἰσιν οἱ γραμματικοί ποῦ εἰσιν οἱ συμβουλεύοντες
	איה ספר את המגדלים	ποῦ ἐστιν ὁ ἀριθμῶν τοὺς συντρεφομένους[113]

As in the MT, the people lament the loss of public officials. Only here in the LXX does συμβουλεύειν translate שקל. However, in v. 19 συνεβουλεύσαντο is the formal equivalent for the MT's נועז, perhaps attesting a *Vorlage* that read נוע (cf. πρὸς τίνα συνεβουλεύσατο || את מי נוע in 40:14), although it is also possible that the mere approximation of נועז to נוע (either graphically or aurally) led the translator to associate the forms. What makes his choice of οἱ συμβουλεύοντες for

---

[112] Ziegler has established beyond doubt the Egyptian provenance of the translation (see below, p. 159). Van der Kooij's argument that the translator worked in Leontopolis is based on his argument about 19:18, on which see below, p. 169. Given the failure of that argument to persuade, Alexandria remains by far the most likely place of origin for LXX-Isaiah.

[113] Ziegler, *Isaias*, reads τοὺς συστρεφομένους ('those gathered together') with אAQΓ 26 106, as well as Verona (*conversantes*) and Syh[mg]. B 88 Syh 109 736 read τρεφομένους (V has στρεφομένους), while Lucianic mss read ἀναστρεφομένους. As Ottley observes, only τρεφομένους "appears to give any sense in connection with the Heb." (*The Book of Isaiah*, 2:273). LXX-Isaiah translates נדלתי with ἐξέθρεψα in 23:4 and נדל with ἐξέθρεψέν in 49:21, so that τοὺς τρεφομένους could reflect an interpretation of המגדלים as the definite article + a passive participle. However, this leaves unexplained the origins of the prefix συσ in other witnesses. Ottley cogently posits that the original reading was συντρεφομένους (attested by 86), which became corrupted to συστρεφομένους (perhaps under the influence of the preceding τους), while ἀναστρεφομένους was a subsequent attempt to improve the reading (ibid.).

שֶׁקֶל in v. 18 more remarkable, however, is that his translation of שֶׁקֶל with ἱστάναι (used as a technical term for weighing out money) in 40:12 and 46:6 shows that he did not lack a suitable equivalent.[114] Because יעץ underlies his choice of συμβουλεύειν and σύμβουλος in each of their other appearances (1:26; 3:3; 19:11; 40:13, 14),[115] and because all other textual witnesses attest שֶׁקֶל,[116] most likely he was casting about for an equivalent that would fit the ranks of officials essential to society and was not content to render שֶׁקֶל with something equivalent to a "banker" or "accountant." His choice of οἱ συμβουλεύοντες for שֶׁקֶל is likely based on reasoning contextually from the theme of "counselors" in v. 19.

Equally striking is ὁ ἀριθμῶν τοὺς συστρεφομένους ('the one numbering those reared together') as the equivalent for סֹפֵר אֶת הַמִּגְדָּלִים. While ἀριθμεῖν translates סֹפֵר fifteen times elsewhere in the LXX (Genesis, 4x; Leviticus, 2x; 2 Kgdms, 1x; 3 Kgdms, 1x; Job, 3x; Ezra, 1x; Chronicles, 3x), this equivalence does not occur elsewhere in LXX-Isaiah.[117] Although ὁ ἀριθμῶν τοὺς συντρεφομένους might be an office contrived to make sense of the Hebrew, it nevertheless is conceivable as an official of state who oversees the youth of the city.[118]

While this occurrence of γραμματικός accords with the common view that the translator worked in Egypt, the most it tells us of this translator is that he considered the γραμματικοί essential to society's wellbeing, since he used it in a passage lamenting the loss of civil officials. On the other hand, even if it is difficult to reason from this to the translator's self-understanding, more might lie behind his translation than just esteem for the γραμματικοί.

Use of the term γραμματικοί commences in the third century B.C.E. Although Strabo classes Eratosthenes (whom Ptolemy III appointed

---

[114] Cf. 2 Kgdms 14:26; 18:12; 3 Kgdms 21(20):39.

[115] συμβουλεύειν most commonly translates יעץ in the LXX (13x), although LXX-Isaiah more frequently renders יעץ with βουλεύειν (10x).

[116] 1QIsaᵃ = MT (this part of the verse stands in a lacuna in 4QIsaᶜ). S reflects a *Vorlage* = MT. V renders איה שֹׁקֵל איה סֹפֵר אֶת הַמִּגְדָּלִים with *ubi legis verba ponderans ubi doctor parvulorum*, both of which seem interpretative, with *ponderans* reflecting a metaphorical understanding of שֶׁקֶל and *legis verba* supplied as the object, while *doctor parvulorum* likely keys in on הַמִּגְדָּלִים as a D-stem participle, 'those rearing up', implying instruction of children. T's translation of the same phrases with איכא חשביא ייתון אם יכלון לחשבא מנין קטילי ריש משרית ניברריא construes שֶׁקֶל and סֹפֵר in the same sense, as having to do with those skilled in computation.

[117] Διηγεῖσθαι || יסֹפּרו, 43:21; λέγε || סֹפֵר, 43:26; ἀνηγγέλη || סֹפֵר, 52:15 (סֹפְרתָם lacks a Greek equivalent in 22:10).

[118] Cf. V's interpretation of this phrase in n. 116, above.

librarian ca. 245) among the γραμματικοί, this is an anachronistic usage. In fact, Eratosthenes coined for himself the term φιλόλογος to designate, as Suetonius phrases it, his exploration of "many and diverse areas of study."[119] It was only in the early second century, when such study became distinct from the work of poets,[120] that Alexandrian scholars claimed the title γραμματικοί (previously applied to "the elementary teacher in writing and reading")[121] to designate themselves as "professional 'men of letters'."[122] Accordingly, the use of γραμματικοί in Isa 33:18 reflects conditions no earlier than the second century. However, the translator's use of γραμματικοί to refer to a class of officials crucial to society may have been spurred by more than simple admiration; it may have arisen from what ensued after Euergetes II took the throne in 145 B.C.E.

Whereas Ptolemy I Soter safeguarded some rights for the Egyptian population—even though he forbade them Alexandrian citizenship, reserving that privilege for immigrants from the Aegean—Philadelphus showed Macedonians and Greeks even more blatant preferential treatment, resulting in social and economic disadvantages for Egyptians that bred pervasive discontent among them.[123] Following the battle of Raphia (217 B.C.E.), when Philopator—with the help of 20,000 Egyptian troops—repelled the advances of Antiochus III, the native population waged a prolonged revolt against their Macedonian overlords.[124] One outcome of this was "the gradual Egyptianization of the [Alexandrian] community."[125] Despite still being barred from citizenship, the increasingly Egyptian population managed to exert their will through "the mob in whose hands, by sheer weight of numbers and by violence, political power lay."[126] Coincidentally, Ptolemaic power and prestige

---

[119] Rudolf Pfeiffer, *History of Classical Scholarship from the Beginnings to the End of the Hellenistic Age* (Oxford: The Clarendon Press, 1968) 158–59. This is also in spite of the fact that Eratosthenes produced two works called Γραμματικά, as well as "twelve or more books Περὶ τῆς ἀρχαίας κωμῳδίας" (ibid.).

[120] Ibid., 171.

[121] Ibid., 157.

[122] P. M. Fraser, *Ptolemaic Alexandria*, 3 vols. (Oxford: The Clarendon Press, 1972) 1:458.

[123] E. G. Turner, "Ptolemaic Egypt," in *The Hellenistic World*, ed. F. W. Walbank, et al., The Cambridge Ancient History, vol. 7:1 (Cambridge: Cambridge University Press, 1984) 155–57.

[124] Fraser, *Ptolemaic Alexandria*, 1:60.

[125] Ibid., 1:82.

[126] Ibid., 1:76–78.

waned by dint of the loss of "most of her overseas empire, and the virtual restriction of this empire to the two home territories of Cyprus and Cyrene."[127] As a result, Alexandria's attraction for scholars who had migrated to it in the third century waned so much that "writers and scientists from overseas...largely disappear[ed], save for the grammarians, whose main activity belongs to this period."[128] But even the haven those γραμματικοί had found in the Museum was about to vanish.

When Ptolemy VI (Philometer) died in 145 B.C.E., strife broke out between his widow, Cleopatra II (along with her son) and Euergetes II, who ruled over the Ptolemaic territory of Cyrene.[129] Slightly more than a year after gaining control of Alexandria, Euergetes II arranged the murder of the Cyrenaeans who had assisted him in usurping power and then turned on the general population, especially those who had been supporters of Philometer.[130]

Alexandrians' hatred for Euergetes was expressed in their sardonic modification of his throne name to Κακεργέτης. Even more biting was the spite the γραμματικοί expressed for him in their use of the epithet Φύσκων ('pot-belly'), "no doubt an allusion to the nickname given by Alcaeus to the hated tyrant Pittacus."[131] Euergetes directed his fury at these scholars, forcing Aristarchus, the librarian, to flee to Cyprus, while one of his students, Dionysus Thrax, took refuge in Rhodes and another star pupil, Apollodorus, initially settled in Pergamum and then joined Diogenes's school in Athens.[132] So great was the dispersion of scholars from Alexandria that Menecles of Barca quipped that ᾿Αλεξανδρεῖς εἰσιν οἱ παιδεύσαντες πάντες τοὺς ῞Ελληνας καὶ τοὺς βαρβάρους ('Alexandrians are the entire cadre instructing the Greeks and

---

[127] Ibid., 1:60–61.

[128] Ibid., 1:78.

[129] Ibid., 1:121.

[130] Among them were the Jews, who had supported Cleopatra II and her son (ibid.). There is reason, however, to conclude that "in course of time the king and the Jews made their peace, for two inscriptions...contain the regular formula of the dedication of a new synagogue in honor of the king" (Victor Tcherikover, *Hellenistic Civilization and the Jews*, trans. S. Applebaum [Philadelphia: Jewish Publication Society of America, 1959] 282). Moreover, even though Jews had already gained prominent positions in the court of Philometer, their numbers increased during Euergetes's reign (Fraser, *Ptolemaic Alexandria*, 1:88).

[131] Pfeiffer, *History of Classical Scholarship*, 211.

[132] Ibid. Pfeiffer reports that Apollodorus's dedication of his Chronicle of the 1,040 years since the fall of Troy to King Attalus II Philadelphus of Pergamum in 144 was "either an attempt to support a request for refuge in Pergamum or an expression of thanks for his reception there" (ibid., 254).

barbarians').[133] This exodus so depleted Alexandria's ranks of scholars that "in the two generations or so after the persecutions of Euergetes we hear little of any intelligentsia, local or immigrant."[134]

In this light, while the translation of ספר by γραμματικοί in Isa 33:18 may simply be a register of the translator's esteem for the grammarians, it seems more likely that his rendering of those verses expressed his dismay at the absence of γραμματικοί as pillars of Alexandrian society after 145 B.C.E. It is difficult to identify a more likely explanation for why, in this passage alone, he elected to use γραμματικοί. In fact, the translation of שׁקל by οἱ συμβουλεύοντες might be equally explicable as reflecting the wholesale dispatching of many who had remained loyal to Philometer's widow.

This inference accords with the perception of earlier scholars that the translation of the book of Isaiah was executed shortly after the middle of the second century B.C.E. Seeligmann stipulated that the *terminus ante quem* must be the Greek translation of Ben Sira in 116, since it shows familiarity with the Greek translation of Isaiah.[135] Van der Kooij, however, insists that the *terminus ante quem* must be raised to 132, since "the translator of the book of Sirach relates in his prologue that he in this year came to Egypt and that at that time the προφητεῖαι were already translated."[136] In the end, however, he agrees with Seeligmann that the OG translation was produced around 140 B.C.E.[137]

As van der Kooij observes, γραμματικός is found in but one other book of the LXX: OG Daniel, where it appears twice in chapter one:

(4)ילדים אשר אין בהם כל מאום	(4)νεανίσκους ἀμώμους
וטובי מראה	καὶ εὐειδεῖς
ומשׂכילים בכל חכמה וידעי דעת	καὶ ἐπιστήμονας ἐν πάσῃ σοφίᾳ καὶ γραμματικοὺς
ומביני מדע	καὶ συνετοὺς καὶ σοφοὺς
ואשר כח בהם לעמד בהיכל המלך	καὶ ἰσχύοντας ὥστε εἶναι ἐν τῷ οἴκῳ τοῦ βασιλέως
וללמדם ספר ולשׁון כשׂדים	καὶ διδάξαι αὐτοὺς γράμματα καὶ διάλεκτον Χαλδαϊκὴν
(17)והילדים האלה ארבעתם	(17)καὶ τοῖς νεανίσκοις
נתן להם האלהים מדע	ἔδωκεν ὁ κύριος ἐπιστήμην

[133] As cited by Fraser, *Ptolemaic Alexandria*, 2:165 n. 324.
[134] Ibid., 1:87.
[135] Seeligmann, *Septuagint Version*, 75.
[136] Van der Kooij, "A Short Commentary," 71.
[137] Ibid., 72. Seeligmann, *Septuagint Version*, 87.

והשׂכל בכל ספר וחכמה   καὶ σύνεσιν καὶ φρόνησιν ἐν πάσῃ
γραμματικῇ τέχνῃ

ודניאל הבין בכל   καὶ τῷ Δανιηλ ἔδωκε σύνεσιν ἐν παντὶ
ῥήματι

חזון וחלמות   καὶ ὁράματι καὶ ἐνυπνίοις καὶ ἐν πάσῃ
σοφίᾳ

As van der Kooij notes, these verses reveal "familiarity with technical terms derived from the scholarly milieu of Alexandria," especially γραμματικός and γραμματικὴ τέχνη, the latter referring "to the ability of a scholar to read and interpret literary texts."[138] However, more than just revealing an Alexandrian milieu, these terms attest familiarity with the type of literary scholarship for which Alexandria gained renown.

Therefore, given the Daniel translator's familiarity with the work of the γραμματικοί and given LXX-Isaiah's apparent reference to them, understanding the Isaiah translator's Alexandrian milieu is important for assessing his approach to his task.[139]

The Museum and its γραμματικοί

While a review of the full history of the museum and its scholars would exceed the scope of this monograph, it is important to understand the ethos of the museum in the translator's era.

When Alexander founded the city that bore his name, it was with a view to its strategic advantages as a base of operations against insurgents, especially through the security its harbor afforded.[140] Even before Ptolemy II Philadelphus undertook building projects "to make the city a wonder of the world," such as the lighthouse and the elaborate mausoleum for Alexander's remains,[141] Ptolemy I Soter had erected in the royal quarter of the city the institution that would bring it special renown: the Μουσεῖα ('shrine of the Muses') and its library.[142]

---

[138] Arie van der Kooij, "The City of Alexandria and the Ancient Versions of the Hebrew Bible," *JNSL* 25 (1999) 142.

[139] Cf. van der Kooij's call for study of not only Jewish exegetical methods but also "welche Berührungspunkte es zwischen diesen Methoden und der Arbeitsweise der alexandrinischen 'grammatici' gab" (*Die alten Textzeugen*, 69).

[140] Turner, "Ptolemaic Egypt," 134.

[141] Ibid., 145.

[142] G. E. R. Lloyd, "Hellenistic Science," in *The Hellenistic World*, ed. F. W. Walbank, et al., The Cambridge Ancient History, vol. 7:1 (Cambridge: Cambridge University Press, 1984) 322. For the topic of the Μουσεῖα, see Pfeiffer, *History of Classical Scholarship*, 50 and 155.

The cultural architect behind Soter's establishment of a Museum and the library housed within it was Demetrius of Phalerum. Soter had initially sought to entice Aristotle's successor, Theophrastus, to assist in establishing Alexandria as a cultural and intellectual center in the Hellenistic world.[143] When, however, Theophrastus was unwilling to leave the Lyceum, Soter was able to draw to his service Theophrastus's erstwhile associate, Demetrius.[144]

Demetrius had been forced to flee Athens after a change of rulers in 308/7. He had been the city's tyrant from 317/16 until 308/7 and had revised its constitution and law code. With those credentials, he became highly influential in Soter's court, especially through the expertise he lent to the development of Alexandria's law code.[145] The Museum also bore his impress, since it was modeled on the one in the Lyceum, where Theophrastus had established a communal life of study dedicated to the Muses.[146] Equally under Demetrius's influence, Soter began collecting scrolls for a library,[147] following the pattern of Aristotle, who innovated the systematic collection of works to enable study of a wide range of topics.[148] The aggressive methods the crown

---

[143] Fraser, *Ptolemaic Alexandria*, 1:315.

[144] Williams contends that while sources report that Demetrius was a pupil of Theophrastus, he may also have studied with Aristotle himself (James M. Williams, "The Peripatetic School and Demetrius of Phalerum's Reforms in Athens," *AncW* 15 [1987] 88).

[145] Ibid., 90.

[146] Fraser judges that this "was probably the particular achievement of Theophrastus and not Aristotle himself" (*Ptolemaic Alexandria*, 1:314).

[147] The earliest reference to the library (*Let. Aris.* 9) places its founding during the reign of Philadelphus, under the oversight of Demetrius. While its association with Demetrius is undoubtedly correct, dating it to the reign of Philadelphus is problematic; it was likely founded under Soter. See Fraser, ibid., 1:321–22. The differentiation of libraries from archives as being "a collection including literary, historical, and perhaps scientific texts, in an institutional building such as a palace or temple or in a private house" is a good rule of thumb, even if it does not always permit clear-cut distinctions (Jeremy A. Black and W. J. Tait, "Archives and Libraries in the Ancient Near East," in *Civilizations of the Ancient Near East*, vol. 4, ed. Jack M. Sasson [New York: Scribner, 1995] 2197).

[148] Williams, "The Peripatetic School and Demetrius," 91. The establishment of libraries long precedes Aristotle, however. The remains of literary collections attached to temples have been found in Sumer, and there was the famed royal library of Assurbanipal, begun by his grandfather, Sennacherib (Black and Tait, "Archives and Libraries," 2206). Royal, temple, and private libraries are also attested for ancient Egypt (ibid., 2198). Moreover, Mesoptoamian librarians developed a system of descriptive colophons to assist cataloguing (ibid., 2199–200), a precursor to the system developed by the Alexandrian scribes (see Fraser, *Ptolemaic Alexandria*, 1:326–29). (Little is known of Egyptian library methods [Black and Tait, "Archives and Libraries," 2200]).

employed to acquire literary works became so infamous that Galen (ca. 130–200 C.E.) preserved stories about the appropriation of scrolls from ships harbored at Alexandria.[149]

Royal sponsorship of the Museum and its library made them, in effect, public institutions, open to those who could read,[150] although by no means should that be understood as a large body of people, since even in Alexandria literacy at this level would have belonged solely to the Macedonian ruling class.[151] While there is no direct evidence that the Museum functioned as a center of instruction, references to students of prominent scholars (e.g., Apollodorus of Athens and Dionysius Thrax as students of Aristarchus),[152] plus the fact that the librarian held congruently the post of tutor of the king's children,[153] suggests that pedagogy was integral to the mission of the Museum. Nevertheless, we should not think of formal courses of study, similar to a modern university. Rather, instruction would have taken the form of "discussion and conversation."[154]

Even with this caveat, the Museum should not be mistaken for a center of research in our sense of the term, any more than we should think of a γυμνάσιον as a health club. Μουσεῖα, as shrines to the Muses, were commonplace throughout the Hellenistic world and functioned primarily as cultic sites, whether as funerary shrines or, increasingly, as centers for literary societies "which met and worshipped the Muses and held literary competitions in the shrine."[155] Accordingly, Strabo reports (*Geography* 793–94) that the Ptolemies appointed priests to oversee the life of the Alexandrian Museum.[156] The establishment of the center of research in a Museum is, therefore, not coincidental, but embodies its sacral character. And every evidence points to the Museum having

---

[149] Fraser, *Ptolemaic Alexandria*, 1:325. In this the Ptolemies parallel Assurbanipal, who wrote an order giving "detailed directions for the (enforced) collection from the temple of Nabu at Borsippa (Birs Numrud) in Babylonia, and from private scholarly collections in that city" (Black and Tait, "Archives and Libraries," 2206).

[150] Pfeiffer, *History of Classical Scholarship*, 103.

[151] See David M. Carr, *Writing on the Tablet of the Heart* (New York: Oxford University Press, 2005) 187–89.

[152] On whom see Pfeiffer, *History of Classical Scholarship*, 252–72.

[153] Ibid., 154; cf. F. E. Peters, *The Harvest of Hellenism* (New York: Barnes and Noble Books, 1970) 194.

[154] Fraser, *Ptolemaic Alexandria*, 1:318.

[155] Ibid., 1:313.

[156] Ibid., 1:315. "The priest was the titular head of the community and particularly responsible for its religious activities," while a civil official was appointed by the king as administrator of its funds (ibid., 1:316).

retained its religious function and significance until the Roman period, when "the Mouseia develop[ed] into secular centres of learning."[157]

The first to hold the post of royal librarian in the Museum (during the first half of the third century) was Zenodotus. It was he who made the first attempt at a critical edition of the text of Homer,[158] no doubt feeling forced to it by the influx of so many differing copies of the Homeric epics.[159] His creation of the obelos as a critical sign to athetize lines whose authenticity he doubted marked "the first time that an editor had provided the serious reader and scholar with an opportunity of appraising his critical judgment."[160] Even if his obelizations at times seem arbitrary (they are typically based on his evaluation of a line as superfluous or indecorous), he nevertheless seems to have had "access to earlier texts of the Homeric poems than were available to his successors,"[161] a consequence of the "hundreds of thousands of papyrus rolls" deposited in the Alexandrian library in the first half of the third century B.C.E.[162]

Equally important in the development of Alexandrian literary scholarship was Callimachus of Cyrene, who flourished in the second quarter of the third century B.C.E. Although he likely never held the official post of librarian,[163] he took on the task of systematizing the mass of literature, not only classifying each by type,[164] but also alphabetizing the works within each class, noting the title and the incipit of each, as well as the number of lines it contained.[165]

---

[157] Fraser, *Ptolemaic Alexandria*, 1:313.

[158] Even if the pre-Hellenistic era Antimachus of Colophon (late fifth century) was the first to produce an edition of Homer, "we have no reason to assume that Antimachus made a 'recension' of the Homeric poems, collating manuscripts and emending the text" (Pfeiffer, *History of Classical Scholarship*, 94).

[159] Ibid., 110.

[160] Ibid., 115.

[161] Fraser, *Ptolemaic Alexandria*, 1:451. Pfeiffer, on the other hand, cautions against assuming too quickly that Zenodotus's choices were arbitrary, offering indications that, at least in points, his text was "based on documentary evidence," even if that does not mean that "he *never* altered the traditional text without external evidence" (Pfeiffer, *History of Classical Scholarship*, 114).

[162] Pfeiffer, *History of Classical Scholarship*, 102.

[163] Cameron observes that the absence of Callimachus's name from the list of librarians in the Oxyrhynchus papyrus settles the question (Alan Cameron, *Callimachus and His Critics* [Princeton: Princeton University Press, 1995] 11). Cf. Fraser, *Ptolemaic Alexandria*, 1:330–31.

[164] Pfeiffer, *History of Classical Scholarship*, 128–29.

[165] Ibid., 126.

Relegating him to the role of a cataloger would be a mischaracterization, however. Even though his various Πίνακες, or 'Tables' (more properly, "Tables of all those who were eminent in any kind of literature and of their writings in 120 books"), enumerated the works stored in the Museum,[166] they also referred to "works only mentioned in earlier literature and to questions of authenticity,"[167] as well as offered lists of distinctive Homeric vocabulary. Callimachus's works also included paradoxographies, descriptions of peculiarities in the natural world, the chief of which was his "Collection of wonders of the world, arranged geographically."[168] Although there is no reason to believe that these are his original observations or that he sought to verify the observations he collated,[169] they attest more than an obsession with cataloging. They are evidence of "the fervent devotion to learning that sprang from the enthusiasm of a great poet,"[170] who drew on these stores of images for his own poetry.[171]

Callimachus asserted a firm divide between the poetry of his day and that of the epics. His dictum, τὸ μέγα βιβλίον ἴσον τῷ κακῷ ('the large book is equivalent to the bad one') epitomizes his rejection of "unity, completeness and magnitude," in place of which he "consciously aimed at a discontinuous form" for which the appropriate characteristic was to be that it was λεπτόν ('subtle'), and the poet was to be recognized as πολυμαθής.[172] As a result, his poetry can best be characterized as creating a web of allusions to earlier works.[173]

A notable area of research in the Alexandrian school was explicit wordplay, even utilizing etymological analysis, a device used by both the

---

[166] Fraser, *Ptolemaic Alexandria*, 1:452–53.
[167] Pfeiffer, *History of Classical Scholarship*, 128.
[168] Fraser, *Ptolemaic Alexandria*, 1:454.
[169] Ibid., 1:455.
[170] Pfeiffer, *History of Classical Scholarship*, 133.
[171] Fraser, *Ptolemaic Alexandria*, 1:455. Thus, Pfeiffer observes that "we are able to find traces of nearly all the learned collections of Callimachus in his poems: fair-sounding names of rivers and islands, of winds and nymphs and birds were picked out of them to embellish the verses" (Pfeiffer, *History of Classical Scholarship*, 135).
[172] Pfeiffer, *History of Classical Scholarship*, 136–38.
[173] I derive this description from Cameron, who cautions against overstating Callimachus's uniqueness, noting that this Alexandrian was "but the most celebrated of an entire generation of learned and allusive poets who flourished in the first half of the third century," many of them outside Alexandria, so that "the label Alexandrian implies rather a common approach and manner" (Cameron, *Callimachus and His Critics*, 24–25).

poets and the later γραμματικοί.[174] Even though Callimachus's works are only fragmentarily preserved, "many passages gloss names by reference to aetiological myths,"[175] as in the explanation of the name Delos with the phrase οὐκετ' ἄδηλος, and the association of the names Dictynna and Dicte with δίκτυα, 'nets,'"[176] while he explains "the origin of the cry ἰή used in worship of Apollo, in telling of Apollo's shooting (ἵημι) of the serpent."[177] Even if such etymologies are not as abundantly attested for Callimachus as for later Alexandrians, his interest in them is consonant with his fascination with lists of names and with his work Αἰτία, that sought to provide explanations for the origins of various phenomena.[178]

The wide-ranging scholarship of Callimachus prepared the way for the γραμματικοί to follow. Upon the departure of the librarian Apollonius, one of Callimachus's students, the post of royal librarian was assumed by Eratosthenes of Cyrene, whose researches ranged more broadly than his predecessors, so that he came to embody a "union nouvelle de l'homme de science, du critique littéraire et du poète."[179] While Callimachus and Apollonius were interested in a broad range of natural wonders, including the study of medicine, Eratosthenes was "the first scholar and poet who was primarily and truly a scientist."[180] In the study of literature, his main attention was given to Old Comedy,

---

[174] Although etymology naturally finds its home among the Stoics, who placed great emphasis on nouns as materially related to their referents (see Anthony A. Long, *Hellenistic Philosophy* [Berkeley and Los Angeles: University of California Press, 1986] 133–34), etymological word play is found in Homer, Hesiod, the pre-Socratics, and Plato (see James J. O'Hara, *True Names: Vergil and the Alexandrian Tradition of Etymological Wordplay* [Ann Arbor: University of Michigan Press, 1996] 7–18).

[175] O'Hara, *True Names*, 30. Not surprisingly, Pfeiffer attenuates the importance of etymological interpretation in Callimachus, cautioning that even if "his verse very often sounds like charming word-play, the poet is never tired of reminding us that everything he is going to tell is true because it is well attested" (Pfeiffer, *History of Classical Scholarship*, 125).

[176] O'Hara, *True Names*, 31–32.

[177] Ibid., 39.

[178] Ibid., 23. As remarkable as this study of lexemes is, the Greeks were not pioneers in this field. Ancient Mesopotamian scribes had already compiled "lexical explications and annotations...[which] were kept separate from the main text" (Fishbane, *Biblical Interpretation in Ancient Israel*, 39).

[179] Christophe Cusset, *La Muse dans la Bibliothèque: Réécriture et intertextualité dans la poésie alexandrine* (CNRS Littérature; Paris: CNRS Éditions, 1999) 16. For Eratosthenes's work in mathematics, which was on a par with that of Archimedes, see Fraser, *Ptolemaic Alexandria*, 1:409–15. For his equally distinguished work in geography, see ibid., 1:525–39.

[180] Pfeiffer, *History of Classical Scholarship*, 152.

for which he sought to establish a trustworthy text through the collation of manuscripts.[181] However, the influence of his scientific bent was
particularly evident in his "approach to matters of literary criticism by
the application of external criteria to solve problems of interpretation,"
thereby displaying "a far more historical conception of literary criticism
than any other of the great Alexandrian scholars."[182] This should not,
however, be construed to mean that he eschewed the sorts of studies
of word plays popular among other Alexandrians. O'Hara notes, for
instance, Eratosthenes's judgment that "φωριαμός (chest, trunk) is so
called because 'secret' (φώριος) things are hidden in it."[183]

Eratosthenes's successor as librarian was Aristophanes, who represented "the rise of 'pure' scholarship, no longer united with poetry, but
an autonomous selfconscious [sic] discipline."[184] In fact, he has left no
trace of his own literary productions and apparently devoted himself
to the study of literature.[185] While three scholars had undertaken the
recension of epic, lyric, and drama in the third century, Aristophanes
himself "made the fundamental recensions of the texts in all these
fields."[186] And in doing so, he expanded the system of critical σημεῖα
beyond the obelus, using the ἀστερίσκος to mark "the lines repeated
from another place in which they appeared to be more appropriate"
and the σίγμα and ἀντίσιγμα to indicate "two consecutive lines having
the same contents and being therefore interchangeable."[187] Following
the example of Zenodotus, Aristophanes used these marginal notations
to indicate his judgments rather than altering the text, thus leaving
text-critical decisions in the hands of the reader.[188]

Aristophanes's skill as a literary critic is evident in his marginal note
that line 296 of Book 23 of the *Odyssey* was the original termination of
the work, a conclusion that still enjoys wide acceptance today.[189] He also
gave attention to marking an understanding of the sense of the text via

---

[181] Fraser, *Ptolemaic Alexandria*, 1:457.
[182] Ibid., 1:458.
[183] O'Hara, *True Names*, 41.
[184] Pfeiffer, *History of Classical Scholarship*, 171.
[185] Fraser, *Ptolemaic Alexandria*, 1:461.
[186] Pfeiffer, *History of Classical Scholarship*, 173.
[187] Ibid., 178.
[188] Ibid.
[189] Ibid., 175–77. Similarly, he followed Apollonius in denying "the Hesiodic origin
of the Χίρωνος Ὑποθῆκαι, and he equally doubted the authenticity of the *Shield of
Heracles*, which Apollonius had maintained" (ibid., 177).

conventions of punctuation known as early as Isocrates and Aristotle.[190] Most impressive is what can be gleaned from the scholiasts' notes about his Λέξεις, a work that "ranged over all fields of literature, prose as well as poetry."[191] Having at his disposal the lexicographic studies of those that preceded him and the *pinakes* of Callimachus, and using his own observations, he sought to establish the meaning not only of archaic words but also problematic lexemes, superceding prior vocabulary lists by inquiring into the eras in which words were used, as well as tracing lexical variation due to dialectical differences.[192]

In short, the extant evidence of Aristophanes's work leaves no doubt about the dramatic changes he introduced in philological study in the Museum. And even though his life ended prematurely (ca. 180 B.C.E.) when he fell out of the king's good graces,[193] the type and intensity of scholarship he established set the tone for those who followed, especially his student Aristarchus of Samothrace, who became the royal librarian in 153 B.C.E.[194]

Unfortunately, remnants of Aristarchus's work survive only in scholiasts' notes.[195] While he produced a thoroughgoing critical recension of Homer that he claimed surpassed those of his predecessors,[196] his distinctive contribution was the writing of commentaries (ὑπομνήματα),[197] a form of literature not previously developed in Alexandria.[198] While Suidas's attribution to Aristarchus of more than 800 ὑπομνήματα is likely inflated, the comment of later copyists that he wrote many com-

---

[190] Ibid., 179–80. Pfeiffer is adamant that "the more elaborate system finally developed in the Hadrianic age by Nicanor should not be dated back to Aristophanes" (ibid., 180). Aristophanes does seem, however, to have originated a system of accentuation (ibid.).

[191] Pfeiffer, *History of Classical Scholarship*, 197.

[192] For Aristophanes's interest in dialectology, see ibid., 200 and 202.

[193] Fraser, *Ptolemaic Alexandria*, 1:461.

[194] Pfeiffer, *History of Classical Scholarship*, 210.

[195] Ibid., 211. For a thorough discussion of the scholiasts' preservation of interpretations by Aristarchus and other Alexandrian scholars see Roos Meijering, *Literary and Rhetorical Theories in Greek Scholia* (Groningen: Egbert Forsten, 1987).

[196] Pfeiffer, *History of Classical Scholarship*, 217–18. Less certain is whether he produced recensions of other texts.

[197] While Aristarchus pioneered the commentary form among Alexandrian scholars, ancient Mesopotamian scribes had already produced interpretative commentaries distinct from the texts they copied (Fishbane, *Biblical Interpretation in Ancient Israel*, 39).

[198] Pfeiffer, *History of Classical Scholarship*, 212. Turner cautions against viewing the ὑπομνήμα as an Alexandrian invention, noting that "it is found fully developed in a papyrus roll recovered at Derveni near Thessaloniki that cannot have been copied later than about 300 B.C." (Turner, "Ptolemaic Egypt," 170).

mentaries (excerpts of which survive in scholiasts' notes in a Venetian codex of the *Iliad*) supports the general claim that his ὑπομνήματα were voluminous.[199] He seems to have commented not only on Homer's epics, but also on "non-Homeric epics, lyrics, and drama, and was the first to comment on a prose author."[200]

Aristarchus's touchstone in interpreting Homer was the question of how a word, phrase, or passage compared with Homer's usage elsewhere.[201] The products of this principle proved salutary, inasmuch as

> he detected in the explanations of glosses errors that had been traditional for centuries, he much improved the distinction of synonyms...and, continuing the research of Aristophanes of Byzantium, he saw how many more words, often quite common ones, had changed their meaning in the interval between the epic age or even the Attic and his own time.[202]

His eye for what was characteristic of Homer likewise led him to distinguish between what was genuinely Homeric (Ὁμηρικώτερον) and what was spurious (κυκλικώτερον).[203] Following the example set by his predecessors, however, Aristarchus did not delete such discrepancies, but annotated them, by means of σημεῖα, as questionable or even κυκλικώτερον.[204] Indeed, the σημεῖα were less text-critical signs than cross-references to his commentaries.[205] It was there that "the bulk of the redaction (and justification) was done—at a safe remove from the body of the texts, which could be left for the most part intact."[206]

Aristarchus's literary judgments were not limited to decisions about what was Ὁμηρικώτερον and what he considered κυκλικώτερον, however. Even if he did not enunciate an overarching theory of poetics, there are terminological and methodological evidences in his writing that he was influenced by Aristotle's *Poetics*,[207] while the scholia attribute

---

[199] Pfeiffer, *History of Classical Scholarship*, 213. For an example of a dispute with an athetization by Zenodotus, see Meijering, *Literary and Rhetorical Theories*, 174.

[200] Pfeiffer, *History of Classical Scholarship*, 219–20.

[201] Fraser, *Ptolemaic Alexandria*, 1:464.

[202] Pfeiffer, *History of Classical Scholarship*, 228.

[203] Ibid., 227. Pfeiffer notes that "the use of the term κυκλικώτερον or κυκλικῶς, reflects the distinction first drawn by Aristotle between the great poet of the *Iliad* and *Odyssey* and the makers of the other early epics, the κυκλικοί....[A]fter Aristotle...everything 'cyclic' was regarded as inferior" (ibid., 230).

[204] Ibid., 231.

[205] Porter, "Hermeneutic Lines and Circles," 69.

[206] Ibid., 68.

[207] Ibid., 74–75.

aesthetic and rhetorical judgments to him.[208] These comments "call attention to the art of composition" or "emphasize the harmony between the speech and character of an epic hero," while other comments address "the specific function of metaphors...or of similes...or of 'not mentioning a thing,'" in each case lauding Homer as a masterful poet.[209] Aristarchus sought to understand Homer's meaning rather than just his words,[210] including an appreciation of his use of poetic or mythic expression, which he saw as a field of thought and art broader than Homer. In Aristarchus's view, "poetic 'licence' is...tightly defined and closely circumscribed by poetic 'rules' and theoretical constraints,"[211] so that myth is never the property of a single author. Consequently, his reading of Homer also entailed comparisons with Hesiod and the tragedians.

The disruption of academic life in Alexandria in the years after 145 B.C.E., mentioned earlier in this chapter, was severe. Aristarchus himself fled to Cyprus, where he died not long after.[212] According to the Oxyrhynchus papyrus, the person appointed to succeed Aristarchus as librarian was Cydas, "One of the Spearmen" (ἐκ τῶν λογχοφόρων), who was "perhaps one of the χιλίαρχοι λογχοφόροι known from contemporary documents," a royal appointee whose job it was simply to administer the library.[213] Moreover, despite Euergetes II's penchant for violence, he (a student of Aristarchus, after all) was devoted to φιλομαθεῖν, "as the fragments of the twenty-four books of his *Memoirs* on a strange variety of subjects disclose."[214] Thus, even though the Museum was bereft of the scholars who had been its lifeblood, it continued to operate during his reign and those of his successors,[215] even if during those times grammatical and literary studies saw "no fundamental reconsiderations of the basic principles of the subject."[216]

The list of Alexandrian librarians contained in the Oxyrhynchus papyrus reports that under Euergetes's successor, Ptolemy IX (Soter II), "there flourished Ammonios and Zeno...and Dokles and Apol-

---

[208] Pfeiffer, *History of Classical Scholarship*, 231.
[209] Ibid., 231–32.
[210] Porter, "Hermeneutic Lines and Circles," 70.
[211] Ibid., 80.
[212] Ibid., 211.
[213] Fraser, *Ptolemaic Alexandria*, 1:333.
[214] Pfeiffer, *History of Classical Scholarship*, 212.
[215] Ibid.
[216] Fraser, *Ptolemaic Alexandria*, 1:807.

lodoros, the grammarians."[217] While Oxyrhynchus is vague about whether Ammonios actually served as librarian,[218] a tradition survives that he 'took over the school of Aristarchus' (διεδέξατο τὴν σχολήν ’Αριστάρχου).[219] Of Ammonios little more than this is known, while knowledge of the other three is even less certain.[220] It was not until the age of Cicero and Antony that another Alexandrian scholar, Didymus, gained prominence.[221]

Summary

The foregoing survey demonstrates the vitality of philology in the Alexandrian Museum down to the pogroms of Euergetes II. Given that these activities would have been familiar to the city's populace, and given that the Greek translation of Isaiah was produced in the wake of Aristartchus's era, this setting merits consideration in exploring the translator's work.

At the same time, we must recognize that the translator was not simply an Alexandrian, but a member of the Jewish community in Alexandria. Chapter two will probe what we know about the city's Jewish community and how the scholarship of the Museum influenced it.

---

[217] Cited in ibid., 1:333.
[218] Fraser opines that the language of "flourishing" suggests that "the author of the list was himself not certain" (ibid.).
[219] Ibid., 2:677 n. 197.
[220] See ibid., 2:492 n. 218.
[221] Pfeiffer, *History of Classical Scholarship*, 275. Cf. Fraser, *Ptolemaic Alexandria*, 1:475, 807.

CHAPTER TWO

ALEXANDRIA AND THE LXX

Discussion of the potential relevance of Alexandrian scholarship on Homer to the translation of Isaiah into Greek is based on the reflection of the Ptolemaic milieu demonstrated by Ziegler in his chapter on "der alexandrinisch-ägyptische Hintergrund der Js-LXX," in which he points out the translation's many "Egyptianisms."[1] For example, noting the translation of ונתן הספר על אשר לא ידע ספר by καὶ δοθήσεται τὸ βιβλίον τοῦτο εἰς χεῖρας ἀνθρώπου μὴ ἐπισταμένου γράμματα in Isa 29:12 (cf. ὃ ἐὰν δῶσιν αὐτὸ ἀνθρώπῳ ἐπισταμένῳ γράμματα || אשר יתנו אתו אל יודע הספר in v. 11), he reports that

> im hellenistischen Ägypten der Ausdruck μὴ ἐπιστάμενος γράμματα und μὴ εἰδὼς γράμματα ganz geläufig war für die Bezeichnung des Analphabeten, namentlich in Unterschriften, die in Vertretung von Analphabeten gegeben wurden: ἔγραψα ὑπὲρ αὐτοῦ διὰ μὴ ἐπίστασθαι αὐτὸν γράμματα.[2]

Although this example does not specifically evince the translator's interest in literary study, it does show his indebtedness to Alexandrian phraseology.

The examples of Ptolemaic terminology and concepts Ziegler found in the translation was so pervasive as to justify his conclusion that LXX-Isaiah "bietet uns so einen lehrreichen Beitrag für die Kenntnis des griechisch-alexandrinischen Ägypten, weil sie den hebr. Text ihrer Vorlage durch das Medium des Hellenismus umgeformt hat."[3] However, there is reason to conclude that the Alexandrian milieu offered more than just new language and vocabulary for this translation. In order to explore this, we need to consider what is known of Alexandrian Judaism.

---

[1] "In keinem anderen Buche der LXX so viele 'Ägyptizismen' stehen als in der Js-LXX" (Ziegler, *Untersuchungen*, 176).

[2] Ibid., 176–77.

[3] Ibid., 212.

Alexandrian Judaism

The origins of the Jewish community in Alexandria are as obscure as other information about the earliest period of the city's existence. That Jews should have settled in the region is not surprising, given evidence of refugees from Judah fleeing there after the Babylonians sacked Jerusalem, as well as evidence of a community of mercenaries at Elephantine.[4] Moreover, we know of the dedication of a synagogue at Schedia to Eugertes I and Bernice, while Aramaic inscriptions in the early Ptolemaic tombs attest Jews in the vicinity of Alexandria.[5] Nevertheless, "there is an almost complete absence of testimony to individual Jews" in the early Ptolemaic period.[6] Although Josephus's report that Alexander himself permitted Jews to settle in Alexandria and that "they gained honor equal to the Macedonians" (καὶ ἴσης παρά τοῖς Μακεδόσι τιμῆς ἐπέτυχον, *Contra Apion* 2.35) has led some to suggest that Jews, *en bloc*, were granted citizenship during Ptolemaic rule, there are sound reasons to reject that surmise, even if "in due course some no doubt acquired Alexandrian citizenship."[7]

While Jews appear to have been among the numerous non-Greeks living in Alexandria, it was not until the second century B.C.E. that the Jewish population burgeoned, largely due to refugees from the upheavals in Judea during the Hellenistic crisis that afflicted Jerusalem.[8] It is likely to that era that the development of the Jewish sector of the city, reported by Strabo, should also be dated, although this was likely "due to private initiative" rather than an official grant of territory.[9]

The favor the Jewish community seems to have attracted from Philometer has long been considered the explanation for the rise of

---

[4] See John J. Collins, *Between Athens and Jerusalem* (The Biblical Resource Series; Grand Rapids: Wm. B. Eerdmans, 2000) 3–4.

[5] Beek notes that "l'inscription, avec laquelle la proseuque de Schédia a été dédiée à la dynastie de Ptolemée III Euergète (247–221) est le plus ancien document que nous possédions d'une proseuque" (Martinus A. Beek, "Relations entre Jérusalem et la diaspora Égyptienne au 2ᵉ siècle avant J.-C.," in *OtSt*, ed. P. A. H. de Boer, vol. 2 [Leiden: Brill, 1943] 133).

[6] Fraser, *Ptolemaic Alexandria*, 1:57.

[7] Ibid., 1:55. Josephus may reflect the fact that in the Roman period citizenship was opened more broadly to non-Greeks (cf. ibid., 1:77).

[8] Sylvie Honigman, *The Septuagint and Homeric Scholarship in Alexandria* (London and New York: Routledge, 2003) 100.

[9] Fraser, *Ptolemaic Alexandria*, 1:56.

a Jewish *politeuma* in Alexandria.[10] However, recently published papyri from Heracleopolis in Middle Egypt have shown that *politeumata* were, first and foremost, rooted in military units rather than constituting a fiefdom granted an ethnic group.[11] And even though Strabo speaks of the Jews of Alexandria being overseen by an ethnarch, his description likely refers to the structure of the *politeuma* rather than a formal organization of the Jewish community as a whole,[12] thereby lessening the impression that they lived in some sort of isolation from the remainder of the city. The notion that Alexandrian Jews formed a "ghetto" cut off from the dominant Hellenistic culture has long since been debunked.[13] No stronger contravening of that notion is to be found than in apparent Jewish affinities for education in the Alexandrian *gymnasia*.

The *gymnasion* stood at the heart of Alexandria, as it did in every πόλις.[14] Fourth century debate in Athens over the content of education had already transformed the *gymnasion* from "a social-athletic club focused on a *palaistra* towards being something far closer to a recognizable secondary school for *paides* (i.e., boys of 12–17)."[15] The export of the *gymnasion* throughout the world made it the supreme vehicle of Hellenistic culture.[16] Education in the *gymnasion* was expanded to embrace the education of young men from ages seven until fourteen or fifteen, "followed by the period of the ephebate which lasted one or two years," after which young men could continue their "instruction in the gymnasium until about the age of twenty."[17]

Fraser reports that "the ephebate, and indeed the whole system of Greek training in the liberal arts and athletics centered on the gymnasion, was probably accessible to most members of the population who

---

[10] See, for instance, ibid., 1:84.

[11] Honigman, *The Septuagint and Homeric Scholarship*, 99. She also points out that *politeumata* "do not appear in these new documents before the reign of Ptolemy IV in the late third century B.C.E. (ibid.).

[12] Ibid., 100.

[13] Ibid., 6 and 94.

[14] Fraser, *Ptolemaic Alexandria*, 1:29.

[15] J. K. Davies, "Cultural, Social and Economic Features of the Hellenistic World," in *The Hellenistic World*, ed. F. W. Walbank, et al., The Cambridge Ancient History, vol. 7:1 (Cambridge: Cambridge University Press, 1984) 308.

[16] Ibid. *Gymnasia* were not, however, the sole property of πόλεις, but were found "even in larger villages, i.e., everywhere that Greeks settled in self-contained groups" (Martin Hengel, *Judaism and Hellenism*, trans. John Bowden, 2 vols. [Philadelphia: Fortress Press, 1974] 1:66).

[17] Ibid.

were Greek-speaking—Hellenized—regardless of race."[18] His comment bears, especially, on the question of Jewish access to the *gymnasion*. We have no direct evidence of Jews enrolled in the Alexandrian
gymnasion, and our only list of ephebes from Alexandria comes from
very late, 134/3 B.C.E., so that information about ephebes in the city's
gymnasion is scant in any case.[19] And while that list of fourteen ephebes
contains only Greek names, by the dawn of the second century B.C.E.
"we find predominately Greek names among the Jews of the Egyptian
Diaspora."[20] What is more, Hengel notes that throughout the Hellenistic
world "Jewish names keep appearing in the lists of ephebes," while
Philo, although admittedly at a much later time, "took it for granted
that well-to-do Jews would be educated at the gymnasium."[21]

More to the point, Jewish approbation of the educational values of
the *gymnasion* is evident in the *Letter of Aristeas*, with its "frequent stress on
the educational ideal of καλοκἀγαθία, so loved in the gymnasium."[22] As
Hengel concludes, "the intellectual elite of the Greek-speaking Jews of
Egypt could not escape this influence [and] developed their own learned
tradition, which lasted over several centuries."[23] This development
seems to have taken root during the reign of Ptolemy VI Philometer
(180–145 B.C.E.) when the number of Jews in Alexandria swelled and
under whose rule (it appears) Alexandrian Jews gained elevated political
status.[24] The affection of Alexandrian Jews for the Ptolemies is apparent
in Aristobulus's dedication of his work Πτολεμαίῳ τῷ Φιλαδέλφῳ καὶ
τῷ τούτου πατρί, while the pseudepigraphic Letter of Aristeas, with
its portrayal of Eleazar and the scribes from Jerusalem as Hellenistic
philosophers whose excellence in reasoning exceeds that of the
Alexandrians, attests the willingness of at least some Alexandrian Jews
to aspire to Hellenistic standards of learning in the second century B.C.E.

Consequently, we should expect to find that scholarship in the library,
which colored the entire city, had an impact on literature studied and

---

[18] Fraser, *Ptolemaic Alexandria*, 1:77.

[19] Ibid., 1:86.

[20] Hengel, *Judaism and Hellenism*, 1:63. Hengel reports that "only about twenty-five
percent of the Jewish military settlers mentioned in the papyri have Jewish names;
in reality the percentage is still lower, as Jewish bearers of Greek names can only be
recognized by the addition of 'Ioudaios', and that was by no means always made"
(ibid.). On the widespread adoption of Greek names in the Diaspora, see Tcherikover,
Hellenistic Civilization, 346.

[21] Hengel, *Judaism and Hellenism*, 1:68.

[22] Ibid.

[23] Ibid., 1:69.

[24] Fraser, *Ptolemaic Alexandria*, 1:55–56.

composed by Alexandrian Jews. Strong evidence of that comes from the (so-called) *Letter of Aristeas*.[25]

The Letter of Aristeas *and the* LXX

The *Letter of Aristeas* purports to recount the translation of the Torah into Greek at the command of Ptolemy II Philadelphus, in response to Demetrius's report of its absence from the royal library (§§9–11). The implausibility of Demetrius serving in the court of Philadelphus is a telltale mark that this work comes from an era later than either of those figures.[26] That is also betrayed by the author's reference to practices undertaken by *"these* kings" (τοῖς βασιλεῦσι τούτοις, §28) and to established procedures for approaching "the kings" (§182), intimating that he wrote in the time of Ptolemy III (246–222) or later.[27] Nevertheless, these inadvertent evidences of the author's ruse offer no help in identifying when he composed his work.

Meecham's suggestion, in 1935, of a date of around 100 B.C.E was adopted by many.[28] However, Bickerman later provided a more precise determination based on the author's "use, in the correct context, of

---

[25] Hadas notes that the description of this work as a letter dates to a fourteenth century manuscript (Moses Hadas, *Aristeas to Philocrates, Dropsie College Edition* [New York: KTAV, 1973] 56 n. 81). He also draws attention to the fact that the form of this work is not that of a letter but of a διήγησις, for which he cites Theon's definition: "a discourse expository of things which happened or might have happened" (ibid., 57). Honigman likewise notes the work's self-identification as a διήγησις and adopts Josephus's title for it as the *Book of Aristeas* (*The Septuagint and Homeric Scholarship*, 1). Wasserstein, however, makes the salient observation that even though the author speaks of his account as a διήγησις, "the introductory words and the general flavour of the phraseology throughout agree with the pattern of the literary epistolary style" (Abraham Wasserstein and David J. Wasserstein, *The Legend of the Septuagint: From Classical Antiquity to Today* [Cambridge: Cambridge University Press, 2006] 23). I will refer to the work either as Pseudo-Aristeas or under the traditional title, *The Letter of Aristeas*, while I will speak of the author as "Aristeas" or simply "the author." Unless otherwise noted, quotations are from Shutt's translation (R. J. H. Shutt, "Letter of Aristeas," in *The Old Testament Pseudepigrapha*, ed. James H. Charlesworth, vol. 2 [New York: Doubleday, 1985]).

[26] Demetrius had advised Ptolemy I Soter to appoint his oldest son heir rather than Philadelphus. After Soter's death, Philadelphus imprisoned Demetrius, who then received a fatal bite from an asp, under suspicious circumstances (Williams, "The Peripatetic School and Demetrius," 92).

[27] Honigman, *The Septuagint and Homeric Scholarship*, 2. Cf. the comments by Fraser, *Ptolemaic Alexandria*, 2:974–75 n. 127.

[28] Henry G. Meecham, *The Letter of Aristeas* (Manchester: Manchester University Press, 1935) 333.

the technical language of the Ptolemaic court and administration."[29] Key for Bickerman were terms like τῶν ἀρχισωματοφυλάκων, whose use in the manner found in *The Letter of Aristeas* began during the reign of Ptolemy VIII, in the year 145.[30] And whereas Meecham appears to have been driven to a date of around 100 by his observation that the phrase χαίρειν καὶ ἐρρῶσθαι (§35) "points to a date at the end of the second or the beginning of the first century B.C., since it is found chiefly in the late Ptolemaic period,"[31] Bickerman compared this formula with Aristeas's use of simple χαίρειν (§41), concluding that the author's use of the former must have preceded the date at which it lost its force as a *Gesundheitsformel*, "das heißt vor ca. 115 v. Chr. und natürlich nach der Erfindung der kürzeren Formel, das heißt nach ca. 170 v. Chr."[32] Such analyses led Bickerman to date the work between 145–125.[33] Hadas, upon reviewing the data, concurred that "nothing in the linguistic evidence compels a dating below the middle of the second century B.C.E."[34] Goodman proposed pushing the upper limit of dating to the beginning of Philometer's reign in 180, but wound up concluding merely that "the author…can be dated with certainty to some time in the second century B.C."[35] Accordingly, Pseudo-Aristeas belongs to the era when LXX-Isaiah was produced, which means that it can provide evidence of how the LXX-Pentateuch was viewed in the translator's day.[36]

---

[29] Fraser, *Ptolemaic Alexandria*, 1:703.

[30] Elias Bickerman, "Zur Datierung des Pseudo-Aristeas," in *Studies in Jewish and Christian History*, ed. Elias Bickerman (Arbeiten zur Geschichte des antiken Judentums und des Urchristentums 9; Leiden: Brill, 1976) 127–28. For a summary of the terms in question, see Fraser, *Ptolemaic Alexandria*, 2:970–71 n. 121.

[31] Meecham, *The Letter of Aristeas*, 333.

[32] Bickerman, "Zur Datierung," 125.

[33] Ibid., 109–36. His lower date is tenuous, since it is based on correlating Eleazar's attitude towards Egyptian Jewry with observations about a change of attitude among the Hasmoneans toward Egyptian Jews datable to 124 (Bickerman, "Zur Datierung," 132), despite the fact that the depiction of Jerusalem and its high priest are idealizations and, thus, can provide no help in dating the work (Honigman, *The Septuagint and Homeric Scholarship*, 129).

[34] Hadas, *Aristeas to Philocrates*, 18.

[35] In Emil Schürer, *The History of the Jewish People in the Age of Jesus Christ*, ed. Geza Vermes, Fergus Millar, and Martin Goodman, vol. III, part 1 (Edinburgh: T&T Clark, 1986) 3.1:683–84. Shutt dates it to "about 170 B.C.," following Jellicoe and Orlinsky (Shutt, "Letter of Aristeas," 9).

[36] For the translator's familiarity with the LXX-Pentateuch, see below, p. 105.

Aristeas's near-contemporary, Aristobulus,[37] likewise attributes the project of translating the Torah to Demetrius's oversight, during the reign of Philadelphus (Eusebius, *Praep. ev.* 13.12.1–2). Fraser posited that this shared errant attribution reveals that Aristobulus was simply dependent on a reconstruction of the translation's history invented by Pseudo-Aristeas.[38] However, Zuntz challenged that conclusion, arguing that because Pseudo-Aristeas seems to have utilized traditions, he was not likely responsible for "so substantial an invention."[39] He posited that the dating of the Torah's translation to Demetrius's day derives from "a legendary tradition current among Alexandrian Jews" with which Aristobulus was also acquainted.[40] Honigman has recently buttressed Zuntz's case by observing that, in a book where the author seems to have carefully chosen theophoric names acceptable for a Jewish audience (e.g., Theodoret, Theopompus), "'Demetrius' stands out as the only theophoric name referring to a pagan deity, the goddess Demeter," which suggests that the author was "dependent on oral tradition that he felt was binding."[41]

Moreover, despite the similarities between Aristobulus and Pseudo-Aristeas, there are substantial differences between them. Most saliently, whereas Aristobulus asserts that Plato and Pythagoras had recourse to and used the Torah, Aristeas makes a point of saying that earlier Greek writers who had attempted to use parts of the Torah had been smitten for their impiety (§§313–316). Contrary to frequent summaries, however,

---

[37] The dating of the fragments of Aristobulus to Philometer's reign has weathered skepticism, leading Adela Yarbro Collins to conclude that "there is no good reason to doubt that Aristobulus wrote during the reign of Ptolemy VI Philometer," probably during the latter part of his reign (155–145 B.C.E.) (Adela Yarbro Collins, "Aristobulus," in *The Old Testament Pseudepigrapha*, ed. James H. Charlesworth, vol. 2 [New York: Doubleday, 1985] 833). For a detailed summary of the objections and their refutation see Schürer, *History of the Jewish People*, 3.1:583–86, and Fraser, *Ptolemaic Alexandria*, 2:964–65. For Wasserstein's undue skepticism that these fragments are late Christian fabrications, see below, pp. 44–46.

[38] Fraser, *Ptolemaic Alexandria*, 1:694.

[39] G. Zuntz, "Aristeas Studies II: Aristeas on the Translation of the Torah," in *Studies in the Septuagint: Origins, Recensions, and Interpretations*, ed. Sidney Jellicoe (New York: KTAV, 1974) 224.

[40] Ibid. Cf. Oswyn Murray, "Aristeas and His Sources," *StPatr* 12 (1975) 115. Tcherikover cites Aristeas's protest against those who "take the contemptible view that Moses enacted this legislation because of an excessive preoccupation with mice and weasels or suchlike creatures" (§ 144) as evidence that Aristeas had Aristobulus in mind (Victor Tcherikover, "The Ideology of the Letter of Aristeas," *HTR* 51 [1958] 72). However, nowhere does Aristobulus adopt this position.

[41] Honigman, *The Septuagint and Homeric Scholarship*, 89–90.

the distinction between these reports does not reside in the question of whether parts of the Torah had been translated previously.

It is commonplace to read that while Aristobulus posits the existence of prior translations, Aristeas asserts that God afflicted those who previously attempted translations.[42] In fact, Wasserstein has argued that this distinction reveals the fragment from Aristobulus to be a fabrication by a Christian apologist concerned to show that Christianity's pedigree accords with Greek thought, so as "to achieve the central purpose of the Christian propaganda argument, based on the pattern of the providential *praeparatio evangelica*."[43] On closer examination, his argument falls due to his adoption of a common misreading of *Let. Aris.* §§312–17:[44]

> All of the version was read by [the king], and he marveled profoundly at the genius of the lawgiver. He said to Demetrius, "How is it that after such great works were (originally) completed, none of the historians or poets took it upon himself to refer to them?" [313]He said, "Because the legislation was holy and had come from God, and indeed, some of those who made the attempt were smitten by God, and refrained from their design." [314]Moreover, he said that he had heard Theopompus declare that, just when he was about to quote in a misleading way some of the previously translated passages from the Law, he had a mental upset for more than thirty days; at its abatement, he besought God to make clear to him the cause of this occurrence. [315]It was revealed to him in a dream that it was due to his meddlesome desire to disclose the things of God to common man, and then—he said—he ceased and so recovered. [316]I have also received from Theodectus the tragic poet (the report) that when he was about to include in a play a passage from what is written in the Bible, he was afflicted with cataract of the eyes. He suspected that this was why the affliction had befallen him, so he besought God for many days and recovered. [317]When the king had received, as I previously mentioned, Demetrius' account on these matters, he bowed and gave orders for great care to be taken of the books and for their hallowed preservation.

Demetrius's initial explanation of why the Torah was not widely known (the holiness of the work brought suffering on those who attempted to use it) and the king's subsequent command "for great care to be taken

---

[42] E.g., Janowitz states that Aristeas "states the opposite" of Aristobulus, explaining "that the writings are not better known due to the deity's opposition to previous attempts at translation" (Naomi Janowitz, "The Rhetoric of Translation: Three Early Perspectives on Translating Torah," *HTR* 84 [1991] 134).

[43] Wasserstein and Wasserstein, *The Legend of the Septuagint*, 34.

[44] Unless otherwise noted, translations are from Shutt, "Letter of Aristeas."

of the books and for their hallowed preservation" emphasize the need
for reverential treatment of these books.

Seemingly distinct is the case of Theopompus, who incurred trouble
because he sought to quote the Torah "in a misleading way." However,
Shutt's translation of ἐπισφαλέστερον in this way is questionable.
While ἐπισφαλής appears only here in *The Letter of Aristeas*, other words
from this root occur: ἀσφάλεια 8x, ἀσφαλῶς 2x, and ἀσφαλίζειν 1x.
Particularly noteworthy is their use in stressing the "safe" accomplish-
ment of the task, as in Eleazar's statement to the king of his hope that
"the translation of the sacred law should progress in a way profitable
and safe for you" (ὅπως γένηται σοι συμφερόντως καὶ μετὰ ἀσφαλείας
ἡ τοῦ ἁγίου νόμου μεταγραφή, §45).[45] Correspondingly, Demetrius's
report of the completion of the translation brought joy to the king,
"because he considered his purpose to have been completed safely"
(τὴν γὰρ πρόθεσιν, ἣν εἶχεν, ἀσφαλῶς ἔδοξε τετελειῶσθαι, §312). In
that light, the report that Theopompus had intended to cite passages
from the Torah ἐπισφαλέστερον likely means "(rather) unsafely."[46] The
danger implied is discernable from the context, in which Theopompus's
punishment is revealed to be "due to his meddlesome desire to disclose the things of God to common man" (ὅτι τὰ θεῖα βούλεται
περιεργασάμενος εἰς κοινοὺς ἀνθρώπους ἐκφέρειν, §315). This is comparable to Theodectus's eye ailment befalling him when "he was about
to include in a play a passage from what is written in the Bible" (§316).
In the context of Aristeas's concern about proper recognition of the
holiness of these books, the "danger" is treating this sacred literature
cavalierly. However, the issue at hand is *not* translation.[47]

Indeed, Theopompus's fault is that he sought to utilize "some of the
previously translated (τινὰ τῶν προηρμηνευμένων) passages of the Law"
(§314).[48] Given this, Demetrius's report that Theodectus's troubles arose

---

[45] Translation mine.

[46] This meaning is consistent with the majority of usages cited by LSJ and with
the noun ἐπισφάλεια, 'precariousness'; while LSJ does attest the meaning, 'making
to fall, misleading' and attaches that sense to the verb ἐπισφάλλειν in Josephus, *B.J.*
3.7.29, the opposition of ἐπισφαλής to ἀσφάλεια and ἀσφαλῶς in *Let. Aris.* favors the
meaning 'dangerous', 'unsafe'.

[47] Honigman seems similarly drawn into this misperception, writing that the
examples of Theopompus and Theodectus show "that not just anyone is entitled to
manipulate the sacred text, either to use it, or to translate or transcribe it" (Honigman,
The Septuagint and Homeric Scholarship, 60).

[48] Bickerman's claim that "here the expression *ta proermeneumena* means 'previously
expounded' and refers to the reading of the Law to the King" will not do (Elias

from his attempt to use "a citation from things written in the book" (τι τῶν ἀναγεγραμμένων ἐν τῇ βίβλῳ)[49] unlikely presupposes that the poet read the material in Hebrew. Accordingly, Aristeas, like Aristobulus, assumes that translations of (at least) parts of the Torah existed prior to the project Philadelphus underwrote. For Aristobulus these provided a means to defend the superiority of Jewish tradition. For Aristeas, on the other hand, they suggested a denigration of the Torah's holiness through the revelation of sacred things to "common men."

The upshot is that the translation of Torah executed in the *Letter of Aristeas* is portrayed as the translation authorized for widespread usage.[50] Even if the anecdotes about Theopompus and Theodectus caution against cavalier use of the Torah, it is nevertheless read by the king, who (with appropriate safeguards) places it in the royal library for public use. Aristeas's concern is for the pedigree of *this* translation, whereas Aristobulus is concerned with the pedigree of the Torah's teachings generally. Both assume that earlier translations existed.

In that light, then, not only does Wasserstein's hypothesis of Eusebius's fragment as the church historian's own fabrication falter, but the outline of events in Aristobulus and Pseudo-Aristeas is more closely aligned. What distinguishes them is the latter's detailing of preparations for the translation, the character of the translators, and the outcome of its acclaim by Alexandrian Jews. What they share is the assertion that the project was undertaken during the reign of Philadelphus, under the superintendence of Demetrius.

Wasserstein regards the whole of Aristeas's story a fabrication that provides "evidence *only* for the existence of *a* translation at the time the *Letter* was composed and for the existence of a wish to ascribe

---

Bickerman, "The Septuagint as a Translation," in *Studies in Jewish and Christian History, part 1*, ed. Elias Bickerman [Arbeiten zur Geschichte des antiken Judentums und des Urchristentums; Leiden: Brill, 1976] 173 n. 14). Not only is the prior reference to a 'public reading' (παρανεγνώσθη) to the king (rather than an exposition), but the translators are called ἑρμηνεῖς (§§310, 318) and their action is ἑρμηνεύειν (§39) or ἑρμηνεία (§3, 11, 32, 120, 301, 308). Accordingly, τινὰ τῶν προηρμηνευμένων refers to 'some of the [passages] previously *translated*'.

[49] Translation mine. As Pelletier notes, this is "the earliest testimony to the use of the expression 'The Book' to designate the Torah" (André Pelletier, "Josephus, the Letter of Aristeas, and the Septuagint," in *Josephus, the Bible, and History*, ed. Louis Feldman and Gohei Hata [Detroit: Wayne State University Press, 1989] 108).

[50] This anticipates Philo's more explicit explanation of the translation of the Torah as owing to the lack of access to the Torah by all humankind (Philo, *Mos.* 2.25–44).

authority of some kind to that translation."[51] Accordingly, he considers "the role of Demetrius Phalereus...an impossibility" that should be excluded from any question of a "kernel of historical truth," although he disavows interest in isolating such a kernel.[52]

On the other hand, Honigman's argument that the use of "Demetrius" (as "the only theophoric name referring to a pagan deity" in Pseudo-Aristeas) signals the author's dependence "on an oral tradition that he felt was binding" does not imply that the tradition of the LXX-Pentateuch owing its existence to Demetrius is a hard datum of history.[53] Demetrius's legendary role in procuring manuscripts of Greek authors may have fostered the association of him with the translation of the LXX in popular lore.[54]

What is more, as Honigman argues, Aristeas tells the story of the translation "in a manner which is both relatively sober and strictly rationalized," while only later, in Philo, do we find "miraculous elements designed to confirm the divine character of the translation"[55] that are subsequently embellished by Christian writers.[56] This does not mean that Aristeas gives us a "historical" account, but it does suggest that he "would not have created his charter myth for the LXX, but would only have given it literary form."[57]

As Honigman argues, the author's own contributions are more tangible in two narrative traditions he reinscribed and intertwined in fashioning his διήγησις.[58] On the one hand, he adopted elements of the plot of the book of Exodus, beginning with a parallel to its story

---

[51] Wasserstein and Wasserstein, *The Legend of the Septuagint*, 25.

[52] Ibid., 23.

[53] Honigman, *The Septuagint and Homeric Scholarship*, 89–90.

[54] Ibid., 90.

[55] Ibid., 3. For the embellishment of the story by Philo, see Wasserstein and Wasserstein, *The Legend of the Septuagint*, 35–45. Josephus's telling of the story, clearly reliant on Aristeas, contains no miraculous elements and omits "all the passages relating to Jerusalem and the Holy Land, to the embassy to Eleazar, the description of the Temple and its service and more...in order to draw the reader's attention away from the failed project of the Jewish Revolt, and instead to draw it on to a different way off viewing the Jews" (ibid., 50).

[56] For subsequent accretions to the tradition that enhance the miraculous even beyond Philo's reformulations, see Pelletier, "Josephus, the Letter of Aristeas, and the Septuagint," 109–12.

[57] Honigman, *The Septuagint and Homeric Scholarship*, 90.

[58] She notes that "this mechanism of literary imitation...is far from isolated in the Hellenistic period.... In all cases of imitation the starting point for the interest in the reference text is not compositional, but topical" (ibid., 76).

of liberation from Egypt in Aristeas's appeal to the king to liberate Jews forced into servitude by his father (§§12–27, 33–37).[59]

The selection of elders from Jerusalem to translate the Torah into Greek (§§46–50) is equally reminiscent of Exodus.[60] Orlinsky had already drawn attention to the parallel between the 72 elders in Pseudo-Aristeas and the 70 elders who accompany Moses, Aaron, Nadab, and Abihu in Exod 24:1, 9–11.[61] However, Honigman points out that the selection of the 72 by the πλῆθος (§45–46), a term denoting "the civic assembly,"[62] makes them "delegates of the whole people of Israel," parallel to the appointment of tribal officials within Greek cities, with each tribe having an equal number of representatives.[63] The formula of six representatives for each of Israel's twelve tribes "was as close as the author of B.Ar. could get to 70 if he wished to keep to a civic model."[64]

The third evocation of the Exodus paradigm is the acclaim accorded the translation by τὸ πλῆθος τῶν Ιουδαίων in Alexandria (§§308–311). While this scene "is not unlike the process of the promulgation of official editions of texts of the classical authors in Greek cities,"[65] even more so it resonates with the assembly's ratification of the Covenant Code in Exod 24:1–8, as Orlinsky observed.[66] More significant, as Orlinsky noted, is the parallel between the assembly's call for a curse on "anyone who should alter the version by any addition or change to any part of the written text, or any deletion either" (§311) and the injunction of Deut 4:2 against adding to or subtracting from any of the LORD's commandments.[67] In Tcherikover's words, "it is as if [the author] transferred the holiness of Mount Sinai from the original Hebrew text to the Greek translation."[68]

---

[59] Ibid., 55.

[60] Ibid., 57.

[61] Harry M. Orlinsky, "The Septuagint as Holy Writ and the Philosophy of the Translators," *HUCA* 46 (1975) 98.

[62] Honigman, *The Septuagint and Homeric Scholarship*, 58. The use of πλῆθος in "an official sense" was first observed by Meecham (*The Letter of Aristeas*, 305) and then adopted by Orlinsky ("The Septuagint as Holy Writ," 96).

[63] Honigman, *The Septuagint and Homeric Scholarship*, 57.

[64] Ibid., 58. She adds that "this explains the number of Elders selected per tribe, six, which is somewhat unparalleled in Greek civic practice" (ibid.). Curiously, the mid-second century Alexandrian scholar Dionysius Thrax records a story of 72 appointed to produce a critically restored text of Homer, although his 72 work in competition with each other (Porter, "Hermeneutic Lines and Circles," 67).

[65] Honigman, *The Septuagint and Homeric Scholarship*, 59.

[66] Orlinsky, "The Septuagint as Holy Writ," 94.

[67] Ibid., 95–96.

[68] Tcherikover, "Ideology," 76.

Taken together, these three passages reinscribe elements of the Exodus story within Pseudo-Aristeas's narrative about the translation of the Torah into Greek. However, it is precisely in the reminiscences of the people's ratification of the Covenant Code and the presence of the seventy elders that Honigman detects another narrative shaping Pseudo-Aristeas's story: the Alexandrian paradigm, which is "linked to royal propaganda about the Library,"[69] such as is preserved in Galen's account of Ptolemy III appropriating the official Athenian edition of the writings of Sophocles, Euripides, and Aeschylus (Galen, 17.1.607–08).[70] While this paradigm is intertwined with the Exodus paradigm,[71] it becomes the dominant motif in the story. Not only the transport of the Hebrew Torah scroll from Jerusalem reflects it, but so do other details of the narrative.

One of the most significant paragraphs is Demetrius's notification of the king regarding the absence of the Torah from the library (§30), which he accounts for as follows:

τυγχάνει γὰρ	For [these books (τοῦ νόμου τῶν Ἰουδαίων
Ἐβραϊκοῖς	βιβλία)] happen to be expressed in Hebrew
γράμμασι καὶ φωνῇ λεγόμενα,	letters and language,
ἀμελέστερον δέ, καὶ οὐχ ὡς ὑπάρχει,	but rather carelessly—and not as they exist—
σεσήμανται,	are written,
καθὼς ὑπὸ τῶν εἰδότων	as by those in the know
προσαναφέρεται·	it is reported,
προνοίας γὰρ βασιλικῆς οὐ τέτευχε.	since they have not come under royal oversight.[72]

The phrase that has sparked debate is καὶ οὐχ ὡς ὑπάρχει, σεσήμανται. The major dispute centers on whether σεσήμανται means 'interpret' (and thus, 'translate') or simply 'write'.[73] Kahle's claim that this refers to prior attempts at rendering the Torah into Greek requires the meaning 'translate'. However, Tcherikover reports that "the verb σημαίνω, as

---

[69] Honigman, *The Septuagint and Homeric Scholarship*, 9.
[70] Ibid., 44.
[71] Ibid., 9.
[72] Translation mine.
[73] Howard reports that Kahle, Thackeray, Hadas, and Jellicoe understand σεσήμανται as "interpreted," while Bickerman, Zuntz, Gooding, and Orlinsky argue that it means "written" (George Howard, "The Letter of Aristeas and Diaspora Judaism," *JTS* 22 [1971] 338).

used in the Letter, never does mean 'translation,'" for which ἑρμηνεύειν is consistently used.[74] Moreover, the context signals the intended meaning of σεσήμανται. The lack of royal oversight implies that the scrolls have not been treated critically, a remediation Demetrius anticipates in the next paragraph: δέον δέ ἐστι καὶ ταῦθ᾽ ὑπάρχειν παρά σοι διηκριβωμένα ('and it is necessary that these also be scrutinized in your care'). As Zuntz notes, this betrays the author's familiarity with the text-critical practices of the library, where the exact wording (τὸ ἀκριβές) was attained through critical examination of the sort envisioned here (διηκριβωμένα).[75] Accordingly, σεσήμανται means 'written' or, as Honigman reasonably renders it, 'transcribed'.[76]

The question is, which texts of the Torah are characterized as "rather carelessly transcribed"? As Zuntz observes, since the first clause of the excerpt from §30 "states that the Law is couched in Hebrew letters and language, the second cannot contain information about any versions but is bound to refer, likewise, to the Hebrew Law."[77] And because the copy of the Torah used to overcome these deficiencies is brought from Jerusalem, the reference to "carelessly transcribed" texts must refer to "Hebrew texts kept by the Alexandrian Jews."[78]

As Zuntz observes, the denigration of these texts as "carelessly transcribed" because they have not been placed under royal oversight—a circumstance tacitly assumed as tautologous with their absence from the library—is odd, since "unimproved by 'royal care', applied to every single book he acquired [but] did not cause them to be 'absent' from the library."[79] And curiously enough, while Demetrius proposes remedying this with help from Jerusalem, neither his proposal nor the king's letter to Eleazar makes any mention of bringing a quality exemplar

---

[74] Tcherikover, "Ideology," 75.

[75] Zuntz, "Aristeas Studies II," 220. Zuntz also notes that the description of the translators reaching agreement "by comparisons" (ταῖς ἀντιβολαῖς, §301) utilizes a nominal form of ἀντιβάλλειν, which is used for the collation of manuscripts among the scholars of the library (ibid., 221). It is for these reasons that I reject Howard's otherwise ingenious suggestion to treat ὡς ὑπάρχει as adverbially modifying σεσήμανται, construed as a middle voice, and translate the sentence, "for they happen to be written in Hebrew characters and in the Hebrew language, but haphazardly, and they have no meaning as they now exist" (Howard, "The Letter of Aristeas," 339–40). Besides overriding the context's interest in textual accuracy, his solution leaves ἀμελέστερον without a clear meaning.

[76] Honigman, *The Septuagint and Homeric Scholarship*, 44.

[77] Zuntz, "Aristeas Studies II," 216.

[78] Ibid. Cf. Schürer, *History of the Jewish People*, 3.1:679 n. 278.

[79] Zuntz, "Aristeas Studies II," 218–19.

from Jerusalem; that arises for the first time in Eleazar's report (and then almost as an afterthought) that the elders will bring the Torah with them (οὓς καὶ ἀπεστείλαμεν ἔχοντας τὸν νόμον).[80]

While the fit between procedures in the museum and the description of the translation of the Torah is inexact, Honigman's identification of the "Alexandrian paradigm" as informing this narrative accounts for these incongruities elegantly:

> The problems about the meaning of ch. 30 disappear if we agree to read it in the light of the Alexandrian paradigm....By informing his account with this paradigm, B.Ar.'s author was, first and foremost, interested in convincing his readers that the translation of the LXX was the best possible one, primarily because it was based on the most authentic original....The reference to careless Hebrew manuscripts in ch. 30 may be understood not as a realistic description but a symbolic one....this reference to careless manuscripts makes no sense unless we remember the situation current in the field of Homeric studies in Alexandria by the time our author wrote B.Ar....The message may be that the Hebrew original can be forgotten now that the LXX has been achieved.[81]

The author reassures readers that the LXX is trustworthy because it has the same sort of moorings as the edition of Homer critically established by the scholars in the Museum.[82] The logical conundrums that strike our analytical reading of §30 are due to allusions to a meta-narrative more familiar to an Alexandrian reader than to us.

The author's goal of reassuring his readers of the trustworthiness of the translation equally illuminates the praise given the elders and the approbation accorded their words by the king and his retinue. Zuntz spotlighted the crucial role the translators play in the narrative, noting that "the individual elders, or at least their detailed views, tak[e] the place of manuscripts collated."[83] Similarly, Orlinsky accounted for the difference between the praise lavished on the elders/translators in Aristeas and the lack of attention given the elders in Exodus 24 by observing that "the elders in the Letter were not mere witnesses to the event of the translation... [but] the authors of the event."[84]

Honigman enriches these observations by linking the praise given the translators with Demetrius's response to the king's question about

---

[80] Ibid., 218.
[81] Honigman, *The Septuagint and Homeric Scholarship*, 48–49.
[82] Ibid., 131.
[83] Zuntz, "Aristeas Studies II," 221.
[84] Orlinsky, "The Septuagint as Holy Writ," 99.

52 CHAPTER TWO

why the Torah was previously unknown in Greek literature. Whereas Aristobulus claims that Plato had access to the Torah thanks to translations produced even "before the conquests of Alexander and the Persians" (*Praep. ev.* 13.12.1), in Aristeas, Demetrius reports that some who had tried to use the Torah for their purposes "were smitten by God, and refrained from their design" (§313). The reason their attempts incurred divine displeasure, explains Demetrius, is that "the legislation was holy and had come from God." Thus, even though Theopompus and Theodectus "bear theophoric names which point to the right God," they run afoul of the Torah's holiness.[85] To transmit the holy Torah requires commensurate piety and divine authorization. Not only the scroll must be exemplary but so also must the translators, which is the point of the praise they receive during the symposium.

By combining the Exodus and Alexandrian paradigms, the author asserts that "the translation was made out of a perfect scroll, was perfect itself, and was acclaimed as such by official recognition, following the regular procedure of ratification and canonization."[86] And he underwrites that by affirming that the translation rested on the highest scholarship of the day, undertaken by scholars whose acuity and holiness were commensurate with both the Torah and the task. Thereby, the author "aimed at endowing the LXX with a charter myth about its origins, with the purpose of giving the LXX the status of a sacred text,"[87] on a par with the Hebrew Torah.[88]

As for royal instigation and patronage of the project, Wasserstein concludes that this motif "is part of Jewish and possibly also Jewish pro-Ptolemaic propaganda but is supported neither by historical evidence

---

[85] Honigman, *The Septuagint and Homeric Scholarship*, 61. While Demetrius asserts that part Theopompus's sin was that he sought to quote from the Law "in a misleading way" (§314), his ultimate fault was "his meddlesome desire to disclose the things of God to common man" (§315). Intriguingly, Theopompus's quotations are said to have been from "the previously translated passages from the Law" (§314), so that Aristeas, like Aristobulus, seems to have a notion of earlier translations. Given the overwhelming results of research on the LXX in the last half century, however, these can hardly be taken as solid evidence for predecessor translations, even if some passages of the Torah likely were rendered into Greek prior to the translation of the whole. In any case, the author's larger point seems to be that transmitting the divinely given Torah in any form requires authorization.

[86] Honigman, *The Septuagint and Homeric Scholarship*, 59.

[87] Ibid., 8.

[88] Cf. ibid., 60: "the new translation is not *equated* with the Law, it *is* the Law, both from now on and retroactively."

nor by any plausible consideration of probability."[89] The association of the crown with the project has long been considered spurious, since (as Fraser argues) "however anxious Philadelphus may have been to obtain Greek translations of Hebrew works, it seems clear that this royal wish was not the cause of the translation," but rather was it spurred by "the need of the Alexandrian Jewish community."[90] The debate over the occasion of the translation of the Torah into Greek has been lengthy and complex, and rehearsing its details here is unnecessary.[91]

More important, for the purposes of this monograph, Pseudo-Aristeas attests the type of esteem in which the LXX-Pentateuch was held in the mid-second century. It assumes that the LXX-Pentateuch is "a free-standing and independent replacement for the Hebrew Pentateuch,"[92] having achieved a status equal to that of the Torah in Hebrew. What is more, Aristeas's depiction of the translation process follows procedures common in the collection and collation of classical texts for the royal library. The author thereby offers reassurance that the translation is to be trusted because it has the same sort of foundation as the critically established text of Homer produced by the likes of Aristarchus.[93] Whether or not this has any relationship to the procedures actually used in the production of the translation, it shows that aligning the process of rendering the Hebrew Torah into Greek with the procedures of the Alexandrian scholars was plausible and laudable in the pseudepigrapher's era.

The import of this observation for study of LXX-Isaiah is that the equation of the translators of LXX-Pentateuch with the scholars of the library buttresses the possibility that the translator of Isaiah modeled his work after that of the γραμματικοί. Indeed, given the association

---

[89] Wasserstein and Wasserstein, *The Legend of the Septuagint*, 15.

[90] Fraser, *Ptolemaic Alexandria*, 1:690. Cf. Wright, who, assuming that the translation was made as a crib to reading the Hebrew Torah, asserts that the *Letter of Aristeas*'s attribution of the LXX's origins to royal instigation is a ploy "to distinguish the translation from its Hebrew parent text *from its very inception*" so as to give the LXX status as a replacement for the Hebrew (Benjamin G. Wright III, "Translation as Scripture: The Septuagint in Aristeas and Philo," in *Septuagint Research: Issues and Challenges in the Study of the Greek Jewish Scriptures*, ed. Wolfgang Kraus and R. Glenn Wooden [Septuagint and Cognate Studies 53; Atlanta: Scholars Press, 2006] 55, emphasis his).

[91] For a summary of the models that have been proposed to explain its origin, see Honigman, *The Septuagint and Homeric Scholarship*, 105–06.

[92] Wright, "Translation as Scripture," 51. This is irrespective of whatever purposes might lay as the motivation for the translation in the first place.

[93] Honigman, *The Septuagint and Homeric Scholarship*, 131.

of the ʟxx-Pentateuch with the library and the procedures of textual
study in the Museum, it is little wonder that the γραμματικοί are among
the pillars of society whose loss is lamented in the translator's rendition
of Isa 33:18, as noted at the outset of this study.

Of course, it is not possible to apply directly to the translator what
(little) we know of the γραμματικοί, especially since it is doubtful that
he would have been devoted to study of classical Greek texts. Moreover,
however "freely" he may have worked at times and however much he
may have been influenced by the work of the literati in the Museum,
he was beholden to precedents set in the ʟxx-Pentateuch. Accordingly,
in order to understand this translator, we are obliged to survey the sorts
of translation procedures he employed.

However, in preparing to explore the *Übersetzungsweise* of the Isaiah
translator, we must also take into account the fact that ʟxx-Isaiah, like
all other ("biblical") books in the Septuagint, is a translation, not an
original composition.

The ʟxx and translation

Even a common sense definition of translation as a rendition of a work
into a language other than the one in which it was composed bears
important implications, not least of which is that a translation is not
a work *de novo*. Of course, on one level this is true of any literature,
inasmuch as each work adopts a recognizable genre, with its characteristic tropes and motifs. Even Callimachus, while repudiating the
epic, patterned his vocabulary after Homer. Accordingly, it would be
unrefined to distinguish translators from authors on the grounds that
the latter have the freedom to create something wholly new.

Nevertheless, the type of reliance on an existing model is of a different sort for authors than translators. Even if Callimachus took Homer's
vocabulary as building blocks, he was free to distribute and combine
those components creatively and to infuse his work with novel features.
According to our common sense definition of translation, the creativity
permitted translators lies solely in selecting words and phrases in the
target language that best express their understanding of the source text.
Even though a translation might differ in the quantity or order of words,
it is expected to convey the meaning(s) of the source text.

Differences between an author's composition and a translation
become more complex when we move beyond this common sense

definition to contemplate the social setting of translation. This consideration raises the question of *why* a work would be translated: whether the impetus originated with the translator or someone who employed him. In either case, the question concerns how the intended audience's needs or interests shaped the translation.[94] Also implied is the question of what relationship the projected audience had to the composition in its source language: could they read (or hear) it in its native language, or was translation necessary because they lacked that ability? And what use was envisioned for the product? Translation of a legal agreement or a royal decree would have had a different application than translation of a literary work, and that difference would likely have affected the character of the translation.

The translation of documents from one language into another had a long pedigree by the Hellenistic era, as evidenced in polyglot monumental inscriptions from the ancient Near East, the translations of Sumerian texts into Akkadian, the numerous renditions of administrative and literary texts in Mesopotamia into different languages, and evidence of Greek translations of texts composed in foreign tongues.[95] Despite this widespread evidence of translation, we have no analytical reflections by translators on how they went about their work prior to the Hellenistic era, and even then such statements are rare.[96]

Translation in the Hellenistic world

Wright has drawn attention to Cicero's remarks on his translations of Demosthenes's orations, *On the Crown*, and Aeschines's *Against Ctesiphon*.[97] These translations, which are no longer extant, Cicero defends in his *De optimo genere oratorum*, disclosing his desire to dispel, through them, misapprehensions about the style of these orations. *Verbum e verbo* translation could not accomplish this; only *sensus de sensu* could give "the general style and force of the language" so as to provide a standard for what

---

[94] See Toury's discussion of the controlling force of the prospective function of a translation (Gideon Toury, *Descriptive Translation Studies and Beyond* [Benjamins Translation Library 4; Amsterdam: John Benjamins, 1995] 12).

[95] See Wasserstein and Wasserstein, *The Legend of the Septuagint*, 1–4.

[96] As observed by Benjamin G. Wright III, "Why a Prologue? Ben Sira's Grandson and His Greek Translation," in *Emanuel: Studies in Hebrew Bible, Septuagint, and Dead Sea Scrolls in Honor of Emanuel Tov*, ed. Shalom M. Paul, et al. (Leiden: Brill, 2003) 633.

[97] Benjamin G. Wright III, "Access to the Source: Cicero, Ben Sira, the Septuagint and their Audiences," *JSJ* 34 (2003) 5–11.

it means to write in the style of the great Attic orators (*De optimo* 14).[98]
To those who might object to his undertaking on the grounds that the
Greek of these orators is readily accessible and, in any case, preferable
to reading it in Latin, Cicero pointed out that Romans regularly used
translations of Greek poetry and challenged his readers to replicate the
force of the rhetoric in Latin better than he had (*De optimo* 18). Cicero
did not translate in order to introduce readers to literature otherwise
inaccessible to them, but to provide them with a guide to understanding
the force of the rhetoric by seeing it replicated in their native tongue.[99]
As Wright observes, while Cicero clearly meant to make a show of his
own virtuosity in Latin through his translation of these speeches,[100] his
stated goal was to assist the student in overcoming misapprehensions of
the orators' styles, the grasp of which he found so elementary that he
attached a condescending disclaimer: "I thought it my duty to under-
take a task which will be useful to students, though not necessarily for
myself" (*De optimo* 13).

Cicero's explanation of his goals and of how he expected his translation to be used provides a useful backdrop for the comments of Ben
Sira's grandson,[101] whose prologue also reflects on the task of translation. Whereas Cicero is more than contented that his translation fits
his purpose, Ben Sira's grandson introduces his translation with an
apology:

[15]παρακέκλησθε οὖν [16]μετ᾽ εὐνοίας καὶ	So, consider yourselves invited to undertake
προσοχῆς [17]τὴν ἀνάγνωσιν ποιεῖσθαι [18]καὶ	reading with goodwill and diligence and to
συγγνώμην ἔχειν [19]ἐφ᾽ οἷς ἂν δοκῶμεν	have compassion for whatever lack of ability
[20]τῶν κατὰ τὴν ἑρμηνείαν πεφιλοπονη-	we may seem to show in some phrases, despite
μένων τισὶν τῶν λέξεων ἀδυναμεῖν [21]οὐ	our diligence in interpreta-tion. For expressions

---

[98] Cicero's imagery here is picturesque: "For I did not think I ought to count them
out to the reader like coins, but to pay them by weight as it were" (*De optimo* 14).
All citations of Cicero's text are from Cicero, *De Inventione, De Optimo Genere Oratorum,
Topica*, trans. H. M. Hubbell, Loeb Classical Library (Cambridge: Harvard University
Press, 1949).

[99] Wright, "Access to the Source," 7. For that reason, Cicero stipulates, "I did not
translate them as an interpreter, but as an orator" (*De optimo* 14).

[100] Ibid., 8.

[101] Ibid., 4.

γὰρ ἰσοδυναμεῖ ²²αὐτὰ ἐν ἑαυτοῖς | in Hebrew do not have equal force in their own

Εβραϊστὶ λεγόμενα καὶ ὅταν μεταχθῇ εἰς | native expression and when they are transposed

ἑτέραν γλῶσσαν ²³οὐ μόνον δὲ ταῦτα | into another language. And that applies not

²⁴ἀλλὰ καὶ αὐτὸς ὁ νόμος καὶ αἱ | only to these instances, but also [to] the Law

προφητεῖαι ²⁵καὶ τὰ λοιπὰ τῶν βιβλίων | itself, and the prophets, and the rest of the

²⁶οὐ μικρὰν ἔχει τὴν διαφορὰν ἐν ἑαυτοῖς | scrolls—the [Hebrew] expressions in their own

λεγόμενα | right show no small difference.

My dynamic equivalence translation assumes Wright's argument that this apology has to do with the translator's misgivings about his Greek style rather than about whether he represented the sense of the Hebrew adequately. Even though his plea for sympathetic reading could be read as a concession that he did not always convey the meaning of the Hebrew, defending himself by pointing out that translations of the scriptures equally fail to communicate the message of the Hebrew would be strange, given his earlier insistence that "those who read the scriptures must not only themselves understand them, but must also as lovers of learning be able through the spoken and written word to help the outsiders" (§§1–2).[102]

Moreover, his comparison of flaws similar to his in Greek translations of scriptures makes sense only if the similar defect was one his audience considered tolerable in authoritative works. It is difficult to see how pointing out a previously unrecognized defect in such translations would engender sympathy for whatever shortcoming Ben Sira's grandson wished excused.

If, on the other hand, we suppose that the grandson here acknowledges blundering his way through his translation, we must presuppose either that the translator did not understand his grandfather's work well, or that he did not know how to express it well in Greek. However, both of these conflict with the reason he gives for translating the work. He extols his grandfather as one who studied and understood the Law, the Prophets, and "the others that followed them" (καὶ τῶν ἄλλων τῶν

---

[102] Ibid., 15.

κατ' αὐτοὺς ἠκολουθηκότων) and wrote about what he had learned so that others might be instructed in the ways of wisdom and "make even greater progress in living according to the law" (§§13–14). It is because of this benefit that he invites his addressees to read his work (παρακέκλησθε οὖν...τὴν ἀνάγνωσιν ποιεῖσθαι), implying that they will derive the benefit from his Greek translation that was intended by his grandfather in composing the Hebrew. This presupposes that he considered himself to understand his grandfather's instruction and was confident that his translation could deliver the benefits his grandfather intended. He underscores this confidence near the conclusion of his preface by saying that his exposure to other instruction in Alexandria convinced him of the *necessity* (ἀναγκαιότατον ἐθέμην) of translating his grandfather's work for the benefit of those who, living as aliens, wished to learn and to live according to the Law (§§34–36). His description of himself applying "great alertness and skill" (πολλὴν ἀγρυπνίαν καὶ ἐπιστήμην) again bespeaks his confidence in his translation skills. Taken together, such statements belie reading his words as a lack of confidence about translating accurately.

Wright argues compellingly that the grandson's sense of vulnerability has to do with the style of his Greek translation.[103] Given the high quality of his Greek in the prologue, his use of "an often wooden Greek translationese for the actual translation" reflects "his expectations of what constitutes translation,"[104] especially since it seems not to have occurred "to him that he could translate any other way."[105] Rather, he appears to have used translations of the scriptures into Greek as his model, as suggested by his ready comparison of the infelicities of his translation with those in the Greek scriptures.[106] His apologies indicate that he had not adopted this procedure for its aesthetic appeal but because it was a model with an authority he could not set aside to express ideas in contemporary idiom, as did Cicero.

What is more, the contrast with Cicero suggests that Ben Sira's grandson did not seek to provide a guide to understanding the Hebrew, but to make his grandfather's work available for the first time for those "living abroad who want to pursue learning" (τοῖς ἐν τῇ παροικίᾳ βουλομένοις φιλομαθεῖν). The fact that a translation of his Hebrew text was neces-

---

[103] Ibid., 16.
[104] Ibid., 12.
[105] Ibid., 20.
[106] Ibid., 19.

sary signals that his translation was meant as *the* text of Ben Sira for those who did not know Hebrew. Providing his co-religionists with his grandfather's wisdom, written in Hebrew, meant using the same sort of procedure that had brought them the biblical books.

Does this imply that the translations of the scriptures were meant as a substitute for Hebrew texts for Egyptian Jews who had lost facility in Hebrew? What, in fact, was the motivation for and purpose of the translation of Hebrew scriptures into Greek?

Translation and the LXX-Pentateuch

As already observed, this is not the place for a review of all proposals for the origins of the LXX-Pentateuch. Nevertheless, we must consider some facets of the recent debate as a backdrop to exploring the work of the Isaiah translator.

The "foreign and clumsy" language of the LXX-Pentateuch led Bickerman to describe the translators as following the methods of the dragomans, experts in translating business and royal texts "who generally clung to the letter."[107] It was adoption of the dragoman's habit of translating "clause for clause, word for word" that produced the Hebraized Greek of the LXX-Pentateuch.[108] The translators did not imitate the dragoman's methods due to their inability to write better Greek ("a poor Jewish granary guard…was able to present his complaint in idiomatic Greek")[109] but because the legal nature of the text led them to adopt the dragoman's word-for-word method as the only way to preserve the legal connotations of the original document.[110]

Translation of legal texts into the languages of foreign rulers was commonplace in the ancient world.[111] Accepting that translation of foreign law codes would have piqued the interests of a Ptolemaic ruler, Bickerman underscored the attraction a translation of the Torah would have held for Philadelphus as "the sole written source of the law of his subjects in Judaea and the sole authority on their history."[112]

Brock objected to Bickerman's analysis on the grounds that the translation style of LXX-Pentateuch is not of a single type (legal), but

---

[107] Bickerman, "The Septuagint as a Translation," 177–78.
[108] Ibid., 180–81.
[109] Ibid., 187.
[110] Ibid., 190.
[111] Ibid., 173.
[112] Ibid., 174.

varies with the genre, such that "specifically legal sections tend to be more literally translated than purely narrative ones."[113] Even if a Greek translation of the Demotic Manual existed early in the Ptolemaic era,[114] "the Pentateuch is by no means a comparable document, since only portions of it are of specifically legal content."[115] Nor should we look to Manetho and Berossus as parallels, since "they did not provide direct translations" and "their works were not even commissioned by official sources."[116] Moreover, as Honigman observes, "given the inconspicuous status of the Jews in early Ptolemaic Alexandria, it is most improbable that the king would have been interested in translating the Jewish Law on his own initiative."[117] Accordingly, the hypothesis that the LXX was translated on royal initiative to serve as an official Jewish legal code is improbable.[118]

That conclusion does not, however, apply equally to the identification of the dragoman model for the translators. In 1968 Rabin advanced an argument for the dragoman model separate from speculation about the purpose of the translation.[119] Rabin's interest, from the outset, was in the process of "recoding" a message into a receptor language. Although the lack of a fit between the source and receptor languages can be so profound that components can lose "their place in the structure relative to other items,"[120] more commonly infelicities arise from the translator's weak familiarity with the source language and his imperfect understanding of the text. In particular, polysemy—at both the lexical and phrase levels—requires that the translator light on a meaning, based on his experience with the source language and his predilections.[121] This process is not undertaken afresh with each locution, however, since "translators tend to render words mechanically by

[113] Sebastian Brock, "The Phenomenon of the Septuagint," in *Witness of Tradition: Papers Read at the Joint British-Dutch Old Testament Conference, Woudschoten, Netherlands, 1970*, ed. Martinus A. Beek (Leiden: Brill, 1972) 20.

[114] Honigman, *The Septuagint and Homeric Scholarship*, 110.

[115] Brock, "The Phenomenon of the Septuagint," 13.

[116] Ibid., 14.

[117] Honigman, *The Septuagint and Homeric Scholarship*, 113.

[118] However, as Honigman notes, this does not mean that it did not come to be utilized that way (ibid., 108–09).

[119] Chaim Rabin, "The Translation Process and the Character of the Septuagint," *Textus* 6 (1968) 1–26.

[120] Ibid., 4.

[121] Ibid., 7.

the receptor-language term on which they first hit."[122] Such automatic "verbal linkage" produces atypical usages in the receptor language, a feature readers tolerate as a staple of translations.[123] At the same time, this sort of tolerance creates a translation "sub-language" that aids "the translator in accomplishing his task efficiently."[124]

Because "Greek society did not go in for translation, but for independent rewriting of information,"[125] and because Jews of the early Ptolemaic period "would certainly not have had access to the schools which catered to the upper-class citizenry,"[126] the LXX translators had no model of literary translation available to them except "in the day-to-day oral translation activity of the commercial and court dragoman (ἑρμηνεύς)," familiar to them from business and legal dealings.[127] Intelligible under this model, argues Rabin, are the "occasional appearance of literal translations which make no sense in Greek" and the LXX-Pentateuch's numerous omissions, since "condensing and omitting phraseology and stylistic ornamentation of the source" accords with "oral business translation, the main purpose of which is to get the message across."[128]

The dragoman theory, as invoked by Bickerman and Rabin, has come in for sharp criticism from Pietersma. Even if the dragoman theory accounts for the woodenness of the LXX-Pentateuch, it fails to explain mechanical and nonsensical translations, as well as transliterations, especially since Rabin stipulated that "the oral dragoman tradition was not averse to omitting words or phrases" in order "to get the message across."[129] One might expect that this factor would eliminate

---

[122] Ibid., 8. Rabin observes that only at a very high degree of sophistication will a translator arrive at the choice of a word because it represents something of the gamut of meaning of the source word in its native structure" (ibid., 7).

[123] Ibid., 9. Rabin refers to this as "semantic tolerance" (ibid.).

[124] Ibid., 13. As Brock observes, Gehman's failure to recognize this as a feature of translation (distinct from *spoken* language) led to his misapprehension of Septuagintal Greek as a "Jewish Greek" of the Alexandrian "ghetto" (Brock, "The Phenomenon of the Septuagint," 32; cf. Albert Pietersma, "A New Paradigm for Addressing Old Questions: The Relevance of the Interlinear Model for the Study of the Septuagint," in *Bible and Computer: The Stellenbosch AIBI-6 Conference.*, ed. Johan Cook [Leiden: Brill, 2002] 355).

[125] Rabin, "Translation Process," 19.

[126] Ibid., 21.

[127] Ibid.

[128] Ibid., 23.

[129] Pietersma, "A New Paradigm," 344. He points out that "in the end Rabin is forced to admit that 'the experienced dragoman would of course learn when to deviate from the mechanical reproduction of the syntax of his source language in order to

mechanical but nonsensical renderings. Given this fault in the dragoman theory, Pietersma has sought another explanation for the characteristics of the LXX-Pentateuch.

Pietersma echoes Aejmelaeus's call to carefully ponder the approach to translation that we assume for these translators, since it informs our judgments about their styles of translation.[130] Implicitly required is that the resultant description encompass "the aspect of unintelligibility as well as that of intelligibility (even literary beauty)" in the LXX.[131] He finds the rudiments of such a theory in Brock's development of "the most elaborate and convincing theory accounting for the linguistic nature of the (translated) Septuagint."[132] While lamenting Brock's failure "to make an explicit connection between the school and Septuagint origins,"[133] he finds that the implications of Brock's argument nevertheless point in that direction.[134]

Speculating about why Brock stopped short of positing an educational paradigm, Pietersma notes Brock's belief "that both as to its original function and as to its later role the Septuagint was a free-standing text that took the place of the original, precisely as Aristeas maintains."[135] In Pietersma's view, this assumption helps account for the failure of mainstream scholarship to advance a satisfactory paradigm.[136] It is essential to distinguish between Septuagintal origins and its reception history, for "the central thrust of the Letter of Aristeas, namely, the independence of the Septuagint *vis-à-vis* the Hebrew, is not a statement about its origins but about its subsequent history."[137]

---

avoid misunderstandings'" (ibid.). However, Pietersma unjustifiably asserts that Rabin makes "favourable reference to Gehman's theory of a Jewish Alexandrian Greek, to the extent that the Jewish community must have been very tolerant of Hebraic Greek" (ibid.). Rabin's assertion that the tolerance of semantic variation in the use of a translation can occasion translation idiom "becoming part of the language" (Rabin, "Translation Process," 11) makes the point that acceptance of such idioms "creates further semantic tolerance, and better reception for translations" (ibid.). This is far different from Gehman's assertion that the Hebraic Greek of the LXX reflected the *spoken* language of Alexandrian Jews.

[130] Pietersma, "A New Paradigm," 338–39.
[131] Ibid., 351.
[132] Ibid., 344.
[133] Ibid., 346.
[134] Ibid., 358.
[135] Ibid., 346.
[136] Ibid., 340.
[137] Ibid., 339–40, quotation from 340. Similarly, Wright argues that the *Letter of Aristeas* attests a reception history in which the translators' intent to offer a crib for studying the Hebrew text had become overwritten by a view of the LXX as "a replacement for the Hebrew" (Wright, "Translation as Scripture," 53).

Pietersma finds grounds for making this distinction in evidence that the strong interference of the source language in the receptor language of the translation reflects a conscious choice to adopt a model of inter-linear translation found in Hellenistic schools. Brock had already noted that while Cicero's distinction between his mode of translation as an *orator* rather than an *interpres* (*De optimo* 14)[138] comes much later than the translation of the LXX, the approach Cicero embraced was already embodied in the bilingual Greek and Aramaic inscription of Asoka's edicts at Kandahar in the third century B.C.E. and in a translation of the Demotic story of Tefnut "in reasonably good Greek style."[139] With these Brock contrasts the "word-for-word translations of legal docu-ments in Egypt and of *senatus consulta* and other government missives originating from Republican Rome," as well as the later "bilingual texts of Vergil and others, for pedagogical use, with the Latin and Greek in parallel columns."[140] Positing that these two modes of translation existed already in the mid-third century, Brock suggested that the translators forged "something of a compromise, in that they are neither consistently literal, nor consistently free."[141]

Especially important to Pietersma is Brock's assertion that the impe-tus for the translation was "not just liturgical, but also, and perhaps primarily, educational," inasmuch as "it would seem only likely that the Pentateuch would have played a very similar role in Jewish education to that of Homer in Greek."[142] This comparison leads Pietersma to observe that Ptolemaic schools required boys to set out Homeric texts in two columns, with Homer's text in the left hand column and a rendition in colloquial Greek in the right.[143] Moreover, he adduces a manuscript from the first century B.C.E. arranged with Homer's text and a colloquial version in alternating lines.[144] Although he refrains from positing that an analogous interlinear Hebrew and Greek text existed, he contends that this conceptual paradigm enlightens the "perceived *linguistic* rela-tionship" between the LXX-Pentateuch and the MT by elucidating the "subservience and dependence of the Greek translation *vis-à-vis* the

---

[138] In *De finibus* 3.15 Cicero disparages them as *interpretes indiserti*, 'ineloquent translators'.

[139] Sebastian Brock, "Aspects of Translation Technique in Antiquity," *GRBS* 20 (1979) 71.

[140] Ibid.

[141] Brock, "The Phenomenon of the Septuagint," 20.

[142] Ibid., 16.

[143] Pietersma, "A New Paradigm," 347.

[144] Ibid., 348–49.

Hebrew parent text."[145] Above all, it helps us understand the occasional
unintelligibility of the LXX, since it shows that the LXX-Pentateuch was
not meant to be a substitute for the Hebrew Torah, given that "for some
essential linguistic information, the parent text needs to be consulted,
since the text as we have it cannot stand on its own feet."[146] Indeed,
the fact that scholars working with the LXX regularly "have recourse
to the parent text in order to account for the translated text" confirms
that the interlinear paradigm best accounts for the LXX.[147]

While many subsequent translations of "biblical" books followed the
model established by the LXX-Pentateuch, not all did. Most notably,
the translation of Job "stands decidedly on the *sensus de sensu* side" of
translation.[148] For Pietersma, this merely confirms that different modes
of translation were available to the translators of LXX-Pentateuch, who
chose a more literal mode of translation due to their social location in
the schools, which motivated them to provide "a study aid to a text in
another language."[149] Much like the student exercise of casting Homer
in colloquial Greek, translation of the Hebrew into Greek was meant
as an aid to understanding the *Hebrew* text. And even as recitation of
Homer in the classrooms utilized the Homeric texts rather than the
students' colloquial renditions, the LXX was not meant to stand on its
own but to point to the Hebrew.[150] It is in this sense Pietersma understands Brock's definition of the function of word-for-word translations
as seeking "to bring the reader to the original" rather than "bringing
the original to the reader."[151] Brock's language "implies *both* that the
source text is the object of study *and* that the receptor language is a
tool in that study."[152]

Pietersma concludes that while "not all translated books in the
Septuagint collection will turn out to be interlinear texts," the dominance of this model in the LXX justifies "a methodological dictum: the
translated books of the LXX are interlinear, until proven otherwise."[153]

---

[145] Ibid., 350, emphasis his.
[146] Ibid., emphasis his.
[147] Ibid., 355.
[148] Ibid., 357.
[149] Ibid., 358.
[150] Ibid.
[151] Brock, "Aspects of Translation Technique in Antiquity," 73; cf. idem, "The
Phenomenon of the Septuagint," 17.
[152] Pietersma, "A New Paradigm," 359, emphasis his.
[153] Ibid., 359.

Moreover, the dominance of this paradigm permits study of the LXX "in order to learn what was happening in the Jewish schools of the Greek speaking diaspora."[154]

Pietersma's hypothesis merits this detailed summary because it serves as the working model for the *New English Translation of the Septuagint*.[155] And correspondingly, I will provide a detailed critique, beginning with Pietersma's use of Brock as the starting point for his theory.

Brock does, in fact, assert that the distinction Cicero draws between two styles of translation was extant in the translators' day.[156] What he does not say, however, is that the translators would have been familiar with the "free" style used in literary texts. In fact, he cautions that the "free" style was "possibly only familiar at that time from oral translation."[157] And he has good reason for his cautious language, since the bilingual Greek and Aramaic inscription of Asoka's edicts at Kandahar, although from the third century B.C.E., is hardly evidence of familiarity with that type of literary translation in distant Alexandria, while the translation of the Demotic story of Tefnut into Greek presents even greater problems.

Not only has the story of Tefnut itself resisted dating, but the Greek translation is extant in a single papyrus of the third century C.E.[158] Moreover, "the vocabulary and style suggest that the translation was made [near] to the date at which the papyrus was written."[159] Accordingly, just as Brock dismissed the translations of Sumerian religious texts into Akkadian as most likely unfamiliar to the translators,[160] so we must discount the literary translations adduced by Brock as evidence that this model was available to the translators.[161] Indeed, as Brock himself contended, it is "very unlikely that they had any real

---

[154] Ibid., 361.

[155] Albert Pietersma and Benjamin G. Wright III, "To the Reader of NETS," in *The Psalms* (The New English Translation of the Septuagint; Oxford: Oxford University Press, 2000) ix.

[156] Brock, "The Phenomenon of the Septuagint," 20.

[157] Ibid.

[158] Stephanie West, "The Greek Version of the Legend of Tefnut," *JEA* 55 (1969) 161.

[159] Ibid., 183.

[160] Brock, "The Phenomenon of the Septuagint," 12.

[161] Thus Barr writes, "truly 'free' translation, in the sense in which this might be understood by the modern literary public, scarcely existed in the world of the LXX, or indeed of much of ancient biblical translation in general" (James Barr, *The Typology of Literalism in Ancient Biblical Translations* [Mitteilungen des Septuaginta-Unternehmens 15; Göttingen: Vandenhoeck and Ruprecht, 1979] 7).

tradition of written translation on which to draw."[162] Equally valid is
Brock's assertion that "no other oriental religious text of such an extent
achieved the honour of translation into Greek," leaving the undertaking
of the translators "entirely without precedent."[163]

Pietersma's citation of Job as evidence that a less literal mode of
translation was available to the translators is tenuous. On the one hand,
the less literal mode of translation in wisdom literature (cf. Proverbs)
may be due to the fact that the genre itself was part of the general store
of ancient Near Eastern traditions, and thus already admitted varied
versions.[164] While this statement is somewhat speculative, we must in
any case acknowledge the peculiarity that it is in wisdom literature that
we find the freest translations.[165]

On the other hand, as we have seen, the frustration expressed by
Ben Sira's grandson suggests that he followed "expectations of what
constitutes translation."[166] It is not just that he took the translation of
the Pentateuch as his model, but that it seems not to have occurred to
him that another approach was available.[167] Perhaps his goal of representing Ben Sira's instruction about living *according to the Law* provoked
him to a more *verbum e verbo* rendition than he might otherwise have
followed.[168] However that might be, the constraints against which Ben
Sira's grandson chafed seem due to his sense that other models were
not open to him.

Pietersma summarizes a second element of Brock's research that he
claims as a base for his own work as follows:

> Brock...suggests that since the Pentateuch was both a legal and a liter-
> ary text, the initial translators found themselves in a dilemma as to the

---

[162] Brock, "The Phenomenon of the Septuagint," 12.

[163] Brock, "Aspects of Translation Technique in Antiquity," 71. Brock repeated this
judgment in his final article on this topic, Sebastian Brock, "To Revise or not to Revise:
Attitudes to Jewish Biblical Translation," in *Septuagint, Scrolls and Cognate Writings*, ed.
George J. Brook and Barnabas Lindars (Septuagint and Cognate Studies 33; Atlanta:
Scholars Press, 1992) 310–11.

[164] Cf. Brock: "Wisdom literature is treated very much more freely, no doubt because
a long tradition of translation of this type of literature was known to the translators of
books such as Proverbs" (Brock, "The Phenomenon of the Septuagint," 19 n. 1).

[165] Of course, Qoheleth is a peculiar instance, since its much more wooden translation is tied to Aquila.

[166] Wright, "Access to the Source," 12.

[167] Ibid., 20.

[168] As Brock observes, "the nature of the text" being translated can affect the
choice of the approach the translator adopts ("Aspects of Translation Technique in
Antiquity," 73).

appropriate style of translation to adopt. Essentially they decided in favour of the legal, literal mode (rather than the literary), and in so doing registered a deliberate choice in its favour.[169]

In the end, Pietersma finds Brock's distinction between "legal" and "literary" modes unsatisfactory for identifying what occasions a *verbum e verbo* translation, and so replaces it with a distinction between "'instructional use' of a text as opposed to 'recreational or edificational use.'"[170]

While Brock does speak of the translators facing a choice of methods, his verdict about their choice is more nuanced than Pietersma suggests:

> Hebraisms in the Greek Pentateuch are in fact far from consistent, and the wavering of the translators between the use of a natural Greek expression and a syntactic calque on the original must simply be attributed to their hesitance in choosing between the literal style of translations of legal documents, and the free periphrastic style used (then orally?) for literary texts.[171]

Similarly, he writes that their

> solution was, not surprisingly, something of a compromise, in that they are neither consistently literal, nor consistently free, although it is interesting to note that *specifically legal sections tend to be more literally translated than purely narrative ones.*[172]

Brock's more subtle assessment provides no foundation for linking *verbum e verbo* translations to an educational setting.[173]

Moreover, when Brock speaks of *verbum e verbo* translations "bringing the reader to the original" he seems to have something different in mind than Pietersma infers. Brock speaks of translations of administrative documents from the Roman Republic as "always point[ing] the reader to the official original in Latin," even though such texts were not meant to help people *read* the Latin,[174] and he speaks of the use of *verbum e*

---

[169] Pietersma, "A New Paradigm," 345.
[170] Ibid., 358.
[171] Brock, "The Phenomenon of the Septuagint," 32.
[172] Ibid., 20, emphasis mine.
[173] While Pietersma notes that Brock attributes a literalistic text like Aquila to a "school environment" (Pietersma, "A New Paradigm," 358), it is clear that Brock *distinguishes* "literal translations...reserved for schoolboy 'cribs'" (which he associates with translators *like* Aquila) from the LXX, which he regards as a mix of translation styles (Brock, "The Phenomenon of the Septuagint," 16–17 and p. 17 n. 1).
[174] Brock, "Aspects of Translation Technique in Antiquity," 74.

verbo translations for sacred texts, where "the need to bring the reader
to the original was felt more than anywhere else" because replicating
its *linguistic structures* brought readers into contact with the sacredness of
the text.[175] Thus, Pietersma's conclusion that Brock's phrase "implies
both that the source text is the object of study *and* that the receptor
language is a tool in that study"[176] forces us to distinguish between
origins and reception history in Pietersma's use of Brock.

It is in the light of this different understanding of "bringing the reader
to the original" that we should understand Brock's oft-cited statement
that "it would seem only likely that the Pentateuch would have played
a very similar role in Jewish education to that of Homer in Greek," as
"the Homer of the Jews."[177] In fact, Honigman reports that Brock, in
personal communication with her, signaled that he viewed "the inte-
gration of the LXX into the educational framework...as a derivative
consequence, not as its primary purpose."[178] By implication, the LXX
was meant as a replacement for the Hebrew text, just as it is viewed
by Pseudo-Aristeas.

A more fundamental problem with the interlinear paradigm is
Pietersma's appeal to the school exercises in Homer. The parallel he
develops is specious, inasmuch as the exercise was a matter of recasting Homer's meaning in the student's vernacular so as to clarify its
cryptic phrases, much as an English teacher might require students to
write paraphrases of Shakespeare. It is not simply the matter of *translation* that distinguishes the LXX from the Homer exercise, but also that
Pietersma's supposition that the translation is intended "as a crib for
the study of the Hebrew."[179] This assumes that the translation was not
an exercise written *by* the student, as when "the pupil gives the equivalents in his own language,"[180] but one written *for* students to acquaint
them with the Hebrew of the Torah. This very different pedagogical
model complicates citing the Homeric exercise as a precedent for the
"interlinear paradigm."

---

[175] Ibid., 75. Following on Brock's discussion of the prestige of the source language
as explanation for a more literal translation, his reference to "bring[ing] the reader to
the original" does not denote study of the source text itself.

[176] Pietersma, "A New Paradigm," 359, emphasis his.

[177] Brock, "The Phenomenon of the Septuagint," 16.

[178] Honigman, *The Septuagint and Homeric Scholarship*, 108 and n. 54.

[179] Pietersma, "A New Paradigm," 360.

[180] Ibid., 347.

Next, although Pietersma finds validation of his claim that the LXX was not intended as a substitute for the Hebrew Torah in the scholarly praxis of checking the MT to clarify tortuous passages in the LXX, broader scholarly praxis undermines this argument. Frequently enough, fine points of arguments in Hermeneia commentaries that have been translated into English from German are better understood by consulting the German, even though the English translation is *meant* as a substitute for the German. Likewise, a particular scholarly monograph was so poorly translated that a colleague declared that one would be better off reading the original German than the translation, even if one did not know German. Perplexing sentence structure and phrases in a translation are not necessarily marks of an aid to reading the source text in its own language. They may be marks of the translator's own perplexity or ineptitude.

A further problem for the "interlinear paradigm" is that while it posits a lively interest in the study of the Hebrew text in the early Ptolemaic era, the earliest examples of Jewish exegetes in Egypt already base their work on the LXX. For example, Demetrius, writing in the latter quarter of the same century the LXX-Pentateuch was created,[181] relied exclusively on that translation. The fact that no evidence has survived of exegesis of *Hebrew* texts by Ptolemaic Jews places us in the awkward position of positing activity for which no shred of evidence has survived except its product that, according to our earliest evidence, had itself become the object of study.

Equally problematic is the claim that a system of Jewish schooling focusing on the Hebrew Torah existed, since we lack evidence to support this. Even if we grant that there must have been a system for educating young Jewish men, we know nothing about Jewish schools in this period.[182] Above all, suggesting that we should extrapolate to their operation on the basis of the "interlinear paradigm" is to advocate building speculation upon speculation.

While I agree with Pietersma that we need an explicitly articulated paradigm of how translators worked, I disagree with his assumption that we can construct a theory that explains all the features in their work. Humans are notoriously (and fortunately) inconsistent and, especially when faced with an undertaking for which there is no clear precedent,

---

[181] See Schürer, *History of the Jewish People*, 3.1:513.
[182] Cf. Dines, *The Septuagint*, 51.

are likely to work somewhat ad hoc rather than execute a reasoned method. Accordingly, we will benefit more from noting the similarities to and differences from the work of dragomans than from faulting the translators for failing to conform to that pattern in every respect. The dragoman remains the only model of translation we can be confident the translators would have known.

Finally, it is necessary to say something about what leads to finding the dominantly "literal" style of translation of the LXX-Pentateuch at home in a school setting: its tendency to reflect the structures of the source language rather than those of the target language. Boyd-Taylor, appealing to Toury's distinction between translations that are expected to conform to the target culture and those which carry more of the marks of their source text,[183] concludes that the conformity of the LXX to the latter paradigm is, "as it happens…the very level at which the school translation works."[184] In his view, it need not be shown that the LXX was used exclusively in a school setting for this affinity to be helpful: "Rather, all that needs to be established is that the text is sufficiently like a school translation that certain inferences regarding its constitutive character can be drawn."[185]

Although I agree with his use of this observation to deny that we can discern the translator's theology or allusions to his historical setting from a more literal translation, this much can be determined without invoking the school model. In fact, in the end it is not clear that the more literal style that pervades the LXX-Pentateuch is a matter of following a specific model of translation. Rather, as Barr already observed, more literal translation was the path of least resistance, a default mode.[186] The

---

[183] In the section Boyd-Taylor cites, Toury distinguishes three types of translation: 1) "linguistically-motivated," a translation "well-formed in terms of the target syntax, grammar and lexicon"; 2) "textually dominated," which is "well-formed in terms of general conventions of text formation pertinent to the target culture"; 3) "literary translation," which "yields more or less well-formed texts from the point of view of the *literary* requirements of the recipient culture, at various possible costs in terms of the reconstruction of features of the sources text" (Toury, *Descriptive Translation Studies,* 171). The first of these is applicable to the more "literal" range of lxx translations, although whether its "translationese" qualifies as "well-formed in terms of the target syntax, grammar and lexicon" is a moot point.

[184] Cameron Boyd-Taylor, "In a Mirror Dimly—Reading the Septuagint as a Document of Its Times," in *Septuagint Research: Issues and Challenges in the Study of the Greek Jewish Scriptures,* ed. Wolfgang Kraus and R. Glenn Wooden (Septuagint and Cognate Studies 53; Atlanta: Scholars Press, 2006) 27–28.

[185] Ibid., 29.

[186] Barr, *The Typology of Literalism,* 26.

degree to which it *happens* to share similarities with school translations is no evidence for its prospective function.

Pietersma's aim is laudable; a heuristic tool that allowed us to reconstruct the origins of the LXX and the philosophy of the translators that bestowed its distinctive text-linguistic texture would be a remarkable advance. However, I am profoundly skeptical about any such attempt, given the sources currently at our disposal. Even if we can say (rightly, in my estimation) that the dragoman provided the model with which the translators were most likely familiar, we are left to explain why the translators of Job and Proverbs worked more freely, or why the translator of Isaiah (to point, for this monograph) at times rendered his *Vorlage* literally, while at other times he diverged from it widely. Moreover, the explanation that the more literal translation style of (much of) the LXX-Pentateuch reflects recognition of the scriptural status of the Torah is an intuition based on subsequent revisions of the LXX attributable to growing assumptions about the importance of each-and-every word of the text. We cannot, however, be certain that such a view guided the translation of the LXX-Pentateuch.[187]

While knowing why the translators proceeded as they did would dispel a plethora of mysteries for us, we simply have no access to the data necessary to construct a "theory of translation" that can explain the varied surface realizations of the translators' work. Nor can we invoke Jonathan Z. Smith's call for a "theory of translation" of the LXX as making the quest for a master paradigm imperative, as Pietersma claims,[188] since Smith clarifies his lament of a lack of a theory among scholars who assume too much semantic freight for individual LXX lexemes[189] by endorsing Barr's call for an

> 'attempt to discover the method by which translators read Hebrew texts and decided on a rendering' as well as making 'the obvious and necessary distinction between two sets of mental processes, those of the translators themselves, whose decisions about meaning were reached from the

---

[187] Cf. Dines's apt criticisms of drawing parallels to Aquila's method of translation (*The Septuagint*, 53).

[188] Albert Pietersma, "Exegesis in the Septuagint: Possibilities and Limits," in *Septuagint Research: Issues and Challenges in the Study of the Greek Jewish Scriptures*, ed. Wolfgang Kraus and R. Glenn Wooden (Septuagint and Cognate Studies 53; Atlanta: Scholars Press, 2006) 37.

[189] Jonathan Z. Smith, *Drudgery Divine: On the Comparison of Early Christianities and the Religions of Late Antiquity*, ed. William S. Green and Calvin Goldscheider (Chicago Studies in the History of Judaism; Chicago: University of Chicago Press, 1990) 77.

Hebrew text, and those of later readers, most of whom did not know the original'.[190]

It is failure to abide by these principles that Smith decries as "the absence of such an attempt to articulate a translation theory."[191]

As a corrective to semantic fallacies common among scholars of early Christian literature in the first half of the twentieth century[192] (as targeted also in Barr's criticisms of the first two volumes of TWNT),[193] Smith's demand is apt. It is hardly, however, a call for the kind of "full-fledged theory of translation" Pietersma seeks to provide. And again, the absence of data necessary to forge such a comprehensive theory places that desideratum out of our grasp at this moment.

Summary

What we are left with, then, are the stilted style of translation found in varying degrees in Septuagintal books and the tradition current in the mid-second century as attested by the *Letter of Aristeas*. The latter is of use for this monograph in helping establish the association between the scholarship of the Museum and a view of translation of Hebrew texts in the era LXX-Isaiah was executed. Nevertheless, that translator seems to have viewed his task differently than those of the Torah. While he often follows their more literal tendencies, he frequently also stands closer to the style of translation we find in Proverbs and Job. The question is how to account for this peculiar mix.

However, before we can evaluate how this translator rendered his *Vorlage*, we must consider the knotty problem of simultaneously reasoning our way back to his *Vorlage* from his translation and reconstructing his approach to translation that guides us in drawing conclusions about what sort of *Vorlage* his renderings presuppose.

---

[190] Ibid., 79.

[191] Ibid.

[192] Two examples of which are detailed by Smith (ibid., 64–71).

[193] James Barr, *The Semantics of Biblical Language* (Oxford: Oxford University Press, 1961).

CHAPTER THREE

RECONSTRUCTING THE *VORLAGE* OF LXX-ISAIAH

The old saw that every translation is also an interpretation finds an apt rejoinder in the observation that interpretation is not of one type, but takes place on different levels.[1] Every translation entails linguistic interpretation: analysis of the semantics and grammar of the source text and recasting them in the lexemes and syntax of the target language. More variable is the degree to which translation involves contextual interpretation.[2] Although selecting an appropriate lexical or syntactic equivalent in the target language can reflect one's perception of the immediate context, contextual interpretation involves a more extensive sculpting of a phrase or sentence according to the sense divined from its broader context. As Tov observes, "the translators' concept of 'context' was wider than ours,"[3] so that decisions about how to translate a phrase or verse may be affected by passages we would consider far afield. Accordingly, contextual interpretation is, itself, of various types, including interpretation in the light of other scriptural passages (both within the book being translated and outside it), liturgical formulae, and the political and geographic realia of the translator's day.

The composite of the translator's interpretative maneuvers on these various levels is often referred to as "translation technique." However, Aejmelaeus has raised cogent objections to this phrase, since "technique" implies a theory of translation, whereas the translators seem to have been driven more "by intuition and spontaneity."[4] Accordingly, what is often called "translation technique" merely describes the *effects* of the translator's work rather than "the system used by the translator."[5]

---

[1] E.g., Barr, *The Typology of Literalism*, 16–18; John W. Wevers, "The Interpretative Character and Significance of the Septuagint Version," in *Hebrew Bible, Old Testament: The History of its Interpretation*, ed. Magne Sæbø (Göttingen: Vandenhoeck & Ruprecht, 1996) 87.

[2] For linguistic and contextual exegeses as the two categories of interpretation involved in translation, see Emanuel Tov, *The Text-Critical Use of the Septuagint in Biblical Research*, second ed. (Jerusalem Biblical Studies 8; Jerusalem: Simor Ltd., 1997), 45, and Barr, *The Typology of Literalism*, 17.

[3] Tov, *Text-Critical Use*, 45.

[4] Aejmelaeus, "Translation Technique," 25; cf. 35 n. 2.

[5] Ibid., 27.

The co-existence of "excellent free renderings and helplessly literal, Hebraistic renderings of one and the same Hebrew expression" within a single book (as is found in LXX-Isaiah) evidences that translators "had no conscious method or philosophy of translation."[6] Accordingly, Aejmelaeus advocates speaking of a translator's *Übersetzungsweise*,[7] a term that allows a more flexible conception of a translator's approach to his *Vorlage*.

Reconstructing a translator's *Übersetzungsweise* would be a simple matter if the translation were consistently transparent to the MT, but that is seldom the case and is certainly not true for LXX-Isaiah. Accordingly, the base line for assessing the Isaiah translator's *Übersetzungsweise* is recovering his *Vorlage*.[8] The complicating factor in this project, however, is that doing so is not merely a prelude to inferring the translator's *Übersetzungsweise*, since the *Vorlage* can be reconstructed only if we already have some sense of his *Übersetzungsweise*.[9] Thus, the task of reconstructing the *Vorlage* and describing the translator's *Übersetzungsweise* must proceed dialectically.[10]

A detailed discussion of the problems and principles of retroversion is needless here, given Tov's masterful, *The Text-Critical Use of the Septuagint in Biblical Research*. Appropriate, however, are some remarks on the possibility of recovering Hebrew variants from LXX-Isaiah. Scholars tend to favor one of two stances: given the wealth of variants revealed by the DSS, some tend to detect a Hebrew variant behind most divergences from the MT, while others, fascinated by signs that the translator wove contextual interpretation into his translation, tend to attribute divergences to the translator's exegesis.

---

[6] Ibid., 25.

[7] The term seems to go back to Frankel's *Vorstudien zu der Septuaginta*, as noted by Emanuel Tov, "The Nature and Study of the Translation Technique of the LXX in the Past and Present," in *VI Congress of the International Organization for Septuagint and Cognate Studies*, ed. Claude E. Cox (Atlanta: Scholars Press, 1987) 343.

[8] As Aejmelaeus stresses, it is only by reconstructing the path the translator took from his *Vorlage* to his translation that we can infer anything about his mental processes (Anneli Aejmelaeus, "Von Sprache zur Theologie," in *The Septuagint and Messianism*, ed. Michael A. Knibb [Leuven, Paris, Dudley, MA: Uitgeverij Peeters, 2006] 21).

[9] "The tracing of the Vorlage is basically the application of all attainable knowledge of the translation technique in the opposite direction" (Aejmelaeus, "What Can We Know?" 62).

[10] Of course, reconstructing all elements of the *Vorlage* is impossible, since retroversion of particles and grammatical features is uncertain, due to the diverse ways translators handled them from case to case (see Tov, *Text-Critical Use*, 59 and 68). There is also frequently doubt about the precise Hebrew lexeme translated by a Greek word.

Based on my experience with the version, I conclude that LXX-Isaiah both contains interpretative elements and attests variants. On the one hand, I find it impossible to attribute transpositions of words and phrases (e.g., καὶ πέσωσιν εἰς τὰ ὀπίσω καὶ κινδυνεύσουσιν καὶ συντριβήσονται καὶ ἁλώσονται ‖ וכשלו אחור ונשברו ונוקשו ונלכדו, 28:13; οὐ γὰρ μὴ σπείρωσιν οὐδὲ μὴ φυτεύσωσιν ‖ אף בל נטעו אף בל זרעו, 40:24) and every interchange or transposition of consonants (e.g., ἡ ψυχή in 21:4 reflects נפש in the translator's *Vorlage* in place of the MT's נשף)[11] to the translator's exegesis. These types of errors are so commonplace in our extant Hebrew manuscripts that denying they stood in the translator's *Vorlage* amounts to special pleading, unless one can mount persuasive arguments about why the translator rendered against the grain of his *Vorlage*.

Ulrich convincingly argues that "in several readings the Qumran Isaiah MSS show that the LXX was not translating from a *Vorlage* like the MT but faithfully attempting to translate a text which was simply a different Hebrew text."[12] 48:17 provides a striking example:

כה אמר יהוה נאלך	οὕτως λέγει κύριος ὁ ῥυσάμενός σε
קדוש ישראל אני יהוה אלהיך	ὁ ἅγιος Ισραηλ ἐγώ εἰμι ὁ θεός σου
מלמדך להועיל מדריכך בדרך	δέδειχά σοι τοῦ εὑρεῖν σε τὴν ὁδόν
תלך	ἐν ᾗ πορεύσῃ ἐν αὐτῇ

The first four phrases are easy enough to align with the MT.[13] Additionally, τοῦ εὑρεῖν σε τὴν ὁδόν is equivalent to MT's מדריכך בדרך, and εὑρεῖν

---

[11] The translator appropriately renders the noun נשף with τὸ ὀψέ in 5:11 and the verb נשף with ἔπνευσεν in 40:24. On the other hand, one can sometimes mount a reasonable argument that the translator, baffled by a word, may have transposed consonants in order to wrench sense from the passage, as in 14:12, where his translation of חולש by ὁ ἀποστέλλων suggests he read the rare word as if it were שולח (חלש occurs elsewhere only in Exod 17:13, where the LXX gives καὶ ἐτρέψατο for ויחלש). However, even in this case we cannot be sure that the more common שולח had not already been substituted for חולש in his *Vorlage*.

[12] Eugene Ulrich, "The Absence of 'Sectarian Variants' in the Jewish Scriptural Scrolls Found at Qumran," in *The Bible as Book: The Hebrew Bible and the Judaean Desert Discoveries*, ed. Edward D. Herbert and Emanuel Tov (London: The British Library and Oak Knoll Press, 2002) 194 n. 20.

[13] Lack of an equivalent for one element of the pair יהוה אלהים occurs elsewhere in this translation: ὅτι ἐγὼ ὁ θεός σου ‖ כי אני יהוה אלהיך (41:13), ὅτι ἐγὼ ὁ θεός σου ‖ למען יהוה אלהיך ולקדוש (51:15), ἕνεκεν τοῦ θεοῦ σου τοῦ ἁγίου Ισραηλ ‖ ואנכי יהוה אלהיך (55:5), διὰ τὸ ὄνομα κυρίου τὸ ἅγιον ‖ לשם יהוה אלהיך ולקדוש ישראל (60:9). The translator used δεικνύναι for למד previously in 40:14: ἢ τίς ἔδειξεν αὐτῷ κρίσιν ‖ וילמדהו בארח משפט.

seems chosen for its semantic compatibility with δέδειχά σοι (cf. the more literal πατῆσαι ποιήσω αὐτούς || אדריכם in 42:16).

On the other hand, the lack of an equivalent for להועיל is remarkable, since the translator renders every other occurrence of יעל√ with ὠφελεῖν or one of its compounds (30:5, 6; 44:9, 10; 47:12; 57:12), and להועיל is preserved in 1QIsaᵃ and 4QIsaᶜ, while S, V, and T integrate it into their renderings.[14] However, we need to consider this minus alongside the phrase ἐν ᾗ πορεύσῃ ἐν αὐτῇ, which lacks a parallel in the MT. The Hebraic structure encourages retroversion to אשר תלך בה, precisely the phrase attested in 1QIsaᵃ: אני יהוה אלהיכה מלמדך להועיל הדריכה בדדך אשר תלך בה.[15]

1QIsaᵃ may not only provide evidence of the Hebrew behind the LXX's prepositional phrase, but also point the way to understand the lack of an equivalent for להועיל. Given the translator's familiarity with יעל√, and given the ease with which he could have rendered his *Vorlage* if it had read מדריכך parallel to מלמדך (as shown by S, V and T), as well as 1QIsaᵃ's reading, הדריכה, his *Vorlage* likely read: אני יהוה אלהיך מלמדך להדריכך בדרך אשר תלך בה.[16]

Thus, in this instance, 1QIsaᵃ provides evidence of the Hebrew that lay before the translator. This is not to say that 1QIsaᵃ as a whole represents the translator's *Vorlage*, for it also differs from the LXX at many points.[17] However, this case does show the importance of comparing the LXX's deviations from the MT to the DSS and the other versions.[18] Accordingly, I agree with Aejmelaeus's dictum that

> the scholar who wishes to attribute deliberate changes, harmonizations, completion of details and new accents to the translator is under the

---

[14] S: ܒܠܗܝ ܐܢܐ ܠܟ ܕܠܐ ܘܗܐ ܡܘܬܪܐ ܐܢܐ ܠܟ ܐܠܗܝܘ (!) ܡܠܦ ; V: *docens te utilia gubernans te in via*; T: מליף לך להנאה מחוי לך באורח.

[15] The only reading 4QIsaᶜ preserves with clarity is תלך, which is followed by ולוא at the start of v. 18. 4QIsaᵈ agrees with the MT throughout the verse, although נאלך יהוה קדוש ישראל אני יהוה falls within a lacuna while the *lāmed* of תלך is uncertain and the final *kāp* stands in a lacuna, thus preserving no evidence of whether it read בה. It should also be noted that it places a significant gap between אלהיך and מלמדך.

[16] It is also possible that it read להועיל להדריכך and that he collapsed the infinitives into a single equivalent.

[17] For a glimpse of the complex relations between the translator's *Vorlage*, the MT, and 1QIsaᵃ see Eugene Ulrich, "The Developmental Composition of the Book of Isaiah: Light from 1QIsaᵃ on Additions in the MT," *DSD* 8 (2001) 288–305.

[18] To avoid further proliferating footnotes, I will report readings in Hebrew mss and the other versions only when the LXX diverges from the MT sufficiently to warrant the comparison. I will not, as a rule, note orthographic differences in Hebrew readings.

obligation to prove his thesis with weighty arguments and also to show why the divergences cannot have originated with the *Vorlage*.[19]

On the other hand, the discoveries of a multitude of previously unknown variants in the DSS does not eliminate the possibility that a distinctive lexeme or phrase reflects the translator's exegesis. Excessive fascination with what is novel can be as much of a pitfall for those enamored of textual variants as for those intrigued by early biblical exegesis. To suppose that, in the light of the DSS, due caution consists of assuming that divergences reflect Hebrew variants is a mirage. To conclude that every divergence attests a Hebrew variant assumes that the translator always understood the Hebrew, always found his *Vorlage* legible, and was never influenced by his community's traditions or by other scriptural passages. We must account for why, at some points, the Isaiah translator took unusual steps in rendering his *Vorlage*.

For example, as has long been recognized, the rendering of צמח by ἐπιλάμψει in Isa 4:2 is based on Aramaic צמחא, 'splendor',[20] even though צמח is translated by ἀνατέλλειν in 42:9, 43:19, 44:4, 45:8, 58:8, and 61:11, as well as by ἐκβλαστάνειν ('to sprout') in 55:10. Similarly, in the same verse he translates לצבי by ἐν βουλῇ,[21] again based on an Aramaic verb, צבא, 'to be willing',[22] despite his rendering of צבי with ἔνδοξος in 13:19, 23:9, and 28:1.[23] While ἐπὶ τῆς γῆς likely reflects על פני הארץ rather than פרי הארץ of the MT in this verse,[24] his appeal to Aramaic for these other words suggests that he interpreted the verse in the light of the theme of the glory of the LORD shining on the land, as described in 40:5 and 60:1–2.[25] Although it is difficult to infer that

---

[19] Aejmelaeus, "What Can We Know?" 71.

[20] Ziegler, *Untersuchungen*, 107.

[21] βουλή is frequently inserted by the translator where it finds no equivalent in the MT in 3:9; 7:5, 7; 10:25; 25:7, and seems to have been a favorite concept with him (see below, pp. 267–68). Even though in this case we can trace his path from צבי to βουλή, his use of Aramaic to achieve this must be seen in light of his evident attraction to this term.

[22] Ziegler, *Untersuchungen*, 107.

[23] While the translator's knowledge of Hebrew lexemes frequently proves deficient, he seems to have had some facility in Aramaic, which "was a more natural source of information for the translators than Hebrew" (Emanuel Tov, "Did the Septuagint Translators Always Understand their Hebrew Text?" in *De Septuaginta*, ed. Albert Pietersma and Claude E. Cox [Mississauga, Ontario, Canada: Benben Publications, 1984] 54 n. 2).

[24] On which see Ziegler, *Untersuchungen*, 108.

[25] See L. H. Brockington, "The Greek Translator and His Interest in ΔΟΞΑ," *VT* 1 (1951) 29. Whether or not this is an example of Tov's observation that "translations

he was trying to score an ideological point here, his rendering suggests familiarity with themes elsewhere in the book.[26]

Similarly, the translator's use of slot words, not merely for unfamiliar lexemes but also for ones he renders well elsewhere, points to interpretative renderings. For instance, while the translator reasonably uses ἡττᾶσθαι for חתת (8:9 [tris]; 20:5; 30:31; 31:4, 9; 51:7), he sometimes uses it when perplexed. Thus, in 13:15 he employs it for a hapax in the book: ὃς γὰρ ἂν ἁλῷ ἡττηθήσεται || ידקר כל הנמצא. Although דקר appears in Num 25:8, where it is appropriately rendered by ἀπεκέντησεν ('he pierced'), the Isaiah translator's unfamiliarity with it is plausible, and ἡττηθήσεται is contextually apt.[27]

However, his use of ἡττᾶσθαι as a slot word even when the vocabulary was familiar is clear in 33:1:[28]

הוי שודד	οὐαὶ τοῖς ταλαιπωροῦσιν ὑμᾶς
ואתה לא שדוד	ὑμᾶς δὲ οὐδεὶς ποιεῖ ταλαιπώρους
ובוגד ולא בגדו בו	καὶ ὁ ἀθετῶν ὑμᾶς οὐκ ἀθετεῖ
כהתמך שודד תושד	ἁλώσονται οἱ ἀθετοῦντες καὶ παραδοθήσονται
כנלתך לבגד יבגדו בך	καὶ ὡς σὴς ἐπὶ ἱματίου οὕτως ἡττηθήσονται

This is the verse Ziegler cites first as an example of lexemes the translator turned to "wenn das hebr. Äquivalent zu undurchsichtig gewesen," using them as "'Lückenbüßer' ('stop-gap words')."[29] Ziegler adduces 33:1 first because it contains three of the words he identifies as "stop-gap words": ἁλίσκεσθαι, παραδιδόναι, and ἡττᾶσθαι.[30]

---

based on Aramaic rather than Hebrew meanings...may nevertheless be literal from the translator's point of view" (*Text-Critical Use*, 24) is immaterial, since the anomalous method the translator employs, together with the consequent similarity of his rendering to passages elsewhere in the book, signals that his translation is exegetical, not simply interpretive (for this distinction, see below, p. 133).

[26] For his explicit borrowing of phrases from other passages in the book, see chapter five.

[27] Cf. his translation of the unfamiliar ימס by ἡττηθήσεται in 19:1.

[28] 1QIsaᵃ reads כהתמכך for כהתמך, ככלותך for כנלתך, and לבנוד for לבגד. S seems to be perplexed, as indicated by its use of ܣܐ ܕ݁ܝ ܚܒ݂ܣܐ for both כהתמך and כנלתך, as well as its modifications in the grammatical number of the pronouns (e.g., ܐܢ݂ܬ݁ܘܢ || ואתה, which also involves construing the pronoun as the direct object); nevertheless, the *Vorlage* seems to have been substantially = מת. V also seems to be at a loss and provides a moralizing paraphrase (e.g., *vae qui praedaris none et ipse praedaberis* || הוי שודד ואתה לא שדוד) in a way similar to T (יי דאתי למבז ויתך לא יבוזון). V and T offer similar guesses for כנלתך: *cum fatigatus desiveris*, כד תלאי.

[29] Ziegler, *Untersuchungen*, 13.

[30] Ibid., 14.

Some peculiar equivalents in this verse point to variants in the *Vorlage*. For example, while the equivalence ἀθετεῖν || בגד is attested throughout Isaiah (21:2 [bis]; 24:16 [bis]; 48:8 [bis]) and in other books (e.g., Exod 21:8; Jer 3:20 [bis]; 5:11 [bis]; 9:1), only with ἡττηθήσονται || יבגדו at the end of v. 1 does the verb בגד find any other equivalent in Isaiah. Accordingly, it is likely that οἱ ἀθετοῦντες in line four, above, attests a *Vorlage* that read בוגד rather than שודד.[31]

Ziegler suggested that the translator's *Vorlage* read כלתך for כנלתך, and in fact, 1QIsaᵃ attests ככלותך here. While Ziegler maintained that the translator simply extrapolated from this reading and his translation of לבגד with ἐπὶ ἱματίου to arrive at the equivalent σής,[32] more likely he lighted on σής due to familiarity with the image of a moth-eaten garment elsewhere in the book (ὡς ἱμάτιον παλαιωθήσεσθε καὶ ὡς σὴς καταφάγεται ὑμᾶς, 50:9; ὥσπερ γὰρ ἱμάτιον βρωθήσεται ὑπὸ χρόνου καὶ ὡς ἔρια βρωθήσεται ὑπὸ σητός, 51:8). In any case, Ziegler is justified in concluding, "hier hat der Übers. offenbar den Sinn seiner Vorlage...nicht erkannt und deshalb sich selbst einen Satz konstruiert, der sich ganz gut verstehen läßt."[33] His use of three slot words is symptomatic of that. Accordingly, ἡττηθήσονται || יבגדו is not grounds for positing a different *Vorlage*, in the way οἱ ἀθετοῦντες points to a variant; it is his use of a favorite word to provide an (admittedly bland) end to the verse.

On the other hand, while the translator uses ἁλίσκεσθαι as a slot-word when the context has to do with warfare,[34] he may have found footing for it here by seeing כהתמך as a form of תמך, whose three other

---

[31] One might argue that ἀθετεῖν was such a key term for the translator in this context that he simply utilized it for שודד, but then how do we explain his resort to ἡττηθήσονται || יבגדו (on which, see below)? On the other hand, even though ταλαιπωρεῖν and ταλαιπώρους translate שדד nowhere else in LXX-Isaiah (as they do at the beginning of v. 1), they do so numerous times in Jeremiah (e.g., 4:13, 20; 9:18; 10:20; 12:12), as well as in Hosea 10:2, Joel 1:10, Micah 2:4, and Zech 11:2–3 (recall Seeligmann's conclusion that the translator of Isaiah was familiar with the Greek translation of the Dodekapropheton [*Septuagint Version*, 73]).

[32] "Frei mit 'Motte' wiedergegeben, indem sie den Stamm כלה in der Bedeutung 'vernichten', 'verzehren' genommen hat" (Ziegler, *Untersuchungen*, 103).

[33] Ibid., 14.

[34] E.g., καὶ σὺ ἑάλως ὥσπερ καὶ ἡμεῖς ἐν ἡμῖν δὲ κατελογίσθης || גם אתה חלית כמונו אלינו נמשלת in 14:10 (he seems to imagine that the Babylonian king died after being captured in battle, just as he translates כל הנמצא ידקר by ὃς γὰρ ἂν ἁλῷ ἡττηθήσεται in 13:15, as noted above); πάντες οἱ ἄρχοντές σου πεφεύγασι καὶ οἱ ἁλόντες σκληρῶς δεδεμένοι εἰσίν || כל קציניך נדדו יחד מקשת אסרו in 22:3, and ἁλώσεται γὰρ νυκτὸς ἡμέρας δὲ πεσεῖται τὸ τεῖχος || פן יפקד עליה לילה ויום אצרנה in 27:3 (τεῖχος is derived from חמה, at the start of v. 4).

occurrences he rendered in different ways: τὰς χεῖρας ἀποσειόμενος ἀπὸ δώρων || כפיו מתמך בשחד (33:15), καὶ ἠσφαλισάμην σε τῇ δεξιᾷ τῇ δικαίᾳ μου || אף תמכתיך בימין צדקי (41:10), and Ιακωβ ὁ παῖς μου ἀντιλήμψομαι αὐτοῦ || הן עבדי אתמך בו (42:1).[35] ἁλώσονται in 33:1 is simply another contextually apt equivalent for תמך.

His translation of תושש by καὶ παραδοθήσονται is another equivalent selected as apt for the context, and thus another example of the translator employing a "stop-gap word."

Thus, some readings in LXX-Isaiah seem best explained as reflecting a Hebrew variant, while others are amenable to observation of the translator's perplexity or his overall conception of the meaning of the verse or passage. At the same time, the discovery of numerous variants in the DSS—most not even suspected previously—places the onus of proof on the scholar claiming that a peculiar equivalent is due to the translator's exegesis.

As is always the case with retroversions, incontrovertible proof that one's reconstructions recover the *Vorlage* is unavailable. Above all, as Tov remarks, retroversion depends on "one's textual judgment, much on one's linguistic feel, and even more on the analysis of the translation techniques involved,"[36] although that itself is a partially intuitive enterprise.[37] Nevertheless, it is the scholar's responsibility to detail her/his arguments for a retroversion.

On the other hand, there are times it is impossible to convince oneself of what lay before the translator, and the honest course is to offer competing arguments without advocating a solution.[38] Above all, we lack an Archimedean platform from which to make "objective" pronounce-

---

[35] His use of ἀντιλαμβάνειν for תמך accords with the use of this equivalence in Gen 48:17; Psalm 40[41]:13; 62[63]:9. His use of ἠσφαλισάμην σε may find a parallel in Prov 28:17 (οὐκ ἐν ἀσφαλείᾳ || אל יתמכו בו), although the fact that ἐν ἀσφαλείᾳ leads into an additional proverb makes the equivalence uncertain.

[36] Tov, *Text-Critical Use*, 61. Tov subsequently reiterates that "in the reconstruction of the *Vorlage* of the LXX, reliance on intuition is as important as consulting equivalents occurring elsewhere in the LXX" (ibid., 71).

[37] Despite Barr's confidence that "a certain subjective and hypothetical element" in this procedure can "be held in check…so long as the investigator…forms his judgement on the basis of extensive experience of the languages involved" (*The Typology of Literalism*, 11), Tov soberly notes that scholarly characterizations of translations embody their own judgments as to what features dominate, while citing examples of opposite tendencies as "exceptions" (*Text-Critical Use*, 25 n. 39).

[38] Fortunately, most of the time—even when the Hebrew behind a particular word resists recovery—the context allows a measure of certainty about how the translator proceeded.

ments, or a method that will guide us unfailingly between the Scylla of assuming the *Vorlage* was entirely like the MT and the Charybdis of multiplying variants baselessly. In particular, despite my admiration for Arie van der Kooij's work, I find that his method for discerning the translator's *Vorlage* offers false hope.

In *The Oracle of Tyre* van der Kooij adumbrates a method that seeks to give the LXX its due as having its own literary structure rather than simply mining it for Hebrew variants.[39] Before outlining that method, however, he reviews the conclusions reached by scholars studying LXX-Isaiah in the past quarter century, beginning with Ziegler's insistence that "um das Verhältnis der Js-LXX zum MT recht zu würdigen, muss zunächst die ganze Persönlichkeit des Übersetzters vor uns erstehen."[40] He concurs with the common characterization of LXX-Isaiah as "a 'free translation' in reflecting a 'free approach' towards its Hebrew original."[41] However, this description says too little, in his estimation, since "the observations made by Ziegler, Seeligmann and others strongly suggest that LXX Isaiah also shows traces of something that goes beyond the border of . . . free translation."[42] In many cases, the translator engages in rewriting, so that "the passage produced by the translator turns out to be, to some extent, a new text or composition."[43]

From Ziegler's sketch, van der Kooij accepts that "a tendency to explication and to paraphrase is typical of this translation," that most minuses are due "to the non-rendering of synonymous words or clauses, whereas most pluses are best understood as part of the tendency of the translator to make things explicit and clear."[44] He also accepts Ziegler's conclusion that the translator "wrote good Koine, in particular in his rendering of images and comparisons,"[45] together with his conclusions about the Egyptian milieu reflected in the translator's lexical choices. He values especially Ziegler's observation that the translator had the whole book so well in mind that his divergences from MT are often

---

[39] Van der Kooij, *The Oracle of Tyre*, 110.
[40] Ziegler, *Untersuchungen*, 7, cited by van der Kooij, *The Oracle of Tyre*, 8.
[41] Van der Kooij, *The Oracle of Tyre*, 12. He defines "free translation" as embodying "the aim of writing good Koine Greek; variety of lexical choices; different word order for reasons of style; grammatical and contextual changes, such as harmonizations" (ibid., 13).
[42] Ibid., 13.
[43] Ibid.
[44] Ibid., 9.
[45] Ibid.

attributable to exegesis of a passage "nach dem ganzen Kontext der Stelle und ihren Parallelen."[46]

From Seeligmann van der Kooij adopts the observation that LXX-Isaiah reflects contemporaneous events so regularly that the translator evidently considered his era the "time for the fulfillment of ancient prophecies."[47] Noting that this perception has been embraced by das Neves, Hanhart, Koenig, and himself, van der Kooij finds a consensus that "LXX Isaiah contains passages where the ancient text of Isaiah has been actualized...in the sense of the updating of a prophecy or oracle of Isaiah."[48]

With this sketch of the translator's *Übersetzungsweise* in view, his four stage method begins with "study of the text of the MT as it stands, grammatically, stylistically, and semantically."[49] Although text-critical difficulties can be noted at this stage, the primary aim is to provide a "comparison between this text and the LXX," so that the distinctive features of the LXX's translation of a passage are clear.[50]

The second stage seeks to understand the passage in the LXX as a literary unit. The pertinent questions at this stage are: "Do significant renderings and passages in the LXX text make sense in relation to each other? Does LXX...present itself as a text with some coherence?"[51] If so, the question becomes the genre to which this literary unit belongs, which "in most cases [will be] that of prophecy."[52] And because *Erfüllungsinterpretation* is, for van der Kooij, a settled characteristic of the translator's handling of prophecy,[53] one must also explore

> whether that passage does not only constitute, as a translation, a trans-formation from the linguistic point of view, but also a transformation in the sense of a reinterpretation of the temporal application of an ancient prophecy....did the translator aim at producing a version of an ancient prophecy which would make sense as an oracle at his time?[54]

---

[46] Ziegler, *Untersuchungen*, 135, cited by van der Kooij, *The Oracle of Tyre*, 9.

[47] Seeligmann, *Septuagint Version*, 4, cited by van der van der Kooij, *The Oracle of Tyre*, 9.

[48] Van der Kooij, *The Oracle of Tyre*, 11.

[49] Ibid., 15.

[50] Ibid., 20.

[51] Ibid., 75.

[52] Ibid., 17.

[53] Ibid., 9–11.

[54] Ibid., 18; cf. 96.

Van der Kooij reserves reconstruction of the LXX's *Vorlage* for the final step so as to permit the LXX "to be taken seriously in its own right."[55] Because decisions about *Vorlage* depend on one's perception of the "style of translation," which have to do with "matters of translation and of interpretation,"[56] the image one holds of the translator's procedure shape these decisions. To this end, van der Kooij stresses that reading the text aloud, essential to reading in the ancient world,[57] must be taken into account in imagining the translator at work. Reading aloud involves creating proper phrasing, itself an interpretative task.[58] Consequently, even though interpretation involves the study of individual elements (words, phrases, and sentences), considered against the background of oral reading such study is not atomistic, since reading leads to greater stress "on the level of clauses and sentences."[59] Accordingly, the goal of this step is

> to reconstruct the 'reading' (ἀνάγνωσις) of the Hebrew on which the translation is based, as well as the 'interpretation' which may account for striking differences between the parent text and the Old Greek version.[60]

For this reason, we should not quickly attribute a difference with the MT to the translator's ineptitude. When viewed from the perspective of ἀνάγνωσις, "it is more plausible to regard such a case as part of the 'reading' of the text that was current in his milieu."[61]

As much as I applaud van der Kooij's desire to do justice to the literary structure of a passage in the LXX and to acknowledge the translator's creation of literary units, I consider his method flawed insofar as it fails to preserve the dialectic between one's sense of the *Übersetzungsweise* of a book and the particular passage under study. Put more colloquially, he stacks the deck.

---

[55] Ibid., 110.

[56] Ibid., 18.

[57] Ibid., 112–15. His discussion seems to bypass the important debate between Barr and Tov over what sort of "reading" the translators employed (see below, pp. 102–04). Moreover, given that the translator's knowledge of Hebrew was (as is generally agreed) more "a product of theoretical study rather than of living experience" (Seeligmann, *Septuagint Version*, 49) it is difficult to imagine him reading his exemplar aloud.

[58] Van der Kooij, *The Oracle of Tyre*, 115–17.

[59] Ibid., 119.

[60] Ibid.

[61] Ibid., 122.

While van der Kooij rightly recognizes that understanding the *Übersetzungsweise* is a prerequisite of text-critical analysis,[62] assaying translation style depends on *all* one's experiences with a translation. It demands continually developing, testing and modifying hypotheses. Specifically, it is illicit to import the assumption of *Erfüllungsinterpretation* into the analysis of a translator's handling of a particular passage.

Van der Kooij's survey of the *status quaestionis* serves as the predicate for his work; he accepts the conclusions noted earlier as the settled principles that guide his study of the translation before entertaining questions of *Vorlage*. Consequently, when he takes up the question of the genre of Isaiah 23, the issue is already decided: it is a prophetic text, and because *Erfüllungsinterpretation* characterizes the handling of prophecy in LXX-Isaiah, this passage, "just as with other prophetic passages in LXX Isaiah, reflects...interest in prophecies as predictions."[63]

In the same way, while van der Kooij begins his study of the *Vorlage* in Isaiah 23 by stating that his assumption in considering this chapter as a literary unit—that the LXX's "parent text w[as] very close to MT"—must now be checked,[64] the ensuing discussion reduces that inquiry to a rhetorical question. By the time van der Kooij approaches this issue he has already concluded that the translator created a meaningful unit in Greek, distinct at points from the MT, but mostly reliant on it, and that he did so largely in the interest of elucidating the fulfillment of the prophet's words. What room is there for variants?

Van der Kooij further telegraphs his conclusions at the outset of his discussion of *Vorlage* by his sketch of the translator as scribe.[65] Having posited that scribes, by reading the text aloud, placed greater stress "on the level of clauses and sentences than on that of single words,"[66] while interpretations of the constituent words and phrases served this larger cause, when he defines the purpose of reconstructing the *Vorlage* as reconstruction of the 'reading' (ἀνάγνωσις) and the consequent interpretation of differences with the MT,[67] all that is left is to play out the paradigm.

---

[62] Ibid., 18.

[63] Ibid., 88.

[64] Ibid., 110.

[65] Ibid., 112–23.

[66] Ibid., 119.

[67] Ibid. Van der Kooij's hypothesis that the translator read the text aloud as the first step of interpretation fails to deal with the widespread recognition that the Isaiah translator's Hebrew was likely weak. See above, n. 57.

In my view, there is no substitute for plunging into the complex and messy task of juggling the LXX, the MT, the Peshiṭta, the Targum, the Vulgate, and all witnesses from the DSS at the same time one wrestles with how to describe the translator's *Übersetzungsweise*. In fact, comparing the LXX to the MT without entertaining the possibility of variants in the LXX's *Vorlage* is not germane to understanding the translator's *Übersetzungsweise*, especially since van der Kooij's execution of his first stage is not simply about comparing the LXX to the MT.

For example, in discussing Isa 23:2 van der Kooij first adjudicates between different interpretations of the MT discussed by modern commentators and, using sound philological reasoning, draws conclusions as to which he prefers.[68] Comparing and contrasting the perceived literary structure of the LXX to that perceived for the MT based on such discussions may be an interesting exercise, but it is difficult to see what *critical* function the MT plays in this task. The only basis for comparing the LXX to the MT is if there is reason to think that the translator's *Vorlage* was like the MT, something that must be established both before and while comparing literary structures in the two works. Otherwise it would be just as useful to compare the LXX with (say) the Peshiṭta. We cannot postpone dealing with the question of variants from the MT, for only by assessing how the translator sought to convey a passage in a *Vorlage* that may or may not be similar to the MT can we work our way from an obscure relationship between the LXX and the MT to accounting for that obscurity. And in doing so we must use *and* test received rules of thumb about the translator's *Übersetzungsweise*.

This dialectical process must now be applied in assessing the *Übersetzungsweise* of the Isaiah translator. The foundational exploration concerns how the translator interpreted the linguistic features of his source text and represented those in Greek. To that question I will turn in the next chapter.

---

[68] Ibid., 20.

CHAPTER FOUR

LINGUISTIC INTERPRETATION IN LXX-ISAIAH

How translators represent the words and syntax of the source text in the target language distinguishes "free" from "literal" translations, for the latter tend to: 1) use stereotyped lexical equivalents; 2) represent constituent elements of words with distinct Greek words (etymological analysis) (e.g., ἐν τῷ ἀκοῦσαι σε || בשמעך[1]); 3) follow the word-order of the source text; 4) represent each Hebrew lexeme with one Greek word (quantitative representation), except when differences in syntactic structure between the source and target languages require etymological analysis.[2] Since each of these features is quantifiable, their frequency in a translation provides a good measure of its relative "literalness" or "freedom."[3]

As Barr has observed, "there are different ways of being literal and of being free, so that a translation can be literal and free at the same time but in different modes or on different levels."[4] Even translations with a well-earned reputation for a "free" translation style, such as LXX-Isaiah, can be remarkably literal at times. Notice, for example, how exactly Isa 7:15–16 corresponds to the MT:[5]

---

[1] As Barr notes, such etymological renderings produce "a Greek sentence substantially more like the *syntax* of the Hebrew sentence" (*The Typology of Literalism*, 21, emphasis mine).

[2] Tov, *Text-Critical Use*, 20–24. I have omitted his criterion of "linguistic adequacy of lexical choices" because, as he admits, this judgment is subjective: "renderings which in our view are incorrect…may nevertheless be literal from the translator's viewpoint" (ibid., 24). The validity of the criterion of "linguistic adequacy" lies in the supposition that a translator who works more literally will "endeavor to provide a linguistically responsible translation" (ibid.), in the sense that he sought to represent the sense of the locution without exegetical embellishment. The classic study of "literal" and "free" translation styles is James Barr's *The Typology of Literalism*.

[3] Tov, *Text-Critical Use*, 25.

[4] Barr, *The Typology of Literalism*, 6.

[5] The slot for ודבש falls in a lacuna in 1QIsaᵃ (which also obscures the end of ה in החמאה), while the ב of MT's בטרם is inserted supralinearly *secunda manu* (which also supplied ו *mater* above both ובחר and תעזב). S, V, and T reflect a *Vorlage* = MT, although T renders מאוס ברע ובחור בטוב metaphorically (לרחקא בישא ולקרבא טבא) both times.

חמאה ודבש יאכל   ¹⁵⁾βούτυρον καὶ μέλι φάγεται

לדעתו מאוס ברע   πρὶν ἢ γνῶναι αὐτὸν ἢ προελέσθαι πονηρὰ

ובחור בטוב   ἐκλέξεται τὸ ἀγαθόν

כי בטרם ידע הנער   ¹⁶⁾διότι πρὶν ἢ γνῶναι τὸ παιδίον ἀγαθὸν ἢ κακὸν

מאס ברע ובחר בטוב   ἀπειθεῖ πονηρίᾳ τοῦ ἐκλέξασθαι τὸ ἀγαθόν

תעזב האדמה אשר אתה קץ   καὶ καταλειφθήσεται ἡ γῆ ἣν σὺ φοβῇ

מפני שני מלכיה   ἀπὸ προσώπου τῶν δύο βασιλέων

The Isaiah translator renders the bulk of these verses literally, as measured by two indices. First, setting aside the plus ἀγαθὸν ἢ κακὸν in v. 16,[6] the Greek accords with the MT's word order, and each Hebrew lexeme can be aligned with a Greek word or phrase.

A second index of literalness relates to lexical equivalents. If we again set aside ἀγαθὸν ἢ κακόν and align the Greek words with the MT's lexemes, we find only two semantic differences: προελέσθαι || מאוס and πρὶν ἢ [γνῶναι αὐτὸν] || ל[דעתו]. The remaining lexical equivalents are standard within the LXX. In this passage, as well as others in the book, the translator uses tactics characteristic of a "literal" *Übersetzungsweise*.

Accordingly, whatever conclusions we reach about this translator's "free" style must take into account such signs of "literal" translation. And here Barr's observation about the LXX translators' working method is apropos:

> Rather than show a definite policy, translators often seem to have worked in an *ad hoc* manner and at any particular point to have opted for a literal or a free rendering, whichever seemed to work out according to the character of the original text and its immediate context.[7]

This means, above all, that we cannot take as a starting point for studying a translation its reputation for being either "literal" or "free," for "the tendency of many early translators was…to combine the two approaches in a quite inconsequential way."[8] Taking this observation to heart is crucial to assessing how the Isaiah translator interpreted his *Vorlage* linguistically.

---

[6] I will consider this plus and the two semantic differences of v. 15 in chapter five.

[7] Barr, *The Typology of Literalism*, 7.

[8] Ibid. Cf. especially Barr's comment that "the 'freer' books had already used the literalist methods in considerable measure: what literalism did was to seek to use these methods more consistently" (ibid.).

We must also consider how semantics and grammar interrelate. We have seen van der Kooij's insistence on interpretation beginning with reading the text. This correctly places the emphasis on the functions of lexemes within the larger project of communication.[9] However, this can hardly be a step *prior* to interpretation, as van der Kooij would have it,[10] inasmuch as reading both assigns meanings to words and intuitively identifies syntactic relationships. Of course, either or both of these might have to be modified in the light of further reflection, since reading proceeds by hypothesizing the meaning of the text and revising it in the light of rereading.[11] The choice of Greek equivalents, then, was not subsequent to reading, but part of it, inasmuch as deciding how to cast the meaning of a passage in a different language entails a fresh rereading.[12]

Grammatical interpretation

While gauging a translator's *Übersetzungsweise* requires considering how he analyzed both individual lexemes and grammar, exploring the issue of grammar first provides a good initial measure of his *Übersetzungsweise* by showing how closely he follows his *Vorlage*'s word order and the degree to which he mimics its syntax.

Variations in tense, voice, number, person and gender (in the case of pronouns) are common in the LXX,[13] including LXX-Isaiah, whose translator "often sacrifices grammatical accuracy to his own stylistic text-formulation."[14] However, we should not explain such modifications solely in terms of his "stylistic text-formulation," for often enough they contribute, as we shall see, to the overall coherence of thought

---

[9] Arie van der Kooij, *The Oracle of Tyre*, 114–17.

[10] Ibid., 117.

[11] See James Barr's "Method A" in his "'Guessing' in the Septuagint," in *Studien zur Septuaginta*, ed. Detlef Fraenkel, Udo Quast, and John W. Wevers (Göttingen: Vandenhoeck & Ruprecht, 1990) 21.

[12] I agree with van der Kooij's distinction between these translators and the dragoman: the translators were not encountering their text for the first time (*The Oracle of Tyre*, 120). Nevertheless, as Barr notes, "even if a translator took a reading tradition into account, at all sorts of points he could and did still conclude to the meaning from the consonantal text" ("'Guessing' in the Septuagint," 28).

[13] See Tov, *Text-Critical Use*, 154–61.

[14] Seeligmann, *Septuagint Version*, 56.

in the literary unit. As such, they are not just "stylistic" devices, but interpretative maneuvers.

The Isaiah translator sometimes avails himself of the more complex word order of Greek.[15] Indeed, while LXX-Isaiah most often follows the verb-subject sequence of its *Vorlage*, a subject-object-verb sequence occasionally appears, as in 1:20 (μάχαιρα ὑμᾶς κατέδεται || חרב תאכלו) and 33:11 (πῦρ ὑμᾶς κατέδεται || אש תאכלכם).[16] Moreover, while Hebrew syntax relies strongly on set sequences in the parts of speech (e.g., nouns in the construct state precede the *nomen rectum*),[17] Greek syntax permits more flexible sequences by dint of case endings that allow syntactically related words to be separated,[18] a feature we sometimes find in LXX-Isaiah. For example, in 5:13 the translator allows a verb (which he supplied) to intervene between πλῆθος and its genitive (καὶ πλῆθος ἐγενήθη νεκρῶν διὰ λιμὸν || וכבודו מתי רעב), while in 30:27 an adjective is removed from the noun it modifies in a way not typical of Hebrew word order (ἰδοὺ τὸ ὄνομα κυρίου διὰ χρόνου ἔρχεται πολλοῦ || הנה שם יהוה בא ממרחק).[19] And although the genitive typically follows the noun it qualifies, in imitation of Hebrew word order,[20] in 10:7 it stands before its noun (καὶ τοῦ ἔθνη ἐξολεθρεῦσαι οὐκ ὀλίγα || ולהכרית גוים לא מעט), as it does in 11:11 (καὶ ἀπὸ ἡλίου ἀνατολῶν || וממשנער), 29:2 (αὐτῆς ἡ ἰσχὺς καὶ τὸ πλοῦτος || תאניה ואניה), and 33:8 (ἐρημωθήσονται γὰρ αἱ τούτων ὁδοί || נשמו מסלות). This pattern is especially marked with pronouns (e.g., ἀπολέσαι αὐτῆς τὴν ἰσχύν || לשמד מעזניה, 23:11)[21] and accords with tendencies in literary Greek.[22] Likewise, while most often modifiers or other adjuncts follow

---

[15] Ziegler notes that the translator conforms his translation to Greek style, observing, "wenn wir also von der Treue der Wiedergabe absehen, müssen wir zugeben, daß der Js-Übers. ein gutes Griechisch schreibt und teilweise ganz vorzüglich seinen Text wiedergibt in der Sprache, die den Lesern seiner Zeit verständlich ist" (*Untersuchungen*, 13).

[16] A thorough study of word order variation in LXX-Isaiah is needed to provide a clearer picture of this aspect of the translation.

[17] J. Merle Rife, "The Mechanics of Translation Greek," *JBL* 52 (1933) 247.

[18] Ibid., 245.

[19] 1QIsaᵃ = MT. S and V reflect a *Vorlage* = MT. T gives an exegetical rendering that reflects MT and (like the LXX) interprets ממרחק temporally (הא שמא דיוי מתגלי כמא דאתנביאו עלוהי נבייא מלקדמין).

[20] Nigel Turner, *A Grammar of New Testament Greek: Vol. III, Syntax* (Edinburgh: T & T Clark, 1963) 349.

[21] 42 times in chapters 1–35 and 40–66 a pronoun in the genitive case precedes its noun (1:24; 3:7; 8:13; 11:16; 23:11; 23:16, 18; 25:2; 26:11; 27:9; 28:5, 18, 22, 25; 29:2, 8; 30:23; 34:3, 9 [bis]; 40:2, 13, 20; 41:26; 43:3; 46:10; 48:8, 9; 49:1, 5; 52:7; 57:6 [bis], 7; 58:2; 59:12; 60:1; 63:17; 65:1; 66:14, 19 [bis]).

[22] See Turner, *Syntax*, 349.

the noun in LXX-Isaiah (as throughout the LXX), sometimes they are embedded between the article and the noun, as in 5:22 (οἱ τὸν οἶνον πίνοντες || יין לשתות) and 33:14 (οἱ ἐν Σιων ἄνομοι || בציון חטאים) (cf. 11:16; 26:19; 29:18; 33:8; 54:10; 59:21).[23] Similarly, in 8:15 we find the striking phrase, ἄνθρωποι ἐν ἀσφαλείᾳ ὄντες || צור. These sorts of accommodations to Greek word order are not the norm and typically occur when the translator reformulates a phrase or inserts words on his own initiative. In any case, the typical accord with Hebrew word order suggests the translator concluded that such word order would be intelligible to his target audience, which accords with Rife's observation that "colloquial Greek in general resembles Semitic more than does literary Greek, in word order."[24]

An equally important criterion for gauging this translator's handling of grammar is his use of conjunctions, for he tends to clarify relationships between clauses through syntaxis rather than parataxis. While the frequency of καί in LXX-Isaiah is near the median for biblical books,[25] this fact tells us little, since the frequency with which καί represents *wāw* in the translator's *Vorlage* is virtually impossible to determine, given the problems of +/- *wāw* in Hebrew manuscripts. On the other hand, the translator's use of other conjunctions sheds light on his approach to rendering Hebrew grammar into Greek.

For instance, while LXX-Isaiah makes less use of δέ than other Septuagintal books,[26] it employs οὐδέ at a rate of 4.02 per 1,000 words, more frequently than any other book, including Job (1.77/1,000) and Proverbs (1.43/1,000). Moreover, its use of οὔτε ten times is matched only by Deuteronomy.[27] The translator's use of οὐδέ and οὔτε signals

---

[23] Turner reports that "in LXX only 4 per cent of the def. articles stand apart from their nouns in books translated from the canonical literature, whereas in the books having no MT as *Vorlage* the percentage is as high as 11 per cent" (ibid., 348). Rife comments that a construction using an "adjective phrase" embedded between the article and its noun suggests "literary effort" (Rife, "The Mechanics of Translation Greek," 248).

[24] Rife, "The Mechanics of Translation Greek," 247.

[25] καί occurs at the rate of 92.66 per 1,000 words in LXX-Isaiah. The lowest frequency is 42.36 per 1,000 (Proverbs), the median is 100.32 per 1,000 (Haggai), and the highest is 137.94 per 1,000 (1 Chronicles).

[26] δέ occurs at a frequency rate of 5.76 per 1,000 words in LXX-Isaiah, whereas it appears at the rate of 26.25 in Genesis, 16.2 in Exodus, 50.21 in Proverbs, and 54.48 in Job.

[27] Exodus and Daniel each have 7 occurrences, Psalms 5, Numbers 4, while Judges and Jeremiah have 2 each.

his interest in coordinating negative phrases with greater refinement
than καί + negative.

The frequency of ἀλλά in Isaiah is among the highest in the biblical
books of the LXX, at 2.03 per 1,000 words (55 occurrences), shy of its
frequency in Job (2.95/1,000 [40 occurrences]) but far above typical
rates.[28] Moreover, only 13 of those 55 occurrences correspond to כי in
the MT, while 20 align with ו, and another 13 lack a formal equivalent.
It appears that the translator was interested in marking strong disjunction for his readers.

The frequency of γάρ in Isaiah is unusually high, appearing at the
rate of 6.79 words per 1,000, second only to Proverbs, where it occurs
at a rate of 9.10/1,000.[29] Of greater significance, however, is which
Hebrew words γάρ represents. As is to be expected, throughout the
LXX it most often translates כי, as reflected in statistics for the Torah:
87% of the occurrences of γάρ in Genesis correspond to כי in the MT,
92% in Exodus, 66% in Leviticus,[30] 90% in Numbers, and 95% in
Deuteronomy. In Isaiah, on the other hand, only 49% of the cases of
γάρ (94/184) correspond to כי in the MT, slightly more than in Job (45%,
94/171), although less than in Proverbs (59%, 42/102). Moreover, in
68 of those instances in Isaiah (37% of all its occurrences) γάρ lacks
a transparent equivalent in the MT.[31] Thus, the translator's use of γάρ
further attests his interest in creating smoother connections between
clauses than would obtain by simply reproducing parataxis.

While the frequency statistics for νῦν are unremarkable,[32] the significance of its use arises when we compare its frequency relative to עתה

---

[28] E.g., among books where ἀλλά appears ten times or more, Genesis has a rate of
0.83, Exodus 0.44, Numbers 0.72, Deuteronomy 1.00, Joshua 1.14, 1 Reigns 1.14, 3
Reigns 0.53, 4 Reigns 0.64, 2 Chronicles 1.08, Psalms 0.29, Proverbs 1.07, Jeremiah
0.83, and Daniel 0.96.

[29] The median is occupied by 1 Samuel, with a rate of 0.10 per 1,000 words, while
Kings, Ezra-Nehemiah, Song, Amos, Joel, Haggai, and Malachi have no occurrences.
For comparison, the frequency rates for the books of the Torah are: Genesis, 3.22;
Exodus, 3.75; Leviticus, 1.89; Numbers, 0.88; and Deuteronomy, 1.70. As Turner notes,
the LXX translators tended to conform to the Semitic style of "avoid[ing] second-place
conjunctions" and so "either placed the conjunction first or else avoided altogether the
second-place conjunctions like γάρ, γε, μέν, δέ, οὖν, τε" (Turner, *Syntax*, 347).

[30] In 12 cases (out of 36) γάρ lacks an equivalent in the MT of Leviticus.

[31] I have excluded here all cases where γάρ could correspond to ו, ל, לכן, הן or any
other word for which it is a natural equivalent.

[32] Isaiah's 1.96 per 1,000 words is less than that of Haggai (4.22), Micah (3.38), and
1 Kingdoms (2.38), but comparable to 2 Kingdoms (1.95) and Genesis (1.50).

in the MT. Looking at the ratio of instances of עתה to occurrences of νῦν, Haggai registers 4:4, Micah 3:3, 1 Kgdms 46:48, 2 Kgdms 30:35, and Genesis 40:49, while the ratio for Isaiah is 29:53.[33] Even though this is but a rough measuring stick, this ratio reinforces the conclusion that the translator sought to clarify clausal relationships.

Two other conjunctions are significant for the fact that they occur at all. The Isaiah translator uses τοίνυν on four occasions: once for כי (3:10), once for לכן (5:13), and twice without an identifiable formal equivalent in the MT (27:4; 33:23). By contrast, τοίνυν occurs in just four passages outside Isaiah: Job 8:13 (|| כי); 36:14 (|| -); 1 Chr 28:10 (|| עתה); 2 Chr 28:23 (αὐτοῖς τοίνυν || להם). Equally noteworthy is τοιγαροῦν in Isa 5:26 (τοιγαροῦν || ונשא), which occurs again only in Job 22:10 (|| על כן), Job 24:22 (τοιγαροῦν οὐ μή || ולא), Prov 1:26 (|| -), and Prov 1:31 (τογαροῦν ἔδονται || ויאכלו). By employing these conjunctions that occur rarely in the LXX, the translator's interest in marking sequences of thought is again evident.

An especially remarkable piece of grammatical interpretation is found in the translator's novel negations of clauses when he (apparently) found himself confounded, as in 3:10:[34]

אמרו צדיק כי טוב εἰπόντες δήσωμεν τὸν δίκαιον ὅτι δύσχρηστος ἡμῖν ἐστι

Tov accounts for the translator's maneuver well: having rendered אסרו (a corruption of אמרו) with δήσωμεν,[35] "the translator felt compelled to render טוב antithetically with δύσχρηστος."[36] This seems a maneuver of last resort to wrest meaning from confusion.[37]

---

[33] Even the more "free" books of Proverbs and Job register 3/3 and 11/18, respectively.

[34] 1QIsaᵃ = MT, although a superlinear ל has been inserted before צדיק. S, V, and T all make צדיק an indirect object (V uses the dative case, S and T mark it with a *lāmed*). T's equivalent for צדיק is in the plural, and it provides a suffix with טוב: לצדיקיא טוביכון טוב.

[35] Tov posits that εἰπόντες δήσωμεν reflects a doublet, אמרי\אמרו אסרו, in the translator's *Vorlage* (*Text-Critical Use*, 139). Ottley and Ziegler entertained that possibility, but also allowed that his *Vorlage* might simply have read אסרו and that he supplied εἰπόντες himself (Ottley, *The Book of Isaiah*, 2:117; Ziegler, *Untersuchungen*, 61), while Seeligmann mentioned only that the translator read אסרו (*Septuagint Version*, 57). Given that the translator supplied λέγων as recently as v. 6, his own insertion of it here is a strong possibility.

[36] Tov, *Text-Critical Use*, 139.

[37] Cf. ibid., 169.

The translator insinuated negations in an equally subtle manner elsewhere by using *alpha* privative, as in 17:10:[38]

כִּי שָׁכַחַתְּ אֱלֹהֵי יִשְׁעֵךְ   διότι κατέλιπες τὸν θεὸν τὸν σωτῆρά σου

וְצוּר מָעֻזֵּךְ לֹא זָכָרְתְּ   καὶ κυρίου τοῦ βοηθοῦ σου οὐκ ἐμνήσθης

עַל כֵּן תִּטְּעִי נִטְעֵי נַעֲמָנִים   διὰ τοῦτο φυτεύσεις φύτευμα ἄπιστον

וּזְמֹרַת זָר תִּזְרָעֶנּוּ   καὶ σπέρμα ἄπιστον

The translator's derivation of ἄπιστον from זָר ascribes a negative nuance to זָר that is apt for the context.[39] In fact this nuance is arrived at in conjunction with a reading of נַעֲמָנִים as נֶאֱמָנִים,[40] leaving him in the lurch, since the clause introduced by לָכֵן is clearly a judgment. Accordingly, he took recourse to inferring a negative meaning for the phrase נִטְעֵי נַעֲמָנִים,[41] providing a good example of the translator resorting to ad hoc modifications due to earlier exegetical decisions.[42]

Seeligmann points to 1:24 as another instance when the translator "forcibly tries to wrench, from passages which he cannot understand, some signification" by insinuating a negation:[43]

---

[38] 1QIsaᵃ reads שכחתי for שכחת, מעוזך for מעזך, נעמונים for נעמנים, וזמורת for וזמרת. 4QIsaᵃ preserves only כי שכחת אלהי, while 4QIsaᵇ is very broken and preserves only שכחת אל[הי] (the *kāp* is marked as uncertain), while *yôd* and *šîn* of ישעך are recorded but uncertain, as is the final *wāw* of תזרענו. S reads ܘܙܪܥܬܐ for כי שכחת, (ܠܐܠܗܐ) ܐܠܗܐ for אלהי ישעך, renders צור metaphorically with ܘܬܩܝܦܐ, translates מעזך with ܥܘܫܢܟ, and gives, as a guess for זמרת, ܘܫܒܫܬܐ. V, similar to S, translates אלהי ישעך with *Dei salvatoris tui* and צור with *Fortis*; following the LXX, it translates נעמנים with *fidelem*. Like S and V, T translates צור with תקיף, although it builds unique and expanded clauses around it. For נעמנים T gives בחירא, while substituting אסנית מקלקלין ועובדין for וזמרת זר תזרענו.

[39] Notice how he extends this theme of σπέρμα ἄπιστον in v. 11: τῇ δὲ ἡμέρᾳ ᾗ ἂν φυτεύσῃς πλανηθήσῃ || ביום נטעך תשגשגי. He effects this by deriving תשגשגי from שנה√. On this translation of זָר, see below, p. 125.

[40] Of course, his *Vorlage* might actually have read נאמנים, although we also know that א and ע often caused confusion of similar words for readers. As Tov observes, "phonetic variants...need not necessarily have been found in the manuscripts used by the translators," who may simply "have understood certain words...as expressing other words of similar phonetic value" (*Text-Critical Use*, 139).

[41] Cf. 18:2 (ἔθνος ἀνέλπιστον καὶ καταπεπατημένον || גוי קו קו ומבוסה), over against 18:7 (ἔθνος ἐλπίζον καὶ καταπεπατημένον || גוי קו קו ומבוסה).

[42] Tov's statement that "these should not be considered deliberate changes of the biblical text, but legitimate maneuverings within the framework of the translator's knowledge" (*Text-Critical Use*, 169) requires some refinement. Obviously they are not "deliberate changes of the biblical text" in the literal sense, but they are deliberate reconstructions of its meaning that the translator must have considered approximations or guesses. Therefore, they are "legitimate maneuverings" only in the guarded sense that they were the only means "the translator's knowledge" left him to offer some representation of the Hebrew in Greek.

[43] Seeligmann, *Septuagint Version*, 57.

לכן נאם האדון יהוה צבאות⁴⁴   διὰ τοῦτο τάδε λέγει ὁ δεσπότης κύριος
σαβαωθ
אביר ישראל הוי   οὐαὶ οἱ ἰσχύοντες Ισραηλ⁴⁵
אנחם מצרי   οὐ παύσεται γάρ μου ὁ θυμὸς ἐν τοῖς
ὑπεναντίοις
ואנקמה מאויבי   καὶ κρίσιν ἐκ τῶν ἐχθρῶν μου ποιήσω

The translation of אנחם with παύσεται finds a precedent in Gen 5:29
(οὗτος διαναπαύσει ἡμᾶς || זה ינחמנו), as well as Jer 26[33]:3, 13, 19;
31[38]:13, 15 (all παύεσθαι). For κρίσιν...ποιήσω || אנקמה,⁴⁶ cf. ὁ
θεὸς ἡμῶν κρίσιν ἀνταποδίδωσιν || אלהיכם נקם בא יבוא in 35:4 (read
as יביא). The translator supplied μου ὁ θυμός as subject of παύσεται,
based on the context. These equivalents prompted the introduction of
a negative to make sense of the statement (cf. 16:8).

Such attempts to derive meaning from difficult texts by the insinuation
of negative particles must be placed in the context of the translator's
treatment of negative particles generally. Orlinsky observed that the
translator of Job "on a number of occasions...rendered a Hebrew
word by a Greek word with the opposite meaning, and then added the
negative particle οὐ or μή to neutralize the Greek word."⁴⁷ The Isaiah
translator frequently adopts that maneuver, as for example with ἐὰν δὲ
μὴ θέλητε || ואם תמאנו in 1:20 and οὐ γὰρ ἠθέλησαν τὸν νόμον κυρίου
σαβαωθ || כי מאסו את תורת יהוה צבאות in 5:24. Especially intriguing
is the way he translated the parallel clauses in 5:7:

ויקו למשפט והנה משפח   ἔμεινα τοῦ ποιῆσαι κρίσιν ἐποίησε δὲ ἀνομίαν
לצדקה והנה צעקה   καὶ οὐ δικαιοσύνην ἀλλὰ κραυγήν

Setting aside the question of whether he read ואקו rather than ויקו,
the fact that his reformulation of the second colon accords with our
understanding of the deep structure is less significant than his use of

---

⁴⁴ In the main, 1QIsaᵃ agrees with MT, although the equivalent of MT's אביר ישראל
stands in a lacuna. Moreover, for MT's מצרי it appears to read מצריו and for מאויבי
it reads מאויבו, while a ה has been placed superlinearly between the מ and א. 4QIsaᶠ
is exceptionally fragmentary but offers no evidence of variants from the MT. S and
V follow a *Vorlage* = MT. Despite T's reformulations and expansions, it too seems to
presuppose a *Vorlage* like the MT.
⁴⁵ Compare to this reformulation the way T handles הוי. First, following its rendering
of אביר ישראל (אביר דישראל תקיפא), it inserts an address to Jerusalem (קרתא ירושלם) and
then the LORD issues a warning: אנא עתיד לנחמותה ברם וי לרשיעיא כד אתגלי.
⁴⁶ The translation of a verb with ποιεῖν + noun is a commonplace. Cf. καλὸν
ποιεῖν || היטב in 1:17.
⁴⁷ Harry M. Orlinsky, "Studies in the Septuagint of the Book of Job, Chapter II,"
HUCA 29 (1958) 231.

a construction with a negative as interchangeable with the syntax of
the preceding clauses. This is a signal case of his willingness to use a
negation to convey what he considered the sense of the statement. And
it is, therefore, not surprising to find him injecting a negative in the
next verse (5:8), in a question expecting a negative response:[48]

הוי מגיעי בית בבית	οὐαὶ οἱ συνάπτοντες οἰκίαν πρὸς οἰκίαν
שדה בשדה יקריבו	καὶ ἀγρὸν πρὸς ἀγρὸν ἐγγίζοντες
עד אפס מקום	ἵνα τοῦ πλησίον ἀφέλωνταί τι
והושבתם לבדכם בקרב הארץ	μὴ οἰκήσετε μόνοι ἐπὶ τῆς γῆς

At other times, he inserts a negative based on the general flow of the con-
text, as in 15:7—μὴ καὶ οὕτως μέλλει σωθῆναι || על כן יתרה עשה[49] —
where the negation arises from the idea developed in the preceding
verse:

כי מי נמרים משמות יהיו	τὸ ὕδωρ τῆς Νεμριμ ἔρημον ἔσται
כי יבש חציר	καὶ ὁ χόρτος αὐτῆς ἐκλείψει
דשא ירק לא היה	χόρτος γὰρ χλωρὸς οὐκ ἔσται

Having deduced that the line of thought is about the failure of vegeta-
tion, the translator uses (and negates) one of his favorite terms, σῴζειν
(see below, pp. 123–28), to fill out the sense.

Even more striking is his rendering of ככבוד בני ישראל יהיו with οὐ
γὰρ σὺ βελτίων εἶ τῶν υἱῶν Ισραηλ καὶ τῆς δόξης αὐτῶν in 17:3,[50] a
reformulation that is part of a restructuring of the entire verse.[51]

Sometimes there is a glimmer of a suggestion that the translator
might have derived a negative particle by etymological reasoning, as
in his translation of בלמדי by τοῦ μὴ μαθεῖν in 8:16, where he perhaps
inferred crasis of למד + בל (cf. ἵνα μὴ ἀναστῶσι || בל יקמו in 14:21
and ἵνα μὴ ἴδῃ || ובל יראה in 26:10), as Koenig suggests,[52] although
Ottley's suggestion that the Vorlage read מלמדי is equally viable.[53]

---

[48] Orlinsky noted the same device in Job (ibid., 242).

[49] 1QIsaᵃ = MT. S recognizes יתרה but offers a periphrastic equivalent for עשה: ܐܠ
ܣܒܪ ܗܘܐ ܕܙܥܘܪ ܗܘ ܣܟܗ. V & T also seem to recognize יתרה, but each gropes its
way towards a rendering: V, secundum magnitudinem operis; T, על כן שאר נכסיהו דקנו
יתבזזון.

[50] 1QIsaᵃ reads יהיה for יהיו. S & V reflect Vorlagen = MT. T expands ככבוד into
ויקרהון כיקר; nevertheless, it reflects a Vorlage = MT.

[51] See below, pp. 100–01.

[52] Jean Koenig, L' Herméneutique, 132–33. Of course, it is equally possible to posit
that his Vorlage read בל למד, although I do not think this is likely, as I will argue in
the next paragraph.

[53] Ottley, The Book of Isaiah, 2:150.

Similarly, in 8:14 he might have arrived at his rendering of וְהָיָה לְמִקְדָּשׁ וּלְאֶבֶן נֶגֶף with ἔσται σοι εἰς ἁγίασμα καὶ οὐχ ὡς λίθου προσκόμματι συναντήσεσθε αὐτῷ by reading וּלְאֶבֶן as crasis of אַל + אֶבֶן. In the same vein, Ottley suggested that the translator derived לֹא from the ל of לְכֵן in some passages (e.g., καὶ οὐχ οὕτως || לְכֵן in 10:15 and οὐχ οὕτως || לְכֵן in 16:6).[54]

These explanations may appeal to us because they seem to give an empirical base for these negative particles unsupported by the MT, but the instances cited in the earlier paragraphs suggest that the translator was more willing to supply negatives for the (perceived) sense than this supposes. It is not an issue of the translator consciously *changing* the meaning of the passage, a notion Orlinsky rightly protests.[55] Even if the result is a rendering that we consider invalid, for the translator the insinuation of a negative may simply have been a way of conveying the only permissible meaning in the context. Seen in that light, δύσχρηστος || טוֹב in 3:10 is no more radical than ἐὰν δὲ μὴ θέλητε || וְאִם תְּמָאֵנוּ in 1:20, or οὐ παύσεται γάρ μου ὁ θυμὸς || אִנָּחֵם in 1:24. The salient point is that the insertions of negative particles or prefixes do not constitute a rule or principle, but are ad hoc maneuvers.

Correlatively, Seeligmann noted that sometimes the translator "neglect[s] a negation which does figure in the Hebrew original."[56] 30:19, for instance, is a passage where the translator struggled to wrest meaning from the Hebrew:[57]

כִּי עַם בְּצִיּוֹן יֵשֵׁב	διότι λαὸς ἅγιος ἐν Σιων οἰκήσει
בִּירוּשָׁלַם בָּכוֹ לֹא תִבְכֶּה חָנוֹן	καὶ Ιερουσαλημ κλαυθμῷ ἔκλαυσεν ἐλέησόν με
יָחְנְךָ לְקוֹל זַעֲקֶךָ	ἐλεήσει σε τὴν φωνὴν τῆς κραυγῆς σου

The translator's rendition of v. 18 found in it a promise that the Kyrios would have mercy on Israel and concluded (in accord with the MT) with a blessing: μακάριοι οἱ ἐμμένοντες ἐν αὐτῷ. While the MT of v. 19 continues the address to Jerusalem begun in v. 18, the translator

---

[54] Ibid., 2:161–62.

[55] Harry M. Orlinsky, "Studies in the Septuagint of the Book of Job, Chapter III (Continued)," *HUCA* 32 (1961) 252–53.

[56] Seeligmann, *Septuagint Version*, 57.

[57] 1QIsaᵃ contains a *wāw* prefixed to בירושלם and, more significantly, reads תבכו חנון חנון יחנך יהוה לקול זעקך for the MT's תבכה חנון יחנך לקול זעקך. S parallels 1QIsaᵃ in reading ܘܡܪܚܡܘ and ܢܪܚܡ. V has *populus enim Sion habitabit in Hierusalem* for the MT's כי עם בציון ישב בירושלם, but otherwise agrees with it. T translates a *Vorlage* = the MT.

understands כִּי as introducing two reasons for the promise of divine mercy issued in v. 18. On the one hand, he finds in עַם בְּצִיּוֹן יֵשֵׁב a forecast of a *holy* people dwelling in Zion—it is their presence that will spur divine mercy—and on the other, he understands בָּכוֹ לֹא תִבְכֶּה to refer to Jerusalem's *past*, tearful petitions. In order to achieve this construal, he inferred that the עַם were "holy" and (in effect) he suppressed לֹא.[58]

Even more striking is how he massages meaning from 7:15–16a:[59]

חֶמְאָה וּדְבַשׁ יֹאכֵל	[15]βούτυρον καὶ μέλι φάγεται
לְדַעְתּוֹ מָאוֹס בָּרָע	πρὶν ἢ γνῶναι αὐτὸν ἢ προελέσθαι πονηρὰ
וּבָחוֹר בַּטּוֹב	ἐκλέξεται τὸ ἀγαθόν
כִּי בְּטֶרֶם יֵדַע הַנַּעַר	[16]διότι πρὶν ἢ γνῶναι τὸ παιδίον ἀγαθὸν ἢ κακὸν
מָאֹס בָּרָע וּבָחֹר בַּטּוֹב	ἀπειθεῖ πονηρίᾳ τοῦ ἐκλέξασθαι τὸ ἀγαθόν

7:15 sharpens the concept of "knowing good or evil" over against the MT by insinuating a human predilection for evil. Whereas v. 16 speaks simply of knowing ἀγαθὸν ἢ κακόν, v. 15 specifies alternative types of engagement: γνῶναι ἢ προελέσθαι πονηρά, 'to know *or* prefer evil(s)'.[60] The juxtaposition of "preferring" and "knowing" suggests that a preference for πονηρά is a common corollary to "knowing." That correlation seems implicit also in the translation of לְדַעְתּוֹ with πρὶν ἢ γνῶναι αὐτὸν in v. 15,[61] parallel to πρὶν ἢ γνῶναι for יֵדַע בְּטֶרֶם in v. 16, thereby equating the period before the child 'knows or prefers evil' with the time before the child "knows good or evil."[62] The question this

---

[58] While he may have rendered the *bêt* of בִּירוּשָׁלַם as a conjunction, it is also possible that his *Vorlage* simply read וִירוּשָׁלַם (cf. the + *wāw* in 1QIsaᵃ & S, noted above).

[59] For the evidence for this passage in the DSS and the other versions, see above, n. 5.

[60] Although the particle ἢ might be understood as interrogative ("before he knows *whether* to prefer evil[s]"), ἢ interrogative is found nowhere else in LXX-Isaiah, so that ἢ more likely marks an alternative. While v. 16 speaks of knowing κακόν and rejecting πονηρία, v. 15 speaks of πονηρά, which are evidently individual instances of πονηρία. The translator's choice of the plural πονηρά to represent רָע here, but πονηρίᾳ in v. 16 attests a nuanced interpretation.

[61] Although it is possible that the LXX's *Vorlage* contained יֵדַע בְּטֶרֶם due to a deliberate or incidental harmonization with v. 16, two observations favor tracing πρὶν ἢ back to לְדַעְתּוֹ in the *Vorlage*. First, the pronoun αὐτόν can be readily aligned with the pronominal suffix of לְדַעְתּוֹ. Second, the translator's interpolation of ἀγαθὸν ἢ κακόν, based on the opposition between 'good and evil' in v. 15, favors understanding πρὶν ἢ as his interpretation of לְ(דַעְתּוֹ). S, T, and V also struggle with לְדַעְתּוֹ. S and V both render it as a purpose clause (ܢܕܥ; *ut sciat*), yielding the curious notion of the child gaining a superior moral bearing from the food. T, like the LXX, interprets לְדַעְתּוֹ in the light of יֵדַע בְּטֶרֶם in v. 16: יֵדַע לֹא עַד.

[62] One consequence is a striking difference in phrasing, compared to MT. Construing

raises, however, is how the translator arrived at this distinction, since προελέσθαι πονηρά and ἀπειθεῖ πονηρίᾳ both correspond to the phrase ברע מאס.[63] Did the translator's *Vorlage* contain a variant?

Προαιρεῖν does not appear again in LXX-Isaiah, but in Prov 21:25 it joins a negative as an equivalent to מאן: οὐ γὰρ προαιροῦνται αἱ χεῖρες αὐτοῦ ποιεῖν τι (|| כי מאנו ידיו לעשות).[64] LXX-Isaiah follows a similar tack on occasion, such as in its translation of כי מאסו with οὐ γὰρ ἠθέλησαν in 5:24 and its rendering of יען כי מאס with διὰ τὸ μὴ βούλεσθαι in 8:6.[65] The obvious difference between these instances and 7:15, however, is the use of a negative adverb.

However, given the translator's willingness to suppress a negative for the sake of the sense, and given that elsewhere he translates מאס by negating a Greek antonym,[66] it would have been but a short step for him to omit the negative with προελέσθαι in 7:15 to gain a sensible meaning. Indeed, his resort to this strategy is determined by the plus, ἀγαθὸν ἢ κακόν, which I will argue (in chapter five) was the translator's own insertion. In any case, it seems that the translator rendered this passage under a conception of this child as eluding even the allure of evil.[67]

Such additions and suppressions of negative particles involve a small number of cases, but effect a profound transformation of meaning, from our point of view. Still more extreme—again, by our metrics—are reformulations of clauses, as in 10:8:[68]

ובחור בטוב as the main clause (headed by *wāw* apodosis), the LXX understands the preceding לדעתו as designating when the action occurred. As a result, it takes המאה ודבש יאכל as an assertion about the child's diet, independent from the time-frame for his choice of τὸ ἀγαθόν.

[63] In 1QIsaᵃ ב of MT's בטרם is inserted supralinearly *secunda manu* (so also ו *mater* above both ובחר and תעזב). S, V, and T reflect a *Vorlage* = MT, although T renders the verbs of מאס ברע ובחור בטוב metaphorically (לדחקא בישא ולקרבא טבא) both times.

[64] Elsewhere it translates חשק (Gen 34.8; Deut 7.7; 10.15) and בחר (Deut 7.6; Prov 1.29).

[65] Cf. ἐὰν δὲ μὴ θέλητε || ואם תמאנו in 1:20, and notice the immediately following μηδὲ εἰσακούσητέ´ μου || ומריתם.

[66] Cf. his reformulation of a negated verb with a simple assertion in 3:9: ἀνήγγειλαν καὶ ἐνεφάνισαν || הנידו לא כחדו.

[67] See Ronald Troxel, "Isaiah 7,14–16 through the Eyes of the Septuagint," *ETL* 79 (2003) 1–22.

[68] 1QIsaᵃ = MT, while 4QIsaᵉ preserves only הלוא אמר[יא]. S provides a paraphrase that appears to presuppose a *Vorlage* = MT: ܗܠܐ ܐܝܟ ܡܠܟܐ ܐܝܟܢܐ ܐܬܝܒ ܕܪܝܐ ܐܟܚܕܐ ܓܠܝ. V accords with MT. Given T's typical translation characteristics, its simile, כמלכין, for MT's מלכים, was likely created by the translator in order to remove the tautology, although one cannot rule out a *Vorlage* that read כמלכים.

כי יאמר הלא שרי יחדו מלכים   καὶ ἐὰν εἴπωσιν αὐτῷ σὺ μόνος εἶ
ἄρχων

At best, this is a paraphrase. Ottley suggests that αὐτῷ arose from the translator reading לא as לו,[69] to which he compares the לא/לו Kethib/Qere in 9:2, 49:5, and 63:9.[70] Here, however, the MT reads not simply לא but הלא, which the translator typically handles by using οὐ/οὐκ/οὐχ in a question, as he does in v. 9, where he omits the subsequent instances of אם לא.[71] On other occasions, he simply omits הלא, as he does in (e.g.) 45:21, τότε ἀνηγγέλη ὑμῖν ἐγὼ ὁ θεός | | הלוא אני יהוה מאז הגידה.[72] Given the other obvious adjustments the translator made in 10:8, the lack of an equivalent for הלא and his supply of αὐτῷ as indirect object are hardly surprising.[73]

An even more thoroughgoing reformulation appears in 17:3:[74]

ונשבת מבצר מאפרים   καὶ οὐκέτι ἔσται ὀχυρὰ τοῦ καταφυγεῖν Εφραιμ
וממלכה מדמשק   καὶ οὐκέτι ἔσται βασιλεία ἐν Δαμασκῷ
ושאר ארם   καὶ τὸ λοιπὸν τῶν Σύρων ἀπολεῖται
כבוד בני ישראל יהיו   οὐ γὰρ σὺ βελτίων εἶ τῶν υἱῶν Ισραηλ καὶ τῆς δόξης αὐτῶν

Ironically, ἀπολεῖται, which lacks an equivalent in the MT, seems a more direct rendering of נשבת(ו) than the circumlocution καὶ οὐκέτι ἔσται used in the first two clauses,[75] even if there is little doubt that καὶ οὐκέτι ἔσται is meant to stress the failure of Damascus (against whom vv. 1–3 are directed) as an aid to Ephraim. The translator specifies the sort of aid Damascus has rendered by modifying ὀχυρά with the explicative infinitive phrase τοῦ καταφυγεῖν. More striking is the reformulation in the final clause, which is transformed into a direct

---

[69] Ottley, *The Book of Isaiah*, 2:160.

[70] Ibid., 2:154.

[71] On his translation of v. 9, see below, pp. 145–47.

[72] 1QIsaᵃ = MT; 45:21 stands in a lacuna in 4QIsaᵇ. V and T accord with MT. S attests a rather different *Vorlage* for this phrase: ܡܢ ܙܒܢܐ ܐܝܟ ܐܝܟ ܐܫܡܥܬ, suggesting that its *Vorlage* read (אני יהוה) מראש in place of MT's (אני יהוה) מאז הגידה הלוא (cf. 41:4, where S translates מראש אני יהוה with ܡܢ ܪܝܫܐ ܐܝܟ ܐܝܟ ܐܫܡܥܬ).

[73] Cf. his supply of καὶ ἐρεῖ, ἔλαβον, and καὶ ἔλαβον in v. 9 to fill out his understanding of its role in the passage.

[74] 1QIsaᵃ reads יהיה for יהיו. S reads ܚܝܠܐ for מבצר, but this is likely a contextual choice (cf. its varied translations in 25:12 & 34:13); *Vorlage* = MT. V reads *adiutorium* for מבצר (cf. S); its *Vorlage* = MT. T reads שלטן for מבצר (cf. S & V), while it expands ושאר ארם into ושאר יחידאין מארם and כבוד into ויקרהון יקר; nevertheless, it reflects a *Vorlage* = MT.

[75] In fact, the translator rendered והשבתי by καὶ ἀπολῶ in 13:11.

address to Damascus and includes a double rendering of כבוד.[76] Even the (somewhat) more literal representation of כ(כבוד בני ישראל) by τῆς δόξης αὐτῶν is integrated into this reformulation. The translator's reformulation of the syntax also required him to insinuate a negative (οὐ), as well as provide γάρ so as to make this clause into an *a fortiori* argument for why Damascus should anticipate such a fate.

As Barr observes such rewriting often "produce[s] a sentiment which is really the translator's idea, connected here and there with the words of the original."[77] Other reformulations in LXX-Isaiah wander farther a field than these examples, but such cases amount to *non*-translations. (I will explore examples of non-translations in the next chapter.)

This survey of the translator's handling of grammar—both the grammar of his *Vorlage* and that of his target language—leads not only to the classification of his *Übersetzungsweise* among the freer translation units of the LXX, but also to the conclusion that he was (to use Brock's phraseology) more interested in bringing the book of Isaiah to his readers than in bringing his readers to the text. For this reason, I find myself at odds with Hanhart's assertion that "as a matter of first principle the Greek translation must be considered as a faithful rendering of the original as far as content and form is concerned, a rendering exact even in grammatical and syntactical details."[78] Even though Hanhart qualifies this statement by allowing the possibility of "freedom as far as formal possibilities are concerned," he sees this merely as a vehicle by which "the essence of the original is rendered more adequately by a formulation that deviates from the formal rules of the original language."[79] This begs the question of what constitutes "the essence of the original," since once a text is abstracted from its particulars, its "essence" is the meaning perceived by the translator. And in cases where the translator was perplexed by his *Vorlage* or rendered it in light of the themes he considered leitmotifs in the book, "the essence of the original" becomes indistinguishable from "the essence of his *interpretation* of the original."

---

[76] On "double renderings," see below, pp. 120–21.

[77] Barr, *Comparative Philology*, 255–56.

[78] Robert Hanhart, "The Translation of the Septuagint in Light of Earlier Tradition and Subsequent Influences," in *Septuagint, Scrolls and Cognate Writings*, ed. George J. Brooke and Barnabas Lindars (Society of Biblical Literature Septuagint and Cognate Studies 33; Atlanta: Scholars Press, 1992) 341.

[79] Ibid.

Thus far, it is clear that the Isaiah translator was concerned to convey the meaning he perceived in the text. The degree to which this entailed further divergences from his *Vorlage* can be measured by studying the semantic equivalences of his translation.

Semantic interpretation

Given that deviations from the syntax of the target language are tolerable in translations, semantics becomes a central issue in the character of a translation. The question is not simply how skillful the translator was at finding suitable Greek equivalents, but also how well he understood the lexemes of his *Vorlage*.

An important question is to what degree this translator was dependent on a tradition of reading Isaiah. As Seeligmann has shown, the Isaiah translator was familiar with the Torah, as indicated by his reuse of locutions from the LXX-Pentateuch, and seems to have been influenced by "traditional homiletics and traditional practice."[80] These factors, however, are different from familiarity with a tradition of reading the Hebrew.

Relevant here is the question of to what degree translators "vocalized" the Hebrew of their *Vorlage*. Barr first raised this question by pointing to examples of translations unlikely to be part of traditional readings, such as the curious ῥάβδος for מטה (MT מִטָּה) in Gen 47:31.[81] He did not deny that the translators vocalized specific words, but argued that their vocalization was not entirely dependent on a *tradition* of vocalization.[82] In reading unpointed text, it is not vocalization that leads to the perception of meaning, but "the perception of meaning that permits and facilitates the choice of vocalization."[83]

Tov raised two salient objections to Barr's hypothesis: 1) the similar transliterations of personal names in the LXX suggest a tradition of vocalization; 2) the "considerable agreement between the LXX and MT in the understanding of consonants...amounts to agreement in

---

[80] Seeligmann, *Septuagint Version*, 45–46, quotation from p. 45.

[81] James Barr, "Vocalization and the Analysis of Hebrew among the Ancient Translators," in *Hebräische Wortforschung*, ed. James Barr (VTSup 16; Leiden: Brill, 1967) 3.

[82] Ibid., 2–3.

[83] Ibid., 4.

vocalization."[84] As for Tov's first objection, Barr responded that the common recognition of vocalization for "the more important persons and places" (e.g., Αβρααμ, Ιερουσαλημ) does not negate the fact that the rendering of place names "is notoriously wild and inaccurate."[85] In the case of LXX-Isaiah, it is striking to find several cases in which a proper noun is translated rather than transliterated, even when the translation makes little sense. For example, in 16:11 the LXX reads καὶ τὰ ἐντός μου ὡσεὶ τεῖχος ὃ ἐνεκαίνισας (|| וקרבי לקיר חרש), even though it rendered the preceding parallel clause sensibly: διὰ τοῦτο ἡ κοιλία μου ἐπὶ Μωαβ ὡς κιθάρα ἠχήσει || על כן מעי למואב כמואב ככנור יהמו.[86] Even more strange is 15:5:

לבי מואב	ἡ καρδία τῆς Μωαβίτιδος
יזעק בריחה עד צער	βοᾷ ἐν ἑαυτῇ ἕως Σηγωρ
ענלת שלשיה	δάμαλις γάρ ἐστι τριετής
כי מעלה הלוחית	ἐπὶ δὲ τῆς ἀναβάσεως τῆς Λουιθ
בבכי יעלה בו	πρὸς σὲ κλαίοντες ἀναβήσονται
בו כי דרך חורנים	τῇ ὁδῷ Αρωνιιμ
זעקת שבר יעערו	βοᾷ σύντριμμα καὶ σεισμός

The translator knows the common מואב and צער, recognizes לוחית as a place name (Jer 31[48]:5 gives Αλαωθ, parallel to the MT's הלחות), as he also does חורנים (Ωρωναιμ in Jer 31[48]:3, 5, and 34, its only other occurrences in the Bible).[87] However, most peculiar is his rendering of ענלת שלשיה with δάμαλις γάρ ἐστι τριετής, despite the awkwardness of the statement in its context and despite the fact that Jer 31[48]:34 transliterates the same phrase as Αγλαθ-σαλισια.

In sum, the equivalent given for קיר in 16:11 and that for ענלת שלשיה in 15:5 undermine the assumption that the Isaiah translator worked from a tradition of vocalizing the Hebrew text.

As for the importance Tov attaches to the widespread agreement between the LXX and the MT, Barr argues that this simply sharpens the question of how to explain "places where deep and flagrant breaches of this agreement take place."[88] The theory that a translator's rendering was based on a tradition of vocalization would require "the possession

---

[84] Tov, *Text-Critical Use*, 108–09.

[85] Barr, "'Guessing' in the Septuagint," 31.

[86] Apparently reading קיר as a noun prompted the translator to read the *rêš* of חרש as a *dālet* (see below on *rêš*/*dālet* confusion among translators).

[87] ἐν ἑαυτῇ || בריחה likely arises from reading the form as בריחה.

[88] Barr, "'Guessing' in the Septuagint," 24, italics his.

in memory...of the phonic text of ...the book being translated, *at every point*," since the issue is not the forms that could be recognized readily enough, "but the unpredictabilities," such as מִטָּה in Gen 47:31.[89] Barr does not deny either that a tradition of reading existed or that the translator "vocalized" words to some extent; at dispute is how complete was his knowledge of a reading tradition.

In fact, Tov's own recognition that translators did not always understand their *Vorlage*, and so resorted to various ways of sidestepping a form or offering conjectural readings, contradicts the supposition of familiarity with a full tradition of vocalization. For example, Tov cites the variation in the way the Isaiah translator renders nearly identical verses in 18:2, 7, including the following examples: ממשך || μετέωρον (v. 2), || τεθλιμμένου (v. 7); ומורט || καὶ ξένον (v. 2), || καὶ τετιλμένου (v. 7); נורא || καὶ χαλεπόν (v. 2), || μεγάλου (v. 7); מן הוא || τίς αὐτοῦ (v. 2), || ἀπὸ τοῦ νῦν (v. 7).[90] Tov's judgment that these are "different attempts of solving lexical problems"[91] undercuts the assumption that the translator followed a tradition of reading.[92] Thus, as Barr concludes, "even if a translator took a reading tradition into account, at all sorts of points he could and did still conclude to the meaning from the consonantal text."[93]

Moreover, even if a choice between rendering מלכו as ἐβασιλεύοντο or as ὁ βασιλεὺς αὐτοῦ implies vocalization as מָלְכוּ or מַלְכּוֹ, this process presupposes neither a tradition of vocalization nor a concrete act of vocalization, as Tov himself acknowledges.[94] Accordingly, while the translator likely had some degree of familiarity with his source text from its use in his religious community and found guidance from "regular" forms and the context, much depended on his construal of the consonants.

Another resource at the translator's disposal would have been prior translations of "biblical" books, chief among them the LXX-Pentateuch.

---

[89] Ibid., 23–24.

[90] For the complete alignment and comparison, see Tov, "Did the Septuagint Translators," 60.

[91] Ibid.

[92] Equally problematic for this theory is Tov's salient observation that the translators sometimes sought to wring sense out of a text in the wake of their misinterpretation of a word or phrase earlier in the verse. He calls such attempts to "rescue" a verse "legitimate maneuverings within the framework of the translator's knowledge" (*Text-Critical Use*, 169).

[93] Barr, "'Guessing' in the Septuagint," 28.

[94] Tov, *Text-Critical Use*, 108.

As Tov notes, translators generally looked to LXX-Pentateuch as a model not only for how to execute a translation,[95] but also for guides to apt lexical equivalents.[96] And yet, although both Seeligmann and Ziegler affirm Thackeray's perception that the translator of Isaiah utilized precedents in the LXX-Pentateuch,[97] Ziegler justifiably tempers his agreement by noting that

> der Js-Übers. an manchen Stellen, wo bereits deutlich im hebr. Text eine Beziehung zum Pent gegeben ist und ganz dieselben Ausdrücke verwendet werden, völlig eigene Wege geht und eine andere Wiedergabe wählt.[98]

A prime example is the translator's rendering of the phrase אֲרֻבּוֹת מִמָּרוֹם ('the lattice windows from above') in 24:18 with θυρίδες ἐκ τοῦ οὐρανοῦ ('windows out of heaven'), in spite of the fact that it is translated "an allen übrigen Stellen mit καταράκται ['waterfalls'] τοῦ οὐρ., vgl. Gn 7,11; 8,2; 4 Rg 7,2.19; Mal 3,10."[99] However, to characterize this as the translator *choosing* to disregard the precedent established by the LXX-Pentateuch would be false. More likely, as Aejmelaeus observes, in such cases "the translator was guided by his intuitive understanding of the requirements of context rather than any word-list he might have had."[100] While the translator was familiar with precedents established by prior translations, he was hardly bound to them if another rendering seemed contextually more apt.

Nevertheless, we should not be surprised to find the Isaiah translator using stock equivalents in the manner of more "literal" translators. Thus, in 5:25 he renders וַיִּרְגְּזוּ הֶהָרִים with καὶ παρωξύνθη τὰ ὄρη (cf. οὖτος ὁ ἄνθρωπος ὁ παροξύνων τὴν γῆν || הֲזֶה הָאִישׁ מַרְגִּיז הָאָרֶץ in 14:16),[101] even though he renders עַל כֵּן שָׁמַיִם אַרְגִּיז by the (slightly) more idiomatic ὁ γὰρ οὐρανὸς θυμωθήσεται in 13:13 and even more sensibly renders

---

[95] Emanuel Tov, "The Impact of the LXX Translation of the Pentateuch on the Translation of the Other Books," in *Mélanges Dominique Barthélemy: Études bibliques offertes à l'occasion de son 60e anniversaire*, ed. Pierre Casetti, Othmar Keel, and Adrian Schenker (Orbis Biblicus et Orientalis 38; Göttingen: Vandenhoeck & Ruprecht, 1981) 578.

[96] Ibid., 587. As Tov observes, "bestimmt standen alle Übersetzer, die die Bücher nach dem Pentateuch übertrugen, in irgendeiner Weise unter dem Einfluss der Pentateuchübersetzung" (Emanuel Tov, "Die Septuaginta in ihrem theologischen und traditionsgeschichtlichen Verhältnis zur hebräischen Bibel," in *Mitte der Schrift? Ein jüdisch-christliches Gespräch*, ed. Martin Klopfenstein, et al. [Bern: Peter Lang, 1987] 240).

[97] H. St. John Thackeray, "The Translators of the Prophetical Book," *JTS* 4 (1903) 583–84, cited by Seeligmann, *Septuagint Version*, 45, and Ziegler, *Untersuchungen*, 103.

[98] Ziegler, *Untersuchungen*, 103.

[99] Ibid.

[100] Aejmelaeus, "Translation Technique," 26.

[101] Seeligmann, *Septuagint Version*, 49.

מפניך נוים ידנזו by ἀπὸ προσώπου σου ἔθνη ταραχθήσονται in 64:2(1).
While 5:25 and 14:16 suggest "a more or less mechanical replacement
of רנ"ז by παροχύνειν, or its synonyms,"[102] his more characteristically
"free" lexical choices make this less likely evidence of a literalistic habit
than of indifference to the effects of his choices in this passage.[103] As
Aejmelaeus states, "the degree of intentionality varies from detail to
detail in a translator's work."[104]

Additionally, the fact that the translator uses a particular lexical
equivalent regularly may be less a mark of his "literalistic" tendency
than an indication that "a particular word was the really natural one
in their language and could be used repeatedly without strain."[105] Stock
equivalents like διδόναι | | נתן and ψυχή | | נפש occur as frequently in
LXX-Isaiah as they do in the Torah. As Seeligmann summarizes,

> certain Greek words had become, in the translator's idiom, fixed versions,
> standard translations in fact, of certain Hebrew ones, which caused them
> to be inserted immediately [when] the translator came across the word in
> question in the Hebrew original, without any notice being taken either of
> the context in which it occurred, or of current Greek idiom.[106]

This is not a matter of method or even deliberation, but is translation
in default mode.[107]

The translator's deviations from equivalences established by the
LXX-Pentateuch is not surprising since, as we have seen, his tendency
towards "free" translation means that, when intent on conveying his
sense of a text, he used available precedents according to his predilections. Indeed, as Ziegler remarks,

> der Js-Übers. nicht ängstlich darauf bedacht ist, seine Vorlage genau,
> Wort für Wort wiederzugeben," but he even shows a willingness to omit
> "schwere, seltene Wörter...wenn dadurch der Sinn des Satzes nicht

---

[102] Ibid.

[103] Tov states his agreement with Seeligmann "dass die Übersetzer der Implikationen
ihrer Wortwahl oft nicht bewusst waren" ("Die Septuaginta," 248). Cf. Aejmelaeus's
comment that "when proceeding by set equivalences, the translator did not consider the
suitability of the equivalent for each individual case" ("Translation Technique," 28).

[104] Aejmelaeus, "Translation Technique," 28.

[105] Barr, *The Typology of Literalism*, 32.

[106] Seeligmann, *Septuagint Version*, 48–49.

[107] Aejmelaeus appropriately adopts Barr's phraseology about the translators' "habit
and the quest of an easy technique rather than...[a] literalist policy" (Barr, *The Typology
of Literalism*, 26, cited in Aejmelaeus, "Translation Technique," 26).

gestört wird, oder auch einen Satz anders einzuteilen und zuasammen-
zuziehen, wenn er nicht mit seiner Vorlage auskommt.[108]

Although this sweeping statement takes us beyond the question of
how he handled lexemes, its (accurate) characterization sheds light on
how he could give mechanical equivalents like καὶ παρωξύνθη τὰ ὄρη
|| וירגזו ההרים in 5:25, could fall back on slot words like ἁλίσκεσθαι,
παραδιδόναι, and ἡττᾶσθαι when bemused by his *Vorlage*, but could also
provide a novel equivalent for a phrase like θυρίδες ἐκ τοῦ οὐρανοῦ
|| ארבות ממרום in 24:18.[109]

As the last instance demonstrates, it would be wrong to characterize
this translator as ham-fisted, for he shows sophistication in translating some lexemes. Thus, for example, in the short span of 3:4–12
he translates four words containing the consonants עלל with four
different Greek words, each of which is chosen to suit its context and
reflects lexical reasoning: καὶ ἐμπαῖκται for ותעלולים in v. 4;[110] μετὰ
ἀνομίας for ומעלליהם in v. 8;[111] τῶν ἔργων for מעלליהם in v. 10;[112] and
καλαμῶνται for מעולל in v. 12.[113] Obviously he had sufficient familiarity
with the semantics possible for עלל to take advantage of what amount
to homonyms.[114]

Consistent with this, we also find him employing etymological exegesis, based on his understanding of Hebrew morphology.[115] Especially
common throughout the LXX are renderings based on an isolation of

---

[108] Ziegler, *Untersuchungen*, 7.

[109] Many of these are cases in which the translator made "a guess when confronted
with a difficult Hebrew word, and based his guess on his—often erroneous—conception
of the context" (Seeligmann, *Septuagint Version*, 54).

[110] Cf. κἀγὼ ἐκλέξομαι τὰ ἐμπαίγματα αὐτῶν || גם אני אבחר בתעלליהם in 66:4
and note ἐμπέπαιχα || התעללתי in Exod 10:2, as well as ἐμπέπαιχάς || התעללת in
Num 22:29.

[111] As Seeligmann suggests, this is likely based on מעל, as in 1 Chr 9:1; 10:13
(*Septuagint Version*, 54).

[112] This equivalence is attested in Ps 76(77):12 and 77(78):7. Seeligmann judges that
sections of Psalms were likely known to the translator and influenced his vocabulary
(ibid., 71–72).

[113] Cf. οὕτως καλαμήσονται αὐτούς for כעוללת in 24:13.

[114] I am using "homonym" in a generic sense that encompasses "homophones,"
"homographs," and "homonymy," as discussed by Jan de Waard, "'Homophony' in
the Septuagint," *Bib* 62 (1981) 551.

[115] Tov, *Text-Critical Use*, 172.

"core consonants,"[116] especially in "forms belonging to the patterns ל״ה, ל״א, ע/י, ע״ע, ע״ע, א פ״נ, פ״א."[117]

Although one could understand how a translator, facing the consonants ישב, might render this cluster somewhat randomly, using κάθησθαι/οἰκεῖν (ישׁב), ἀποστρέφειν (שׁוב), or πνεῖν (נשׁב), congruence between the LXX's translation and MT's pointing is the norm.[118] The question of whether a reading tradition helped guide the translator is moot,[119] as we have seen, and more important is the role that context plays, particularly since verbs like שׁוב and ישׁב typically appear in distinct semantic environments.[120] At times, however, the context is not as helpful, such as in Isa 7:19, where the translator renders ובאו ונחו כלם with καὶ ἐλεύσονται πάντες καὶ ἀναπαύσονται, deriving (ו)נחו as from נוח rather than נחה. While there the translator had to make a choice with few data, the case is different with his rendering of כי אצק מים על צמא ונזלים על יבשה by ὅτι ἐγὼ δώσω ὕδωρ ἐν δίψει τοῖς πορευομένοις ἐν ἀνύδρῳ in 44:3,[121] where ונזלים is construed as from אזל, evidently in light of the theme of wandering in the wilderness.[122]

---

[116] As Barr observes, consonant sequences "do not make clear which consonants are 'root consonants' and which are not" (Barr, *Comparative Philology* 197). See further below, pp. 111–12.

[117] Tov, *Text-Critical Use*, 174. However, such confusion was probably not quite as widespread as is often assumed. For example, there is little reason to deny that συναγάγετε γενήματα ἐνιαυτὸν ἐπ᾽ ἐνιαυτόν || שׁנה על שׁנה ספו in 29:1 (1QIsaᵃ סַפֵּי; S & V = MT) actually reflects אספו in the *Vorlage*, since his translation would seem to suffer nothing from using προστιθέναι. (T's משׁרין כנישׁת cannot be adduced in support of this, since it seems to easily interchange יסף and אסף, as it does again [with virtually the same formulation] in 15:9: נוספות || משׁרייין כנישׁת.)

[118] Barr points out that the LXX's καὶ συνεκάθισεν αὐτοῖς in Gen 15:11 indicates that the translator construed אתם וישׁב as וַיֵּשֶׁב אתָם (ישׁב√), rather than MT's וַיַּשֵּׁב אתָם (נשׁב√) (Barr, "Vocalization," 3). This is quite understandable, especially since this is the only occurrence of נשׁב in the MT's Torah. ישׁב רוחו in Ps 147:7 (147:18) is translated with πνεύσει τὸ πνεῦμα αὐτοῦ, although this might be a contextually chosen equivalent, especially since the only other occurrence of נשׁב (Isa 40:7) is part of a lengthy minus in the LXX.

[119] See above, pp. 102–04.

[120] E.g., note how the translator distinguishes between two identical verbs in Gen 22:19: ἀπεστράφη δὲ (וישׁב) Αβρααμ πρὸς τοὺς παῖδας αὐτοῦ καὶ ἀναστάντες ἐπορεύθησαν ἅμα ἐπὶ τὸ φρέαρ τοῦ ὅρκου καὶ κατῴκησεν (וישׁב) Αβρααμ ἐπὶ τῷ φρέατι τοῦ ὅρκου. Despite the identical forms, the context determines which verb is appropriate. For semantic clarity within a given context, see David Weissert, "Alexandrinian Analogical Word-Analysis and Septuagint Translation Techniques," *Textus* 8 (1973) 34.

[121] 1QIsaᵃ (ונזלים) = MT (in lacuna in 4QIsaᶜ). S, V, T reflect a *Vorlage* = MT.

[122] So Ziegler, *Untersuchungen*, 126. The translator may have been as unfamiliar with נזל, as the translators of the Torah seem to have been (Exod 15:8; Num 24:7; Deut

The translator's rendering of 29:1 likely exhibits similar reasoning:[123]

| הוי אריאל אריאל קרית חנה דוד | οὐαὶ πόλις Αριηλ ἣν Δαυιδ ἐπολέμησεν |
| ספו שנה על שנה | συναγάγετε γενήματα ἐνιαυτὸν ἐπ’ ἐνιαυτόν |

It is easy enough to recognize a reformulation in the first clause, with the translator preserving only one instance of אריאל and transferring his equivalent of קרית before Αριηλ for the sake of the target language.[124] His insertion of the relative pronoun (ἣν) for his target language is paralleled in S, V, and T, while his translation of חנה by ἐπολέμησεν already discloses his interpretation of this passage as a matter of an assault on the city.

Ottley concludes that the translator, having misconstrued ספו as from אסף, "lost [his] direct connection with 'year to year,' and supplied γενήματα."[125] However, even if we posit that the translator's *Vorlage* actually read אספו (on which see below), it is not clear why he could not have rendered the phrase with something like συναγάγετε ἐνιαυτὸν ἐπ’ ἐνιαυτόν, which would amount to the same thing as προστίθετε ἐνιαυτὸν ἐπ’ ἐνιαυτόν. Therefore, γενήματα was triggered by something other than συναγάγετε.

γενήματα renders two words in its four other appearances in LXX-Isaiah: פרי in 3:10, 32:12, and 65:21; and תבואת in 30:23. While γενήματα here could reflect a corrupt dittography of ספו as פרי, the graphic confusion that would produce this cannot be explained via typical scribal errors. Despite this, the equivalent quantity of consonants favors this corruption as the source of γενήματα. (Stranger cases than this survive in the textual witnesses of the Hebrew Bible.)

32:2). Cf. his translation of הויל למו by ἐξάξει αὐτοῖς in 48:21. His translation of ושחקים יזלו צדק by καὶ αἱ νεφέλαι ῥανάτωσαν δικαιοσύνην in 45:8 is hardly evidence to the contrary, since ῥανάτωσαν would be an apt contextual rendering under the assumption that the verb was אזל.

[123] 1QIsa^a reads ספי for ספו, but otherwise = MT, and 1QIsa^b shows no differences from MT. While 4QIsa^k is very fragmentary, it does preserve [דו]ד ספי שנ[ה], although it is difficult to distinguish whether *yôd* or *wāw* is proper reading of the letter following ספ. V accords with the MT, while T is so expansionistic and periphrastic as to render little help (e.g., מדבחא || אריאל is metonymic for Jerusalem). Thus, even though it reads כנישת for MT's ספו, this may also be exegetical.

[124] Cf. his repositioning of הוי in 1:24: οὐαὶ οἱ ἰσχύοντες Ισραηλ || אביר ישראל הוי.

[125] Ottley, *The Book of Isaiah*, 2:246.

This may, in fact, help explain the translator's συναγάγετε ||
סּפוּ. While the textual critic's reflexes immediately urge positing that
the translator's *Vorlage* read אספּוּ (given the semantic match between
συνάγειν and אסף), if the *Vorlage* read סּפוּ פרי, that might have prompted
reading סּפוּ as an apocopated form of אספּוּ. Of course, it would be
equally reasonable to conclude that a scribe had made that leap before
the translator, writing אספּוּ. This would be a natural surmise, if it were
not for 15:9, where the translator uses a similar equivalence:

כי מי דימון מלאו דם	τὸ δὲ ὕδωρ τὸ Ρεμμων πλησθήσεται
	αἵματος
כי אשית על דימון	ἐπάξω γὰρ ἐπὶ Ρεμμων Ἄραβας
נוספות לפליטת מואב אריה	καὶ ἀρῶ τὸ σπέρμα Μωαβ καὶ Αριηλ

We will look at this verse more carefully in chapter five. For the moment
what is of interest is καὶ ἀρῶ τὸ σπέρμα Μωαβ as the formal equivalent of נוספות לפליטת מואב. The translator appears to have arrived at
ἀρῶ by construing נוספות as from אסף, for which αἴρειν serves as the
equivalent in 10:14 (bis); 16:4, 10; and 57:1 (bis). In the light of the
translator's assumption about the apocopation of אזל, demonstrated
above, it is likely that in both 15:9 and 29:1 the translator detected
אסף within what we recognize as פ"י forms.[126]

Such tacks have antecedents in the use of paronomasia within the
Bible,[127] particularly in etymological explanations of names, such as the
derivation of Eve's name from חיה in Gen 3:20: ויקרא האדם שם אשתו
חוה כי הוא היתה אם כל חי; or the explanation of Noah's name offered
by Lamech: ויקרא את שמו נח לאמר זה ינחמנו (Gen 5:29).[128] Still more
relevant is the twofold etymology implied for the name יוסף in Gen
30:23–24, based on two roots containing ס/ף: אסף אלהים את חרפתי
(v. 23) and יסף יהוה לי בן אחר (v. 24).[129] Given these precedents, it

---

[126] While it would be reasonable to posit that one of these forms had suffered the
insertion of א, it is highly unlikely that it occurred in *both* verses.

[127] Paronomasia also stands behind Amos's vision of קיץ, which is said to signify an
imminent קץ for Israel (Amos 8:2), while the interpretation of Jeremiah's vision of a
שקד is: שֹׁקֵד אני על דברי לעשׂתו (Jer 1:12).

[128] Barr, *Comparative Philology*, 47.

[129] As noted by van der Kooij, *Die alten Textzeugen*, 69. While the first of these is not
specifically marked as an explanation of יוסף, a similar double etymology is found in
the story of Esau, with one specifically marked the other not. Esau's identity as the
patriarch of Edom is explicitly explained in Gen 25:30 as due to his request to eat
(על כן קרא שמו אדום) מן האדם האדם הזה. However, another explanation of this name
is presupposed in the earlier story of his parents naming him: ויצא הראשׁון אדמוני כלו
כאדרת שׂער ויקראו שמו עשׂו (25:25). The unused element, אדמוני, has no function in the
story and likely was an alternative ground for the identification of Esau as Edom.

would be pedantic to assume that all renderings based on associations of Hebrew words with common consonants in LXX-Isaiah derive from the *Vorlage*,[130] even if the question of whether a particular rendering is based on the *Vorlage* or is attributable to the translator is often insoluble.

Weissert argues that etymological theories refined by the Alexandrian γραμματικοί likely played a role in such maneuvers. While Aristophanes had already noted "recurrent patterns in the Greek declension" that allowed reasoning by analogy (ἀναλογία),[131] Aristarchus made this his "guiding principle of . . . interpretation" in explaining unique forms he regarded as Homeric, despite their singularity.[132] Weissert cites examples of Aristarchus tracing problematic verbal forms to their present tense stems, which Alexandrian grammarians regarded as the base form of the verb,[133] and using analogies from similar Greek verbs to resolve conundrums.[134] Since "we may assume that the translators of the OT had learned Greek grammar . . . and that they would have been able to find without difficulty the present indicative of most of the Greek verbs then used," they would have been familiar with syncopation of infixed *iota* and *lamda*, the variable final *nu*, the prefixing of *epsilon* (syllabic augmentation) in past tenses, reduplication of initial consonants in the perfect, and loss of reduplicated consonants in certain forms (e.g., ἔδωκα < δίδωμι).[135]

Not only that, but they would have been aware of similar phenomena in Hebrew words, such as the seeming appearance and disappearance of (infixed) ה and ש, reduplication of consonants, as well as the appearances and disappearances of ו, י, נ, and other consonants. As Barr observes, their grasp of these changes would have been intuitive rather than analytical, since

> conceptions which are today familiar to the beginner in Hebrew, such as the triliteral root, the distinctiveness of root consonants from affirmatives,

---

[130] Just as Talmon notes that the use of *'al tiqre* readings in Midrash became "a mere exegetical *Spielelement*" (Shemaryahu Talmon, "Aspects of the Textual Transmission of the Bible in the Light of Qumran Manuscripts," *Textus* 4 [1964] 128), so also Talshir speaks of "the almost Midrash-like use of 'double translation'" in some cases (Zipora Talshir, "Double Translations in the Septuagint," in *Sixth Congress of the International Organization for Septuagint and Cognate Studies, Jerusalem, 1986*, ed. Claude E. Cox [Atlanta: Scholars Press, 1987] 44).

[131] Pfeiffer, *History of Classical Scholarship*, 202.

[132] Ibid., 229.

[133] Weissert, "Alexandrinian Analogical Word-Analysis," 35–36.

[134] Ibid., 36.

[135] Ibid.

and the conditions under which certain consonants seem to disappear
or to reappear in different places, were unknown or poorly known to
the ancient translators.... It was only after the vocalized forms had been
carefully registered by the Massoretes that grammarians were able by
induction to produce the rules.... In antiquity the changes must have
seemed arbitrary.[136]

Accordingly, the translators likely reasoned analogically from morphological changes familiar in Greek to an understanding of changes to
root forms in perplexing Hebrew words.

This perception helps explain the translation of תשגשני by πλανηθήσῃ
in Isa 17:11. The translator assumed a reduplicated form of שָׁנָה,
'to wander', and used the same Greek verb he used to translate שָׁגוּ
(πεπλανημένοι εἰσίν) in 28:7.[137] Likewise, the translation of אל תשתע
by μὴ πλανῶ in 41:10 seems based on the translator identifying the
root as תעה,[138] which he renders by πλανᾶν elsewhere (e.g., 3:12; 9:15;
16:8). Similarly explicable under this theory is his translation of ישעה
by πεποιθὼς ἔσται in 17:7 and by πεποιθότες ὦσιν in 17:8 (cf. ἦσαν
πεποιθότες || שָׁעוּ in 31:1 and καὶ οὐκέτι ἔσονται πεποιθότες ἐπ᾽
ἀνθρώποις || ולא תשעינה עיני ראים in 32:3),[139] which suggest that the
translator identified ישעה as from שען,[140] under the assumption that ל/ן
could be lost in conjugation, as happens in inflected forms of נתן.

Further evidence of etymological reasoning comes from two different
sets of renderings for מעוז: τοῦ βοηθοῦ σου || מעזך in 17:10, βοηθός
|| מעוז in 25:4, and οὐκ ἐπηρώτησαν τοῦ βοηθηθῆναι || לא שאלו לעוז
במעוז in 30:2 on the one hand, and ἡ ἰσχύς || מעוז in 23:4 and τὸ
ὀχύρωμα ὑμῶν || מעזכן in 23:14, on the other. The translator seems to
have detected two semantic fields in מעוז: 'strength', which he derived
from עזז (cf. πόλις ὀχυρά || עז עיר in 26:1 and ἔνδυσαι τὴν ἰσχὺν ||
לבשי עז in 51:9),[141] and 'help'. While it is possible that he reasoned

---

[136] Barr, "Vocalization," 9–10.

[137] As suggested by Ottley, *The Book of Isaiah*, 2:192. The MT points the verb as תשגשני,
'to make increase', from שָׂגָא, a bi-form of the Aramaic verb שְׂגָא.

[138] Ibid., 303.

[139] The only other occurrence of שעה in Isaiah is 22:4, where על כן אמרתי שעו is
rendered remarkably: διὰ τοῦτο εἶπα ἄφετέ με.

[140] For πέποιθα || שען, cf. (οὐκέτι μὴ) πεποιθότες ὦσιν || (ל)השען and ἀλλὰ
ἔσονται πεποιθότες || ונשען in 10:20.

[141] In 10:31 ישבי הגבים העיזו is rendered as a summons: καὶ οἱ κατοικοῦντες Γιββιρ
παρακαλεῖτε, the content of which comfort is given in v. 32: σήμερον ἐν ὁδῷ τοῦ
μεῖναι (|| עוד היום בנב לעמד). It is possible that the translator derived παρακαλεῖτε
from העיזו by semantic extension ("make strong" = "encourage").

semantically from "strength" to "help" that comes from strength, it is also possible that he related מעוז to עזר, the Hebrew word he most frequently renders with βοηθεία (עזרה in 20:6; 31:1; עזר in 30:5), βοηθεῖν (עזרה in 10:3; עזר in 31:3; 41:10, 14; 44:2; 49:8; 50:9; 60:15), and βοηθός (עזר in 50:7; 63:5). And it is worth adding that he renders לתעודה with εἰς βοήθειαν in 8:20, which points to לתעזרה in either his *Vorlage* or his mind.[142] Because a translator, needing to convey the sense of his *Vorlage* to his readers, does not have the luxury of reproducing forms whether or not they make sense, the inducement to perceive לתעודה as לתעזרה may have been strong. The surmise that the meaning of לתעודה in this context was likely obscure to him is reinforced by his rendering of the only other occurrence of this noun in Isaiah, four verses earlier (τότε φανεροὶ ἔσονται || צור תעודה).[143] Moreover, note his reformulation of the entire locution (לתורה ולתעודה) with νόμον γὰρ εἰς βοήθειαν ἔδωκεν.

As Tov reasons, even though the translators were not paleographers, experience would have taught that one cannot always distinguish a ד from a ר, or a ו from a י.[144] Accordingly, when faced with a problematic text that could be eased by reading one letter rather than the other, they might well have convinced themselves that the contextually sensible reading was correct.

Barr notes, especially, that differences of ד and ר, which "existed within the Hebrew written text itself, existed in even greater amount as between the Hebrew and the LXX."[145] While there are numerous instances where the translator's *Vorlage* likely read one of these in place of the other,[146] Tov plausibly suggests that ד and ר were especially prone to interchange "in order to create words which would fit the context."[147]

---

[142] Ottley posits that the translator "read עזר 'help,' for עוד 'testimony'" (*The Book of Isaiah*, 2:150).

[143] For discussion of this phrase in 8:16, see below, p. 232 n. 134.

[144] Tov, *Text-Critical Use*, 163–64.

[145] Barr, "'Guessing' in the Septuagint," 30. Scholz enumerates nineteen cases of ד/ר confusion in LXX-Isaiah (*Die alexandrinische Übersetzung*, 40). But cf. Vaccari, who counts 26 "casi *certi* di scambio fra ד e ר" (A. Vaccari, "ΠΟΛΙΣ ΑΣΕΔΕΚ Is. 19, 18," *Bib* 2 [1921] 354–55).

[146] E.g., καὶ τὰ ἐντός μου ὡσεὶ τεῖχος ὃ ἐνεκαίνισας || וקרבי לקיר חרש in 16:11. Even though 1QIsaᵃ, S, and V all attest חרש (T's דוון is likely a metaphorical translation), it seems certain that the LXX's *Vorlage* read חדש. Cf. Ρεμμων || דימון in 15:9 (bis) (cf. S ܪܡܘܢ).

[147] Tov, "Did the Septuagint Translators," 61. Elsewhere he cites cases he regards as likely instances of manipulation (Tov, *Text-Critical Use*, 164–67).

We need not assume deliberate manipulation of consonants to allow that translators may have read graphically similar letters in a way that fit their comprehension of the context.[148]

A case in point is the translation of מי יגור לנו by τίς ἀναγγελεῖ ὑμῖν twice in 33:14:[149]

פחדו בציון חטאים   ἀπέστησαν οἱ ἐν Σιων ἄνομοι
אחזה רעדה חנפים   λήμψεται τρόμος τοὺς ἀσεβεῖς
מי יגור לנו אש אוכלה   τίς ἀναγγελεῖ ὑμῖν ὅτι πῦρ καίεται
מי יגור לנו מוקדי עולם   τίς ἀναγγελεῖ ὑμῖν τὸν τόπον τὸν αἰώνιον

The ad hoc character of this translation is evident in several ways. First, while it generally mirrors the MT in word order and syntax,[150] ὑμῖν | | לנו in the interrogative clauses reflects the translator's desire to resume the second person address begun in v. 11:[151]

תהרו חשש תלדו   νῦν ὄψεσθε νῦν αἰσθηθήσεσθε
קש רוחכם   ματαία ἔσται ἡ ἰσχὺς τοῦ πνεύματος ὑμῶν
אש תאכלכם   πῦρ ὑμᾶς κατέδεται

I will postpone briefly comment on the divergences from the MT in this verse,[152] except to note that the translator's *double* insertion of νῦν, in an echo of v. 10 (νῦν ἀναστήσομαι λέγει κύριος νῦν δοξασθήσομαι νῦν

---

[148] Aejmelaeus considers Tov to have gone "too far in suggesting that the translators manipulated their *Vorlage* in order to create words that would better suit the context" (Aejmelaeus, "What Can We Know?" 66–67 n. 17). Tov himself seems to have some ambivalence about this, since in a subsequent article he wrote, "obwohl die Annahme paläographischer Exegese nicht unmöglich ist, ist sie in den meisten Fällen unwahrscheinlich, und ich nehme eher an, dass es sich um unabsichtliche graphische Vertauschungen handelt, auch wenn viele Wissenschaftler dies anders sehen" (Tov, "Die Septuaginta," 261). On the other hand, even though he places a question mark in the title of the second excursus of his book—"Tendentious Palaeographical Exegesis?" (Tov, *Text-Critical Use*, 100)—he nevertheless allows that a translator, faced with a problematic text, "would probably have been strongly tempted to render [a *daleth*] as if it were written with a *resh*" (ibid., 164).

[149] 1QIsaᵃ = MT. S reformulates אחזה רעדה חנפים as ܪ̈ܫܝܥܐ ܠܒܟ ܐܚܕܬ but reflects a *Vorlage* = MT. V translates the first מי יגור לנו with *quis poterit habitare de vobis* and the second with *quis habitabit ex vobis*, each an equivalent shaped for the target language. T is expansionistic but reflects a *Vorlage* = MT.

[150] The phrase οἱ ἐν Σιων ἄνομοι is formulated in accord with Greek syntactic style, and the future tense λήμψεται stands for the perfect form אחזה.

[151] 1QIsaᵃ reads החשש for MT's תחשו, but otherwise = MT. S reflects a *Vorlage* = MT. V has *ardorem* for MT's תחשו, which seems to be a guess, since in 5:24 he renders it with *calor*. T diverges from MT too drastically to allow a judgment.

[152] The absence of an equivalent for תחשו matches the omission of it in 5:24 (διὰ τοῦτο ὃν τρόπον καυθήσεται καλάμη ὑπὸ ἄνθρακος πυρὸς καὶ συγκαυθήσεται ὑπὸ φλογὸς ἀνειμένης ἡ ῥίζα αὐτῶν | | לכן כאכל קש לשון אש וחשש להבה ירפה שרשם), its only other occurrence in the book.

ὑψωθήσομαι || אקום יאמר יהוה עתה ארומם עתה אנשא),[153] signals his exegetical interest. The salient observation at the moment is that this statement warns the addressees that they will recognize the vanity of their strength, (for) fire will devour them. Correspondingly, after vv. 12–14a describe fire consuming the nations and the effects news of that will have on the wicked, 14b resumes the idea of the addressees learning the vanity of their strength by asking *who* will announce the fire to them. Given the translator's set-up of this scenario in v. 11, there is little doubt that he conformed the 1cp suffix of לנו in both instances to the address of the group.[154]

In this light, the rendering of both occurrences of מי ינור with τίς ἀναγγελεῖ involves two graphic ambiguities considered thus far: י/ו and ד/ר.[155] The translator shows his familiarity with נור in his translation of ינורו בך with παροικήσουσίν σοι in 16:4 and of לנור with παροικῆσαι in 52:4.[156] In the present context, where he has already found v. 11 to speak of the addressees' futility in the face of consuming fire, the inducement was probably strong to shape this verse, which also speaks of אש אוכלה, in terms of the announcement ὅτι πῦρ καίεται. Accordingly, it was but a small step to construe מי ינור in both cases as מי יניד.

As for his work on the semantic plane in v. 14, his rendering of פחדו by ἀπέστησαν is remarkable, since he translates forms of פחד with φοβέσθαι in 12:2, 19:17, 51:13, and 61:5. However, in 44:11 he translates יפחדו יבשו יחד with ἐντραπήτωσαν καὶ αἰσχυνθήτωσαν ἅμα, evidently accepting a nuance for פחד that accorded with its companion verb, יבש.[157] Similarly, his rendering of פחדו by ἀπέστησαν likely reflects a finessing of פחד, especially since LSJ (s.v.) reports that ἀφιστάναι can be used absolutely in the sense, "*stand aloof, recoil* from fear, horror, etc.," a meaning well suited to v. 14.

In the case of τὸν τόπον τὸν αἰώνιον || מוקדי עולם, did the translator's *Vorlage* read מקום עולם or is this the translator's interpretation?

---

[153] For the translator's insinuation of particles elsewhere, see above, pp. 91–96.

[154] For this translator's frequent willingness to modify pronouns to fit the context, see below, pp. 219–22, 265.

[155] As suggested by das Neves, *A Teologia*, 117.

[156] Similar to his exegetical finessing of פחדו with ἀπέστησαν in v. 14 and of יפחדו with ἐντραπήτωσαν in 44:11, is his translation of ורג זאב עם כבש with καὶ συμβοσκηθήσεται λύκος μετὰ ἀρνός in 11:6.

[157] While καὶ στήτωσαν ἅμα || יעמדו in the preceding clause might suggest that the translator read יחדו for יפחדו, the fact that he provides verbs corresponding to both יפחדו and יבשו suggests, rather, that he supplied ἅμα, parallel to the ἅμα || יחד.

Given that his rendering of יְקֹד in 10:16 (πῦρ καιόμενον καυθήσεται
|| אֵשׁ) and 65:5 (יְקֹד יֵקַד כִּיקוֹד) and 65:5 (πῦρ καίεται ἐν αὐτῷ πάσας τὰς ἡμέρας
|| אֵשׁ יֹקֶדֶת כָּל הַיּוֹם) suggests that he was familiar with יְקֹד, and given
that a more literal translation might have served the translator's interest in the announcement of "consuming fire," one could argue that
his *Vorlage* already contained מְקוֹם עוֹלָם. Viewed in isolation from other
considerations, this inference is compelling. However, מוּקַד is a hapax,
and given what we have already observed about the translator's shad-
owy knowledge of morphology, we cannot assume that the relationship between מוּקְדֵי and יְקֹד would have been as apparent to him as
it is to us. What is more, the translator elsewhere employs τόπος for
atypical Hebrew equivalents. Thus, in 4:5 he renders כֹּל מְכוֹן הַר with
πᾶς τόπος τοῦ ὄρους, parallel to his rendering of וַאֲבִיטָה בִמְכוֹנִי with
ἀσφάλεια ἔσται ἐν τῇ ἐμῇ πόλει in 18:4 (on which see below, p. 127),
even though the more frequent equivalents for מְכוֹן throughout the
LXX are ἕτοιμος and ἑτοιμασία. Similarly noteworthy is his rendering
of וְנָתַתִּי לָהֶם בְּבֵיתִי וּבְחוֹמֹתִי יָד וָשֵׁם with δώσω αὐτοῖς ἐν τῷ οἴκῳ μου
καὶ ἐν τῷ τείχει μου τόπον ὀνομαστόν in 56:5. Moreover, he injects
τόπος as part of his rendering in 5:1 (ἐν τόπῳ πίονι || בֶּן שָׁמֶן), 10:26
(ἐν τόπῳ θλίψεως || בְּצוּר), and 30:23 (τόπον πίονα καὶ εὐρύχωρον ||
כַּר נִרְחָב).[158] Accordingly, we cannot preclude that τὸν τόπον τὸν αἰώνιον
is his interpretation of מוּקְדֵי עוֹלָם.

While on a first reading τὸν τόπον τὸν αἰώνιον seems obscure and
contextually inapt, das Neves notes the attention given Jerusalem in
v. 20 and, particularly, the characterization of Zion as τὸ σωτήριον
ἡμῶν || קִרְיַת מוֹעֲדֵנוּ.[159] Whether Seeligmann correctly identifies this as
an interpretative rendering[160] or מוֹשִׁיעֵנוּ stood in the *Vorlage* (see below,
p. 126),[161] we should note that v. 21, after extolling Jerusalem (under the
image of unshakable tents, v. 20), claims that τὸ ὄνομα κυρίου μέγα ὑμῖν
τόπος ὑμῖν ἔσται (שָׁם אַדִּיר יְהוָה לָנוּ מָקוֹם ||),[162] so that the description
of Jerusalem as a τόπος appears again in this context (although that
could be equally used to argue that a scribe was thereby motivated to

---

[158] Less remarkable is his translation of צַר לִי הַמָּקוֹם נְשָׁה לִי with στενός μοι ὁ τόπος
ποίησόν μοι τόπον in 49:20, since the latter phrase is simply an interpretation of the
oblique נְשָׁה לִי based on the preceding clause.

[159] Das Neves, *A Teologia*, 118.

[160] Seeligmann, *Septuagint Version*, 115.

[161] T & V = MT, 1QIsaᵃ and S read the plural (מוֹעֲדֵינוּ / ܡܘܥܕܢ); 4QIsaᶜ preserves only קִרְיוֹן.

[162] Das Neves, *A Teologia*, 118.

change מוּקְדֵי to מָקוֹם). Also noteworthy is that, following the declaration of Zion as τὸ σωτήριον ἡμῶν, v. 20 exclaims, οἱ ὀφθαλμοί σου ὄψονται Ιερουσαλημ (|| עֵינֶיךָ תִּרְאֶינָה יְרוּשָׁלַ͏ִם), echoing the introduction of v. 11's announcement by νῦν ὄψεσθε νῦν αἰσθηθήσεσθε (|| תֶּחֱרוּ חֲשָׁשׁ תֵּלְדוּ). Given that τίς ἀναγγελεῖ ὑμῖν ὅτι πῦρ καίεται in v. 14 looks back to v. 11, under which influence the translator rendered לָנוּ with ὑμῖν, there is reason to conclude that in the phrase, τίς ἀναγγελεῖ ὑμῖν τὸν τόπον τὸν αἰώνιον, the translator anticipated the depiction of Jerusalem as τόπος ὑμῖν in v. 21, and so offered τὸν τόπον τὸν αἰώνιον as an interpretation of מוֹקְדֵי אוֹלָם.

This suggestion is lent some plausibility by the perplexing course he took in offering ματαία ἔσται ἡ ἰσχὺς τοῦ πνεύματος ὑμῶν || קְ רוּחֲכֶם in v. 11. Both Ziegler and Seeligmann drew attention to the similar phraseology of 30:15:[163]

| 164וּבְבִטְחָה | ὅτε ἐπεποίθεις ἐπὶ τοῖς ματαίοις |
| תִּהְיֶה נְבוּרַתְכֶם | ματαία ἡ ἰσχὺς ὑμῶν ἐγενήθη |

Ziegler noted the similar phrasing in 59:4: πεποίθασιν ἐπὶ ματαίοις || בָּטוֹחַ עַל תֹּהוּ.[165] In light of that passage, it appears likely that the translator derived ματαία from תִּהְיֶה, reading it as תֹּהוּ, as suggested by Ottley.[166] In fact, it may well be that this is (as Ziegler suggested) a double rendering of תִּהְיֶה—once as תֹּהוּ (ματαία) and once as תִּהְיֶה (ἐγενήθη)[167]—although it is also possible that the translator simply supplied ἐγενήθη, since it comes much later in the clause. However that might be, Ottley is likely correct that ἐπὶ τοῖς ματαίοις was "introduced to match" ματαία,[168] while Ziegler is equally right to suggest, "wird der Übers. durch 59,4 zu seiner Wiedergabe angeregt zu sein."[169]

As Ziegler concludes, the translator's rendering of 30:15 influenced his rendering of קְ רוּחֲכֶם by ματαία ἔσται ἡ ἰσχὺς τοῦ πνεύματος

---

[163] Ziegler, *Untersuchungen*, 147; Seeligmann, *Septuagint Version*, 46.

[164] 1QIsaᵃ = MT [4QIsaᶜ preserves only נבורת]; S, V and T reflect a *Vorlage* = MT (T renders ובבטחה expansively as תשרון לרוחצן, even as it rendered the preceding בהשקט with תשקטון).

[165] Ziegler, *Untersuchungen*, 147.

[166] Ottley, *The Book of Isaiah*, 2:256. Cf. μάτην δὲ σέβονταί με || ותהי יראתם אתי in 29:13, which Driver had already suggested was based on a reading ותהו (S. R. Driver, *Notes on the Books of Samuel*, lxxxvi), cited by Swete, *Introduction*, 321.

[167] Ziegler, *Untersuchungen*, 147.

[168] Ottley, *The Book of Isaiah*, 2:256.

[169] Ziegler, *Untersuchungen*, 147.

ὑμῶν in 33:11,[170] although in both passages he may well have been influenced by a reminiscence of Lev 26:20 (καὶ ἔσται εἰς κενὸν ἡ ἰσχὺς ὑμῶν || וחם לריק כחכם), as both Ziegler and Seeligmann posit.[171] And if the translator was willing to draw inspiration for his translation of קש רוחכם from beyond the immediate context, then his interpretation of מוקדי עולם in the light of v. 21 is feasible.

As for other peculiar equivalents in v. 11, while αἰσθηθήσεσθε stands parallel to the MT's תלדו, his foundation for it is obscure.[172] On the other hand, ὄψεσθε most likely arises from paleographic ambiguity, with the translator reading תחזו for תהרו.[173]

The translator's confronting of graphic ambiguities might also lie behind some of the double renderings in the book. A case in point is 29:3, where he shows familiarity with two forms of a word, based on ד/ר interchange:

וחניתי כדור עליך[174]	καὶ κυκλώσω ὡς Δαυιδ ἐπὶ σὲ
וצרתי עליך מצב	καὶ βαλῶ περὶ σὲ χάρακα
והקימתי עליך מצרת	καὶ θήσω περὶ σὲ πύργους

Earlier we noted that the translator treated v. 1a as a recollection of David's attack on Ariel, as he signaled by his rendering of חנה with ἐπολέμησεν. And in v. 1b he construed a *Vorlage* that read ספו פרי as a call to store up produce for a siege, given the Kyrios's stated intent (v. 2) to afflict Ariel (ἐκθλίψω γὰρ Αριηλ || והציקותי לאריאל), resulting in his

---

[170] Ibid.

[171] Ibid.; Seeligmann, *Septuagint Version*, 46.

[172] Did he relate it to ידע, for which he employs αἰσθάνομαι in 49:26 (καὶ αἰσθανθήσεται πᾶσα σάρξ ὅτι ἐγὼ κύριος ὁ ῥυσάμενός σε || וידעו כל בשר כי אני יהוה מושיעך) or did his *Vorlage* read a form of ידע that has escaped attestation in our other textual witnesses?

[173] For *rêš*/*zayin* confusion, cf. 25:4, where ἐγένου γὰρ πάσῃ πόλει ταπεινῇ βοηθός || כי היית מעוז לדל מעוז, discussed below, p. 125.

[174] 1QIsaᵃ reads כדור, with the *rêš* thick and black, while 4QIsaᵏ clearly reads וחניתי כדו, but lacks a clear reading for the crucial letter. Additionally, 1QIsaᵃ reads מצודות for MT's מצרת and 4QIsaᵏ reads מצו, while the fourth letter is illegible, the next is in a lacuna, and the left leg of the *tāw* is possible but uncertain. While S's ܐܟܪܟ (|| וצרתי, as if from צרר) could reflect והצרת, more likely it was chosen in light of והציקותי in v. 2, which it translated with ܐܥܝܩ. The nominal complement to the verb, ܟܐܒܫܟܐ (which Payne-Smith identifies as some sort of "engine of war") is chosen in light of the context, with (instrumental) *bêt* prefixed to express the means of affliction. Otherwise, S reflects a *Vorlage* = MT. V's *et iacam contra te aggerem* || וצרתי עליך מצב may have been influenced by the LXX's καὶ βαλῶ περὶ σὲ χάρακα, while its *et munimenta ponam in obsidionem tuam* || והקימתי עליך מצרת is certainly in the same vein; both are likely renderings of a *Vorlage* = MT. A similar conclusion pertains to T's periphrastic ואשרי עלך משרין ואבני עלך כרקום ואצבור עלך מליתא.

seizure of αὐτῆς ἡ ἰσχὺς καὶ τὸ πλοῦτος (|| האניה ואניה).[175] Similarly, χάρακα || מצב and πύργους || מצרת seem to be chosen in view of the notion of a siege.[176] We must now consider καὶ κυκλώσω ὡς Δαυιδ || והניתי כדור against that backdrop.

The translation of והניתי by καὶ κυκλώσω shows that דור stood in the *Vorlage*, since had he wanted simply to extrapolate investment of the city from חנה, he could have chosen a more elegant equivalent, such as πολιορκεῖν (cf. ὡς πόλις πολιορκουμένη || כעיר נצורה, 1:8; καὶ οὐκ ἠδυνήθησαν πολιορκῆσαι αὐτήν || ולא יכל להלחם עליה, 7:1). κυκλώσω attests his knowledge of דור, while ὡς Δαυιδ reflects a reading based on כדוד. Ziegler posits that "die Wiedergabe verdankt ihre Entstehung dem V. 1, wo David genannt ist."[177] The phrase הנה דוד there, similar to והניתי כדור here, might have encouraged a double rendering of כדור.

However, as Ziegler acknowledges, it is also possible that the translator's rendering attests that he found *both* כדור and כדוד in his *Vorlage*.[178] If so, it is a reading peculiar to his *Vorlage*, since 1QIsaᵃ and 1QIsaᵇ read only כדור,[179] while S and V give equivalents attesting the same reading (ܐܝܟ ܐܣܟܪܐ [ܐܝܟܪܐ], [*et circumdabo*] *quasi spheram*) and T's (אשרי עלך משרין), while oblique, does not presuppose כדור.

On the other hand, the translator's incorporation of both דור and דוד into the syntax does not necessarily attest distinct words in his *Vorlage*,[180] for in 17:3 he works similarly, even though it is clear that the word translated twice appears but once in his *Vorlage*:[181]

---

[175] For detailed consideration of vv. 1c–2, see below, pp. 134–36.

[176] The case for this is that 1) even though χάραξ is an appropriate equivalent for מצב, the translator was likely not familiar with מצב, given his translation of והדפתיך ממצבך וממעמדך by καὶ ἀφαιρεθήσῃ ἐκ τῆς οἰκονομίας σου καὶ ἐκ τῆς στάσεώς σου in 22:19, the only other occurrence of this consonant series in the book; 2) χάραξ occurs again only in the periphrastic 31:9: πέτρα γὰρ περιλημφθήσονται ὡς χάρακι || וסלעו ממנור יעבור; 3) πύργος otherwise renders מגדל (2:15; 5:2; 30:25), save in 9:10(9) and 10:9, where it is inserted in a "free association" with the story of the tower of Babel (see below, pp. 145–48).

[177] Ziegler, *Untersuchungen*, 147.

[178] Ibid.

[179] Skehan and Ulrich argue that the top of the right side of the fourth letter preserved in 4QIsaᵏ "is high enough to favor *dalet* over *reš*" but sensibly regard this as too insubstantial to include it among their list of variants in this ms (Eugene Ulrich et al., eds., *Qumran Cave 4 X: The Prophets* [DJD XV; Oxford: Clarendon Press, 1997] 126).

[180] As Talshir notes, "a translator could have deliberately created a doublet that ended up looking like a mechanical fusion of variants" ("Double Translations in the Septuagint," 29).

[181] 1QIsaᵃ reads יהיה for יהי. S, V = MT. T expands ככבוד into ויקרדון כיקר, but otherwise reflects a *Vorlage* = MT.

ככבוד בני ישראל יהיו   οὐ γὰρ σὺ βελτίων εἶ τῶν υἱῶν Ισραηλ καὶ τῆς
                          δόξης αὐτῶν

To arrive at οὐ γὰρ σὺ βελτίων εἶ he appears to reason from comparing Damascus to the "glory" of Israel, to the inferiority of Damascus.
On the other hand, καὶ τῆς δόξης αὐτῶν represents כבוד literally, but
enmeshed within the same syntactic structure as the first rendering of
it by οὐ γὰρ σὺ βελτίων εἶ,[182] thanks to the appended αὐτῶν, which
comports with the translator's tendency to insert pronouns.

41:15 presents a seemingly analogous case:

הנה שמתיך למורג חרוץ   ἰδοὺ ἐποίησά σε ὡς τροχοὺς ἁμάξης
חדש בעל פיפיות תדוש הרים   ἀλοῶντας καινοὺς πριστηροειδεῖς καὶ
                           ἀλοήσεις ὄρη

Here the translator renders תדוש with ἀλοήσει, so that ἀλοῶντας
suggests he read הדש rather than חדש, while καινούς appears to be a
double rendering of the same word, read this time as חדש. It is less
likely that both הדש and חדש stood juxtaposed in his *Vorlage* than that
familiarity with the graphic ambivalence of ה/ח led him to render it
both ways, although without inextricably binding both renderings in
a syntactic unit.

Here we must distinguish formally between the similar phenomena
of translation doublets and double renderings. Translation doublets are
two equivalents (typically juxtaposed) for a single word that are *syntactically independent* of each other,[183] as is the case in 41:15. Each rendering
provides a distinct solution about how to render a single lexeme.[184]

31:4 contains another example of a translation doublet. The Hebrew
syntax of the verse, which is admittedly complex, seems to have baffled
the translator, prompting him to take advantage of the ambiguous
derivation of יקרא from קרה or קרא:[185]

---

[182] For his insertion of οὐ, see above, p. 96.

[183] A chief criterion for double renderings is that "each of the two renderings now
joined in the 'double translation' could have been an independent equivalent to the
relevant Vorlage-item.... When only the two combined translation-items together can
function as an equivalent for the single Vorlage-item we are no longer dealing with
'double translations' proper " (Talshir, "Double Translations in the Septuagint," 23).

[184] Ibid., 26. Seeligmann notes that the issue of such doublets is "probably the
most thorny part in the history of the Septuagint tradition," since one must ferret
out those that are due to subsequent revisions during transmission, with the second
rendering designed to more closely align the translation with the MT (Seeligmann,
Septuagint Version, 31).

[185] 1QIsaᵃ shows no lexical differences with the MT, although ה (article) is written

כַּאֲשֶׁר יֶהְגֶּה הָאַרְיֵה וְהַכְּפִיר   ὃν τρόπον ἐὰν βοήσῃ ὁ λέων ἢ ὁ σκύμνος
עַל טַרְפּוֹ אֲשֶׁר יִקָּרֵא עָלָיו   ἐπὶ τῇ θήρᾳ ᾗ ἔλαβε καὶ κεκράξῃ ἐπ' αὐτῇ
מְלֹא רֹעִים מִקּוֹלָם   ἕως ἂν ἐμπλησθῇ τὰ ὄρη τῆς φωνῆς αὐτοῦ

The ambiguity of יִקְרָא in this context prompted both ἔλαβεν and κεκράξῃ, which function parallel to but independent of each other and, thus, constitute a translation doublet.[186]

By contrast, a "double rendering" is the conjoining of two equivalents in a *single syntactic unit*, as in 17:3. This is the case with κυκλώσω ὡς Δαυιδ in 29:3, where κυκλώσω reflects interpretation of כַדּוּר as verbal coordination, making room for the comparative ὡς Δαυιδ. However, whereas Talshir uses the distinction between syntactic independence and dependence to exclude what she regards as simple exegetical amplifications from her category of "double translations,"[187] each of these can arise because the translator deems it advantageous to translate one Hebrew word two ways. Accordingly, I will use "double rendering" and "translation doublet" to distinguish the *effects* of two ways of implementing that decision.

Of course, "translation doublets" may in fact reflect doublets in the Hebrew *Vorlage*, and the same may be said of "double renderings," since a translator could easily fold a Hebrew doublet into a unified syntactic locution. The DSS have demonstrated how often variant readings entered manuscripts to produce conflate readings.[188] However, the fact that the DSS have yielded evidence of doublets that arose through variants conflation[189] is insufficient grounds for assuming that all doublets in LXX-Isaiah reflect doublets in the *Vorlage*. Only if this translation were consistently literal could we do so. LXX-Isaiah's characteristically "free" *Übersetzungsweise* means that doublets may have arisen from its *Vorlage*, from the translator's familiarity with a tradition that

---

superscript above אַרְיֵה, it reads טרפיו for MT's טרפו and מלאו for מלא. S, through mildly periphrastic equivalents (e.g., ܠ ܡܛ ܢܬܒ || טרפו עַל), reflects the MT. T's paraphrase, though more oblique than S's (e.g., כמא דמכלי || כַאֲשֶׁר יהגה), does not seem to presuppose a different *Vorlage*. V's *cum occurrerit* reflects Jerome's identification of יקרא with קרה.

[186] Of course, we cannot rule out the possibility that his *Vorlage* actually read אשר יקרה, even if it would be the only witness to do so.

[187] "When only the two combined translation-items together can function as an equivalent for the single Vorlage-item we are no longer dealing with 'double translations' proper " (Talshir, "Double Translations in the Septuagint," 23).

[188] See especially Talmon, "Aspects of the Textual Transmission."

[189] Ibid., 107–17.

preserved a reading similar to but different from the one in his *Vorlage*, or from his own exegesis.[190]

Returning to the case of 29:3, the translator's production of a "double rendering" in 17:3 strengthens the possibility that he rendered כדור twice, first as καὶ κυκλώσω (in conjunction with והניתי) and then as ὡς Δαυιδ, in the light of הנה דוד in v. 1. While certainty is unattainable,[191] the lack of attestation of כדור in contemporary textual witnesses and the examples of this translator employing similar maneuvers elsewhere favor this solution.

Besides using "literal" equivalents, reasoning etymologically, and exploiting paleographic ambiguities, the translator also shows some degree of semantic sophistication, frequently basing an equivalent on a meaning appropriate for the context, despite familiarity with the "literal" meaning of the word. Thus we saw him render פחדו with ἀπέστησαν in 33:14 and יפחדו with ἐντραπήτωσαν in 44:11. We also noted his translation of וגר זאב עם כבש with καὶ συμβοσκηθήσεται λύκος μετὰ ἀρνός in 11:6, extrapolating from גור to the kind of coexistence pertinent to the context, as evident also from his insinuation of a verb from the same root in the next clause: καὶ μοσχάριον καὶ ταῦρος καὶ λέων ἅμα βοσκηθήσονται || ועגל וכפיר ומריא יחדו, based on καὶ βοῦς καὶ ἄρκος ἅμα βοσκηθήσονται || ופרה ודב תרעינה יחדו in v. 7.[192]

Also significant is the translator's creation of compound words that represent an extended meaning for some Hebrew words. Tov has cited nine such cases in his tables of compound words that translate two or more Hebrew words,[193] such as ἀμέτρητον for רחב ידים in 22:18, ἀλλόφυλοι for בן נכר in 61:5, ὁπλομάχοι for כלי זעם in 13:5, and ὑπέρθυρον for אמות הספים in 6:4.

---

[190] Tov, *Text-Critical Use*, 129. Talmon has isolated superscripted words in 1QIsaᵃ that appear as variants conflation in the мт, but that he considers scribal additions rather than preserved variants (Talmon, "Aspects of the Textual Transmission," 118).

[191] As Talshir observes, in such matters "there always remains an area of doubt between processes that take place on the level of the Vorlage and processes that take place on the level of the translation" ("Double Translations in the Septuagint," 23).

[192] As suggested by Ziegler, *Untersuchungen*, 64. This seems more likely than his alternative suggestion (followed by "?") that βοσκηθήσονται is derived from reading ומריא as ירעו, especially since that involves assuming that καὶ ταῦρος "ware dann spätere Einfügung nach dem мт" (ibid.). The textual evidence shows that hexaplaric manuscripts correct the lxx's order, καὶ ταῦρος καὶ λέων, to agree with the мт's וכפיר ומריא (see the apparatus in Ziegler, *Isaias*).

[193] Emanuel Tov, "Compound Words in the LXX Representing Two or More Hebrew Words," *Bib* 58 (1977) 206–12.

Equally noteworthy is the translator's employment of some words even when they override the semantics of the Hebrew. For example, Seeligmann observes that σῴζειν, σωτήριον, and σωτηρία are "introduced in various places in the Greek text, either in partial or in complete divergence from the Hebrew original."[194] Thus, even though μετὰ γὰρ κρίματος σωθήσεται ἡ αἰχμαλωσία αὐτῆς || במשפט תפדה ושביה in 1:27 might not initially raise eyebrows (since ἡ αἰχμαλωσία αὐτῆς simply assumes a different pointing of ושביה than in the MT and σωθήσεται || תפדה seems a sensible enough equivalence), פדה "is rendered by this verb in only one other place, i.e. Job 33.28,"[195] while it is rendered variously in its other three appearances in the book.[196] Similarly, in 10:22 τὸ κατάλειμμα αὐτῶν σωθήσεται renders שאר ישוב בו,[197] with σωθήσεται expanding the semantics of ישוב.[198]

In 14:32, יחסו עני עמו is translated σωθήσονται οἱ ταπεινοὶ τοῦ λαοῦ,[199] the only time in the LXX that σῴζειν translates חסה. The dominant equivalents for חסה elsewhere are ἐλπίζειν and πεποιθέναι, which the Isaiah translator uses in rendering מחסה in 28:15 (τὴν ἐλπίδα ἡμῶν || מחסנו) and 28:17 (οἱ πεποιθότες μάτην || מחסה כזב).[200] Comparable is his translation of על כן יתרה עשה by μὴ καὶ οὕτως μέλλει σωθῆναι in 15:7,[201] while Seeligmann's description of 51:14 (ἐν γὰρ τῷ σῴζεσθαί σε οὐ στήσεται οὐδὲ χρονιεῖ || מהר צעה להפתח ולא ימות לשחת ולא יחסר לחמו)[202]

---

[194] Seeligmann, *Septuagint Version*, 114.
[195] Ibid.
[196] ἐπὶ τὸν οἶκον Ιακωβ ὃν ἀφώρισεν ἐξ Αβρααμ || אל בית יעקב אשר פדה את אברהם, 29:22; καὶ συνηγμένοι διὰ κύριον ἀποστραφήσονται || ופדויי יהוה ישבון, 35:10; and, in a different rendering of the same phrase as in 29:22, καὶ λελυτρωμένοις ὑπὸ γὰρ κυρίου ἀποστραφήσονται || ופדויי יהוה ישובון, 51:11.
[197] 1QIsaᵃ = MT. The *Vorlagen* of V, S, and T = MT, although S expands כחול הים slightly, into ܐܝܟ ܘܚܠܐ, and T expands שאר ישוב בו into שאר דלא חטו ודתבו מחטאה.
[198] Cf. Ottley's conclusion that "σωθήσεται explains 'shall return'" (*The Book of Isaiah*, 2:163).
[199] 1QIsaᵃ = MT. S accords with MT. V follows a lexical equivalence established in the LXX, translating יחסו with *sperabunt*, while T gives a translation doublet: יתרחצון ויחדון.
[200] חסה appears twice more in Isaiah, first in 30:2, where καὶ σκεπασθῆναι ὑπὸ Αἰγυπτίων translates ולחסות בצל מצרים, an equivalence found also in Ps 61[60]:5 and paralleled in the translation of מחסה in Isa 4:6 (καὶ ἐν σκέπῃ || ולמחסה) and 25:4 (σκέπη ἀπὸ ἀνθρώπων πονηρῶν || מחסה מזרם). The translator's rendering of והחוסה בי by οἱ δὲ ἀντεχόμενοί μου in 57:13 is perhaps contextually chosen; cf. 48:2: καὶ ἀντεχόμενοι τῷ ὀνόματι τῆς πόλεως τῆς ἁγίας καὶ ἐπὶ τῷ θεῷ τοῦ Ισραηλ || כי מעיר הקדש נקראו ועל־אלהי ישראל.
[201] See above, p. 96.
[202] 1QIsaᵇ = MT, but 1QIsaᵃ reads צרה rather than צעה. S seems perplexed by its *Vorlage*, giving ܡܣܬܪܗܒ ܕܢܬܦܬܚ ܠܡܥܒܕ for the MT's מהר צעה להפתח. V seems

remains apt: "a text which was evidently obscure to the translator... and which he rendered more or less colourlessly, apparently following a line of thought with which he was familiar."[203] This verdict means that this is really a non-translation: a Greek locution that shows no relationship to the Hebrew and functions as a substitution for a translation.

In this light, the insinuation of a verb for salvation in 25:4–5a, which contains a number of interesting differences from the мт, is not surprising:[204]

⁽⁴כי היית מעוז לדל מעוז
לאביון בצר לו מחסה
מזרם
צל מחרב כי רוח עריצים

כזרם קיר
⁽⁵כחרב בציון שאון זרים

⁴ἐγένου γὰρ πάσῃ πόλει ταπεινῇ βοηθὸς
καὶ τοῖς ἀθυμήσασι διὰ ἔνδειαν σκέπη
ἀπὸ ἀνθρώπων πονηρῶν ῥύσῃ αὐτούς
σκέπη διψώντων καὶ πνεῦμα ἀνθρώπων
ἀδικουμένων
⁵ὡς ἄνθρωποι ὀλιγόψυχοι
διψῶντες ἐν Σιων ἀπὸ ἀνθρώπων ἀσεβῶν

The phrase ῥύσῃ αὐτούς, which lacks a Hebrew equivalent, follows on the distinctive translation of מזרם by ἀπὸ ἀνθρώπων πονηρῶν, while כזרם קיר is translated with ὡς ἄνθρωποι ὀλιγόψυχοι in v. 5. These equivalents stand within a hymn addressed to κύριε ὁ θεός μου (v. 1) that praises him for having made cities a heap (ἔθηκας πόλεις εἰς χῶμα || שׂמת מעיר לנל, v. 2), making its "foundations" (τὰ θεμέλια|| ארמון)[205] fall, and depopulating "a city of impious men" (τῶν ἀσεβῶν πόλις || זרים מעיר), who have oppressed "the poor people" (ὁ λαὸς ὁ

---

similarly baffled at this point, giving a fairly bland *cito veniet gradiens ad aperiendum*, while T reads מוחי פורענא לאתגלאה and supplies צדיקיא as the subject for ימותון || ימות.

[203] Seeligmann, *Septuagint Version*, 114.

[204] 1QIsaᵃ = мт. S renders the first מעוז with ܚܝܠܐ and the second with ܣܬܪܐ (on which see below, n. 209). Its ܟܠ ܡܕܝܢܬܐ at the start of v. 5 suggests that its *Vorlage* read כצל בחרב rather than כזרב כציון (cf. its rendering of the later חרב בצל עב with ܛܠܠܐ ܡܢ ܚܘܡܐ). V's *spes* || מחסה is interpretative, as is its insertion of a verb in the phrase, *quasi turbo inpellens parietem*, 'like a whirlwind striking a wall' (|| כזרם קיר) (cf. V). Like S, T translates the second מעוז with סעיד, 'help', while it interprets מחסה מזרם with כמא דמטמרין מן קדם זרמית מטרא, 'like those who hide themselves from a rain storm'. Furthermore, T interprets and expands כי רוח עריצים into כין מלי רשיעיא לצדיקיא, 'thus are the words of the wicked to the righteous', and (like V) supplies a verb in the final phrase of v. 4 כזרמית דשקפא בכתול, 'like a rain storm which strikes against a wall'), while it expands בציון of v. 5 into בארע ציהא.

[205] Seeligmann notes that the variety and confused equivalents given for ארמון throughout the lxx indicates that its meaning was unknown in Alexandria (*Septuagint Version*, 52). Tov points out that θεμέλια appears as an equivalent for ארמון again in Jer 6:5; Hos 8:14; Amos 1:4, 7, 10,12, 14; 2:2, 5 ("Did the Septuagint Translators," 58).

πτωχός || עז עם,[206] v. 3), the "cities of afflicted men" (πόλεις ἀνθρώπων ἀδικουμένων || קרית גוים עריצים).

Coste concludes that the translator derived πάσῃ πόλει in v. 4 from a *Vorlage* that read מעיר לדל rather than מעזו לדל.[207] In support of this, one might point to the translation of מעיר לנל by πόλεις εἰς χῶμα in v. 3, parallel to τῶν ἀσεβῶν πόλις || זרים מעיר in v. 2, for which could be posited the variants ערים לנל and זרים עיר, respectively. Haplography would account for the latter case, and perhaps all these variants could be attributed to something of a chain reaction. However, we need to weigh these alongside additional differences with the MT.

The list of variants that might be traced to graphic errors in these verses includes also ὁ πτωχός || עז, which could attest עני (v. 3), and ἀδικουμένων || עריצים, read as ערוצים[208] in vv. 3 and 4. ἀδικουμένων || עריצים is especially interesting, inasmuch as in both instances the full phrase is ἀνθρώπων ἀδικουμένων, with no Hebrew counterpart for ἀνθρώπων present in v. 4, while its counterpart in v. 5 is גוים, the only place in LXX-Isaiah this equivalence is found. Moreover, βοηθός || מעזו in v. 4 is one of three passages where he accords this meaning to this noun, likely based on etymological reasoning, as discussed above (p. 112).[209] Similarly, ἀπὸ ἀνθρώπων πονηρῶν || מזרם in v. 4 is clarified by τῶν ἀσεβῶν || זרים in v. 2, showing that the translator construed מזרם as מ(ז)רם,[210] thereby extending the pejorative sense of זר to include impiety.[211] Curiously, however, his translation of קיר כורם at the end

---

[206] Scholz already classified πτωχός || עז under "Verwechslung ähnlich aussehender Buschstaben," viz., similarity between ז and נ induced the translator to read עז as עני (*Die alexandrinische Übersetzung*, 40).

[207] J. Coste, "Le texte Grec d'Isaie xxv:1–5," *RB* 61 (1954) 42–43, although this was already suggested by Ottley, *The Book of Isaiah*, 2:225.

[208] So Ottley, *The Book of Isaiah*, 2:225.

[209] Although S similarly renders this מעזו with ܪܘܚܐ, it translates the first מעזו with ܬܘܩܦܐ, suggesting that it chose to render both metaphorically. V translates both with *fortitudo*; T renders the first by תקוף, the second by סעיד.

[210] So Ottley, *The Book of Isaiah*, 2:224.

[211] Explaining these as based on זר is preferable to Coste's judgment that the translator read זרים as זדים (Coste, "Le texte Grec," 40). The only occurrence of זר in the MT of Isaiah (13:11) is rendered ἀνόμων, an equivalence paralleled only in Ps 85[86]:14 and 118[119]:85, both of which translate זדים with παράνομοι, although these are exceptions to LXX-Psalm's typical equivalent, ὑπερήφανος (5x), all of which are in Ps 118(119) (Jer 53[43]:2 gives no equivalent for הזדים). On the other hand, the equivalent for MT's זריך in 29:5 is τῶν ἀσεβῶν, while in 17:10 καὶ σπέρμα ἄπιστον translates וזמרת זר, parallel to the immediately preceding φύτευμα ἄπιστον || נטעי נעמנים (see above, p. 94) זרים is rendered with ἀλλότριοι in 1:7 (bis), 43:12, and 61:5. For πικρίας || זר in 28:21, see below, pp. 281–82.

of v. 4 is ὡς ἄνθρωποι ὀλιγόψυχοι,[212] where he now construes זרם as referring to those oppressed by the ἀσεβεῖς, rather than the ἀσεβεῖς themselves, who were identified as the referent of זרם in v. 2. Note also his rendering of ייראוך as εὐλογήσουσίν σε in v. 3,[213] in accord with his translation of יכבדוך by εὐλογήσει earlier in the verse.

This series of exegetical readings is so intertwined as to all but preclude that all of the detected graphic misreadings stood in the translator's *Vorlage*. Even if it is reasonable to posit that his *Vorlage* read זרים עיר in place of זרים מעיר in v. 2, the translator's handling of this passage suggests that he was capable of isolating עיר in the remaining forms. This inference is strengthened by noting the lack of an equivalent for the *lāmed* of לדל in v. 4 (πάσῃ πόλει ταπεινῇ || מעוז לדל), resulting in a separation of בצר לו לאביון from the preceding מעוז, as guaranteed by a prefixed a copula: καὶ τοῖς ἀθυμήσασιν διὰ ἔνδειαν. This, in turn, forced the translator to continue the new clause with the following מחסה מזרם.

In accord with this pastiche of interpretative readings, then, is his insertion of ῥύσῃ αὐτούς. While Ottley suggests that this insertion is due to reading צל both as 'shadow' (= σκέπη) and as √נצל,[214] given the translation of יחסו with σωθήσονται in 14:32, it is equally possible that ῥύσῃ is a second rendering of מחסה. In any case, it is clear that the translator has found in this passage a celebration of the salvation of the pious from the impious, an illustration of Brockington's observation that "the translation of Isaiah has a marked soteriological emphasis."[215]

In a similar vein, Seeligmann regards ἰδοὺ Σιων ἡ πόλις τὸ σωτήριον ἡμῶν || חזה ציון קרית מועדנו in 33:20 as evincing the translator's exegesis.[216] While we might infer a variant reading along the lines of מושענו, four considerations favor attributing τὸ σωτήριον to the translator. First, as we have seen, he incorporates several exegetical elements into his rendering of 33:11–20 (see above, pp. 114–18).

Second, while the translator gives an apt equivalent for ומועדיכם in 1:14 (καὶ τὰς ἑορτὰς ὑμῶν), he renders it oddly in 14:31 (ὅτι καπνὸς

---

[212] This phrase is found three other times in the book, although for different Hebrew phrases: οἱ ὀλιγόψυχοι τῇ διανοίᾳ || לנמהרי לב (35:4); καὶ ὀλιγόψυχον || ועצובת רוח (54:6); καὶ ὀλιγοψύχοις || ושפל רוח (57:15).

[213] 1QIsa^a = MT, while S, V, and T equally accord with MT.

[214] Cf. Ottley, *The Book of Isaiah*, 2:225.

[215] Brockington, "Greek Translator, 30.

[216] Seeligmann, *Septuagint Version*, 115. T & V = MT, 1QIsa^a and S read the plural (הגאבדני /מועדינו); 4QIsa^c preserves only ציון קר.

ἀπὸ βορρᾶ ἔρχεται καὶ οὐκ ἔστι τοῦ εἶναι || כִּי מִצָּפוֹן עֹשֶׁן בָּא וְאֵין בּוֹדֵד
(בְּמוֹעֲדָיו) and gives a peculiar equivalent for the phrase in which it stands
in 14:13 (καθιῶ ἐν ὄρει ὑψηλῷ ἐπὶ τὰ ὄρη τὰ ὑψηλὰ τὰ πρὸς βορρᾶν
|| וְאֵשֵׁב בְּהַר מוֹעֵד בְּיַרְכְּתֵי צָפוֹן)[217].[218] Accordingly, his overwriting of
מוֹעֲדֵנוּ with τὸ σωτήριον ἡμῶν in 33:20 is comparable to two of the
other three occurrences of מוֹעֵד in the book.

Third, given the translator's tendency to read one passage in the light
of another (as will be discussed in detail in chapter five), his rendering
may have been guided by 26:1, where he gives a similar rendering:
ἰδοὺ πόλις ὀχυρὰ καὶ σωτήριον ἡμῶν || עִיר עָז לָנוּ יְשׁוּעָה.

Finally, the likelihood that the translator is responsible for τὸ σωτήριον
ἡμῶν is increased by comparing his distinctive rendering of 18:4:[219]

כִּי כֹה אָמַר יְהוָה אֵלַי	ὅτι οὕτως εἶπέ μοι κύριος
אֶשְׁקוּטָה Q) אֶשְׁקֳטָה) וְאַבִּיטָה בִמְכוֹנִי	ἀσφάλεια ἔσται ἐν τῇ ἐμῇ πόλει
כְּחֹם צַח עֲלֵי אוֹר	ὡς φῶς καύματος μεσημβρίας

מָכוֹן occurs elsewhere in Isaiah only in 4:5, where the translator renders
it with τόπος. And in fact, this is the only place in the LXX that πόλις
translates מָכוֹן, which is most often rendered by ἕτοιμος, as it is in Exod
15:17 (its only occurrence in the LXX-Pentateuch). Similarly, ἀσφάλεια
|| אֶשְׁקוּטָה is singular in the LXX, where שקט is most frequently rendered
by ἡσυχάζειν (e.g., Isa 7:4). It is noteworthy that in 14:6 the translator renders נָחָה שָׁקְטָה כָּל הָאָרֶץ with ἀνεπαύσατο πεποιθὼς πᾶσα ἡ γῆ
(an equivalence found elsewhere only in Jer 48[31]:11), for we find a
semantic overlap with the phrase ἄνθρωποι ἐν ἀσφαλείᾳ ὄντες in 8:15,
which the translator seems to have supplied as a subject:[220]

וְנִלְכָּדוּ   καὶ ἁλώσονται ἄνθρωποι ἐν ἀσφαλείᾳ ὄντες

---

[217] The א and the בּ of וְאֵשֵׁב are apparent in 1QIsaᵃ, but the שׁ stands within a tear,
while there is clearly no initial wāw (N.B. MT's preceding כִּסֵּא), which is also read in
1QIsaᵃ). 4QIsaᶜ attests only the sequence [בּ]הַר מוֹ[עֵד], although the wāw is uncertain.
4QIsaᵉ has a lacuna in the place this phrase would stand. S reads ܒܛܘܪܐ ܪܒܐ for בְּהַר
מוֹעֵד. V & T accord with the MT.

[218] The mountains' height is likely emphasized in light of the foregoing εἰς τὸν
οὐρανὸν ἀναβήσομαι ἐπάνω τῶν ἄστρων τοῦ οὐρανοῦ θήσω τὸν θρόνον μου and
invokes the sense of height that goes unexpressed in the translation of אָרִים כִּסְאִי
with θήσω τὸν θρόνον μου. For a more detailed discussion of this verse, see below,
p. 216.

[219] 1QIsaᵃ reads אֶשְׁקוֹטָה for אֶשְׁקֳטָה. S attests a Vorlage = MT, as does V, which gives
a periphrastic rendering of כְּחֹם צַח עֲלֵי אוֹר similar to the LXX's: sicut meridiana lux clara
est. T's paraphrase presupposes a Vorlage like MT, especially in its rendering of וְאַבִּיטָה
בִמְכוֹנִי by וְאִתְרְעֵי מִמְּדוֹר קֻדְשִׁי לְאוֹטָבָא לְהוֹן.

[220] See below, p. 245.

This comparison suggests an association between being at ease and enjoying safety[221] that might help explain the equivalence ἀσφάλεια || אשקוטה in 18:4.

As for the lack of an equivalent for ואביטה, it may have been lacking in the *Vorlage* due to parablepsis (homoioarchton) or the translator may have omitted it as superfluous to the thought he detected in the sentence. However that might be, the translator forged this rendering deliberately, since an equivalent like ἡσυχάσω ἐν τῷ ἐμῷ τόπῳ would appear more ready to hand. Accordingly, 18:4 betrays the translator's interest in the theme of Jerusalem as a source of salvation, providing strong support for the supposition that ἡ πόλις τὸ σωτήριον ἡμῶν || קרית מועדנו in 33:20 reflects the same interest.

Based on all four of these considerations—other exegetical maneuvers in this context, the handling of מועד elsewhere, the translator's tendency to read one verse in light of another (26:1 being the likely template here), and his derivation of the theme of Jerusalem as a source of security in 18:4—ἡ πόλις τὸ σωτήριον ἡμῶν || קרית מועדנו in 33:20 expresses the translator's interest in the theme of salvation.

Of equal importance to the translator was the δόξα word group. Forster drew attention to the fact that, in Isaiah, δόξα translates sixteen of the twenty-five Hebrew words it represents throughout the LXX, and eight of those equivalents are unique to LXX-Isaiah,[222] while another three are found only in Isaiah and one other book.[223] As in the rest of the LXX, the word most frequently translated by δόξα is כבוד (29x), which is also rendered by ἔνδοξος in 22:24 and 59:19, and by δοξάζειν in 24:23. However, כבוד is also rendered by τιμή in 11:10 and 14:18, and the translator chooses more contextually apt renderings on three

---

[221] Cf. ἐκεῖ ἐνόσσευσεν ἐχῖνος καὶ ἔσωσεν ἡ γῆ τὰ παιδία αὐτῆς μετὰ ἀσφαλείας || שמה קננה קפוז ותמלט ובקעה ודגרה בצלה in 34:15.

[222] A. Haire Forster, "The Meaning of Δόξα in the Greek Bible," *ATR* 12 (1929/30) 312. Those eight are καὶ πλήρης ὁ οἶκος τῆς δόξης αὐτοῦ || ושוליו מלאים את ההיכל in 6:1, οὐ κατὰ τὴν δόξαν κρινεῖ || ולא למראה עיניו ישפוט in 11:3, καὶ τὰ πίονα τῆς δόξης αὐτοῦ σεισθήσεται || ומשמן בשרו ירזה in 17:4, καὶ ἀφαιρεθήσεται ἡ δόξα ἡ ἐπ' αὐτόν || ונכרת המשא אשר עליה in 22:25, τὸ ἄνθος τὸ ἐκπεσὸν ἐκ τῆς δόξης || וציץ נבל צבי תפארתו in 28:1, καὶ πᾶσα δόξα ἀνθρώπου ὡς ἄνθος χόρτου || וכל הסדו כציץ השדה in 40:6, ἀπὸ πολλῆς δόξης καὶ ἐν κράτει ἰσχύος οὐδέν σε ἔλαθεν || מרב אונים ואמיץ כח איש לא נעדר in 40:26, and καὶ ἡ δόξα σου ἀπὸ τῶν ἀνθρώπων || ותארו מבני אדם in 52:14.

[223] Ibid., 313. עז in Isa 12:2, 45:24, and Ps 67[68]:35; יפי in 33:17 and Lam 2:15; תהלה in Isa 61:3 and Exod 15:11. Forster also lists גאון, which appears in Isa 14:11, 24:14, 26:10, Exod 15:7, and Micah 5:4.

other occasions. In 5:13 he renders וכבודו מתי רעב והמונו צחה צמא by καὶ πλῆθος ἐγενήθη νεκρῶν διὰ λιμὸν καὶ δίψαν ὕδατος, where δόξα or τιμή would be nonsensical. Similarly, in the translation of חיל גוים תאכלו ובכבודם תתימרו by ἰσχὺν ἐθνῶν κατέδεσθε καὶ ἐν τῷ πλούτῳ αὐτῶν θαυμασθήσεσθε in 61:6, πλοῦτος concretizes the meaning of the metaphor ἰσχὺν ἐθνῶν κατέδεσθε, making clear what sort of benefit Israel gains from the nations that makes it a marvel.[224] The rendering of קלון ושמה מרכבות כבודך by καὶ θήσει τὸ ἅρμα σου τὸ καλὸν εἰς ἀτιμίαν in 22:18, is more difficult to parse, since one might have expected τιμή, given ἀποστελεῖ κύριος σαβαωθ εἰς τὴν σὴν τιμὴν ἀτιμίαν in 10:16.[225]

Brockington interpreted these data as showing δόξα to be the term the translator used to denote the effect of the divine "on those who experience God's presence," much as δόξα can denote humans' "outward appearance, usually with a sense of being something worth seeing" (e.g., 11:3; 40:6).[226] This is especially evident in Isaiah 6. Whether the translator rendered ושוליו מלאים את ההיכל in 6:1 by καὶ πλήρης ὁ

---

[224] This assessment seems to me more likely than Forster's speculation that the translator reasoned from the "root idea" of כבוד as 'weight, importance' to 'wealth' as what "usually gives importance" (ibid., 315). Ottley similarly attempted to divine a common semantic base for the equivalents εἰς τὴν σὴν τιμὴν || במשמני in 10:16, τὸ κῦδος αὐτῶν || סבלו in 14:25, and ἡ δόξα || המשא in 22:25 by positing that all three rest on the notion of a weight borne, parallel to the meaning of "be heavy" for כבד (*The Book of Isaiah*, 2:151, 181–82). Although Ottley's reasoning was subsequently endorsed by Seeligmann (*Septuagint Version*, 50), LXX-Isaiah's translations of neither סבל nor שמן inspire enough confidence to permit this conclusion. The rendering of כי את עֻל סבלו by διότι ἀφαιρεθήσεται ὁ ζυγὸς ὁ ἐπ' αὐτῶν κείμενος in 9:4(3) seems a guess, as is reinforced by ἀφαιρεθήσεται ὁ φόβος αὐτοῦ || יסור סבלו in 10:27 (cf. 53:4), despite the fact that the parallel ועֻלו might have given him a clue as to the meaning of סבל (equivalents in 46:4 and 53:11 seem shaped by context). And even though the translator elsewhere rendered שמן "literally," in 28:4 his rendering of על ראש גיא שמנים with ἐπ' ἄκρου τοῦ ὄρους τοῦ ὑψηλοῦ is made all the more striking by the fact that he translated על ראש גיא שמנים as ἐπὶ τῆς κορυφῆς τοῦ ὄρους τοῦ παχέος in v. 1. His rendering of שמנים in v. 4 seems as determined by the image of a mountain as τοῦ ὄρους || גיא was by על ראש. Similarly, his translation of משתה שמרים שמנים ממחים by πίονται εὐφροσύνην πίονται οἶνον χρίσονται μύρον in 25:6–7 seems based on context.

[225] Outside this range of semantic equivalents lies his rendering of וכבוד by ἀποσβεσθήσεται in 10:18. When seen in the light of the periphrastic translation he gives for the first half of the verse (ἀποσβεσθήσεται τὰ ὄρη καὶ οἱ βουνοὶ καὶ οἱ δρυμοὶ καὶ καταφάγεται ἀπὸ ψυχῆς ἕως σαρκῶν || וכבוד יערו וכרמלו מנפש ועד־בשר יכלה), ἀποσβεσθήσεται is likely derived from כבוד by associating it with כבה, which is frequently translated by σβεννύναι (e.g., καὶ οὐκ ἔσται ὁ σβέσων || ואין מכבה, 1:31; καὶ οὐ σβεσθήσεται || לא תכבה 34:10).

[226] Brockington, "Greek Translator," 26–28.

οἶκος τῆς δόξης αὐτοῦ because he was unfamiliar with שׁוּלָיו (despite the translation of שׁוּלֵי by λῶμα, 'hem', in Exod 28:34; 39:24, 25, 26) or because he recoiled at so pronounced an anthropomorphism,[227] clearly he patterned his translation (including word order) after 6:3: πλήρης πᾶσα ἡ γῆ τῆς δόξης αὐτοῦ || מְלֹא כָל־הָאָרֶץ כְּבוֹד. In any event, δόξα here designates the effect of God's presence.

In 4:2 the divine δόξα becomes something that "shines upon the earth"[228] (ἐπιλάμψει ὁ θεὸς ἐν βουλῇ μετὰ δόξης ἐπὶ τῆς γῆς) so as "to exalt and to glorify the remnant of Israel" (τοῦ ὑψῶσαι καὶ δοξάσαι τὸ καταλειφθὲν τοῦ Ισραηλ || לִגְאוֹן וּלְתִפְאֶרֶת לִפְלֵיטַת יִשְׂרָאֵל). Ziegler points out that the phrase μετὰ δόξης in 4:2 "kehrt auch 30,27 und 33,17 wieder, wo ebenfalls von einer Theophanie gesprochen ist."[229] In fact, he numbers these among translations derived from the "gegenseitige Beeinflussung sinnverwandter Stellen," noting that the translator employed this phrase in 30:27 (καιόμενος ὁ θυμός μετὰ δόξης || בֹּעֵר אַפּוֹ וּכֹבֶד) and 33:17 (βασιλέα μετὰ δόξης ὄψεσθε || מֶלֶךְ בְּיָפְיוֹ תֶּחֱזֶינָה) because they were embedded in theophanies.[230]

Equally important, in the light of 4:2, is the association of δόξα with Israel's salvation,[231] as is evident in the translation of 40:5:[232]

וְנִגְלָה כְּבוֹד יְהוָה	καὶ ὀφθήσεται ἡ δόξα κυρίου
וְרָאוּ כָל־בָּשָׂר יַחְדָּו	καὶ ὄψεται πᾶσα σάρξ τὸ σωτήριον τοῦ θεοῦ
כִּי פִּי יְהוָה דִּבֵּר	ὅτι κύριος ἐλάλησεν

---

[227] As suggested by Charles T. Fritsch, "The Concept of God in the Greek Translation of Isaiah," in *Biblical Studies in Memory of H. C. Alleman*, ed. O. Reimherr, Jacob M. Myers, and H. N. Bream (Locust Valley, NY: J. J. Augustin, 1960) 165–66. The question of how the translator handled anthropomorphisms has been vigorously debated. Orlinsky responded to Fritsch with a survey of anthropomorphic images that the translator rendered without reservation (Harry M. Orlinsky, "The Treatment of Anthropomorphisms and Anthropopathisms in the Septuagint of Isaiah," *HUCA* 27 [1956] 193–200). However, Lust isolated passages that he concluded were modified to avoid implying "an 'immoral' character" for God (Johan Lust, "The Demonic Character of Jahweh and the Septuagint of Isaiah," *Bijdragen* 40 [1979] 3). While 6:1 does not fall into that category, it is possible that the anthropomorphism proved too bold for the translator.

[228] See above, p. 77.

[229] Ziegler, *Untersuchungen*, 108.

[230] Ibid., 137. In 30:27, καιόμενος ὁ θυμός μετὰ δόξης follows the announcement, ἰδοὺ τὸ ὄνομα κυρίου διὰ χρόνου ἔρχεται πολλοῦ (|| הִנֵּה שֵׁם־יְהוָה בָּא מִמֶּרְחָק), while 33:17, part of the proclamation of what the people will see that we have examined previously (above, pp. 114–15).

[231] Cf. Brockington's perception that δόξα, as characteristically used by this translator, "was associated, directly or indirectly, with God's redemptive work among men" ("Greek Translator," 26).

[232] 1QIsaᵃ = MT. Likewise, S, V, and T presuppose a *Vorlage* = MT.

As Ziegler deduces, the translator seems to have forged this rendering in accord with 52:10b:[233]

וראו כל אפסי ארץ.   καὶ ὄψονται πάντα τὰ ἄκρα τῆς γῆς
את ישועת אלהינו   τὴν σωτηρίαν τὴν παρὰ τοῦ θεοῦ.

The similar heading of the clauses in 40:5 and 52:10 by וראו and the parallel between כל בשר and כל אפסי ארץ likely inspired the translator to align his rendering of 40:5 with 52:10.[234] The result is a close association of the revelation of divine δόξα and the arrival of τὸ σωτήριον τοῦ θεοῦ,[235] thereby portraying, as Seeligmann inferred, "the deliverance of Israel as a theophany."[236]

The implications of this δόξα for Israel's salvation are stated more clearly elsewhere. We have already seen that in 4:2 the appearance of the Kyrios μετὰ δόξης ἐπὶ τῆς γῆς results in the glorification of Israel's remnant (τοῦ ὑψῶσαι καὶ δοξάσαι τὸ καταλειφθὲν τοῦ Ισραηλ || לגאון ולתפארת לפליטת ישראל). More explicit and striking is the proclamation of 44:23 that ἐλυτρώσατο ὁ θεὸς τὸν Ιακωβ καὶ Ισραηλ δοξασθήσεται (|| גאל יהוה יעקב ובישראל יתפאר). Even if this reformulation is so slight as to raise the question of whether the translator did not stumble upon it almost reflexively, 4:2 and 40:5 show that even that reflex was part of his notion of what would constitute Israel's salvation.[237] Thus, as Brockington concludes, the translator's distinctive "concern for salvation was never very far from the use of the noun δόξα or the verb δοξάζω."[238]

At the same time that the translator's exploitation of the themes of δόξα and salvation are good examples of "theological exegesis" as Tov

---

[233] Ziegler, *Untersuchungen*, 150. So already Zillessen, "Bermerkungen, 242.

[234] It is not as clear to me as it is to Ziegler that the translator justified this association by reading יחדו as יהוה in 40:5 (*Untersuchungen*, 150). Needless to say, it remains possible that his *Vorlage* read וראו כל את ישועת יהוה, already under the influence of 52:10, although this would be a singular reading among all our witnesses and seems less likely in light of the translator's interest in the topic of σωτήριον.

[235] Cf. Frederic Raurell, "La «Doxa» com a Participació en la Vida Escatológica," *RevCT* 7 (1982) 76.

[236] Seeligmann, *Septuagint Version*, 115.

[237] Raurell concludes that "there appears to be a very close relationship of equivalence between *doxa* and *sôtêrion*" ("La «Doxa»," 76, translation by Prof. Mary Lou Daniel).

[238] Brockington, "Greek Translator," 32. While Raurell rightly agrees that δόξα embodies the theme of salvation, his perception that δόξα adopts "el significant teològico-escatològic, caracteristic d'Is-LXX" ("La «Doxa»," 75) overstates its role. For my objections to the widespread perception that eschatology dominates LXX-Isaiah, see below, pp. 179–88.

has described it,[239] they are not themes brought into the book from
the outside, but were essential elements of the book that the translator
appropriated as leitmotifs in his interpretation of the whole. It is in
this sense that Hanhart is correct to say that "the LXX…is interpretation only insofar as a decision is made between various possibilities of
understanding which are already inherent in the formulation of the
Hebrew *Vorlage* and thus given to the translator."[240] In effect, this is a
matter of Ricouer's "surplus of meaning" that arises from the meaning
a text can engender from within the reader's frame of reference. This
translator seems to have been willing to make clear for his readers, at
points, the frame of reference within which the book of Isaiah could
be read aright.

Summary

The Isaiah translator appears to have been familiar enough with literary Greek to formulate sentences in its style, suggesting that he was
among the well educated, although we must suspect that to be true, in
any case, for a person undertaking the task of translation. His choices
of conjunctions, his reformulations of sentences, and his interpretation of passages in the light of theologoumena he perceived essential
to the book show that he was less concerned to bring his readers to
the Hebrew text of Isaiah than to bring the book to them. The fuller
extent of this will become apparent in chapter five.

   The translator's freer *Übersetzungsweise* permits us to ask how his work
compares to that of other literati in his world. We have already noted
affinities between his linguistic interpretation and exegetical impulses
attested for the Alexandrian γραμματικοί. Chapter five will open another
vista on his similarities to their work.

---

[239] Tov, "Die Septuaginta," and idem, "Theologically Motivated Exegesis Embedded
in the Septuagint," in *Translation of Scripture: Proceedings of a Conference at the Annenberg
Research Institute, May 15–16, 1989* (Philadelphia: Annenberg Research Institute,
1990).
[240] Hanhart, "The Translation of the Septuagint," 342.

CONTEXTUAL INTERPRETATION IN LXX-ISAIAH

Linguistic interpretation, which is basic to translation, does not necessarily entail "exegesis" in our sense of the word. In fact, Pietersma
reasonably refuses to apply the word "exegesis" to linguistic interpretation,[1] for exegesis exists only "when one acts deliberately, systematically,
and purposefully."[2]

One could take issue with this definition by pointing out that linguistic interpretation is both deliberate and purposeful. However, it
certainly is not "systematic" in the sense of steadily working according
to a strategically organized *Übersetzungsweise*. Moreover, while the Isaiah
translator works deliberately, he also invests varying degrees of intention in the passages he translates, as we have seen. Even if we cannot
deny that linguistic renderings that are transparent to their *Vorlage* lack
intention, "exegesis" involves a deliberate unpacking of more than the
linguistic features of a text. Accordingly, I concur with Pietersma's plea
to reserve "exegesis" for particular kinds of interpretation embodied
in a translation.[3]

However, the qualifying phrase, "embodied in a translation," is significant, inasmuch as the only access we have to the translator's exegesis
of a passage is what he reveals in his translation. Most importantly,
the act of translation is not the same as writing a commentary. What
a *translator* offers is bound, to one degree or another, to what his source
text says and does not necessarily entail anything beyond linguistic
interpretation. As long as a translator renders his source text "literally,"
we have no way of perceiving his exegesis.[4]

---

[1] Albert Pietersma, "Exegesis in the Septuagint," 45.

[2] Ibid., 35.

[3] I part company with Pietersma in his insistence that divining exegesis must be
based on a "full-fledged theory of translation" that begins with the identification of
the "(prospective) position & function of a translation" (ibid., 37). For my criticisms of
Pietersma's program, see above, pp. 71–72.

[4] Cf. Aejmelaeus's insistence that "the intended meaning is the meaning that can
be read from the translation" ("Translation Technique," 30).

It becomes appropriate to speak of "exegesis" only when the translation departs from any likely *Vorlage* to the degree it suggests the translator *substituted* a phrase or a clause for what lay in his *Vorlage*. Because
it is reasonable to assume that the translator provided material that
he considered in accord with the context, it is equally reasonable to
view such "contextual interpretation" as embodying his exegesis of the
passage in its context.

We have already seen the translator consider context in choosing
lexical equivalents and in reformulating clauses and sentences. However,
"contextual interpretation," as studied in this chapter, means not simply
that the translator takes into account the ambient phrase or sentence, but
the larger picture of the paragraph, the chapter, or the book. Because,
as Tov observes, "the translators' concept of 'context' was wider than
ours," they created "relationships between words not only when they
occurred in the immediate context, but also when they occurred in
remote contexts."[5] Moreover, a translator could be prompted by the
text to inject themes we would consider tangential, or to relate the passage before him to his socio-political milieu. Accordingly, "contextual
interpretation" itself comprises different types of exegesis.

Reformulations and non-translations

In chapter four I noted Barr's remark that reformulations of phrases
and clauses yield "a sentiment which is really the translator's idea,
connected here and there with the words of the original."[6] However,
because connections with the *Vorlage* are traceable, the sentiment produced is not simply "the translator's idea" but one that arises under
the inspiration of the source text. At the same time, as I noted, other
reformulations wander farther a field from the source text and, thus,
cannot be considered translations. They are "non-translations."

A prime example is 29:1–2:

הוי אריאל אריאל קרית חנה דוד	[1]οὐαὶ πόλις Αριηλ ἣν Δαυιδ ἐπολέμησεν
ספו שנה על שנה	συναγάγετε γενήματα ἐνιαυτὸν ἐπ᾽ ἐνιαυτόν
חנים ינקפו	φάγεσθε γὰρ σὺν Μωαβ

---

[5] Tov, *Text-Critical Use*, 45.
[6] Barr, *Comparative Philology*, 255–56.

והציקותי לאריאל והיתה תאניה ואניה	²⁾ἐκθλίψω γὰρ Αριηλ καὶ ἔσται αὐτῆς ἡ ἰσχὺς
והיתה לי כאריאל	καὶ τὸ πλοῦτος ἐμοί

While examining 1a-b in chapter four, I noted that the translation of חנה by ἐπολέμησεν signals the translator's interpretation of this passage as a matter of an assault on the city. Moreover, I argued that his *Vorlage* likely read ספו פרי שנה על שנה and that the translator, working under the image of an attack on the city, construed this as a call to gather (ספ[א]) produce in preparation for the siege. His rendering of תאניה ואניה by αὐτῆς ἡ ἰσχὺς καὶ τὸ πλοῦτος ἐμοί was probably also shaped by the image of a siege and the types of plunder taken in capturing a city.[7]

This reconstructed train of thought helps explain why the translator resorted to φάγεσθε γὰρ σὺν Μωαβ for חגים ינקפו in the final clause of the verse.[8] Given the image of gathering produce in preparation for a siege left him stumped when he came to חגים ינקפו, no doubt partly because he was unfamiliar with נקף, as his equivalents for it elsewhere reveal (καὶ πεσοῦνται || ונקף, 10:34; συνῆψε γὰρ || כי הקיפה, 15:8; ὡς ῥῶγες ἐλαίας || כנקף זית, 17:6; ἐάν τις καλαμήσηται ἐλαίαν || כנקף זית, 24:13). However, this does not explain how he arrived at the notion of Ariel eating the produce σὺν Μωαβ.

Ziegler finds the likely solution to this conundrum by pointing to 15:9:

---

[7] The translator appears to have collapsed the two occurrences of והיתה in v. 2 into one (καὶ ἔσται). While his path to αὐτῆς ἡ ἰσχὺς καὶ τὸ πλοῦτος || תאניה ואניה is obscure, it is at least noteworthy that the translator renders שאנן with πλούσιος in 32:9 and 33:20, and with πλοῦτος in 32:18 (cf. καὶ οἱ πλούσιοι || ושאננה in 5:14), equivalences found nowhere else in the LXX. Perhaps he arrived at τὸ πλοῦτος for אניה by analogy with שאנן. More likely, however, he arrived at this pair as common words to designate plunder taken from a captured city. Cf. the discussion of χάρακα || מצב and πύργους || מצרת in v. 3 (above, p. 119).

[8] Neither 1QIsaᵃ nor 1QIsaᵇ show any differences from the MT in 1c–2, and the same is true of V, whose *et circumvallabo* ('and I will besiege [Ariel]') is likely a contextually chosen equivalent for והציקותי (cf. its rendering of המצקים לה by *et praevaluerunt adversus eam* in v. 7). 4QIsaᵏ may have read תהיה[ו] for והיתה in v. 2, although only the lower left leg of the *tāw* is visible, leaving the reading uncertain. S preserves no equivalent for לי in v. 2 (ܠܝ ܐܝܟ ܘܬܗܘܐ), whether because its *Vorlage* lacked it or because the translator regarded it dispensable in the target language. Its ܘܬܗܘܐ ܐܝܟ for חגים ינקפו shows the translator's familiarity with the noun, which likely influenced his choice of ܘܬܗܘܐ. His familiarity with נקף is evinced by 15:8: ܡܛܠ ܕܐܬܩܪܒ ܩܠ ܓܒܘܠ ܡܘܐܒ את הזעקה הקיפה כי .כי הקיפה הזעקה את נבול מואב || ܠܓܒܘܠܐ ܘܥܕܡܐ. T's rendering is too expansionistic and periphrastic to provide help. For v. 1a–b see above, p. 108, n. 122.

כי מי דימון מלאו דם⁹   τὸ δὲ ὕδωρ τὸ Ρεμμων πλησθήσεται αἵματος
כי אשית על דימון   ἐπάξω γὰρ ἐπὶ Ρεμμων Ἄραβας
נוספות לפליטת מואב אריה   καὶ ἀρῶ τὸ σπέρμα Μωαβ καὶ Αριηλ
ולשארית אדמה   καὶ τὸ κατάλοιπον Αδαμα

While we need not address all differences between LXX and MT in this
verse, we must note the insertions of Ἄραβας and Αριηλ. Given the
translator's distinctive rendering of המת by ᾽Αραβία in 10:9 and 11:11
(see below, p. 146), he likely inserted Ἄραβας as the foe brought against
Ρεμμων. In that light, καὶ Αριηλ is most likely due to the translator
than to ואריאל in his *Vorlage* and, as posited by Ziegler and Seeligmann,
is based on 2 Sam 23:20, which explicitly connects Ariel and Moab.[10]
In any event, 15:9 explains why, in 29:1, the translator phrased Ariel's
eating as shared with Moab: it is a matter of contextual exegesis.[11]

33:11, which we also encountered in chapter four, provides another
example of the impact of a previously translated phrase on a later
one:

תהרו חשש תלדו   νῦν ὄψεσθε νῦν αἰσθηθήσεσθε
קש רוחכם   ματαία ἔσται ἡ ἰσχὺς τοῦ πνεύματος ὑμῶν
אש תאכלכם   πῦρ ὑμᾶς κατέδεται

As noted in the prior discussion of that passage (above, p. 117), both
Seeligmann and Ziegler drew attention to the similar phraseology in
30:15:[12]

ובבטחה   ὅτε ἐπεποίθεις ἐπὶ τοῖς ματαίοις
תהיה גבורתכם   ματαία ἡ ἰσχὺς ὑμῶν ἐγενήθη

Ziegler cogently contended that the translator's rendering of 30:15
influenced his rendering of קש רוחכם by ματαία ἔσται ἡ ἰσχὺς τοῦ
πνεύματος ὑμῶν in 33:11,[13] although in both passages he may have

---

⁹ 1QIsaᵇ comports with MT, while 1QIsaᵃ's only difference is נוספת for נוספות. V
reflects a *Vorlage* = MT, as does T, despite its expansions. S correctly construes נוספות as
the direct object (ܐܚܘܢܐ ܢܒܥܐ ܠ ܢܒܥܐ ܘܝ) and then gives ܘܐܪܝܡ ܠ ܐܪܝܩ,
ܐܪܥܐ ܡܢ ܘ ܕܝ ܕܣܒܪ for לפליטת מואב אריה, basing ܐܪܝܩ on אריה, perhaps reading
(or thinking of Aramaic) ארעה.
¹⁰ Ziegler, *Untersuchungen*, 68; Seeligmann, *Septuagint Version*, 78.
¹¹ Cf. Ziegler, *Untersuchungen*, 68. It is unnecessary to posit, with Ziegler, that the *Vorlage*
contained ואכלו את מואב as "eine Glosse oder Variante" (ibid.). That begs the question
of why the translator *substituted* this phrase for the other and overlooks the problems
חנים ינקפו presented him.
¹² Seeligmann, *Septuagint Version*, 46; Ziegler, *Untersuchungen*, 147.
¹³ Ziegler, *Untersuchungen*, 147.

been influenced by Lev 26:20 (καὶ ἔσται εἰς κενὸν ἡ ἰσχὺς ὑμῶν ||
ותם לריק כחכם), as both Ziegler and Seeligmann suggested.[14]

40:5 also utilizes a phrase borrowed from elsewhere, although later
in the book:

ונגלה כבוד יהוה[15]	καὶ ὀφθήσεται ἡ δόξα κυρίου
וראו כל בשר יחדו	καὶ ὄψεται πᾶσα σὰρξ τὸ σωτήριον τοῦ θεοῦ

As Ziegler deduced, the translator seems to have forged this rendering
in accord with 52:10b:[16]

וראו כל אפסי ארץ	καὶ ὄψονται πάντα τὰ ἄκρα τῆς γῆς
את ישועת אלהינו	τὴν σωτηρίαν τὴν παρὰ τοῦ θεοῦ.

The similar heading of the clauses in 40:5b and 52:10a by וראו and the
parallel between כל בשר and כל אפסי ארץ likely triggered his alignment of 40:5 with 52:10.

These cases substantiate Ziegler's observation that the translator
"scheint überhaupt sein Buch sehr gut dem Inhalte nach im Gedächtnis
gehabt zu haben," inasmuch as "es begegnen viele Wiedergaben, die
sich nur auf Grund der Exegese nach sinnverwandten Stellen erklären
lassen."[17] While instinct might suggest that a translator would work
verse-by-verse, not taking into account other verses or passages, cases
like those just cited confirm Ziegler's perception.

However, the translator's intertextual readings also exceed the
bounds of Isaiah. Beyond using lexical equivalents found in the LXX-
Pentateuch, he interpreted some Isaianic passages in the light of the
LXX-Pentateuch,[18] as is evident in 2:6:[19]

---

[14] Ibid.; Seeligmann, *Septuagint Version*, 46.
[15] 1QIsaᵃ = MT. S, V, and T presuppose a *Vorlage* = MT.
[16] Ziegler, *Untersuchungen*, 150.
[17] Ibid., 135.
[18] Hanhart cites examples of this in LXX-Amos 9:13 and Dan 11:30 (both G and
θ′) ("The Translation of the Septuagint," 360–63).
[19] 1QIsaᵃ reads לא מלאו for כי מלאו. 4QIsaᵇ preserves clearly only [ו]בית יעקב כי מלא,
although Skehan and Ulrich find grounds in the photograph for concluding that the
fragment lacked the final *hê* of נמשׁתה (Eugene Ulrich et al., eds., *Qumran Cave 4 X*, 23).
S's expansionistic equivalents for בית יעקב (ܕܒܝܬ ܝܥܩܘܒ) and מקדם (ܡܢ ܩܕܝܡ) show
that its ܘܐܬܡܠܝܘ ܐܪܥܗܘܢ ܡܢ ܩܨܡܐ for ועננים כפלשתים is an interpretive rendering of
a *Vorlage* = MT. V supplies a verb for ועננים: *et augures habuerunt ut Philisthim*. T
gives a literal rendering of ועננים כפלשתים, but also offers, as part of an expansion of
כי מלאו מקדם, the clause ארי אתמליאת ארעכון מטען כיד מלקדמין, similar to the LXX's
ἐνεπλήσθη ὡς τὸ ἀπ᾽ ἀρχῆς ἡ χώρα. Quite likely the *Vorlagen* of the LXX and T read
something like כי מלאת מקדם ארצם.

כי נטשתה עמך בית יעקב	ἀνῆκεν γὰρ τὸν λαὸν αὐτοῦ τὸν οἶκον τοῦ Ισραηλ
כי מלאו מקדם	ὅτι ἐνεπλήσθη ὡς τὸ ἀπ' ἀρχῆς
ועננים	ἡ χώρα αὐτῶν κληδονισμῶν
כפלשתים	ὡς ἡ τῶν ἀλλοφύλων

The translator likely conformed the personal pronouns to the ensuing context, since v. 7 likewise speaks of the land being filled, although using 3ms pronominal suffixes (ἡ χώρα αὐτῶν || ארצו, ἡ γῆ || ארצו, τῶν ἀρμάτων αὐτῶν || למרכבתיו). The plus ἡ χώρα αὐτῶν may reflect מלאת מקדם ארצם in the *Vorlage*, a scribal harmonization with ותמלא ארצו in v. 7.[20] In any case, τοῦ Ισραηλ attests ישראל rather than the MT's יעקב.

While κληδονισμῶν is a semantically apt equivalent for עננים, this is the sole occurrence of this word (as well as κληδονίζειν or κληδών) in LXX-Isaiah, including 57:3, where it might have been expected:

ואתם קרבו הנה בני עננה	ὑμεῖς δὲ προσαγάγετε ὧδε υἱοὶ ἄνομοι
זרע מנאף ותזנה	σπέρμα μοιχῶν καὶ πόρνης

In fact, κληδονίζειν and κληδών are used in only four other passages in the LXX. 4 Kgdms 21:6 and (the parallel) 2 Chr 33:6 render ועונן with καὶ ἐκληδονίζετο. However, they, along with Isa 2:6, seem to have taken their cue from Deut 18:10 and 14:

18:10	לא ימצא בך מעביר	οὐχ εὑρεθήσεται ἐν σοὶ περικαθαίρων
	בנו ובתו באש	τὸν υἱὸν αὐτοῦ ἢ τὴν θυγατέρα αὐτοῦ ἐν πυρί
	קסם קסמים מעונן	μαντευόμενος μαντείαν <u>κληδονιζό-μενος</u>
	ומנחש ומכשף	καὶ οἰωνιζόμενος φαρμακός
18:14	כי הגוים האלה	τὰ γὰρ ἔθνη ταῦτα
	אשר אתה יורש אותם	οὓς σὺ κατακληρονομεῖς αὐτούς
	אל מעננים ואל קסמים ישמעו	οὗτοι <u>κληδόνων</u> καὶ μαντειῶν ἀκού-σονται
	ואתה לא כן נתן לך יהוה אלהיך	σοὶ δὲ οὐχ οὕτως ἔδωκεν κύριος ὁ θεός σου

---

[20] While it is possible that the translator effected the harmonization as part of his modification of the pronouns of v. 6, T's similar ארי אתמליאת ארעכון increases the likelihood that it is based on a scribal harmonization already found in the *Vorlage*.

The claim, in Isa 2:6, that the Kyrios rejected Israel because its land was full of things that characterize the ἀλλόφυλοι could easily have prompted recollection of Deut 18:10 and 14, as Ziegler suggested.[21]

An even more striking example of the influence of the LXX-Pentateuch on the Isaiah translator is 7:15–16:

חמאה ודבש יאכל	[15]βούτυρον καὶ μέλι φάγεται
לדעתו מאוס ברע	πρὶν ἢ γνῶναι αὐτὸν ἢ προελέσθαι πονηρὰ
ובחור בטוב	ἐκλέξεται τὸ ἀγαθόν
כי בטרם ידע הנער	[16]διότι πρὶν ἢ γνῶναι τὸ παιδίον ἀγαθὸν ἢ κακὸν
מאס ברע ובחר בטוב	ἀπειθεῖ πονηρίᾳ τοῦ ἐκλέξασθαι τὸ ἀγαθόν

As noted in chapter four, aside from ἀγαθὸν ἢ κακόν in v. 16, the LXX follows the MT's word order, and each of the MT's lexemes can be aligned with a Greek word or phrase. Moreover, aside from ἀγαθὸν ἢ κακόν, there are only two semantic differences: προελέσθαι | | מאוס and πρὶν ἢ [γνῶναι αὐτὸν] | | [דעתו]ל. The remaining lexical choices are standard within the LXX.

Therefore, ἀγαθὸν ἢ κακόν in v. 16 is a remarkable plus. Even though a contrast between "good and evil" is inherent in these verses, the phrase טוב ורע is lacking in all extant Hebrew witnesses, as well as S, V, and T. While the translator of Isaiah elsewhere supplies a subject or object for a verb in the interest of clarity,[22] this plus likely arises from speculation current in the translator's day that is attested by interpolations in two passages of LXX-Numbers, as well as by the LXX's translation of Deut 1:39.[23] Patient exploration of these will provide good reason to conclude that the plus of Isa 7:16 can be attributed to such a strain of thought.

Num14:23 contains a lengthy plus (absent from MT, S, V, T, and SP)[24] identifying those exempt from the Lord's vow to annihilate the people:

---

[21] Ziegler, *Untersuchungen*, 107.

[22] As Ziegler notes, the translator inserts elements "manche Stellen durch die Angabe des Subj. und des Obj. zu verdeutlichen" (ibid., 59).

[23] Whether the translator was exposed to such speculation as a member of the Alexandrian community or by virtue of his reading the LXX-Pentateuch need not be resolved here. Whichever be the case, the subtle changes he makes to infuse these verses with this ideology attests that it had become so native to his own thought that divining its presence here was intuitive.

[24] SP contains a plus of לתת להם after לאבתם. None of the 11 mss of Numbers among the DSS preserves chapter 14.

אִם יִרְאוּ אֶת הָאָרֶץ   ἦ μὴν οὐκ ὄψονται τὴν γῆν
אֲשֶׁר נִשְׁבַּעְתִּי לַאֲבֹתָם   ἣν ὤμοσα τοῖς πατράσιν αὐτῶν
                ἀλλ' ἢ τὰ τέκνα αὐτῶν ἅ ἐστιν μετ' ἐμοῦ ὧδε
                ὅσοι οὐκ οἴδασιν ἀγαθὸν οὐδὲ κακόν
                πᾶς νεώτερος ἄπειρος τούτοις δώσω τὴν γῆν
וְכָל מְנַאֲצַי לֹא יִרְאוּהָ   πάντες δὲ οἱ παροξύναντές με οὐκ ὄψονται αὐτήν

While Wevers judges this plus "a corrective based on information given later in the chapter (vv. 29–35),"[25] comparison of those verses undermines his conclusion.

Within that section, v. 31 shows the greatest affinities to the plus of v. 23. And yet, while that verse vows that the rebels' children shall enter and possess the land,[26] it shares little else with the plus of v. 23. On the other hand, that plus shows greater affinities with Deut 1:39. Not only does its definition of the children as ὅσοι οὐκ οἴδασιν ἀγαθὸν οὐδὲ κακόν align more precisely with Deut 1:39 (אֲשֶׁר לֹא יָדְעוּ הַיּוֹם טוֹב וָרָע), but even more strikingly, while Num 14:31 promises that the children κληρονομήσουσιν τὴν γῆν (= MT) v. 23 promises to *give* them the land (τούτοις δώσω τὴν γῆν), in accord with Deut 1:39: וְלָהֶם אֶתְּנֶנָּה.[27]

Additional evidence that the plus of 14:23 is based on Deut 1:39— either deriving from the Septuagint translation of that passage or, if it reflects material already interpolated into the translator's *Vorlage*, translated similar to LXX-Deut 1:39—is the phrase πᾶς νεώτερος. Elsewhere

---

[25] John W. Wevers, *Notes on the Greek Text of Numbers* (Atlanta: Scholars Press, 1998) 223. Cf. Gilles Dorival, *La Bible d'Alexandrie: Les Nombres* (Bible d'Alexandrie 4; Paris: Cerf, 1994) 323, and idem, "Les phénomènes d'intertextualité dans le livre Grec des Nombres," in *KATA TOUS O´/Selon les Septante*, ed. Gilles Dorival and Olivier Munnich (Paris: Cerf, 1995) 266. Dorival regards any affinities with Deut 1:39 as matters of "simples parallélismes, et non d'emprunts" (*Les Nombres*, 323). His insistence that the LXX's plus was constructed from Num 14:26–35 suggests he means the parallels with Deut 1:39 are simply fortuitous.

[26] As for the differences between the LXX and MT in v. 31, καὶ κληρονομήσουσιν is likely attributable to a (superior) reading of וְיָרְשׁוּ in LXX's *Vorlage* (so also Dorival, *Les Nombres*, 326), while εἰς τὴν γῆν either reflects a scribal interpolation of אֶל הָאָרֶץ in the *Vorlage* or the translator's own clarification. On the other hand, the translation of בָּהּ מְאַסְתֶּם by ἣν ὑμεῖς ἀπέστητε Dorival attributes to "une tendance dont on a vu d'autres exemples, la LXX atténue, euphémise, le TM" (ibid., 99). Accordingly, LXX-Numbers translates the only other occurrence of מָאַס in the book (11:20) as follows: ὅτι ἠπειθήσατε κυρίῳ || יַעַן כִּי מְאַסְתֶּם אֶת יהוה. As Dorival observes in commenting on 14:11, "nous avons affaire ici à une exégèse qui considérait comme impossible que l'homme puisse témoigner du mépris à Dieu" (ibid., 98).

[27] Gray notes that S attests the influence of these passages upon one another, reporting that in v. 31 S "inserts from Dt. 1³⁹ *and your children who this day have no knowledge of good or evil, they shall enter the land*" (George Buchanan Gray, *Numbers* [ICC; Edinburgh: T & T Clark, 1903] 162).

in the Torah νεώτερος is used only as a comparative adjective in speaking of the younger/youngest of siblings, and on such occasions it translates קטן or צעיר (e.g. Gen 19:31, 34; 27:15, 42; 29:16, 18; 42:13, 15).[28] While the substantival use of νεώτερος in Num 14:23 is, thus, exceptional in the Torah, it bears a striking similarity to LXX-Deut 1:39, whose translation of וטפכם with καὶ πᾶν παιδίον νέον (unparalleled in other witnesses) is likely due to "free rendering," as Wevers concludes.[29] While παιδίον translates טף elsewhere (Gen 45:19; Num 14:3, 31; Deut 3:6; Josh 1:14; 8:35), only here is it qualified by νέον, yielding a striking resemblance to νεώτερος in Num 14:23, and expressing the same belief that *young* children know "neither good nor evil."

νεώτερος further undermines Wevers's supposition that the interpolation of Num 14:23 was extrapolated from vv. 29–35, since v. 29 uses a different way of specifying the children's age: מבן עשרים שנה ומעלה, which the LXX dutifully translates with ἀπὸ εἰκοσαετοῦς καὶ ἐπάνω. The translator's choice of the less exact νεώτερος, with its closer ties to LXX-Deuteronomy's equivalent for טף in 1:39, weakens Wevers's assertion that Num 14:23 draws on vv. 29–35.[30]

Also indicating a relationship between the plus of Num 14:23 and Deut 1:39 is the similarity between the restrictive relative clause ὅσοι οὐκ οἴδασιν ἀγαθὸν οὐδὲ κακόν in Num 14:23 and אשר לא ידעו היום טוב ורע in Deut 1:39, while Num 14:29–35 lacks a parallel to this. Moreover, LXX-Deuteronomy's translation of וטפכם with καὶ πᾶν παιδίον,[31] thus characterizing *each* person who will enter the land, is paralleled by πᾶς νεώτερος in Num 14:23.

Finally, Num 14:23 and LXX-Deut 1:39 betray a like understanding of the phrase טוב ורע. While these words are elsewhere conjoined with καί (Gen 2:9, 17; 3:5; 2 Sam 14:17; Jer 49:6), both Num 14:23 and Deut 1:39 portray them as alternatives, with Deut 1:39 translating אשר לא

---

[28] Typical substantives for a young person in the Torah are παῖς (for both males and females), παιδάριον, παρθένος, νεανίσκος, and νεάνις. Outside the Torah, νεώτερος is used substantivally to designate a young person in Judges 8:20 (A & B); 18:3 (A; B uses νεανίσκου); and 2 Chr 13:7, each time for נער, while in 2 Chr 10:14 τῶν νεωτέρων translates הילדים.

[29] John W. Wevers, *Notes on the Greek Text of Deuteronomy* (Atlanta: Scholars Press, 1995) 23.

[30] His interpolation of οἱ ἐπιστάμενοι τὸ κακὸν καὶ τὸ ἀγαθὸν in 32:11 follows the phrase ἀπὸ εἰκοσαετοῦς καὶ ἐπάνω (|| מבן עשרים שנה ומעלה).

[31] Whether the *Vorlage* actually read וכל טפכם in Deut 1:39 is immaterial for my argument, for which the important issue is the distinctive formulation with πᾶς in both passages.

ידעו טוב היום ורע with ὅστις οὐκ οἶδεν σήμερον ἀγαθὸν ἢ κακόν,[32] and Num 14:23 reading ἀγαθὸν οὐδὲ κακόν.[33] The fact that οὐδέ accords with lxx-Deut 1:39 in this detail suggests that the translator developed his interpolation from a common understanding of Deut 1:39.[34]

The interpolation of Num 14:23 goes beyond Deut 1:39, however, by qualifying νεώτερος with ἄπειρος, thus defining those exempt from judgment in terms not only of age, but also (in)experience.[35] ἄπειρος appears only here in the Torah and but two other times in the rest of the lxx. In Zech 11:15 קח לך כלי רעה אולי is translated λαβὲ σεαυτῷ σκεύη ποιμενικὰ ποιμένος ἀπείρου, with ἀπείρου apparently a guess for אולי.[36] ῎Απειρος appears again only at Jer 2:6, where ὁ καθοδηγήσας ἡμᾶς ἐν τῇ ἐρήμῳ ἐν γῇ ἀπείρῳ καὶ ἀβάτῳ renders המוליך אתנו במדבר בארץ ערבה ושוחה. However the translator found his way from ערבה to ἀπείρῳ,[37] this is a different sense for ἄπειρος (≈ 'untried') than in Num 14:23, where the phrase νεώτερος ἄπειρος suggests that ἄπειρος connotes "inexperienced." In that context, "knowing good or evil" suggests consciousness of a choice that renders one accountable, so that ἄπειρος is tantamount to "innocent."

Thus, "knowing good or evil" in Num 14:23 and Deut 1:39 specifies culpability acquired at a certain stage of maturation. The importance of this concept for these translators is evident from the lengthy plus of Num 14:23, the correspondence between lxx-Deuteronomy's translation of וטפכם with (καὶ πᾶν) παιδίον νέον and Num 14:23's νεώτερος, and the latter's qualification of the νεώτερος as ἄπειρος. The passages expound similarly what merits the children's exemption from judgment.

---

[32] More revealing of their interpretation of the phrase טוב ורע...ידעו לא are T, לא ידעו דין טב וביש, and V, boni ac mali ignorant distantiam (S = mt).

[33] lxx-Numbers blurs the distinction between οὐδέ and οὔτε (cf. Num 11:19; 20:5, 22), as is common in Koine.

[34] The translator's reliance on Deut 1:39 comports with his habit of interpreting verses in light of other passages in the Torah, as noted by Dorival, Les Nombres, 66–72.

[35] The phrase νεώτερος ἄπειρος is difficult to trace back to an original Hebrew construction, not only because there is no obvious Hebrew equivalent for ἄπειρος, but more so because the whole phrase lacks a parallel in the Hebrew Bible.

[36] Cf. Ps 106(107):17, where ἀντελάβετο αὐτῶν is a conjecture for אולים (ἀντελάβετο αὐτῶν ἐξ ὁδοῦ ἀνομίας αὐτῶν || אולים מדרך פשעם), and Hosea 9:7, where ὥσπερ reveals the translator's perplexity over אולים (καὶ κακωθήσεται [reading ירעו] Ισραηλ ὥσπερ ὁ προφήτης ὁ παρεξεστηκώς || ידעו ישראל אויל הנביא משנע).

[37] ἀπείρῳ καὶ ἀβάτῳ are likely a double rendering of ערבה.

LXX-Numbers 32:11 also contains an interpolation of the phrase "to know good and evil," in this case describing those barred from seeing the land:

אם יראו האנשים העלים	εἰ ὄψονται οἱ ἄνθρωποι οὗτοι οἱ ἀναβάντες
ממצרים מבן עשרים שנה ומעלה	ἐξ Αἰγύπτου ἀπὸ εἰκοσαετοῦς καὶ ἐπάνω
	οἱ ἐπιστάμενοι τὸ κακὸν καὶ τὸ ἀγαθὸν
את האדמה אשר נשבעתי	τὴν γῆν ἣν ὤμοσα
לאברהם ליצחק וליעקב	τῷ Αβρααμ καὶ Ισαακ καὶ Ιακωβ
כי לא מלאו אחרי	οὐ γὰρ συνεπηκολούθησαν ὀπίσω μου

As in the surrounding context, the translator rendered his *Vorlage* rather literally,[38] not only following the Hebrew word order, but even using εἰ to represent אם in an oath (cf. 14:30), making the plus (absent also from S, V, T, SP, and DSS) remarkable. While Wevers and Dorival posit that the translator imported the plus from 14:23,[39] more is involved than the transfer of a phrase.

On the one hand, the wording indicates that the translator freshly formulated the phrase for this context. Rather than using οἶδα, as in 14:23 (and as in LXX-Deut 1:39), he chose ἐπίσταμαι, and in place of the anarthrous κακόν and ἀγαθόν of 14:23, he used τὸ κακόν and τὸ ἀγαθόν. More significantly, as Wevers notes, the translator transposed the sequence, placing τὸ κακόν before τὸ ἀγαθόν.[40] Accordingly, whatever the relationship of this plus to 14:23, it is not a matter of perfunctory harmonization. And while this phrase was interpolated into the same type of context as the plus of 14:23, it was not modeled on a particular biblical passage.

Given the more extemporaneous construction of this plus, the unusual position of "evil" before "good" likely implies their greater familiarity with τὸ κακόν,[41] as befits this passage's focus on the rebels.

---

[38] Budd's judgment that "G appears to be generally interpretative and expansionist in this section," based on this plus and what he considers the addition of ὁ διακεχωρισμένος in v. 12, is unwarranted (Phillip J. Budd, *Numbers* [WBC 5; Waco: Word Books, 1984] 337). ὁ διακεχωρισμένος is not a plus, but an etymological interpretation of הקנו, even as in v. 9 נחל אשכול is rendered Φάραγγα βότρυος. The translator's approach in these verses is "literal."

[39] Wevers, *Numbers*, 532, and Dorival, *Les Nombres*, 536. Derivation from Deut 1:39 was suggested already by Gray, *Numbers*, 431.

[40] Wevers, *Numbers*, 532.

[41] Wevers notes the unusual order, without venturing an explanation (ibid., 532).

Moreover, while translation of טוב and רע with ἀγαθός and κακός is typical in LXX-Numbers and LXX-Deuteronomy (in contrast to the rest of the Torah),[42] the juxtaposition of *articular* τὸ κακὸν and τὸ ἀγαθόν is distinctive,[43] suggesting that κακόν and ἀγαθόν are not general concepts, but sharply delimited categories. Thus, we should understand this plus to mean, "those who know what is evil and what is good." The translator's creativity in formulating this interpolation suggests, once more, the importance to him of this idea.

In summary, the LXX's pluses in Num 14:23; 32:11 and its translation of Deut 1:39 evince exegetical reflection on the meaning of "knowing good and evil," finding in it an adolescence-era threshold leading from innocence to accountability. Not only does this give foundation for suggesting that the plus of ἀγαθὸν ἢ κακόν in Isa 7:16 is based on a commonly shared notion, but it also provides grounds for concluding that this plus derives from LXX-Deuteronomy 1:39.

The case for this begins with the exceptional use of κακόν in Isa 7:16. While ἀγαθός is used twice in vv. 15 and 16 (beyond the ἀγαθός of the plus), κακόν in the plus contrasts with πονηρά and πονηρία in vv. 15 and 16, and is the exception to the otherwise exclusive use of πονηρός for "evil" in chapters 1–12 (1:4, 16; 3:9, 11; 5:20; 7:5, 15–16; 9:16). Moreover, every other occurrence of κακός in the whole of LXX-Isa is in the neuter plural, denoting "calamities" (13:11; 26:15; 28:9; 31:2; 45:7; 46:7; 57:12) rather than the abstract notion of "evil." The fact that κακόν in v. 16 is anomalous both in terms of usage in chapters 1–12 and semantics throughout LXX-Isaiah favors the conclusion that even though ἀγαθὸν ἢ κακόν was interpolated by the translator, it was not formulated by him, but was imported as a set phrase *in Greek*. Moreover, the notion of the child knowing "good *or* evil" is reminiscent of the interpolations of Numbers and the unique translation of the *wāw* conjunction of טוב ורע in Deut 1:39 (ἀγαθὸν ἢ κακόν). While certainly the idea of a choice between good and evil is present in the

---

[42] Gen 2:9, 17; 3:5, 22; Lev 27:10, 12, 14, 33 use καλός and πονηρός, while Gen 24:50 uses καλός and κακός. Never are ἀγαθός and κακός paired in translating this phrase, even though ἀγαθός appears independently 8x in Gen through Lev.

[43] The only other instance of these articular adjectives juxtaposed is in Deut 30:15, where ואת הטוב ואת המות ואת הרע translated τὴν ζωὴν καὶ τὸν θάνατον τὸ ἀγαθὸν καὶ τὸ κακόν. Since the articular forms accord with MT, and since it is not possible to determine whether the redistribution of words to create the pairing τὸ ἀγαθὸν καὶ τὸ κακόν is attributable to the translator or his *Vorlage*, we cannot draw any conclusions to aid in considering Num 32:11.

Hebrew of Isa 7:15–16, and while the interpretation of this choice as moral has been frequently assumed, the idea of "knowing *good or evil*" is not native to the Hebrew, nor is the phrase טוב ורע found anywhere in Isaiah.

Consequently, given the evidence that this phrase was imported as a Greek formulation that utilized the conjunction ἤ, the distinctive translation in LXX-Deuteronomy 1:39 is its likely source,[44] whether the translator drew it directly from there or found it mediated in a use of the phrase γνῶναι ἀγαθὸν ἢ κακόν based on speculation tied to Deut 1:39. Moreover, this phrase is integral to the translator's rendering of לדעתו מאוס ברע by πρὶν ἢ γνῶναι αὐτὸν ἢ προελέσθαι πονηρά in v. 15, inasmuch as διότι πρὶν ἢ γνῶναι τὸ παιδίον ἀγαθὸν ἢ κακὸν offers the explanation for why the child will select the good without even knowing about evil. Therefore, this phrase, taken from Deut 1:39, was most likely inserted by the translator himself.

At least as striking is the way the translator interprets the Assyrian king's claim to have captured territories in 10:9:[45]

הלא ככרכמיש	οὐκ ἔλαβον τὴν χώραν τὴν ἐπάνω βαβυλῶνος
כלנו	καὶ Χαλαννη οὗ ὁ πύργος ᾠκοδομήθη
אם לא כארפד חמת	καὶ ἔλαβον Ἀραβίαν
אם לא כדמשׂק שמרון	καὶ Δαμασκὸν καὶ Σαμάρειαν

Seeligmann suggests that the translator spoke in general terms about "a country above Babylon for lack of familiarity with ככרכמיש (a *hapax* in Isaiah).[46] However, that does not explain why he chose a description of the location rather than a simple transliteration, an expedient he resorts to frequently (see chapter six). The answer is allied with his identification of כלנו with כלנה, a city mentioned in Gen 10:10

---

[44] ἤ shows that the translator did not rely on the LXX's translation of טוב ורע in Gen 2:9, 17 and 3:5, 22, or even the plus of Num 32:11, since all those passages use καί. Moreover, the verses in Gen 2 and 3 all translate טוב with καλός and רע with πονηρός.

[45] For חמת 1QIsaᵃ has a large gap after כארפד, followed by מח (it also reads כדרמשׂק for כדמשׂק). 4QIsaᵉ preserves only a ל that likely belongs to לא and the final three letters of שמרון. S renders הלא with ܐܠܐ and omits an equivalent for both instances of לא אם, substituting for it simple *waw*. It reads ܒܠܝ ('they became worn out') for כלנו, and reads ܘܐܝܟ ܐܪܦܕ for כארפד. For כארפד לא אם V reads simply *et ut Arfad*. T is expansionistic, but reflects a *Vorlage* = MT.

[46] Seeligmann, *Septuagint Version*, 78. In the same passage, Seeligmann supports this contention by pointing out that the translator of 2 Chr 35:20 renders בכרכמיש על פרת by borrowing from 4 Kgdms 23:29 (ἐπὶ τὸν βασιλέα Ασσυρίων ἐπὶ τὸν ποταμὸν Εὐφράτην), indicating he construed כרכמיש as the name of an Assyrian king.

(Χαλαννη ἐν τῇ γῇ Σεννααρ), with which the translator correlated the story of the tower in Genesis 11 (οὗ ὁ πύργος ᾠκοδομήθη).[47] Thus, his reference to a land ἐπάνω βαβυλῶνος is related to his identification of כלנה/כלנו with Mesopotamia.

The story of Genesis 11 exerts an influence again in Isa 11:11:

והיה ביום ההוא	καὶ ἔσται τῇ ἡμέρᾳ ἐκείνῃ
יוסיף אדני שנית ידו	προσθήσει κύριος τοῦ δεῖξαι τὴν χεῖρα αὐτοῦ
לקנות את שאר עמו	τοῦ ζηλῶσαι[48] τὸ καταλειφθὲν ὑπόλοιπον τοῦ λαοῦ
אשר ישאר מאשור...	ὃ ἂν καταλειφθῇ ἀπὸ τῶν' Ασσυρίων...
ומשנער ומחמת ומאיי הים[49]	καὶ ἀπὸ ἡλίου ἀνατολῶν καὶ ἐξ' Αραβίας

Just as the story of the tower influenced the translation of כלנו in 10:9, so also the translator rendered ומשנער in 11:11 by καὶ ἀπὸ ἡλίου ἀνατολῶν, due to the location specified for the tower in Gen 11:2 (ἀπὸ ἀνατολῶν εὗρον πεδίον ἐν γῇ Σεννααρ).[50] The fact that the translator substitutes this phrase for שנער, rather than transliterating it with Σεννααρ and appending the phrase ἀπὸ ἡλίου ἀνατολῶν (comparable to his qualification of Χαλαννη by οὗ ὁ πύργος ᾠκοδομήθη in 10:9), suggests that he was more concerned to locate the action than to identify the site with precision, even as he was content to render כרכמיש with τὴν χώραν τὴν ἐπάνω βαβυλῶνος in 10:9.

This observation sheds light on another anomaly in 10:9. After the reference to "the land above Babylon" and the identification of Χαλαννη as οὗ ὁ πύργος ᾠκοδομήθη, the translator reprises the verb he supplied at the outset (καὶ ἔλαβον) and renders חמת with Αραβίαν, leaving כארפד without a formal equivalent.[51] If his concern was to set the actions of these passages in Mesopotamia generally, due to the influence of the story of the tower, then he might well have considered a translation of ארפד unessential in 10:9, even as he regarded τὴν χώραν τὴν ἐπάνω βαβυλῶνος a sufficient representation of ככרכמיש.

[47] Ibid., 47.
[48] As discussed previously, this reflects לקנאה in the *Vorlage*.
[49] 1QIsaᵃ = MT. 4QIsaᵃ does not preserve this verse. T reads ומבבל for ומשנער. S & V reflect a *Vorlage* = MT.
[50] Seeligmann, *Septuagint Version*, 47. Cf. Koenig, *L' Herméneutique*, 100.
[51] ארפד is transliterated Αρφαδ in 36:19, 37:13 (= 2 Kgdms 19:13), and Jer 30:29 (49:23).

Equally intelligible, in this light, is Βαβυλωνία || פתרוס in 11:11, the only place this equivalence appears.[52] Given the translator's insertion of Βαβυλων as part of his rendering in 10:9 (τὴν χώραν τὴν ἐπάνω Βαβυλῶνος), where Gen 11:2 was again his pedagogue, his employment of Βαβυλωνία for פתרוס should occasion no surprise, especially since that provides a Mesopotamian power as the counterpart to Αἰθιοπία, just as 'Ασσυρίων is the counterpart to Αἰγύπτου.[53]

This perception of the influence of the story of the tower finds further support from the rendering of 9:10(9),[54] where we find other unusual equivalents:[55]

לבנים נפלו	πλίνθοι πεπτώκασιν
וגזית נבנה	ἀλλὰ δεῦτε λαξεύσωμεν λίθους
שקמים נדעו וארזים	καὶ ἐκκόψωμεν συκαμίνους καὶ κέδρους
נחליף	καὶ οἰκοδομήσωμεν ἑαυτοῖς πύργον

The correspondence between the LXX and the MT in the first line is transparent, and there are equally perceptible correspondences in lines two and three;[56] the only Hebrew word without a clear equivalent is נחליף. Koenig suggests the translator transposed נבנה and נחליף, construing the latter in the light of an Aramaic homonym meaning "to cut down."[57] This merely trades one problem for another, however, since line three already has a recognizable Hebrew equivalent for ἐκκόψωμεν (נדעו).

The solution is more likely found in addressing the question of the plus, ἑαυτοῖς πύργον, which bears a striking resemblance to LXX-Gen

---

[52] The four remaining appearances (all outside Isaiah) are transliterated Παθ-ουρης.

[53] The only other place βαβυλωνία (or βαβυλων) does not correspond to בבל in the MT is 14:23, where the LXX translates ושמתיה with καὶ θήσω τὴν Βαβυλωνίαν. However, this clarification of the 3rd fem. sing. suffix simply compensates for the translation of והכרתי לבבל שם by καὶ ἀπολῶ αὐτῶν ὄνομα in the previous verse.

[54] As recognized by Koenig, L'Herméneutique, 98; Ottley, The Book of Isaiah, 2:156; Seeligmann, Septuagint Version, 78; Ziegler, Untersuchungen, 63 and 109.

[55] 1QIsaᵃ = MT. 4QIsaᶜ preserves only שוקמי נבנה, whose final incomplete form leaves the editors in a quandary as to whether the waw is an orthographic difference or makes it a variant (Ulrich et al., eds., Qumran Cave 4 X, , 47). S's ܪܒܝܢ for נפלו likely reflects haplography in its Vorlage (N.B. וגזית following), causing it to render the remainder accordingly: ܘܢܒܢܐ ܠܢ ܩܣܛܪܐ ܘܡܓܕܠܐ ܢܣܒ ܘܢܣܩ. V's Vorlage = MT, while T departs too widely to assess.

[56] The idea of cutting stones is semantically related to גזית, while its prefixed waw has been rendered by ἀλλά. ἐκκόψωμεν corresponds to נדעו, συκαμίνους to שקמים, and καὶ κέδρους to וארזים, while οἰκοδομήσωμεν corresponds to נבנה, even if its place in the sentence differs.

[57] Koenig, L'Herméneutique, 94–95.

11:4a: καὶ εἶπαν Δεῦτε οἰκοδομήσωμεν ἑαυτοῖς πόλιν καὶ πύργον. The hypothesis that LXX-Isaiah translated 10:9(10) under the influence of Gen 11:4 explains not only the plus, but also why οἰκοδομήσωμεν stands at a later point than נבנה; and it accounts for another, more minor plus: δεῦτε.[58]

The influence of Genesis 11 is already apparent with λαξεύσωμεν λίθους, reminiscent of Gen 11:3: (δεῦτε) πλινθεύσωμεν πλίνθους. Like that phrase, this one is introduced by δεῦτε and is constructed of a volative + cognate external accusative. Given the clear impress of Gen 11:4 on the end of the verse, it is likely that the shape of this phrase equally bears its impress.[59]

It is evident, therefore, that in 9:10(9), 10:9, and 11:11 the translator looked to the story of the tower in Genesis for both phraseology and a means of casting whole verses. Koenig's protest that this reduces the translator to "un amateur d'antiquités bibliques"[60] misunderstands its significance as evidence that the Isaiah translator did not set out simply to render his *Vorlage* into Greek, but on occasion expounded it in its broader web of relationships to the Torah. As Hanhart states, "the theologoumenon that the Torah is the origin of the canon and the basis of the נביאים ראשנים, אחרנים and of the כתובים is actualized and confirmed in the translation of the LXX itself."[61]

These examples give good reason, then, to endorse Seeligmann's perception that a line inserted at the end of 48:21 evidences the translator borrowing from the LXX-Pentateuch:[62]

---

[58] As already observed by Ziegler, *Untersuchungen*, 63.

[59] Even though I cannot agree with Koenig's conclusion that the translator infused 9:10(9) with reminiscences of the story of the tower so as to discredit the Samaritan community, he has correctly identified the influence of Genesis 11 here, thus showing the extent to which the translator was affected by that story (*L'Herméneutique*, 92). Van der Kooij has pointed out the fallacy in Koenig's assumption that "Samaria" would have univocally raised the specter of the Samaritan schism, noting that the Greek text of Ben Sira 50:26 distinguishes between οἱ καθήμενοι ἐν ὄρει Σαμαρείας and ὁ λαὸς ὁ μωρὸς ὁ κατοικῶν ἐν Σικίμοις ("Accident or Method?" 370). He also notes that Koenig fails to pay adequate attention to equally striking and significant differences with the MT in the context of v. 9 (ibid.).

[60] Koenig, *L' Herméneutique*, 101 n. 30.

[61] Hanhart, "The Translation of the Septuagint," 359–60.

[62] 1QIsaᵃ reads הוליכו for הוליכם, and הזיב for הזיל. 4QIsaᵈ preserves only בחרבות הזיל, הוליכם מים מצר, and it must be noted that בחרבות is written superlinearly over הוליכם, while only the tops of צר הזיל are visible, leaving some uncertainty about the readings. S lacks an equivalent for ולא צמאו, while its ܐܘܪ would be a good equivalent for either הזיל (MT) or הזיב (1QIsaᵃ). V's *Vorlage* = MT, despite the syntactic reformulation of ולא צמאו בחרבות הוליכם: *non sitierunt in deserto cum educeret eos* (≠ יוציאם; cf. *qui*

וְלֹא צָמְאוּ בָּחֳרָבוֹת הוֹלִיכָם	καὶ ἐὰν διψήσωσιν δι' ἐρήμου ἄξει αὐτούς
מַיִם מִצּוּר הִזִּיל לָמוֹ	ὕδωρ ἐκ πέτρας ἐξάξει αὐτοῖς
וַיִּבְקַע צוּר וַיָּזֻבוּ מָיִם	σχισθήσεται πέτρα καὶ ῥυήσεται ὕδωρ
----------	καὶ πίεται ὁ λαός μου

As Zillessen had already detected, the final clause was drawn from
Exod 17:6:[63]

וְהִכִּיתָ בַצּוּר וְיָצְאוּ מִמֶּנּוּ מַיִם	καὶ πατάξεις τὴν πέτραν καὶ ἐξελεύσεται
	ἐξ αὐτῆς ὕδωρ
וְשָׁתָה הָעָם	καὶ πίεται ὁ λαός μου

While one might posit that καὶ πίεται ὁ λαός μου in 48:21 reflects a
harmonization in the *Vorlage* or is a scribal interpolation predating our
ms evidence, the foregoing examples justify Seeligmann's assertion that
this phrase provides "decisive evidence that our translator quoted the
Greek text of the Pentateuch."[64]

The translator's interest in reading Isaiah in the light of the Torah
(and helping others to do so) finds parallels in other Jewish literature
of the era. Elsewhere we find intertextual readings based on analogy,
as in *Liber antiquitatum biblicarum* 17, where Moses' collection of staffs
from the tribes (Num 17) leads to a comparison with the story of Jacob
setting up rods via which he acquired sheep for himself from Laban's
flock (Gen 30:37–39). Likewise, 4QFlor 1:14–16a interprets Psalm 1:1
in the light of Isa 8:11, explicitly marking the comparison with Isaiah.
In these cases, however, the analogy is explicit, differentiating them from
what we find in LXX-Isaiah, even if the phenomenon of intertextual
interpretation is the same.

A closer parallel is the way *Liber antiquitatum biblicarum* refash-
ions Joshua's farewell address with a series of phrases drawn from
Deuteronomy, Job, and Isaiah. Whereas Josh 24:1 introduces Joshua's
valedictory with the messenger formula (כֹּה אָמַר יהוה אֱלֹהֵי יִשְׂרָאֵל),
in *L.A.B.* 23:2 Joshua begins his address with the words of Deut 6:4,
followed by language with a similarly Deuteronomic ring: "Hear, O
Israel. Behold I am establishing with you a covenant of this Law that
the LORD established for your fathers on Horeb." The author does not

---

eduxit || מוֹלִיךְ in 63:12). T's *Vorlage* = MT, although it translates the first four verbs as
imperatives (וּבוֹזֵע, אָפִיק, דברינון, וְלֹא אַצְהִינוּן).
[63] Zillessen, "Bermerkungen," 243–44. Ziegler notes this in his apparatus and places
καὶ πίεται ὁ λαός μου in brackets, although without giving sufficient manuscript evidence
to place its textual validity in doubt.
[64] Seeligmann, *Septuagint Version*, 46.

dispense entirely with the messenger formula, however. We are told that after adjourning the assembly,

> Joshua rose up in the morning and gathered all the people and said to them, "The Lord says this: 'There was one rock from which I quarried out your father. And the cutting of that rock bore two men whose names are Abraham and Nahor, and out of the chiseling of that place were born two women whose names are Sarah and Melcha, and they lived together across the river. And Abraham took Sarah as a wife, and Nahor took Melcha.'" (23:4)

Notably, this paragraph comprises an exposition of Job 24:2, Isa 51:1–2, and Gen 11:29, extending the scriptural pastiche already evident in Joshua's valedictory.

Likewise, Jubilees 17 introduces into its recounting of the ʿaqedah the motif of Prince Mastema goading God to demand that Abraham sacrifice Isaac in order to "know whether he is faithful in everything in which you test him" (Jub 17:16), under the influence of Job 1–2. Conversely, in *Liber antiquitatum biblicarum* 40 Jephthah's daughter explains her willingness to submit to sacrifice by referring to the ʿaqedah (*LAB* 40:2). That use of this character's words to introduce the analogy is as subtle as the Isaiah's translator's insertion of οὗ ὁ πύργος ᾠκοδομήθη into Isa 10:9.

Even more noteworthy is a comparison between the translator's reading Isaiah in the light of the Torah and the way Alexandrian γραμματικοί read Homer in the light of other revered Greek poets. Particularly important is Aristarchus, who by the first century B.C.E. had acquired such esteem that Athenaeus has Ulpian refer to him as Ἀρίσταρχος ὁ γραμματικώτατος (Deipnosophistae 15.671–672). Aristarchus assumed that Homer adhered strictly to a set of poetic principles, so that he wrote as a φιλότεχνος ('artist').[65] The τέχνη by which he considered Homer to have written was, above all, concerned with the poet's purpose of moving the plot towards a specific end,[66] so that in editing Homer it is necessary to ask whether the line in question is necessary (ἀναγκαῖος) or superfluous (οὐκ ἀναγκαῖος), serves a purpose (πρὸς ὠφέλειαν) or is pointless (πρὸς οὐδέν).[67]

---

[65] Meijering, *Literary and Rhetorical Theories*, 173.
[66] Ibid., 182.
[67] Ibid., 173.

Given his assumption that Homer consistently sought to achieve meaning through the use of poetic τέχνη, Aristarchus took it as his principle to interpret Ὅμηρον ἐξ Ὁμήρου ('Homer from Homer'),[68] although that cannot be reduced to simple comparisons of Homeric phraseology or even comparisons of passages within Homer alone.[69] For Homer, as a practitioner of a poetic τέχνη, participated in a larger phenomenon, poetry itself.[70] Accordingly, Aristarchus is cited in a scolium to *Iliad* 23.638–41, where Nestor speaks of having been defeated by the twin "sons of Aktor," as interpreting that line by a parallel from Hesiod,[71] while "elsewhere, Aristarchus isn't averse to drawing confirming parallels, whether mythological or philological, from Hesiod, and on occasion even from the tragedians."[72] Aristarchus sought to understand Homer's *meaning*, rather than just his words, without abandoning the conviction that his words were the only path to his meaning.[73] To follow that path involved considering Homer's use of poetic or mythic expression, which was not his unique property, but the shared store of all poets. Accordingly, for Aristarchus "poetic 'licence' is never totally 'free' or permissive; it is tightly defined and closely circumscribed by poetic 'rules' and theoretical constraints."[74] When Aristarchus sought "a poetical solution to an interpretive scandal,"[75] therefore, he pursued that solution (λύσις) at the level of mythic composition, for which reason his reading of Homer could be intertextual, even beyond the boundaries of the Homeric corpus.

Accordingly, the fact that the translator of Isaiah should look for the meaning of Isaiah in analogies to other books within the collection his community held sacred is not surprising. The form of contextual interpretation we have seen him engage in by drawing on passages in the Torah is quite explicable under the hypothesis of his familiarity with the work of the Alexandrian γραμματικοί and accords with the use of intertextuality as an interpretative ploy in other Jewish compositions of the Hellenistic era.

---

[68] Pfeiffer's dispute of this as authentically Aristarchean (*History of Classical Scholarship*, 73) is refuted by Porter, "Hermeneutic Lines and Circles," 73–74.

[69] Porter, "Hermeneutic Lines and Circles," 80.

[70] Ibid., 75–76.

[71] Cited by Porter in ibid., 82.

[72] Ibid., 83.

[73] Ibid., 70.

[74] Ibid., 80.

[75] Ibid., 71.

"Contemporizing" Interpretation

As the survey of literature in chapter one recounted, a form of contextual interpretation frequently considered basic to the translator's
Übersetzungsweise is "contemporization." The context, in this case, is not
literary but the translator's historical and political milieu. The idea that
a translator would engage in *Erfüllungsinterpretation* seems peculiar, on
the face of it. But then, this translator's reformulations, substitutions,
and insertions of phraseology from other sources ill accord with what
we consider permissible translation tactics. Therefore, the issue is not
whether we regard "contemporization" as appropriate for a translator,
but whether the phenomena of the translation support this surmise.
If evidence of "contemporization" exists, we must make room for it.
But first we need a clear understanding of "contemporization" and
its parameters.

Eight years before publishing *The Septuagint Version of Isaiah*, Seeligmann included in an essay on "Problems and Perspectives in Modern
Septuagint Research" a section entitled, "Hellenization and Actualization
of the Bible in the Septuagint,"[76] in which he addressed three topics:
"Forms of Hellenization in the Septuagint," "Hellenistic Theology of
the Septuagint," and "Actualization of the Bible in the Septuagint."

Under the first rubric he posited that the translation of the Bible
into Greek transposed it "into an entirely different world of concepts
and notions" than the Hebrew authors "wanted to arouse in the mind
of their contemporaries."[77] For example, whereas Hebrew fused "the
concept of iniquity and punishment" in words like עון and חטא, translation into a language that lacks that fusion brought with it a modification of such concepts, as evident in Num 32:23, where the translator
renders ודעו חטאתכם אשר תמצא אתכם by supplying a different subject
for תמצא—καὶ γνώσεσθε τὴν ἁμαρτίαν ὑμῶν ὅταν ὑμᾶς καταλάβῃ τὰ
κακά—thereby dissecting the sin from its punishment.[78]

Taking up Deissmann's observation that the Septuagintal translators appropriated technical terms of Ptolemaic society, Seeligmann
postulated that the translators "attained, more or less consciously, a

---

[76] I. L. Seeligmann, "Problems and Perspectives in Modern Septuagint Research,"
trans. Judith H. Seeligmann, *Textus* 15 (1990) 169–232.

[77] Ibid., 220.

[78] Ibid., 221.

transposition from the ancient biblical into the Hellenistic atmosphere."[79]
He noted Ziegler's catalogue of ways that the translator of LXX-Isaiah
used the nomenclature of Ptolemaic Egypt to represent in Greek the
world depicted by the Hebrew text. For example, while the Hebrew
of Isa 19:2 describes kingdoms engaging each other in battle ממלכה
בממלכה, the LXX, reflecting its Ptolemaic environment, translates this
phrase with νομὸς ἐπὶ νομόν.[80]

Correspondingly, Seeligmann defined his references to a "Hellenistic
theology" embedded in the Septuagint by explaining that "when the
translators theologized, theirs was a *Jewish* theology" minted under
the impress of life in the Hellenistic era.[81] Especially expressive of this
Jewish "Hellenistic theology" is the identification of תורה so exclusively
with νόμος that "in Psalms about fifteen expressions for wickedness and
impiety are translated by ἀνομία," so that piety comes to be defined
as living according to the νόμος.[82] Likewise, the translators' awareness
of the distinction between Israel and the gentiles is embodied in their
frequent use of λαός "to indicate God's people as opposed to ἔθνη,"[83]
thus elaborating a distinction between עם and גוים sometimes found
but not regularized in the Bible. In the same vein, the translators use
ἅγιον for the temple, but never ἱερόν, the word typically used for Greek
temples, while מזבח is translated with different terms, depending on
whether it designates an Israelite or gentile altar,[84] with θυσιαστήριον
used for the former and βωμός for the latter.[85] Moreover, some texts
explicitly reflect this strong sense of a divide between Jews and Gentiles,
as in Isa 54:15, where הן גור יגור אפס מאותי מי גר אתך עליך יפול is
translated ἰδοὺ προσήλυτοι προσελεύσονταί σοι δι' ἐμοῦ καὶ ἐπὶ σὲ
καταφεύξονται.[86]

While one might expect that the rubric of "Actualization of the Bible
in the Septuagint" would pertain to the translators' perceptions that
prophecies had been fulfilled in their day, Seeligmann defined this "as
continuation and completion of the discussion about the Hellenization

---

[79] Ibid.
[80] Ibid.
[81] Ibid., 223, emphasis mine.
[82] Ibid.
[83] Ibid., 226.
[84] Ibid., 223.
[85] Cf. Hanhart, "The Translation of the Septuagint," 346.
[86] Seeligmann, "Problems and Perspectives," 227.

of Jewish theology in the Septuagint."[87] "Actualization" was his term for the embodiment in the LXX of "the religious praxis and the homilies of Judaism."[88] Siding with Freudenthal's postulation of an indigenous Alexandrian "Hellenistic midrash," against Frankel's hypothesis of the influence of "Palestinian midrash" on Alexandrian Judaism, he cited passages in the LXX that address concerns pertinent to those living within a dominantly Hellenistic city.[89] Thus, for instance, he noted that while LXX-Deuteronomy 23:18 prohibits cultic prostitution, it also "adds a warning against initiation into mysteries"—καὶ οὐκ ἔσται τελισκόμενος ἀπὸ υἱῶν Ισραηλ[90]—thereby embodying "a typical Hellenistic halakah as well as a magnificent example of actualization of the word of the Thorah."[91] Similarly, καὶ τῶν ἐπιλέκτων τοῦ Ισραηλ οὐ διεφώνησεν οὐδὲ εἷς || ואל אצילי בני ישראל לא שלח ידו in Exod 24:11 "obviously derives from a sermon in the Alexandrian synagogue aiming at glorifying the inspired origin of the Septuagint."[92]

In the context of this discussion he adduced examples of what has become central to recent use of the terms "contemporization" and "actualization," especially his perception that LXX-Isaiah 8:8, 14:19–20, and 10:13–15 are actualizing interpretations in which Antiochus Epiphanes "was identified with the ancient kings of Assyria and Babylon," as evidenced by

> the conspicuous fact that ארץ, in all other instances in which it stands for earth or world, is always translated as γῆ, however, in Isa 10, 13, 14 and 37 (also in 23–24), which refer to the world-embracing dominion of the Assyrian-Babylonian king, the rendition is always actualized into οἰκουμένη.[93]

In the final paragraph of the essay, Seeligmann stated what he considered the grounds for positing this sort of Alexandrian "Hellenistic midrash":

> The origin of the Septuagint was in the synagogue, and its uses in synagogal homilies and sermons allow us to qualify it as a Targum; its exegesis is that of the midrash and the very essence of true midrash is

---

[87] Ibid., 228.
[88] Ibid.
[89] Ibid., 228–29.
[90] Ibid., 229.
[91] Ibid.
[92] Ibid., 230.
[93] Ibid., 230–31.

actualization. The Septuagint is a testimony to the awareness which obviously was alive in Alexandrian Jewry...[that] from the Bible the voice of God is daily anew perceivable.[94]

In this statement, "contemporization" and "actualization" are functions of the worshipping community that help to explain the origins of *all* the Greek translations of Hebrew scriptures.

The breadth of Seeligmann's approach to "contemporization" in this essay was replicated in his subsequent tome on LXX-Isaiah, where his chapter on "The Translation as a Document of Jewish-Alexandrian Theology" comprised three rubrics: 1) "epithets and attributes ascribed to God," 2) "other aspects of [the translator's] religiosity," and 3) "God's intervention in history and the fate of Israel."[95]

Under the first rubric he explored how the translation of images and themes in the Hebrew were filtered through Hellenistic ideas, just as he had in his earlier essay. For example, he characterized 65:11's address of those who, forsaking the Kyrios, are ἑτοιμάζοντες τῷ δαίμονι τράπεζαν καὶ πληροῦντες τῇ τύχῃ κέρασμα (|| הערכים לגד שלחן והממלאים למני ||
ממסך) as "a daring contemporization" that juxtaposes "the Hellenistic cult of these two...worshipped as arbiters of fate ('Αγαθὸς) Δαίμων and Τύχη."[96] And he explored the possibility "that certain passages in the Septuagint of Isaiah have been formulated under the influence of the liturgy in the Jewish-Alexandrian milieu,"[97] observing, for example, that ἅγιος ὁ θεὸς ὁ κατοικῶν ἐν ὑψηλοῖς || נשגב יהוה כי שכן מרום in 33:5 "gives the impression of a liturgical text, which impression is confirmed by the singular rendering נשגב by ἅγιος, and by ἐν ὑψηλοῖς."[98] Even more so, he finds in 57:15 evidence of "liturgical influences" that can "hardly be evaded":[99]

כי כה אמר רם ונשא	τάδε λέγει κύριος ὁ ὕψιστος
שכן עד וקדוש	ὁ ἐν ὑψηλοῖς κατοικῶν τὸν αἰῶνα ἅγιος ἐν ἁγίοις
שמו מרום וקדוש אשכון	ὄνομα αὐτῷ κύριος ὕψιστος ἐν ἁγίοις ἀναπαυόμενος

---

[94] Ibid., 232.
[95] Seeligmann, *Septuagint Version*, 96–103, 103–10, and 110–20, respectively.
[96] Ibid., 99.
[97] Ibid., 101.
[98] Ibid., 102.
[99] Ibid.

He found confirmation that the phrase ἅγιος ἐν ἁγίοις arose from the liturgy in its subsequent use in 3 Macc 2:2 (ἅγιε ἐν ἁγίοις μόναρχε παντοκράτωρ) and 2:21 (προπάτωρ ἅγιος ἐν ἁγίοις), as well as in *Ascen. Isa.* 6:8, where the LXX's translation of Isa 57:15 "is quoted as a hymnic prayer."[100]

Also in the course of these comments he noted that Flashar's observations about the prominent role of νόμος in the Psalms, accompanied by a prodigious use of ἄνομος and ἀνομία, apply equally to LXX-Isaiah, whose translator "resorted to the term ἀνομεῖν whenever he was in need of a synonym, or wished to give the Greek equivalent of a term he found difficult to translate, e.g. אָוֶן, שֶׁקֶר, שֹׁדֵד, פֶּשַׁע, חָנֵף," and used ἀνομία for "both current and rare Hebrew words signifying vice or evil."[101] It was in this context that he discussed passages in which the translator attacks "irreligiousness and disloyalty as the denial of the law," such as 24:16's οὐαὶ τοῖς ἀθετοῦσιν οἱ ἀθετοῦντες τὸν νόμον (|| אוֹי לִי בֹּגְדִים בָּגָדוּ וּבֶגֶד בּוֹגְדִים בָּגָדוּ) and, even more poignantly, 8:16's τότε φανεροὶ ἔσονται οἱ σφραγιζόμενοι τὸν νόμον τοῦ μὴ μαθεῖν (|| צוֹר תְּעוּדָה חֲתוֹם תּוֹרָה בְּלִמֻּדָי), as well as its broader context, where "one gets the impression that the translator is polemizing [sic] against a certain group of people who fail to recognize the binding force of the law, or refuse to see in it more than the face value of the words."[102] For the translator and his religious community, on the other hand, νόμον γὰρ εἰς βοήθειαν ἔδωκεν (sc. ὁ θεός) || לְתוֹרָה וְלִתְעוּדָה (8:20).[103]

Also of significance for Seeligmann were indications of the translator's view of prophecy. Although he conceded that LXX-Isaiah does not permit a full reconstruction of the translator's understanding of prophecy, he found sufficient grounds "to make a few marginal notes."[104] Thus, in providing a rendition of 21:10 "practically independent of the Hebrew text," the translator "must have had in mind his exiled compatriots" as the true referents of Isaiah's words:[105]

---

[100] Ibid.
[101] Ibid., 105.
[102] Ibid., 105–06.
[103] Ibid., 106. On this passage, see below, p. 231.
[104] Ibid., 109.
[105] Ibid.

מדשתי ובן גרני	ἀκούσατε οἱ καταλελειμμένοι καὶ οἱ ὀδυνώμενοι
אשר שמעתי מאת יהוה צבאות	ἀκούσατε ἃ ἤκουσα παρὰ κυρίου σαβαωθ
אלהי ישראל הגדתי לכם	ὁ θεὸς τοῦ Ισραηλ ἀνήγγειλεν ἡμῖν

Even more important for understanding the translator's view of prophecy, in Seeligmann's view, was that the translator, in contrast to the biblical assumption that prophesy *occasions* what happens, viewed prophecy as "only foretelling that which is yet to happen," as evident in the rendering of 42:9 (καὶ καινὰ ἃ ἐγὼ ἀναγγελῶ καὶ πρὸ τοῦ ἀνατεῖλαι ἐδηλώθη ὑμῖν || וחדשות אני מגיד בטרם תצמחנה אשמיע אתכם), where the prophet himself speaks of announcing "new things" that were revealed (ἐδηλώθη) by God himself.[106] Such proclamations are the revelation of "an age-old plan" (as stated in 37:26: οὐ ταῦτα ἤκουσας πάλαι ἃ ἐγὼ ἐποίησα ἐξ ἀρχαίων ἡμερῶν συνέταξα νῦν δὲ ἐπέδειξα || הלוא[107] שמעת למרחוק אותה עשיתי מימי קדם ויצרתיה) that amount to "announcing God's intervention in the fate of the peoples."[108]

Seeligmann opined that the translator's interest was not just in anticipated fulfillments but also in prophecy already fulfilled, such that he viewed "God's Judgment, proclaimed by the prophet as an impending threat…as the actualized reality of Galuth."[109] This, he claimed, opens a unique window on "the Galuth psychology of Alexandrian Jewry," since LXX-Isaiah breathes the atmosphere of the διασπορά suffering under foreign oppressors.[110] In that milieu, the translator's interest in the theme of salvation comes to bear "the meaning of 'liberation from a powerful political enemy'…and this could quite naturally evolve into 'deliverance from exile,'"[111] even as "we read in 44.23, of Israel liberated from exile: ὅτι ἐλυτρώσατο ὁ θεὸς τὸν Ιακωβ καὶ Ισραηλ δοξασθήσεται (Massoretic text: ובישראל יתפאר)."[112] Similarly, 11:16's proclamation of a path from Assyria for Israel's survivors is transformed into a promise to those *in Egypt*—καὶ ἔσται δίοδος τῷ καταλειφθέντι μου λαῷ ἐν Αἰγύπτῳ || והיתה מסלה לשאר עמו אשר ישאר מאשור—just as 19:25 pronounces a benediction on those who are *in* Egypt and Assyria—εὐλογημένος ὁ

---

[106] Ibid.
[107] Ibid., 110.
[108] Ibid., 109
[109] Ibid., 110
[110] Ibid., 111–12, quotation from 111.
[111] Ibid., 114.
[112] Ibid., 116.

λαός μου ὁ ἐν Αἰγύπτῳ καὶ ὁ ἐν ᾽Ασσυρίοις | | ברוך עמי מצרים ומעשה
ידי אשור—which suggests that the translator "regarded the diaspora in
Egypt, to which he himself belonged, as the rightful recipient of the
prophetically promised salvation."[113]

Five observations on Seeligmann's detection of "contemporization"
and "actualization" are salient. First, his identification of a Ptolemaic
background and a Hellenistic strain of Jewish thought betrayed by
lexical items and images is beyond doubt, at least in principle if not
always in its details.

Second, Seeligmann's reconstruction of the *Weltanschauung* of Alexandrian Jews through divergences between the LXX and the MT would
be untenable if offered today, insofar as his direct comparison of the
two textual traditions has been undermined by the discoveries from
the Judean desert. Even if at points in his monograph he recognizes
that the translator found variants in his *Vorlage*, Seeligmann could confidently reconstruct his "Jewish Hellenistic theology" from the wide
divergences with the MT that struck him as indubitably originating with
the translator.

In light of the discoveries in the caves of the Judean desert, we
know too much to work as Seeligmann did. Only if we are willing to
allow that such divergences may point to a divergent *Vorlage* and take
into consideration all the textual witnesses among the DSS and the
other versions (on which Seeligmann is virtually silent) can we hope
to ascertain to what degree apparently "free" renderings may point to
ideas attributable to the translator.

Third, Seeligmann's uses of "contemporization" or "actualization"
were very broad, for they were vehicles, in his view, to recover the ethos
of the Alexandrian Jewish community and to reconstruct the ideology
of the translator. Strikingly, the space he devotes to Jewish-Alexandrian
"theology" and the community's milieu is greater than his detection
of allusions to political realia in the translator's day. For Seeligmann,
mantological exegesis is but one component of what he terms the
translator's midrashic approach, not its essence.

Moreover, it is difficult to gainsay many of Seeligmann's observations
of what the translation reveals of his community's assumptions and
ideas. For example, Flashar's observations about the use of the νόμος
word group that Seeligmann saw embodied in LXX-Isaiah are easy

---

[113] Ibid., 117.

enough to confirm, as we will find in chapter seven.[114] Additionally, as Seeligmann noted, Ziegler had already provided an impressive catalog of *Ägyptizismen* from the realms of agriculture, topography, irrigation, "die ägyptische Tierwelt," official terms for weights and measures, "Fachwörter gewerblicher Art," legal terminology, Ptolemaic "Beamtenbezeichnungen," Egyptian geography, and the general milieu of second century Ptolemaic Egypt.[115] His survey left no doubt about the general influence of the Alexandrian milieu on the translation.

Neither is there reason to doubt the impact of the translator's worshipping community on his work, including the possibility that some of the phrases Seeligmann identified actually derive from liturgical life, just as Ulrich Luz has isolated phrases in the Gospel of Matthew's redaction of the Jesus tradition that likely reflect confessions and liturgical formulations used within the redactor's religious community.[116] Seeligmann's detection of glimpses of the translator's milieu through his renderings remains plausible, whatever the fate of his observations about reflections of the historical-political circumstances of the Alexandrian Jewish community.

Consequently (and fourth), it is significant that Seeligmann reconstructs "Jewish-Alexandrian theology" from sporadic intimations rather than considering them a readily retrievable product of an exegetical agenda. This is the significance of his skepticism about "particularly ingenious and particularly purposeful efforts to discover logical connexions in any chapter or part of a chapter in our Septuagint-text," in place of which he found reason to try "to discover, in isolated, free renderings, certain historical allusions or expressions of the translators own views and ideas."[117] For Seeligmann, because the translator was essentially "a slave to the text he was translating,"[118] windows into his Jewish Alexandrian milieu are available only through "alterations in meaning" that are "very subtle in character," or through instances

---

[114] Cf. Olley's report that "ἀνομία and ἄνομος are used of Israel in 38 out of 42 occurrences, the exceptions being 13:11 and 24:20 (both being general references), and possibly 59:4, 6 (the people amongst whom the Jews are living)" (John W. Olley, *'Righteousness' in the Septuagint of Isaiah* [Septuagint and Cognate Studies 8; Missoula: Scholars, 1979] 122).

[115] Ziegler, "Der alexandrinische-ägyptische Hintergrund der Js-LXX," in idem, *Untersuchungen,* 175–212.

[116] Ulrich Luz, *Matthew 1–7* (Minneapolis: Augsburg Press, 1989) 77.

[117] Seeligmann, *Septuagint Version,* 41.

[118] Ibid., 120.

when "the translator did not understand the Hebrew text before him, and arbitrarily altered it, or gave an erroneous interpretation of it," in which cases his (and his community's) views were "introduced—probably unconsciously—as a result of the theological attitude in which the translator approached the Hebrew text, and which, in effect, suggested certain misinterpretations to his mind."[119] For Seeligmann, glimpses into "Alexandrian-Jewish theology" are fortuitous, not the result of a program or a method.

Finally, Seeligmann's belief in the Isaiah translator's occasional revelation of contemporary circumstances operated within his theory about the origins of the LXX as a whole. He did not argue that the Isaiah translator's *Übersetzungsweise* was different from other translators, even if that translator's frequent perplexities spurred renditions that allowed his milieu to peak through more often than in other books. The perception of allusions to the translator's milieu were tied to a liturgical model for the origins of the LXX as a whole.

Indeed, it is notable that the perdurance of Seeligmann's perception of "contemporizations" is due, in part, to the identification of a different model to account for them. Das Neves, van der Kooij, and Koenig have pointed to the *pesharim* as the template for understanding the "contemporization" or "actualization" Seeligmann first noted in LXX-Isaiah. Moreover, the stress on the literary unity achieved by the translator as suggested by Coste and raised to a principle by van der Kooij has taken the parallel with the *pesharim* to the point of suggesting that the translator undertook his translation of whole units with an eye to accentuating their fulfillment in the translator's era.[120] As noted in chapter one, Koenig's study of parallels in the interpretation of Isaiah at Qumran and in LXX-Isaiah (*L' Herméneutique*) sought to detect a "method" behind both. And despite reservations about Koenig's procedures in positing the persons or events to which an actualizing rendering referred, van der Kooij has agreed in principle with Koenig's conclusion that "variant-readings in LXX Is are intentional, if they serve the actualization of the prophecies aimed at by the translator."[121] The

---

[119] Ibid., 96.

[120] With regard to Coste, I am thinking especially of his "Le texte Grec," particularly his treatment of 25:1–5 under the rubric, "Le texte comme unité littérarire" ("Le texte Grec," 45–51). For van der Kooij, see particularly his early article, "A Short Commentary," 36–37.

[121] Van der Kooij, "Accident or Method?" 371.

upshot has been that, over the past quarter century, "contemporization" and "actualization" have become equivalent to *Erfüllungsinterpretation*, elevating a subsidiary aspect of Seeligmann's program to prominence and placing questions about other sorts of "contemporization" in the background.

This elevation of *Erfüllungsinterpretation* is understandable in light of the fascination the *pesharim* and the form(s) of exegesis used in them have inspired. Once Seeligmann isolated what he saw as allusions to the historical-political circumstances of the translator's community, and once the Habakkuk *pesher* came to light (again, a resource not known to Seeligmann when he wrote his monograph), viewing Seeligmann's perceptions through the lens of the *pesharim* became virtually inevitable.[122]

The recognition of this shift is not a verdict that the focus on *Erfüllungsinterpretation* is baseless, but it is important to draw attention to Seeligmann's original focus on *various* forms of "contemporization." And in doing so, I want to raise the question of how we might recognize any type of "contemporization," although especially *Erfüllungsinterpretation*. What are the marks that the translator's social, historical-political, and religious environments have created interference in his rendering of Isaiah?

Van der Kooij's five step method for recognizing *Erfüllungsinterpretation* proceeds from (1) establishing the text of the LXX, through (2) alignment of formal Greek-Hebrew lexical equivalents, through (3) assessment of the translator's interpretation of the semantics and grammar of his *Vorlage* and whether that resulted in a meaningful literary unit, through (4) comparison of the lexical equivalents to identify indications of exegesis or the translator's reliance on parallel passages, to (5) identifying the contemporary referents implicit in the translator's exegesis, what van der Kooij terms "the level of actualization."[123] However, as with the three

---

[122] As Hanhart and Spieckermann point out, Seeligmann's own fascination with the political and social perils of the Jews in the Hellenistic era were not a matter of detached scholarly investigation but accord with the circumstances of his own life as a Jew in the Netherlands of the 1940's. While noting that Seeligmann largely excluded references to those events from his writings (although see the preface to his *Septuagint Version*), they observe that "the careful reader...will realize that the history of Israel during the Hellenistic period...serves as the background for the interpretation of the history of the Jewish people in his own time" (Robert Hanhart and Hermann Spieckermann, eds., *The Septuagint Version of Isaiah and Cognate Studies* [Forschungen zum alten Testament 40; Tübingen: Mohr Siebeck, 2004] v).
[123] Van der Kooij, "Accident or Method?" 368–70.

step method detailed in his *The Oracle of Tyre*, van der Kooij assumes that "contemporization" enlivens every stage of the translator's rendering of his source text. As a result, he rarely concludes that the translator's *Vorlage* read anything different than the MT and always argues that the translator's divergences from it embody *Erfüllungsinterpretation*.

If, on the other hand, we do not start with the assumption that divergences from the MT reflect exegesis or, if exegesis occurs, do not necessarily reflect *Erfüllungsinterpretation*, how are we to recognize cases of contemporization? And here the point at issue is how to test the hypothesis of *Erfüllungsinterpretation*, since contemporizations that involve substituting Hellenistic toponyms for ancient ones or use Ptolemaic *Beamtenbezeichnungen* lie on the surface and, thus, are easily detectable. The tricky matter is how to determine whether a rendering attributable to the translator's exegesis reflects perception of prophecy fulfilled in events of his era.

The issue is defining what sorts of textual markers are sufficient to conclude that the translator deliberately alluded to events in his world as the "true" referent of the prophet's oracle. Van der Kooij argues that key to recognizing these is "a good knowledge of the history of the Hellenistic period, and of the literature, biblical and non-biblical, Jewish and non-Jewish, of this period."[124] Undoubtedly that is true, but satisfying that requirement may do little more than equip one to find correlations between the text and history that rely on an insubstantial correspondence.

The problem with comparing the supposed *Erfüllungsinterpretation* of the translator with the *pesharim* is that the latter are explicit in their alignment of the text with contemporaneous events, whereas we have to extrapolate from oblique statements in a translation to what the translator might have had in view, which raises the thorny issue of intention. When we are dealing with a work whose substance is derived from its Hebrew exemplar, how can we ascertain what mental process created what we perceive as a historical allusion?

Boyd-Taylor has drawn attention to this problem, calling for "a principled distinction between translational and non-translational discourse."[125] Because a translation has an already existent text as its base, "the evidential value of a translation is categorically different from

---

[124] Ibid., 369.
[125] Boyd-Taylor, "In a Mirror Dimly," 16.

assessing that of a non-translational text."[126] Citing Barr's maxim that one must "attempt to discover the method by which translators read Hebrew texts and decided on a rendering,"[127] Boyd-Taylor contends that one cannot assume that a divergent rendering is mantological exegesis without considering what linguistic factors might have led to the translation.[128] This is, indeed, the minimum requirement.

Hanhart has addressed the same issue, contending that "the LXX is the actualization of the contemporary history of the translator only when the choice of the Greek equivalent is capable of doing justice both to the factuality and history of the original Hebrew witness and also to the contemporary history of the translator."[129] However, this raises the question of how we know that the translator *intended* to allude to contemporary events or persons if his rendering also "does justice" to "the original Hebrew witness." What do we do once we have concluded that the translator arrived at his rendering with an eye to literary context in a way that can also be aligned with circumstances or events we know of from the Hellenistic era?

Here Aejmelaeus's dictum about gauging the translator's intention is relevant: "The intended meaning is the meaning that can be read from the translation. As a matter of fact, it is only through the translated text that we know anything about the intentions of the translator."[130] She has since provided a useful clarification of this principle by insisting that understanding the translator's intent, whether in matters of theology or contemporization, can be accomplished "nur in Vergleich zum hebräischen Original und als Ergebnis des Übersetzungsprozesses."[131] And such comparison is useful only when the translation deviates from the *Vorlage*, for

> erst durch das Hinzukommen von interpretativen Elementen, durch Nuancierung oder Verschiebung oder Änderung der einzelnen Aussagen im Vergleich zum Original wird es möglich, dass der Zweck oder der Kontext der Übersetzung veratten wird.[132]

---

[126] Ibid., 17.
[127] Barr, "Common Sense," 379.
[128] Boyd-Taylor, "In a Mirror Dimly," 21.
[129] Hanhart, "The Translation of the Septuagint," 342–43.
[130] Aejmelaeus, "Translation Technique," 30.
[131] Idem, "Von Sprache zur Theologie," 24.
[132] Ibid., 21.

Embracing this principle requires a minimalist approach: only if the translator can be shown to refer deliberately to people, countries, ethnic groups, circumstances, or events by deviating from his *Vorlage* is it legitimate to entertain the possibility that he sought to identify such entities as the "true" referents of his Hebrew exemplar. More stringently, it must be shown that the translator did not arrive at a rendering by reasoning from the immediate or broader *literary* contexts, but that he fashioned it with an eye to circumstances or events in his day.

The minimum threshold for explicitness needed to draw such a conclusion is illustrated by the Gospel of Matthew's modifications of Q tradition in the parable of the banquet (Matt 22:1–14 || Luke 14:15–24) to reflect knowledge of the Roman sack of Jerusalem.[133] I adduce this example because this redactor, like the translator of Isaiah, utilizes a tradition he has received but reshapes it to reflect events of his day (albeit retaining the source language).

In this parable, which tells of a host's extension of invitations to a banquet, Matthew and Luke agree that the guests rebuffed the invitation, but Matthew alone has the host reissue it (v. 4).[134] On the other hand, while Matthew alludes to the reasons the guests declined the original invitation, Luke catalogs their specific excuses (vv. 18–20). However, Matthew alone has the invitees abusing and even killing the messengers who bring the renewed invitation (v. 6). Similarly, although both Matthew and Luke portray the host piqued by his guests spurning his invitation, only Matthew has him sending troops against them to burn their city (v. 7). And even though Matthew, like Luke, has the host summon a new set of guests, Luke's story of the host's desperate search for alternate dinner guests among the lower classes makes better narrative sense than Matthew's scenario of mistreatment of the servants bringing the renewed invitation, leading to the host's launch of a military campaign against them, and then the extension of an

---

[133] See W. D. Davies and Dale C. Allison, *The Gospel according to St. Matthew*, vol. 1 (ICC; Edinburgh: T & T Clark, 1988) 131–22.

[134] Even taking into account evidence of heavy editing in Mathew and some in Luke, most likely each derived this from independent traditions (Ulrich Luz, *Matthew 21–28* [Hermeneia; Minneapolis: Fortress Press, 2005] 47). The same judgment applies to the similar parable in Gos. Thom. 64 (W. D. Davies and Dale C. Allison, *The Gospel According to St. Matthew*, vol. 3, [ICC; Edinburgh: T & T Clark, 1997] 195). Davies and Allison conclude that "the thoroughly Matthean character of Mt. 22:1–10 suggests to us that the First Evangelist adopted oral tradition" (ibid., 194).

invitation to new guests.[135] The military campaign seems particularly out of place in that scenario.

To understand the distinctive elements in Matthew's story we must compare with this parable the earlier parable of the wicked tenants (Matt 21:33–46), inasmuch as it has influenced the shape of Matt. 22:1–14.[136]

That parable describes a landowner setting up a vineyard (based on Isaiah five's song of the vineyard) and leaving it in the care of farmers who mistreat two sets of servants sent to collect the owner's share at harvest time and ultimately kill the owner's son. When Jesus asks the crowd what they think the landowner should do with these mutinous tenets, they reply that he should destroy them and replace them with tenets who will give the owner his due (v. 41). It is in this parable that we find the theme of sending out a second wave of messengers and a report that the servants were mistreated or even killed, both distinctive features in Matthew's parable of the banquet. We also find here the theme of destroying those who mistreat the messengers, a motif present in Matthew's parable of the banquet, but absent from Luke's version. There is little doubt that Matthew imported these themes from that parable into his parable of the banquet.

However, this doesn't account for all the wrinkles in Matthew's banquet parable. In Luke the invitations are issued by the owner of an estate who has servants at his disposal. Matthew, by contrast, identifies the host as a king (22:2), a motif not found in Matthew's parable of the wicked tenants. Moreover, in contrast to the parable of the wicked tenets in Matthew 21, where the landowner κακοὺς κακῶς ἀπολέσει αὐτούς, the king of Matthew 22 not only destroys his servants' murderers, but also has his troops set fire to their city. The assumption that all the invited guests are from the same city permits the king's wrath to be expended against a city rather than disparate guests, but this is unique to Matthew.[137]

These distinctive features are best accounted for as reflecting Matthew's knowledge of the sack of Jerusalem by Titus's army.[138] By conceiving

---

[135] Cf. Davies and Allison: "Matthew's version is even more removed from the original—as well as from the real world" (Davies and Allison, *Matthew*, vol. 3, 196).

[136] Ibid., 197. Cf. Luz, *Matthew 21–28*, 47.

[137] Cf. Anthony J. Saldarini, *Matthew's Christian-Jewish Community* (Chicago Studies in the History of Judaism; Chicago: University of Chicago Press, 1994) 63.

[138] Davies and Allison, *Matthew*, vol. 3, 201–02; Luz, *Matthew 21–28*, 54.

an attacking army as an agent of divine judgment (a motif common among Israel's prophets), Matthew invests a parable about Israel's rejection of divine emissaries with new significance as an explanation for the fall of Jerusalem to the Romans. His redaction exemplifies not only the tactic of intertextual reading but also reformulation of a unit in the light of current events.

Parallel to the method posited for the Isaiah translator, Matthew does not explicitly point to Jerusalem's fall as a fulfillment of the speaker's words, but simply interweaves what he knows of Jerusalem's fate into his redaction. It is only Matthew's introduction of features absent from his sources but relevant to the Roman's destruction of Jerusalem in 70 c.e. that discloses his intent to contemporize the traditions he had received.

Identifying "contemporizations" in LXX-Isaiah, on the other hand, presents special hurdles. Detecting Matthew's reflections of his era is simplified by our ability to assume that he understood the traditions he received, since they were in the same language in which he composed his work. That assumption allows us to infer that changes to the warp and woof of a pericope reflect his intention. For the same reason, we can assume that recurring vocabulary, phrases, and grammatical structures unique to his gospel (among the Synoptics) embody his intention. On the other hand, because LXX-Isaiah is a translation, we must always consider whether a divergence from the MT reflects the translator's misunderstanding of the Hebrew or an attempt to complete a verse when his construal of its initial words have set him on a difficult course. Additionally, the fact that deviations from the MT recur in several passages may mean nothing more than that the translator followed similar paths in trying to rescue verses he found inscrutable, as evidenced by "stop-gap" words like ἡττᾶσθαι. And above all, given the complex textual history of the Hebrew Bible, we must consider whether a divergence reflects a variant in the translator's *Vorlage*. All of these special problems are raised by the fact that this is a translation, and they compel raising the bar for identifying contemporizations beyond what suffices for Matthew.

It is not enough that a passage that differs from the MT—even one demonstrably not based on a *Vorlage* different from the MT—can be aligned with circumstances or events of the Hellenistic period. It must be shown that the translator did not arrive at his rendering by reasoning from the immediate or broader contexts but that he fashioned it with an eye to conditions or events in his day, as indicated by vocabulary or

images that can be explained in no other way. Measured by this standard, most suggested cases of *Erfüllungsinterpretation* fail to persuade.

For example, much has been made of the translator's rendering of
עִיר הַהֶרֶס by πόλισ-ασεδεκ in 19:18:[139]

בַּיּוֹם הַהוּא יִהְיוּ חָמֵשׁ עָרִים בְּאֶרֶץ מִצְרַיִם	τῇ ἡμέρᾳ ἐκείνῃ ἔσονται πέντε πόλεις ἐν Αἰγύπτῳ
מְדַבְּרוֹת שְׂפַת כְּנַעַן	λαλοῦσαι τῇ γλώσσῃ τῇ Χανα-νίτιδι
וְנִשְׁבָּעוֹת לַיהוה צְבָאוֹת	καὶ ὀμνύουσαι τῷ ὀνόματι κυρίου
עִיר הַהֶרֶס יֵאָמֵר לְאֶחָת	πόλισ-ασεδεκ κληθήσεται ἡ μία πόλις

The obstacles Wildberger justly raises to understanding וְנִשְׁבָּעוֹת לַיהוה
צְבָאוֹת as bespeaking Jewish settlements[140] do not apply to καὶ ὀμνύουσαι
τῷ ὀνόματι κυρίου, since in 48:1 the people of Israel and Judah
are called οἱ ὀμνύοντες τῷ ὀνόματι κυρίου (|| הַנִּשְׁבָּעִים בְּשֵׁם יהוה),
which clearly means "those who swear *by* the name of the Kyrios."[141]
Accordingly, the cities of chapter 19 are evidently conceived of as (at
least substantially) Jewish communities.

---

[139] 1QIsaᵃ has a tear that obliterates the וֹ of הַהוּא, while it reads הַהֶרֶס rather
than הַחֶרֶס. 4QIsaᵇ likewise reads הַהֶרֶס, while the remainder of its text (at least those
characters not in lacunae) = MT. S attests a *Vorlage* = MT, including its rendering of עִיר
הַהֶרֶס יֵאָמֵר לְאֶחָת with ܐܓܪ ܡܬ݂ܐܡܪܐ ܠܚܕܐ ܡܕ, in which the lack of an equivalent
for עִיר is likely a stylistic omission of an element considered redundant. V accords
with 1QIsaᵃ and 4QIsaᵇ in reading *civitas Solis* for עִיר הַהֶרֶס, but in the remainder it
follows the MT. T accords largely with the MT, but for עִיר הַהֶרֶס reads קִרְתָּא בֵּית שֶׁמֶשׁ
דַּעֲתִידָא לְמֶחֱרַב, suggesting familiarity with *both* חֶרֶס and הֶרֶס. The transliteration given
by both Theodotian and Aquila, αρες, could support either reading, while Symmachus
reads ἡλίου, in accord with הַחֶרֶס.

[140] Wildberger rejects the inference that all Egyptian Jews lived in just five cities, for
which, in any case, "the construction בְּ נשבע (swear by) would have been used," rather
than לְ נשבע, which "has to refer either to Egyptians who had associated themselves
with Judaism or to Jewish communities that sought to win proselytes" (Hans Wildberger,
Isaiah 28–39 [Continental Commentary; Minneapolis: Fortress Press, 2002] 268).

[141] *Pace* Monsengwo-Pasinya, who argues that this Greek phrase means, "those who
swear *to* the name of the Lord," citing Deut 10:20; Isa 48:1; Jer 12:16; 51(44):26;
Zech 5:4 and Mal 3:5 as examples of נשבע בשם meaning "to swear *to* the name" and
rendered by ὀμνύναι τῷ ὀνόματι (Laurent Monsengwo-Pasinya, "Isaïe 19:16–25 et
universalisme dans la LXX," in *Congress Volume, Salamanca* [VTSup 36; Leiden: Brill,
1985] 200). While there insufficient space to review all the passages he cites, in Jer 12:16
(וְהָיָה אִם לָמֹד יִלְמְדוּ אֶת־דַּרְכֵי עַמִּי לְהִשָּׁבֵעַ בִּשְׁמִי חַי יהוה || καὶ ἔσται ἐὰν μαθόντες
μάθωσιν τὴν ὁδὸν τοῦ λαοῦ μου τοῦ ὀμνύειν τῷ ὀνόματί μου ζῇ κύριος) the formula
ζῇ κύριος makes it clear that this is a matter of taking an oath בְּשֵׁם יהוה.

As for the other textual witnesses, S accords with the MT's עִיר הַהֶרֶס, while 1QIsaᵃ and 4QIsaᵇ read עִיר הַחֶרֶס, a reading attested also by V's *civitas solis* and Symmachus's ἡλίου. To Aquila and Theodotian is attributed the ambivalent transcription, αρες, while T is familiar with both readings: קרתא בית שמש דעתידא למחרב ('city of the house of the sun which will be destroyed'). The LXX stands out not simply because it attests neither הַהֶרֶס nor הַחֶרֶס, but also because (like Aquila and Theodotian) it entails *transliteration* rather than translation.

Cheyne suggested that the original text read הַחֶרֶס, referring to Heliopolis, and that this was altered by Ptolemaic Jews to הַצֶּדֶק, in support of the temple at Leontopolis, and to הַהֶרֶס by those who condemned it.[142] However, this does not address why הַצֶּדֶק would have been transliterated, given that the LXX provides a translation for each of the 67 occurrences of a noun or verb from צדק in the MT.

F. C. Burkitt proposed that the original reading of the LXX was ασεδ, as attested by the first hand of א, ασεδ ἡλίου, within which he considered ἡλίου a duplicate rendering, based on familiarity with the reading חרס.[143] Underlying ασεδ, he asserted, stood חסד. Aside from the problems raised by Burkitt's cherry picking of ασεδ from א without due attention to the overwhelming attestation of ασεδεκ in the Alexandrian manuscripts, ασεδ raises the question of why the translator would have transliterated חסד, when he provided a Greek equivalent for it in each of its other eight occurrences.[144]

Seeligmann contended that הַצֶּדֶק was the original reading and became displaced by הַהֶרֶס, which he judged a gloss signaling that Heliopolis was the true referent of עִיר הַצֶּדֶק, while הַהֶרֶס reflects a denigration of Heliopolis.[145] However, van der Kooij has justly questioned why the rare חרס would have been chosen as a gloss over שמש.[146] And while Seeligmann calls ασεδεκ a "remarkable transcription," he does not take up the question of why we find a transcription.

---

[142] Cited by Ottley, *The Book of Isaiah*, 2:201.

[143] Cited by Ottley, ibid.

[144] ἔλεος in 16:5; 54:8, 10; 63:7 (¹חסד). δίκαιος in 57:1 and δικαιοσύνη in 63:7 (²חסד). δόξα in 40:6. τὰ ὅσια Δαυιδ τὰ πιστά || הנאמנים דוד חסדי in 55:3.

[145] Seeligmann, *Septuagint Version*, 68. Simons, likewise, argued that עִיר הַהֶרֶס is "a deliberate pejorative alteration…of the original reading עִיר הַצֶּדֶק" (Jan J. Simons, *The Geographical and Topographical Texts of the Old Testament* [Leiden: Brill, 1959] 438). Curiously, Zeigler makes no comment on 19:18.

[146] Van der Kooij, *Die alten Textzeugen*, 53.

Van der Kooij, for his part, noting that ασεδεκ is found only in an Egyptian witness, while all Palestinian witnesses contain חרס or הרס, concludes that the translator interpreted a *Vorlage* that read עיר ההרס in the light of עיר הצדק in 1:26 to provide scriptural support for the Oniad temple at Leontopolis.[147] Noting Josephus's report that Onias IV appealed to Isa 19:19 to justify a temple there (*Ant.* 13.68), van der Kooij posits that "auch V. 18 in diesem Zusammenhang eine wichtige Rolle spielte" in Onias's argument, and he concludes, "es liegt deshalb nahe, die Bezeichnung πόλις ασεδεκ in LXX Jes 19,18 als Legitimation von Leontopolis als Stadt eines jüdischen Tempels zu verstehen."[148] The predicate for this endorsement is the conviction that

> der Tempel von Jerusalem, sei es infolge der Entweihung im Jahr 167 v.Chr., oder sei es wegen eines nicht zum Oniadengeschlecht gehörigen und deshalb 'illegitimen' Hohenpriesters wie Menelaos…, nicht mehr als legitime Stätte angesehen werden konnte.[149]

Although van der Kooij allows that the translator may have been helped to this interpretation by a *Vorlage* that (like 1QIsa[a] and 4QIsa[b]) read הההרס, the motivation remains that the translator regarded the temple at Leontopolis as the only legitimate temple. Noting that Isa 36:7 embodies the notion "dass es nur *eine* legitime Stätte für die Verehrung Gottes gebe," he concludes, "M.E. hat der Übersetzer wegen seiner positiven Einstellung gegenüber dem Oniastempel in Leontopolis auf eine Wiedergabe der entsprechenden Passage verzichtet."[150] What this proposal leaves unanswered, however, is why the translator chose to transliterate הצדק, whereas he translated it in 1:26.

Monsengwo-Pasinya, in attributing ασεδεκ to a *Vorlage* that read הצדק, argues that the translator "a-t-il évité de donner a la ville égyptienne le meme attribute qu'à Jérusalem," although he assigns no motive for this.[151] However, it seems that, under this hypothesis, the translator did not avoid the attribution, but made it more radical by preserving the Hebrew word, thereby suggesting that the Egyptian city is the *true* "city of righteousness." This seems unlikely, however, since in 1:26 he not only translated הצדק, but also, by applying μητρόπολις to Jerusalem, voiced

---

[147] Ibid., 54.
[148] Ibid., 54–55.
[149] Ibid., 55.
[150] Ibid.
[151] Monsengwo-Pasinya, "Isaïe 19:16–25," 201.

his esteem and affection for the city, rather than signaling rejection of it. In short, it is not clear what sort of differentiation the translator would have intended by transliterating הצדק in 19:18.

Alternatively, one might posit that πόλις ασεδεκ had become something of a technical term in Alexandria and Leontopolis for the Oniad temple as the legitimate worship site (no one has done so, as far as I know). However, this proposal already faces an uphill battle, inasmuch as it assumes that v. 18 was an important justification for the temple at Leontopolis, whereas Josephus reports only that Onias appealed to v. 19. Moreover, under that hypothesis, it is not clear why we wind up with the hybrid, πόλις ασεδεκ, since that claim would hinge on the phrase עיר הצדק, in which עיר is not equivalent to a linguistic determinative but is important to the semantic freight of the phrase. One might suggest that the use of πόλις was a concession to the political importance of the πόλις in the Hellenistic world, but granting such a concession begs the question of why transliteration of הצדק would have been considered more advantageous than translation.

In the end, attempts to attribute πόλις ασεδεκ to "contemporization" falter primarily in their inability to explain why the translator should have transliterated הצדק. As we shall soon see, this translator resorts to transliteration when he considers a word a technical term or a proper noun, as in 5:2, where ויטעהו שרק is rendered καὶ ἐφύτευσα ἄμπελον σωρηχ, even though in 16:8 שרוקיה is rendered with τὰς ἀμπέλους αὐτῆς. Similarly, five times he follows the pattern established in the Pentateuch of transliterating שכר with σικερα (5:11, 22; 24:9; 28:7; 29:9). Most frequently transliterated in Isaiah are toponyms, roughly 80% of which are so handled.[152] Given that עיר in 19:18 suggests that what follows could be a name, one can understand why it might be transliterated, but only if it were a standard equivalent for a recognized toponym or if the translator had been unfamiliar with the name.[153]

Already in 1921 Vaccari proposed a satisfactory solution to this problem. Drawing attention to the alternation between תמנת חרס in Judg 2:9 and תמנת סרח in Josh 19:50,[154] and noting Scholz's observation of how frequently the Isaiah translator reads ר as ד, as well as cases in which the LXX transliterates ח with *kappa*, he concluded that the translator's

---

[152] See below, p. 190.
[153] See below, pp. 190–91.
[154] A. Vaccari, "ΠΟΛΙΣ ΑΣΕΔΕΚ Is. 19, 18," *Bib* 2 (1921) 354.

Vorlage contained עיר הסרה, which the translator misread as עיר הסדה.[155] Of course, attributing ד/ר interchanges exclusively to misreading by the translator is tenuous, given what we know about the frequent confusion of these consonants among scribes. In any case, explaining ασεδεκ as a transliteration of הסדה is compelling, not simply because of the graphic similarity, but also because הסדה can be understood as a tendentious modification.

George F. Moore suggested that תמנת חרס in Judg 2:9 was the original toponym ('Timnah of the Sun') and that תמנת סרה in Josh 19:50 and 24:30 is not an accidental transposition of *sāmek* and *ḥêt*, but a tendentious alteration meant to obliterate intimations of solar worship. Kutscher suggested that the readings עיר ההרס and עיר ההרס in Isa 19:18 reflect the same dynamic, with ההרס meant as an aspersion on the original ההרס.[156]

Merging these observations with Vaccari's proposal, it is likely that another scribe altered עיר ההרס to עיר הסרה for the same reason, and that in the translator's *Vorlage* the *rêš* proved impossible to distinguish from a *dāleth*, prompting him to transliterate the unfamiliar word with ασεδεκ. This reconstruction, which I adopt, more credibly explains how the LXX wound up with the transliteration ασεδεκ than supposing that the translator, while reading (or importing) עיר הצדק, forsook the rendering he had used for that phrase in 1:26.[157] Speculating about πόλις ασεδεκ by positing contemporizing exegesis might make for a more intriguing theory of the translator's *Übersetzungsweise*, but it raises problems that cannot be resolved as readily as they can via this philological explanation.

In the end, there seem to be inadequate grounds for positing "contemporization" of any sort as the explanation for πόλις ασεδεκ. Suggesting that Onias would have found in v. 18 a basis of legitimacy for his temple at Leontopolis simply because Josephus reports that Onias cited v. 19 to that effect is mere speculation, even as positing that ασεδεκ is a transliteration of צדק, drawn in as an interpretation of הרס/הרס in the light of 1:26 is also groundless speculation.

---

[155] Ibid., 355–56.

[156] E. Y. Kutscher, *The Language and Linguistic Background of the Isaiah Scroll (1QIsaᵃ)* (Leiden: Brill, 1974) 116.

[157] The primary drawback I see is the transliteration of ח by κ, although even that finds parallels elsewhere in the LXX, as he notes (Vaccari, "ΠΟΛΙΣ ΑΣΕΔΕΚ," 355).

The rejoinder to this dismissal of contemporization in 19:18 would undoubtedly be that it must be considered in light of the dominant tendency of the Isaiah translator to employ *Erfüllungsinterpretationen*, especially ones that find forecasts of events during the Hellenistic crisis of early second century Jerusalem. Here we come up against the same sort of dialectic that makes determining the *Vorlage* so problematic: one's conception of the translator's *Übersetzungsweise* determines how one perceives a particular instance, while the case at hand must contribute to a sketch of the *Übersetzungsweise*. The only way to engage this rejoinder is by taking up the topic of "contemporization" in lxx-Isaiah more directly, as I will in the next two chapters.

CHAPTER SIX

A CRITIQUE OF CONTEMPORIZATION

If the translator sought to interpret Isaiah as prophecy fulfilled in his day, that project will have left tangible marks. We should, for example, expect to find evidence that the translator believed that he was living in "the last days," as most of those who assert the translator's fascination with *Erfüllungsinterpretation* posit. An equally telling mark would be his translation of toponyms with Hellenistic place names, so as to help his readers connect the oracles of Isaiah with their own day. This chapter will probe evidence of such tendencies that would confirm the translator's commonly posited interest in "contemporization."

Eschatology in LXX-Isaiah

Although Seeligmann concluded that the translator considered himself living in the "time for the fulfillment of ancient prophecies"[1] and that he "combined Isaiah's expectations regarding the future with his own,"[2] he stopped short of declaring the translator an enthusiast of eschatology. Nevertheless, his description of "contemporization" prompted others to detect evidence of the translator's fascination with eschatology.

Shortly after Seeligmann published his study, J. Coste characterized Isa 25:1–5 as "un chant d'action de grâces à horizons messianiques."[3] A more full-throated assertion of the translator's captivation with eschatology came with das Neves's claim that, because the prophecies interpreted as being realized "se rapportent aux derniers temps," the translator viewed "les temps eschatologiques commencent dès maintenant."[4] Shortly after das Neves's study appeared, but independently of him, Frederic Raurell concluded that entire pericopae had been rendered from "una perspectiva escatològico-messiànica"[5] and that

---

[1] Seeligmann, *Septuagint*, 4.
[2] Ibid., 116.
[3] Coste, "Le texte Grec," 51.
[4] Das Neves, *A Teologia*, 283.
[5] Frederic Raurell, "«Archontes» en la interpretació midràshica d'Is-LXX," *RevCT* 1 (1976) 332.

the translator had given chapters 3 and 14, in particular, "un accent fortament escatologic."[6] Similarly, in his initial study of LXX-Isaiah, Arie van der Kooij asserted that "der Autor der LXX Jes war vom Glauben getragen, die entscheidende Periode (vgl. τὰ ἔσχατα) der Geschichte sei angebrochen."[7] And throughout subsequent studies, van der Kooij has maintained that "Ereignisse zur Zeit des Übersetzers vom Propheten Jesaja vorausgesagt worden waren, und daß also die Zeit der letzten Ereignisse angefangen hat."[8] Accordingly, the past few decades have seen a sustained characterization of the translator as propounding an eschatological interpretation of Isaiah's oracles.

Given this perception, the frequent comparison of LXX-Isaiah with the Qumran *pesharim* is understandable. Like the *pesharim*, with their highly charged belief in the impending arrival of the ideal age and their identification of features in prophetic passages with events and persons in the interpreter's day, the translator of LXX-Isaiah (in this view) saw himself on the cusp of the new era and found people and events of his own day presaged in the prophetic text.

Eschatology Defined

Before assessing whether this is an accurate characterization of LXX-Isaiah, however, we must find a usable definition of "eschatology," a term commonly applied to descriptions of "the skies roll[ing] up like a scroll" (Isa 34:4) or expectations of "a new heaven and a new earth" (Isa 65:17). It is also applied to passages that voice hopes for an ideal era, such as we find in Isa 2:1–4, even though, far from positing an "end to history," this passage envisions the gradual pacification of nations under the LORD's oversight, ruling from an elevated, but quite this-worldly Jerusalem. Given the diverse scenarios to which "eschatology" is applied, we need to define the term before asking whether the Isaiah translator was captivated by it.

As Collins has pointed out, even though the word "eschatology" derives from ἔσχατος, passages typically considered eschatological are

---

[6] Ibid., 371. Cf. Raurell's discussion of "el rol escatològic de «doxa»" in chapter 26, in his "La «Doxa»," 64–88.

[7] Van der Kooij, *Die alten Textzeugen*, 64. While Koenig does not describe the translator as having a fascination with eschatology, he does repeatedly speak of "une utilization oraculaire" of passages, such that "tantôt le texte a été appliqué à des faits contemporains, tantôt on y a lu des indications concernant l'avenir" (*L'Herméneutique*, 44).

[8] Van der Kooij, "Zur Theologie," 16.

not concerned with an "end" but with the arrival of an ideal world.[9] Above all, such passages do not anticipate an "end of history," if "history" means the unfolding of events in the human world.[10] Most passages thought to focus on "the end of the world" are concerned not with its destruction but with one sort of transformation or another. Even the assertion of 2 Pt 3:10 that "the heavens will pass away with a loud noise, and the elements will be dissolved with fire, and the earth and everything that is done on it will be disclosed" is followed not by visions of incorporeal existence, but by a substitute world with a new-and-improved character.[11] Thus, Lindblom was on the right track in concluding that

> Eschatologie am besten als Bezeichnung solcher Vorstellungen benutzt werden soll, die sich auf eine Zukunft beziehen, wo die irdischen Verhältnisse so verändert werden, dass man von etwas wirklich Neuem und »ganz anderem« sprechen muss, gleichgültig ob sich das Neue innerhalb oder ausserhalb des Rahmens der Geschichte abspielt.[12]

Such a new era is not fully (or even predominantly) discontinuous with the previous era, even if talk of (say) "a new heaven and earth" implies that the current era is irredeemably corrupt. Thus, while Isa 25:6 portrays a banquet at which the Lord "will swallow up death forever," Isa 65:20 views the ideal era as lacking an "infant that lives but a few days, or an old person who does not live out a lifetime." There a remedy is desired not for death itself but for the injustice of dying short of a ripe old age. The important issue is that the new era is an idealized state for a specified spectrum of conditions, whose make up and range varies from passage to passage. A definition of eschatology, therefore, must make room for both discontinuity and continuity by avoiding descriptions of the climax as an "end."[13]

---

[9] John J. Collins, "Apocalyptic Eschatology as the Transcendence of Death," *CBQ* 36 (1974) 27.

[10] Ibid. 26.

[11] This is the case even in the passage Collins considers the classic case of expectation of "the cosmological end of the world," 4 Ezra 7:30–31: "Then shall the world be returned to primeval silence seven days, like as the first beginning.... And it shall be, after seven days, that the age which is not yet awake shall be aroused, and that which is corruptible shall perish" (ibid., 25).

[12] J. Lindblom, "Gibt es eine Eschatologie bei den alttestmentlichen Propheten?" *ST* 6 (1953) 82. Cf. the similar stress placed on discontinuity by Thomas M. Raitt, *A Theology of Exile* (Philadelphia: Fortress Press, 1977) 215–16.

[13] Cf. Collins, "Apocalyptic Eschatology," 29. Von Rad's conclusion that the break between the old and new eras "goes so deep that the new state...cannot be understood

Equally essential to a definition is that the new area brings a *defini-tive* amelioration of prior ills.[14] No portrait of an ideal age sees it as merely a temporary respite from the bitterness of life. While reversals of natural phenomena were accepted in ancient Israel (such as the raising of the Shunammite's son in 2 Kgs 4), these were seen as ad hoc interventions. Eschatological language, on the other hand, speaks of life on the other side of a boundary set between life as commonly experienced and transformed life. For the term "eschatology" to have any meaning, it must designate the definitive transformation of a world persistently flawed in some respect(s).[15]

A further assumption of eschatology is that God introduces the ideal age. Because the new era is deliverance from human and cosmologi-cal flaws, the only effective agent is God. Even when divine agency is not expressly stated, the changed circumstances presuppose divine action. Thus, 2 Peter 3 might not say that the "new heavens and new earth where righteousness dwell" are created by the deity, but no other means of their appearance could be envisioned. Similarly, when Isaiah 2 declares, "the mountain of the LORD's house shall be established as the highest of the mountains, and shall be raised above the hills," this transformation is implicitly wrought by the LORD.

Finally, because such portraits of an ideal age are projections, they are *visions* of a future era. It is the futurity of these visions that accounts for the use of phrases like באחרית הימים and ἐν ταῖς ἐσχάταις ἡμέραις. Even when such phrases do not appear, there is an assumption that such conditions can exist only in an envisioned era.

In accord with these observations, the definition used in this study is that "eschatology is a vision of a new era, to be introduced by God, that will definitively realize the loftiest divine and/or human ideals."[16]

Given that stock temporal phrases placing a vision in the future (especially באחרית הימים and ἐν ταῖς ἐσχάταις ἡμέραις) often introduce

---

as the continuation of what went before" (Gerhard von Rad, *Old Testament Theology*, 2 vols. [New York: Harper, 1962–1965] 2:115) correctly accentuates the decisive nature of the transformation but tends to overstate the discontinuity.

[14] Cf. Collins's observation that "in the Prophets, the 'End of Days' implies a defini-tive transformation of Israel in the distant future" (John J. Collins, "Eschatology," in *Encyclopedia of the Dead Sea Scrolls*, ed. Lawrence H. Schiffman and James C. VanderKam, 2 volumes [Oxford and New York: Oxford University Press, 2000] 1:256).

[15] Collins, "Apocalyptic Eschatology," 28.

[16] The distinction between "divine and/or human ideals" functions on a literary plane: ideals that mirror divine criticisms of human behavior or that address human laments of abysmal conditions (such as death prior to one's time).

or punctuate eschatological scenes, and given that such phrases occur in Isaiah, we must investigate their use. While obviously the phrase crucial for LXX-Isaiah is ἐν (ταῖς) ἐσχάταις ἡμέραις, it will be useful first to understand the Hebrew phrase this translates.

The Meaning(s) of באחרית הימים

באחרית הימים occurs 13 times in the Bible, and corresponding to it is the Aramaic phrase באחרית יומיא in Dan 2:28. Linguistically, this phrase simply locates events in the future, without specifying when they will occur.[17] As Seebass has observed, however, some of its uses lay the foundation for באחרית הימים as a technical term of eschatology, inasmuch as they do not forecast events in the normal course of history, but introduce descriptions of circumstances that break decisively with previous conditions.[18] For example, in Isaiah 2 || Micah 4, באחרית הימים precedes a description of dramatic topographic change for Jerusalem in which it becomes the locus of divine rule that draws the peoples of the nations to it for instruction that leads to idyllic peace amongst them. In spite of the eschatological tenor of the passage, however, באחרית הימים functions as a temporal phrase equivalent to "in the future."[19]

On the other hand, Hos 3:5 forecasts the reunification of north and south under a Davidic ruler באחרית הימים. Although this expectation is less dramatic than the transformation of Jerusalem in Isaiah 2, the redactor's insertion of ואת דוד מלכם paints an ideal era, at least from a Judean perspective.[20] What makes באחרית הימים in this passage interesting is the tension between it and אחר at the outset of the verse. Whereas אחר designates the period when the lessons of deprivation will have been learned, so that Israel "will seek the LORD their God," באחרית הימים designates the future in a general way, without specifying

---

[17] For this linguistic analysis see George Wesley Buchanan, "Eschatology and the 'End of Days'," *JNES* 20 (1961) 188–93; Hans Kosmala, "At the End of the Days," *ASTI* 2 (1963) 27–37; and Jean Carmignac, "La notion d'eschatolgie dans la Bible et a Qumrân," *RevQ* 7 (1967) 17–31.

[18] Horst Seebass, "אַחֲרִית," in *Theological Dictionary of the Old Testament*, vol. 1, ed. G. Johannes Botterweck and Helmer Ringgren (Grand Rapids: Wm. B. Eerdmans, 1974) 211.

[19] Cf. van der Ploeg's conclusion that באחרית הימים in Isa 2 "has no technical 'eschatological' meaning, though those days coincide with the time of future happiness and salvation" (J. P. M. van der Ploeg, "Eschatology in the Old Testament," *OtSt* 17 [1972] 90).

[20] For the argument that a redactor supplied ואת דוד מלכם, see Hans Walter Wolff, *Hosea* (Hermeneia; Philadelphia: Fortress, 1974) 63.

it as the dénouement of a remedial program.[21] Thus, באחרית הימים in
this case designates an era in which ideal conditions prevail.

Comparable, as Seebass contends, is Ezek 38:16, part of a forecast
of the LORD's incitement of Gog against Israel, resulting in the LORD's
vindication in the sight of the nations.[22] Whereas v. 14 sets the time
for this attack as ביום ההוא בשבת עמי ישראל לבטח, v. 16 designates the
time of Gog's aggression as באחרית הימים, suggesting that the redactor
regarded אחרית הימים as a final period of crisis.

While I am not as convinced as Seebass that באחרית יומיא functions
as a technical term of eschatology in Dan 2:28,[23] באחרית הימים in 10:14
seems to be so used, since the divine attendant tells Daniel not only
that he has come to reveal את אשר יקרה לעמך באחרית הימים, but further
defines that revelation by adding, כי עוד חזון לימים, in which case לימים
has evident demonstrative force ("for *those* days") that makes אחרית הימים
designate a particular era rather than some indeterminate time.[24]

This use of אחרית הימים for the time of eschatological events is full-
blown in the Qumran literature, where outside the "biblical" texts it
occurs—with one possible exception—only in literature composed by
the community.[25] Moreover, with the exception of 1QSa 1.1, it always
appears "in the context of Scripture interpretation,"[26] and mostly in
the *pesharim*.[27] As Steudel has shown, the community's authors used
אחרית הימים to designate a period which, in their view, had already
begun.[28] Indeed, not only is "the present time of the community's own

---

[21] While Wolff's argument that באחרית הימים "belongs to Judaic eschatology" (ibid.)
is circular, he is right to observe that this "solemn formula clashes with the simple
word אחר at the beginning of the sentence" (ibid., 57), even if "solemn" is not quite
the right word.

[22] Seebass, "אַחֲרִית," 211.

[23] Ibid. Dan 2:28's description of Nebuchadnezzar's vision of the destruction of all
kingdoms by the superior kingdom of God as מה די להוא באחרית יומיא stands parallel
to אחרי דנה מה די להוא in v. 29, both phrases simply designating events to occur in
the future.

[24] Making this evident as the intent is the fact that in drawing on כי עוד חזון למועד
from Hab 2:3, the only change the author made was לימים for למועד.

[25] Annette Steudel, "אחרית הימים in the Texts from Qumran," *RevQ* 16 (1993) 227.
The one possible exception is an occurrence in 4Q504, on which see ibid., 227 n. 14.

[26] Ibid.

[27] Steudel reports that the thematic *pesharim* 4Q174 (4Qflorilegium) and 4Q177
contain "one third of all אחרית הימים references in the Qumran texts" (ibid., 228).

[28] Ibid., 228–30. With this we might compare their conviction that only with
them have the promises of a renewed covenant been realized (Shemaryahu Talmon,
The 'Dead Sea Scrolls' or 'The Community of the Renewed Covenant' [The Albert T. Bilgray
Lecture; Tuscon: University of Arizona, 1993] 17), making them the זרע ישראל and
the זרע הקדש (ibid., 19) who alone can claim to continue Israel's life (ibid., 18).

existence…dated to the אחרית הימים," but so also are "the coming of the messiahs and the final judgment."[29] Accordingly, the frequent occurrence of אחרית הימים in the *pesharim* is a mark of their eschatological orientation.

Nevertheless, as this survey demonstrates, one cannot assume that every occurrence of באחרית הימים bears eschatological freight; each case must be considered in its context. How much more so, then, is it necessary to consider the semantic content of ἐν (ταῖς) ἐσχάταις ἡμέραις in LXX-Isaiah rather than simply assume that it is a technical phrase of eschatology.

ἐν (ταῖς) ἐσχάταις ἡμέραις in LXX-Isaiah

Several occurrences of ἔσχατος in LXX-Isaiah seem, on first blush, to attest a fascination with eschatology. Isa 2:2 is the premier example, for it sets Jerusalem's exaltation ἐν ταῖς ἐσχάταις ἡμέραις. Because the conditions described in 2:2–4 are undeniably "eschatological," as they are in the Hebrew, this phrase is readily assumed to be an eschatological idiom.[30] Moreover, one might infer that because this phrase varies from the typical LXX rendering of באחרית הימים (by ἐπί + the genitive) it reflects the translator's sensitivity to ἔσχατος as a technical term of eschatology.[31] The use of τὰ ἔσχατα in 41:22 and 46:10 seem to support this surmise:

(41:22) ἐγγισάτωσαν καὶ ἀναγγειλάτωσαν ὑμῖν ἃ συμβήσεται ἢ τὰ πρότερα τίνα ἦν εἴπατε καὶ ἐπιστήσομεν τὸν νοῦν καὶ γνωσόμεθα τί τὰ ἔσχατα καὶ τὰ ἐπερχόμενα εἴπατε ἡμῖν.
(46:10) ἀναγγέλλων πρότερον τὰ ἔσχατα πρὶν αὐτὰ γενέσθαι καὶ ἅμα συνετελέσθη.

---

[29] Steudel, "אחרית הימים in the Texts from Qumran," 231. Steudel rightly compares the use of ἐν (ταῖς) ἐσχάταις ἡμέραις in early Christian literature (ibid., 232). The most striking comparison (though one Steudel does not use) is the temple sermon of Acts 2, where Peter interprets the glossolalia for the crowd as the fulfillment by appeal to Joel's prophecy that ἐν ταῖς ἐσχάταις ἡμέραις, λέγει ὁ θεός, ἐκχεῶ ἀπὸ τοῦ πνεύματός μου ἐπὶ πᾶσαν σάρκα, καὶ προφητεύσουσιν οἱ υἱοὶ ὑμῶν καὶ αἱ θυγατέρες ὑμῶν (Acts 2:17). Cf. Heb 1:1–2: Πολυμερῶς καὶ πολυτρόπως πάλαι ὁ θεὸς λαλήσας τοῖς πατράσιν ἐν τοῖς προφήταις ἐπ' ἐσχάτου τῶν ἡμερῶν τούτων ἐλάλησεν ἡμῖν ἐν υἱῷ.

[30] Buchanan notes that the LXX's use of ἔσχατος in rendering באחרית הימים has contributed to the assumption that באחרית הימים "is a technical term used only in eschatological literature" (Buchanan, "Eschatology and the 'End of Days'," 189).

[31] Elsewhere באחרית הימים is rendered with ἐπ' ἐσχάτου τῶν ἡμερῶν (Num 24:14; Jer 23:20; 49:39 [25:19]; Dan 10:14), ἐπ' ἐσχάτων τῶν ἡμερῶν (Gen 49:1; Deut 4:30; Jer 37[30]:24; Ezek 38:16; Dan 2:28; Hos 3:5; Micah 4:1), and ἔσχατον τῶν ἡμερῶν (Deut 31:29).

Van der Kooij, having detected *Erfüllungsinterpretationen* in lxx-Isaiah, suggests that the translator interpreted Isaiah "im Geist von Sir 48,24f." and its interest in τὰ ἔσχατα:[32]

> ²⁴πνεύματι μεγάλῳ εἶδεν τὰ ἔσχατα καὶ παρεκάλεσεν τοὺς πενθοῦντας ἐν Σιων.
> ²⁵ἕως τοῦ αἰῶνος ὑπέδειξεν τὰ ἐσόμενα καὶ τὰ ἀπόκρυφα πρὶν ἢ παραγενέσθαι αὐτά.

Like Ben Sira, the translator understood Isaiah's oracles as "Vorhersagen der 'kommenden Ereignisse' (τὰ ἐπερχόμενα: 41,4.22f.; 44,7; 45,11), und diese Ereignisse sind τὰ ἔσχατα (41,22f.; vgl. auch 46,10)" that constitute "die entscheidende Periode (vgl. τὰ ἔσχατα) der Geschichte," that is, "die Endzeit."[33] However, is it justifiable to assume that ἔσχατος in these texts signifies "die Endzeit"?[34]

In Classical Greek, ἔσχατος always denotes, in spatial terms, "das 'letzte', das 'äußerste' in verschiedener Hinsicht."[35] lxx-Isaiah's use of ἔσχατος in geographical expressions accords with this. For instance, ἕως ἐσχάτου τῆς γῆς ('to the end [= the farthest reaches] of the earth') translates עד קצה הארץ in 48:20 and 49:6, and אל קצה הארץ in 62:11. In 8:9 ἐπακούσατε ἕως ἐσχάτου τῆς γῆς corresponds to the mt's והאזינו כל מרחקי ארץ. This idiom is peculiar for Greek, and thus is not likely to have been invented by the translator. His *Vorlage* probably read והאזינו אל מרחקי ארץ.[36] In any case, ἕως ἐσχάτου τῆς γῆς again means 'to the farthest reaches of the earth.'

---

[32] Van der Kooij, *Die alten Textzeugen*, 63.

[33] Ibid., 63–64. Cf. van der Kooij's assertion that τὰ ἔσχατα (translating אחרית) in Sir 48:24 signifies "die Endzeit" (ibid., 21).

[34] It is unacceptable to claim, as van der Kooij does, that since scholars have found lxx-Isaiah to employ "actualizations" of Isaianic oracles and these reflect the translator's belief that his era was "the 'last' period of history," passages containing τὰ ἔσχατα "are to be taken as referring to the final and decisive period of history as understood by the translator" (van der Kooij, "'Coming' Things and 'Last' Things: Isaianic Terminology as Understood in the Wisdom of Ben Sira and in the Septuagint of Isaiah," in *The New Things: Eschatology in Old Testament Prophecy, Festschrift for Henk Leene*, ed. Ferenc Postma, Klaas Spronk, and Eep Talstra [Maastricht: Uitgeverij Shaker, 2002] 140). Besides begging the question of whether the translator, in fact, engages in widespread "actualizing" interpretation, it is methodologically improper to decide on the meaning of a word without observing how it is used in its contexts. Indeed, such information must help shape an understanding of the translator's mindset.

[35] W. C. van Unnik, "Der Ausdruck ἙΩΣ ἘΣΧΑΤΟΥ ΤΗΣ ΓΗΣ (Apostelgeschichte 1:8) und sein alttestamentlicher Hintergrund," in *Studia Biblical et Semitica*, ed. W. C. van Unnik and A. S. van der Woude (Wageningen, the Netherlands: H. Veenman en Zonen N. V., 1966) 343.

[36] כל is attested by 1QIsa (כול), as well as S, T and V. This part of the phrase stands

In 45:22 ἐπιστράφητε πρός με καὶ σωθήσεσθε οἱ ἀπ᾽ ἐσχάτου τῆς γῆς corresponds to the MT's פְּנוּ אֵלִי וְהִוָּשְׁעוּ כָּל אַפְסֵי אָרֶץ. Most likely כֹּל was absent from the LXX 's *Vorlage*,[37] while οἱ ἀπ᾽ ἐσχάτου τῆς γῆς is a paraphrase of אַפְסֵי אָרֶץ,[38] just as οἱ σῳζόμενοι ἀπὸ τῶν ἐθνῶν paraphrases פְּלִיטֵי הַגּוֹיִם in v. 20. Οἱ ἀπ᾽ ἐσχάτου τῆς γῆς means 'those who hail from the farthest reaches of the earth.'[39]

Finally, in 37:24 τὰ ἔσχατα τοῦ Λιβάνου translates יַרְכְּתֵי לְבָנוֹן[40] and, like the Hebrew phrase, means 'the far reaches of Lebanon.' Thus, in geographical expressions ἔσχατος remains true to the meaning 'the extreme' or 'last.'

The five remaining appearances of ἔσχατος in LXX-Isaiah are in temporal expressions and translate either אַחֲרִית (4x) or אָחוֹר. The best window for understanding ἔσχατος in these passages is 46:10, where the Kyrios describes himself as

| מַגִּיד מֵרֵאשִׁית אַחֲרִית | ἀναγγέλλων πρότερον τὰ ἔσχατα |
| וּמִקֶּדֶם אֲשֶׁר לֹא נַעֲשׂוּ | πρὶν αὐτὰ γενέσθαι καὶ ἅμα συνετελέσθη |

Although much of the second line is difficult to reconcile with the MT,[41] the relationship between συνετελέσθη and נַעֲשׂוּ is transparent, since συντελεῖν translates עשׂה in 32:6, 44:24, and 55:11. Moreover, πρίν for וּמִקֶּדֶם is reminiscent of 23:7, where קַדְמָה stands behind an equally oblique translation:

| קַדְמָתָהּ יוֹבִלוּהָ רַגְלֶיהָ מֵרָחוֹק לָגוּר | πρὶν ἢ παραδοθῆναι αὐτήν |

---

in a lacuna in 4QIsaᵉ. Cf. 62:11, where κύριος ἐποίησεν ἀκουστὸν ἕως ἐσχάτου τῆς γῆς translates יְהוָה הִשְׁמִיעַ אֶל קְצֵה הָאָרֶץ.

[37] כֹּל is attested by 1QIsaᵃ (כול), as well as S, T and V. The phrase stands in a lacuna in 4QIsaᵇ. Cf. 52:10, where the translator translates וְרָאוּ כָּל אַפְסֵי אָרֶץ with καὶ ὄψονται πάντα τὰ ἄκρα τῆς γῆς.

[38] Cf. T's handling of 52:10: וְיֶחֱזוֹן כָּל דְּבִסְיָפֵי אַרְעָא יָת פּוּרְקָנָא דֶּאֱלָהָנָא || וְרָאוּ כָּל אַפְסֵי אָרֶץ אֵת יְשׁוּעַת אֱלֹהֵינוּ.

[39] As das Neves suggests, the LXX probably has in mind the diaspora (*A Teologia*, 244–45).

[40] Ἔσχατος renders ירכה again only in Jer 6:22; 27(50):41; 32(25):32; 38(31):8 (all ἀπ᾽ ἐσχάτου τῆς γῆς || מִירְכְּתֵי אָרֶץ); Ezek 38:6 (ἀπ᾽ ἐσχάτου βορρᾶ || יַרְכְּתֵי צָפוֹן); 38:15; 39:2 (both ἀπ᾽ ἐσχάτου βορρᾶ || מִירְכְּתֵי צָפוֹן). ירכה occurs again in Isaiah only in 14:15, which the LXX renders it with τὰ θεμέλια. ירך does not appear in the book.

[41] 1QIsaᵃ and 1QIsaᵇ = MT. In place of אַחֲרִית, 4QIsaᶜ read אַחֲרוֹנוֹת (only the letters ונות are clearly visible, although the left-most end of a line is visible that could well be the remnants of a *rêš* and the form precedes וּמִקֶּדֶם אֲשֶׁר, although only the top of the final letter (quite likely *rêš*) is preserved). 4QIsaᵈ preserves only אֲשֶׁר לֹא נַעֲשׂוּ.

Flint suggests that the LXX's *Vorlage* read קדמת for קדמתה,[42] comparing
Ps 128(129):6, where the translator renders שקדמת שלף יבש with ὃς πρὸ
τοῦ ἐκσπασθῆναι.[43] However that may be, this translation of קדמת with
πρὶν ἤ in 23:7 likely explains πρίν in 46:10, as well.[44]

However, Ziegler perceived another factor at work here. He suggested
that the translator's choice of πρὶν αὐτὰ γενέσθαι was influenced by
48:5:[45]

| ואניד לך מאז | καὶ ἀνήγγειλά σοι τὰ πάλαι |
| בטרם תבוא השמעתיך | πρὶν ἐλθεῖν ἐπὶ σὲ ἀκουστόν σοι ἐποίησα |

Actually, there is no conflict between Ziegler's perception and the surmise that πρίν was derived from ומקדם. While the translator may have
justified πρίν by ומקדם, nowhere else in LXX-Isaiah does πρίν translate
מקדם or קדם.[46] Moreover, the affinity to 48:5 runs deeper than πρίν, for
46:10, like 48:5, stresses the announcement of events *in advance*. This
notion, imported from 48:5, led the translator not only to choose πρίν
for ומקדם, but also to supply αὐτὰ γενέσθαι.[47]

---

[42] Peter W. Flint, "The Septuagint Version of Isaiah 23:1–14 and the Massoretic
Text," *BIOSCS* 21 (1988) 41. As for the remainder of the line, Ziegler notes that "die
LXX hat Kap. 23 vielfach abwegig und gekürzt wieder gegeben" and concludes that the
translator provided παραδοθῆναι αὐτήν either because his *Vorlage* was poor or because
"sie kam mit ihrer Vorlage nicht zurecht" (*Untersuchungen*, 49). As he notes, the translator
frequently used παραδιδόναι when he was perplexed (ibid., 13–14).

[43] Flint, "The Septuagint Version," 41 n. 36. This is the only occurrence of קדמה
in Isaiah.

[44] Cf. the translation of קדם with ἔμπροσθεν in 2 Esdr 4:18, Jb 29:2, Mic 7:20,
Lam 5:21, and Ezek 38:17.

[45] Ziegler, *Untersuchungen*, 155. Ziegler (ibid.) suggested that 48:5 may also have been
translated in the light of 44:7 (καὶ τὰ ἐπερχόμενα πρὸ τοῦ ἐλθεῖν ἀναγγειλάτωσαν
ὑμῖν || ואתיות ואשר תבאנה ינידו למו), although he allowed that the LXX's *Vorlage* may
have read בטרם for ואשר.

[46] מקדם is translated ἀπ' ἀρχῆς in 2:6 and 45:21, and ἀφ' ἡλίου ἀνατολῶν in
9:12(11). Cf. τοὺς ἀφ' ἡλίου ἀνατολῶν || את בני קדם (11:14), ἐξ ἀρχαίων ἡμερῶν ||
מימי קדם (37:26), ὡς ἐν ἀρχῇ ἡμέρας || כימי קדם (51:9), υἱοὶ βασιλέων τῶν ἐξ ἀρχῆς
|| בן מלכי קדם (19:11), and ἀπ' ἀρχῆς || מימי קדם (23:7).

[47] A parallel case is the translation of השמעתיך מעתה חדשות ונצרות with ἀλλὰ καὶ
ἀκουστά σοι ἐποίησα τὰ καινὰ ἀπὸ τοῦ νῦν ἃ μέλλει γίνεσθαι in 48:6. Ziegler suggested that the translator paraphrased ונצרות as ἃ μέλλει γίνεσθαι ("'das Aufbewahrte' =
die Zukunft" [cf. πόλις πολιορκουμένη || עיר נצורה in 1:8 and 27:3, and καὶ τὴν
διασπορὰν τοῦ Ισραηλ || ישראל ('Q) נצירי (ונצירי in 49:6]) in the light of 47:13, where
τί μέλλει ἐπὶ σὲ ἔρχεσθαι renders עליך יבאו מאשר (although the LXX's *Vorlage* probably
read אשר) (*Untersuchungen*, 160). Here also the notion of the proclamation of the future
inspired the translator to emphasize this theme, paraphrasing his *Vorlage* but also borrowing elements of another text.

As for καὶ ἅμα, this adverb occurs twelve times in LXX-Isaiah without an equivalent in the MT. While three (if not four) of these are attributable to the *Vorlage*,[48] in one case (59:11) the translator supplied ἅμα under the influence of another passage,[49] while in others he seems to have supplied it in order to stress either simultaneous action (3:16 [2x]; 19:14) or joint participation in an action (13:3; 24:14; 36:12). Similarly, καὶ ἅμα in 46:10 stresses joint participation in completion: *all* τὰ ἔσχατα predicted have been fulfilled (συνετελέσθη).[50]

Accordingly, while the MT of 46:10 depicts God announcing future events, the LXX stresses the *certainty* of his forecasts by emphasizing that all τὰ ἔσχατα announced in advance have been fulfilled.[51] These ἔσχατα are not events at the "end of history," but simply events yet future when announced.[52] Thus, here τὰ ἔσχατα refers to the future only in a general sense ('things to occur later'), much as the spatial use of ἔσχατος in the phrase οἱ ἀπ᾽ ἐσχάτου τῆς γῆς in 45:22 refers to those living at a great, but indeterminate distance.

Τὰ ἔσχατα in 47:7 is similar. As in the MT, this verse accuses the "virgin daughter of Babylon" of insolence:

ותאמרי לעולם אהיה גברת עד	καὶ εἶπας εἰς τὸν αἰῶνα ἔσομαι ἄρχουσα[53]
לא שמת אלה על לבך	οὐκ ἐνόησας ταῦτα ἐν τῇ καρδίᾳ σου
לא זכרת אחריתה	οὐδὲ ἐμνήσθης τὰ ἔσχατα

---

[48] Ἅμα in 41:5 reflects יחדו for יחרדו in the *Vorlage*, just as in 44:1 it is due to יחדו for יפחדו. In 42:22 the LXX reads ἡ γὰρ παγὶς ἐν τοῖς ταμιείοις πανταχοῦ καὶ ἐν οἴκοις ἅμα ὅπου ἔκρυψαν αὐτούς for the MT's הפח בחורים כלם ובבתי כלאים החבאו. Ἅμα may represent a second כלם (a corruption of כלאים) in the LXX's *Vorlage* (cf. πανταχοῦ || כלם). In 11:7, the appearance of ἅμα, without an equivalent in the MT, in two clauses parallel to one where ἅμα translates יחדו, is attributable to either the translator or his *Vorlage*.

[49] See Ziegler, *Untersuchungen*, 166–67.

[50] Cf. the insertion of ἅμα in 24:14, where it accents the unified rejoicing of οἱ καταλειφθέντες: οἱ δὲ καταλειφθέντες ἐπὶ τῆς γῆς εὐφρανθήσονται ἅμα τῇ δόξῃ κυρίου || ירנו בגאון יהוה (on the LXX of 24:14 see ibid. 59–60).

[51] τὰ ἔσχατα may reflect אחרונות in the *Vorlage*, a reading attested by 4QIsaᶜ (see above, n. 41), and cf. τὰ ἔσχατα || אחרונות in 1QIsaᵃ (אחריתן in MT) in 41:22.

[52] This conclusion is valid even if one construes συνετελέσθη as a gnomic aorist. The prediction of eschatological events which are *regularly* accomplished would be meaningless.

[53] V and S also fail to represent עד; 1QIsaᵃ reads עוד. It was likely lacking in the translator's *Vorlage*.

Τὰ ἔσχατα[54] are not something she should have predicted, but recalled.[55] Given the context, which enumerates calamities to befall Babylon because of its deeds, it is implausible that τὰ ἔσχατα denotes "die Endzeit." Rather, like אחריתה, τὰ ἔσχατα refers to the future in the general sense of "outcome."[56]

Those two occurrences of τὰ ἔσχατα illuminate 41:22–23:

יגישו ויגידו לנו	[22]ἐγγισάτωσαν καὶ ἀναγγειλάτωσαν ὑμῖν[57]
את אשר תקרינה	ἃ συμβήσεται
הראשנות מה הנה הגידו	ἢ τὰ πρότερα τίνα ἦν εἴπατε
ונשימה לבנו	καὶ ἐπιστήσομεν τὸν νοῦν
ונדעה אחריתן	καὶ γνωσόμεθα τί τὰ ἔσχατα
או הבאות השמיענו	καὶ τὰ ἐπερχόμενα εἴπατε ἡμῖν
הגידו האתיות לאחור	[23]ἀναγγείλατε τὰ ἐπερχόμενα ἐπ' ἐσχάτου
ונדעה כי אלהים אתם	καὶ γνωσόμεθα ὅτι θεοί ἐστε

The referent of τὰ ἔσχατα is ambiguous.[58] The particle ἤ—whether supplied by the translator or due to his *Vorlage*[59]—gives a choice as to what is to be announced: ἃ συμβήσεται or τὰ πρότερα. In either case, the listeners will weigh the words carefully and know τί τὰ ἔσχατα.

---

[54] While the *Vorlage* may have lacked the 3fs suffix of אחריתה, the translator frequently omits suffixes with articular nouns if the person is clear from the context (e.g., καὶ ἐπιστήσομεν τὸν νοῦν || ונשימה לבנו in 41:22). This explanation is bolstered by τὰ ἔσχατα || אחריתן in 41:22 (although 1QIsaᵃ reads אחרונות; 1QIsaᵇ = мт).

[55] Cf. Lam 1:9: ἀκαθαρσία αὐτῆς πρὸς ποδῶν αὐτῆς οὐκ ἐμνήσθη ἔσχατα αὐτῆς (טמאתה בשוליה לא זכרה אחריתה ||).

[56] Cf. τὰ ἔσχατα in Job 8:13: οὕτως τοίνυν ἔσται τὰ ἔσχατα πάντων τῶν ἐπιλανθανομένων τοῦ κυρίου (|| כן ארחות כל־שכחי אל; the *Vorlage* no doubt read אחרית for ארחות).

[57] Ὑμῖν || לנו (1QIsaᵃ and 1QIsaᵇ = мт) is probably an adjustment of the pronoun to the preceding context (v. 21: ἐγγίζει ἡ κρίσις ὑμῶν λέγει κύριος ὁ θεός ἤγγισαν αἱ βουλαὶ ὑμῶν λέγει ὁ βασιλεὺς Ιακωβ). Cf. 5:2: περιέθηκα καὶ ἐχαράκωσα καὶ ἐφύτευσα ἄμπελον σωρηχ καὶ ᾠκοδόμησα πύργον ἐν μέσῳ αὐτοῦ καὶ προλήνιον ὤρυξα ἐν αὐτῷ || ויעזקהו ויסקלהו ויטעהו שרק ויבן מגדל בתוכו וגם־יקב חצב בו (due to v. 1: τῷ ἀμπελῶνί μου || לכרמי, where the Lxx's *Vorlage* probably read לכרמי). Even more striking is 8:21: καὶ ἥξει ἐφ' ὑμᾶς σκληρὰ λιμός καὶ ἔσται ὡς ἂν πεινάσητε λυπηθήσεσθε καὶ κακῶς ἐρεῖτε τὸν ἄρχοντα καὶ τὰ παταχρα || ועבר בה נקשה ורעב והיה כי ירעב והתקצף וקלל במלכו ובאלהיו. The translator conformed the pronouns to אליכם (πρὸς ὑμᾶς) and דרשו (ζητήσατε) of v. 19.

[58] Although it is possible that the *Vorlage* lacked the 3fp suffix (1QIsaᵃ reads או אחרונות; 1QIsaᵇ =мт), cf. n. 54.

[59] As usual, it is virtually impossible to discern if a *wāw* or או stood before הראשנות in the *Vorlage* (cf. καὶ τὰ ἐπερχόμενα || או הבאות at the beginning of v. 23). It is not represented in the other versions, nor is it present in 1QIsaᵃ (but cf. 1QIsaᵃ's || אחריתן או אחרונות). In any case, the presence or absence of a particle in the *Vorlage* is immaterial to the point, which is the meaning of τὰ ἔσχατα, given the presence of ἤ in the Greek sentence.

Consequently, τὰ ἔσχατα does not appear to be as specific as "die End-zeit," since it can refer to τὰ πρότερα as well as ἃ συμβήσεται.

Moreover, while the neuter plural interrogative pronoun, τίνα, requests the *detailing* of τὰ πρότερα, the neuter singular τί (which the translator probably supplied under the influence of מה)[60] calls for more *general* information: τὰ ἔσχατα as a body of data rather than details,[61] suggesting something less than a fascination with the culmination of history as a schematized set of events.

While τὰ ἐπερχόμενα ἐπ' ἐσχάτου (|| הָאֹתִיּוֹת לְאָחוֹר, v. 23) might appear to signify events at the "end of time," ἐπ' ἐσχάτων in Deut 32:20 is evidence to the contrary:

וַיֹּאמֶר אַסְתִּירָה פָנַי מֵהֶם	καὶ εἶπεν ἀποστρέψω τὸ πρόσωπόν μου ἀπ' αὐτῶν
אֶרְאֶה מָה אַחֲרִיתָם	καὶ δείξω τί ἔσται αὐτοῖς ἐπ' ἐσχάτων

The succeeding verses depict both God's punishment of Israel, scatter-ing them among the nations, and the punishment of those who capture Israel—events well within "normal" history—so that ἐπ' ἐσχάτων means simply 'later' or 'in the future'. Similarly, τὰ ἐπερχόμενα ἐπ' ἐσχάτου in Isa 41:23 most likely means 'the things to occur in the future'.[62]

This conclusion is reinforced by LXX-Isaiah's translation of 42:23:

מִי בָכֶם יַאֲזִין זֹאת	τίς ἐν ὑμῖν ὃς ἐνωτιεῖται ταῦτα
יַקְשֵׁב וְיִשְׁמַע לְאָחוֹר	εἰσακούσεται εἰς τὰ ἐπερχόμενα

The translator construes לְאָחוֹר—for which he chose ἐπ' ἐσχάτου in 41:23[63]—as denoting the future in a general sense: 'Who is there among you who will pay attention to these things, (who) will listen to the things to come?'[64] This translation of לְאָחוֹר cautions against construing

---

[60] Even if his *Vorlage* contained מה, that would make no difference to the present point, since it was the *translator's* decision to use the neuter plural and the neuter singular.

[61] See Herbert W. Smyth, *Greek Grammar* (Cambridge: Harvard University, 1956) 310 §1246: "τί is used for τίνα as the predicate of a neuter plural subject when the general result is sought and the subject is considered as a unit....τίνα emphasizes the details."

[62] Cf. 2 Kgdms 24:25, where ἐπ' ἐσχάτῳ means "later."

[63] LXX-Isaiah translates אחור with εἰς τὰ ὀπίσω in 28:13; 42:17; 44:25, and ὀπίσω in 59:14. It paraphrases אחור לֹא נְסוּגֹתִי with οὐδὲ ἀντιλέγω in 50:5, and translates פְּלִשְׁתִּים מֵאָחוֹר as καὶ τοὺς Ἕλληνας ἀφ' ἡλίου δυσμῶν in 9:12(11) (on which, see below, pp. 192–93). It offers no equivalent for נֹזְרוּ אָחוֹר in 1:4.

[64] Cf. 44:7 (above), where τὰ ἐπερχόμενα means "the things to come," and 41:4, where τὰ ἐπερχόμενα means "the future": ἐγὼ θεὸς πρῶτος καὶ εἰς τὰ ἐπερχόμενα ἐγώ εἰμι || אֲנִי רִאשׁוֹן וְאֶת אַחֲרֹנִים אֲנִי הוּא.

τὰ ἐπερχόμενα ἐπ᾽ ἐσχάτου (|| האתיות לאחור) in 41:23 as an eschato-
logical idiom. At the very least, the translator failed to exploit לאחור in
42:23 for his (putative) eschatological interests by translating it with εἰς
τὰ ἔσχατα. This is, however, but one of numerous instances in which
he let such an opportunity pass.

The same failure to employ ἔσχατος appears in the translation
of אחרון in 41:4 (ἐγὼ θεὸς πρῶτος καὶ εἰς τὰ ἐπερχόμενα ἐγώ εἰμι ||
אני יהוה ראשון ואת אחרנים אני הוא), 44:6 (ἐγὼ πρῶτος καὶ ἐγὼ μετὰ ταῦτα
|| אני ראשון ואני אחרון), and 48:12 (ἐγώ εἰμι πρῶτος καὶ ἐγώ εἰμι εἰς τὸν
αἰῶνα || אני ראשון אף אני אחרון). While ἔσχατος is the most frequent
equivalent for אחרון outside of Isaiah,[65] never does LXX-Isaiah avail
itself of it.[66] If the translator had been as sensitive to the usefulness
of ἔσχατος for eschatological themes as an initial reading of the book
might suggest, these deviations would be difficult to understand.

Finally, we return to Isa 2:2:

והיה באחרית הימים	ὅτι ἔσται ἐν ταῖς ἐσχάταις ἡμέραις
נכון יהיה הר בית יהוה	ἐμφανὲς τὸ ὄρος τοῦ κυρίου καὶ ὁ οἶκος τοῦ θεοῦ
בראש ההרים ונשא	ἐπ᾽ ἄκρων τῶν ὀρέων καὶ ὑψωθήσεται
מגבעות	ὑπεράνω τῶν βουνῶν
ונהרו אליו כל הגוים	καὶ ἥξουσιν ἐπ᾽ αὐτὸ πάντα τὰ ἔθνη

---

[65] Eight of eleven times in the Pentateuch, 26 of 35 elsewhere. The LXX renders
the first אחרנים of Gen 33:2 with ὀπίσω, the second with ἐσχάτους. It translates
ועד הים האחרון in Deut 11:24 with καὶ ἕως τῆς θαλάσσης τῆς ἐπὶ δυσμῶν, and הדור
האחרון in Deut 29:21 with ἡ γενεὰ ἡ ἑτέρα. The last equivalent occurs again in Ps
48(47):14; 78(77):4, 6; 102(101):19. Ὕστερον appears twice (Jer 27[50]:17; 1 Chr
29:29), while Dan 8:4(3) (G) has μετὰ δὲ ταῦτα for באחרנה (θ´: ἐπ᾽ ἐσχάτων), and
Job 19:25 reads οἶδα γὰρ ὅτι ἀέναός ἐστιν ὁ ἐκλύειν με μέλλων ἐπὶ γῆς for the MT's
ואני ידעתי גאלי חי ואחרון על עפר יקום.

[66] 30:8 reads ὅτι ἔσται εἰς ἡμέρας καιρῶν ταῦτα καὶ ἕως εἰς τὸν αἰῶνα for the MT's
ותהי ליום אחרון לעד עד עולם. While the pleonastic ἕως εἰς might be due to לעד עד,
with καιρῶν translating אחרון, this would be the only time καιρός translates √אחר in
the LXX. On the other hand, καιρός corresponds to לעד again in Isa 64:9(8) (καὶ μὴ
ἐν καιρῷ μνησθῇς ἁμαρτιῶν ἡμῶν || ואל לעד תזכר עון), where the LXX's *Vorlage* doubt-
less read לעת, as does 1QIsa[a] (cf. Jer 11:4). The LXX's *Vorlage* probably contained some
form of עת in 30:8, as well, and lacked אחרון. Similarly perplexing is the rendering
of the only other text containing אחרון in Isaiah, 9:1(8:23): τοῦτο πρῶτον ποίει ταχὺ
ποίει χώρα Ζαβουλων ἡ γῆ Νεφθαλιμ ὁδὸν θαλάσσης καὶ οἱ λοιποὶ οἱ τὴν παραλίαν
κατοικοῦντες καὶ πέραν τοῦ Ιορδάνου Γαλιλαία τῶν ἐθνῶν || כעת הראשון הקל ארצה.
זבלון וארצה נפתלי והאחרון הכביד דרך הים והאחרון הכביד seems to have been absent
from the LXX's *Vorlage*, unless καὶ οἱ λοιποὶ οἱ τὴν παραλίαν κατοικοῦντες represents
this (dislocated) clause. However, this would be the only time λοιπός translates אחרון.
Seeligmann suggests that καὶ οἱ λοιποὶ οἱ τὴν παραλίαν κατοικοῦντες "was literally
taken over from Ezek 25.16, without definite sanction from the Hebrew text" (*Septuagint
Version*, 80).

One problem in evaluating ἐν ταῖς ἐσχάταις ἡμέραις here is that the context is of little help. Despite minor variations from the MT,[67] the depiction of Jerusalem as the center of the earth is just as eschatological as the MT's. However, the translator's failure to exploit ἔσχατος to mark eschatological thought makes it difficult to conclude that he chose ἐν ταῖς ἐσχάταις ἡμέραις for באחרית הימים because it resonated for him as an idiom of eschatology. Since nowhere else in the book is ἔσχατος a technical term of eschatology, and since the translator does not seem intent on exploiting ἔσχατος to create such idioms, ἐν ταῖς ἐσχάταις ἡμέραις in 2:2 is best construed as 'in days to come' ('*later* days'). While this phrase may *introduce* an eschatological scene, it was likely not, itself, an eschatological idiom in the translator's mind.[68]

Accordingly, when ἔσχατος appears in temporal expressions in LXX-Isaiah, it connotes the future only in a general sense. This is not to say that there is no eschatology in LXX-Isaiah; there may be. However, the translator did not use ἔσχατος as a technical term of eschatology, nor does his use of ἔσχατος suggest he was dominated by expectation of "die Endzeit." On these grounds, we should not suspect too strong a similarity with the Qumran *pesharim*, whose mantological exegesis of the prophetic texts is motivated by eschatological fervor. Similarly, we are not likely to find numerous *Erfüllungsinterpretationen* of Isaianic oracles.[69]

A second means of confirming or overturning this judgment is to explore to what degree the translator equated places, people, and events

---

[67] Ἐμφανές is probably the translator's interpretation of נכון (Mic 4:1 reads ἕτοιμον). This finds support in 65:1, the only other occurrence of ἐμφανής in LXX-Isaiah: ἐμφανὴς ἐγενόμην τοῖς ἐμὲ μὴ ζητοῦσιν || נדרשתי ללוא שאלו. Elsewhere LXX-Isaiah renders כון with βουλεύεσθαι (51:13), διορίζειν (45:18) διωρθοῦν (16:5; 62:7) ἑτοιμάζειν (14:21; 30:33), ἱστάναι (40:20), κατορθοῦν (9:6) and οἰκοδομεῖν (54:14). As for τὸ ὄρος τοῦ κυρίου, the LXX's *Vorlage* probably read הר יהוה in place of the MT's הר יהיה. Καὶ ἥξουσιν is simply the translator's attempt to translate ונהרו (cf. ἥξει || תהרף in 18:6).

[68] The two other occurrences of ἐν (ταῖς) ἐσχάταις ἡμέραις in the LXX are of little help. Prov 31:26(25) renders ליום אחרון with ἐν ἐσχάταις ἡμέραις, while Dan 11:20 (G and θ′) renders ובימים אחדים with ἐν ἐσχάταις ἡμέραις (doubtless reading אחרים). While in both cases it is difficult to perceive the meaning of the phrase, the context of Proverbs 31 does not suggest an eschatological idiom, while Daniel uses such phrases as ἐπ' ἐσχάτου in texts with a clearer eschatological ring (e.g., 10:14: || ἦλθον ὑποδεῖξαί σοι τί ὑπαντήσεται τῷ λαῷ σου ἐπ0 ἐσχάτου τῶν ἡμερῶν [cf. 2:28, 45]). In any case, LXX-Isaiah's use of ἔσχατος must be the yardstick for understanding ἐν ταῖς ἐσχάταις ἡμέραις in Isa 2:2.

[69] Unless, of course, it expresses a type of mantological exegesis that, contrary to other examples from this period, is not driven by eschatological expectation.

in Isaiah's oracles with those of his own era. And a test case for this is his translation of Isaiah's toponyms.

Translation of Toponyms in LXX-Isaiah

Seeligmann considered LXX-Isaiah's toponyms (including allied ethnic names) "eminently suited to giving one an impression of the translator's mental and spiritual horizons," inasmuch as they reveal the translator's "conscious or unconscious tendency to rediscover, in the text he was translating, the world of his own period."[70] For example, because the translator

> replaces, on more than one occasion, the Assyrian king of the Hebrew text by the action of Antiochus Epiphanes, we may be justified in regarding the Greek translation of 10:24 (μὴ φοβοῦ ὁ λαός μου οἱ κατοικοῦντες ἐν Σιων ἀπὸ Ασσυρίων...πληγὴν γὰρ ἐγὼ ἐπάγω ἐπὶ σὲ τοῦ ἰδεῖν ὁδὸν Αἰγύπτου) as echo of the idea of a Jewish emigration from Palestine to Egypt to escape the religious persecution of Antiochus Epiphanes.[71]

In this case, Ασσυρίων does not refer to the ancient Mesopotamian empire, but serves as a cipher for the Seleucids.

Van der Kooij endorsed this inference and sought to give it firmer footing by pointing out that in 10:5 אשור is translated as referring to a people (Ασσυρίων), not a country, and positing that the translator equated the Assyrian king addressed in the succeeding verses with a Seleucid ruler.[72] While van der Kooij disputed Seeligmann's assertion that 10:24 refers to a persecution under Antiochus IV, considering it more likely that "viel eher verband er damit das Unheil, das das Gottesvolk in Jerusalem vor allem 167 v.Chr. getroffen hat, und dieses Unheil scheint eine Flucht nach Ägypten ausgelöst zu haben,"[73] he still found in it a reflection of an event affecting Jerusalem during the early second century B.C.E. Similarly, in the translation of תרשיש by Καρχηδόνος in 23:1, 6, 10, and 14 he has detected an updating of the oracle against Tyre so as to reflect the fall of Carthage to the Romans in 146 B.C.E.[74]

---

[70] Seeligmann, *Septuagint Version*, 76, 79. Cf. Henry Redpath, "The Geography of the Septuagint," *AJT* 7 (1903) 291.

[71] Seeligmann, *Septuagint Version*, 85. Cf. Koenig, *L'Herméneutique*, 45.

[72] Van der Kooij, *Die alten Textzeugen*, 35–36.

[73] Ibid., 39.

[74] Van der Kooij, *The Oracle of Tyre*, 96–98.

Koenig likewise concluded that LXX-Isaiah applied Ἀσσύριοι "aux Syriens de l'époque séleucide" and perceived the translation of תרשיש by Καρχηδόνος in 23:1, 6, 10, and 14 to be "un indice oraculaire très visible."[75] Indeed, for Koenig, "l'interprétation oraculaire de noms géographiques, ethniques ou personnels établit sans conteste que le livre d'Is a été utilisé par G à des fins oraculaires contemporaines."[76]

The question is whether this perception is right: did the translator of LXX-Isaiah treat the toponyms of his *Vorlage* as references to political or ethnic entities in his own day? As a first step towards an answer, we must survey how he rendered the book's 108 different toponyms, which occur an aggregate of 558 times.

In only four instances would I conclude that the translator's *Vorlage* contained a variant vis-à-vis the MT, beyond merely orthographic variants. In 8:14 Ἰακώβ attests יעקב, in place of the MT's ישראל; in 11:16 ἐν Αἰγύπτῳ reflects במצרים in contrast to MT's מאשור; and in 66:19 Φουδ attests פוד in the *Vorlage*, opposite MT's פול. More significantly, in 30:4 the LXX's μάτην suggests its *Vorlage* read חנם rather than MT's חנס. This last case reduces the number of toponyms available to the translator by one, to 557.

Twenty-four of these lack a clear Greek equivalent, but since my interest is in how the translator *represented* toponyms, it is unimportant whether each of these cases is due to an absence from the *Vorlage* or to omission by the translator. For that reason, I will deduct these 24 from the total, leaving 533 instances the translator represents a Hebrew place name.

There are also instances when the translator seems to have found a toponym in his *Vorlage* that is not attested in the MT. The first is in 1:21, where corresponding to איכה היתה לזונה קריה נאמנה the LXX reads πῶς ἐγένετο πόρνη πόλις πιστὴ Σιων. It would appear that a scribe had already inserted ציון as a gloss, since there is no perceptible reason to attribute it to the translator.

Two other instances are similar and adjacent to each other. In 22:1, parallel to the MT's משא גיא חזיון, 'an oracle of the valley of vision', the LXX reads τό ὅραμα τῆς φάραγγος Σιων, 'the word of the valley of Zion'. Similarly, in v. 5 the LXX reads ἐν φάραγγι Σιων parallel to the

---

[75] Koenig, *L'Herméneutique*, 44.
[76] Ibid., 45.

MT's בניא חזיון. There is no convincing reason to deny that the LXX's *Vorlage* read הציון in both places.[77]

Two cases where lexical confusion was a factor are 25:5 and 32:2, where both times the LXX reads ἐν Σιων for the MT's בציון 'in the desert'. These are the only occurrences of ציון in the Tanach, so that the translator can be forgiven for reading the more common proper name.

In all five of these cases, then, the translator can reasonably be said to have found in his *Vorlage* toponyms not attested in the MT. Accordingly, we must increase the number of toponyms available to him to 538.

Of that number, 22 (or 4.1%) are translated with common nouns. E.g., in 15:8 באר אילים is rendered with τοῦ φρέαρτος τοῦ Αιλιμ '*well of Elim*', consistent with the LXX's pattern of translating באר in compound names.[78]

On the other hand, the preponderance of toponyms in Isaiah—430 (79.9%)—are transliterated,[79] in accord with Seeligmann's observation that the translator "shows a preference . . . for transcriptions from Hebrew names of towns and countries above the Hellenistic nomenclature."[80] The transliterations used are most often standard throughout the LXX. Thus, ציון is always rendered by Σιων and ירושלם by Ιερουσαλημ,[81] while דמשק is invariably rendered by Δαμασκός, לבנון by Λίβανος, and בבל by Βαβυλών or Βαβυλωνία. Not only are these place names common in the LXX, but they are also used by such authors as Strabo and Didorus Siculus.[82]

Equally noteworthy are the *hapax legomena* the translator recognized as place names and transliterated. For example, נלים is found in Isaiah

---

[77] Cf. 10:31, where the LXX reads Μαδεβηνα for the MT's מדמנה, apparently finding מדבנה in its *Vorlage*. It is fruitless to deny that the translator's *Vorlage* contained variants. For example, ἅμα in 41:5 clearly reflects יחדו for יחרדו in the *Vorlage*, just as in 44:1 it is due to יחדו for יפחדו. The only reason to maintain that the translator manipulated graphic similarities or the like is a prejudice against finding variants.

[78] Similarly, in 15:1 קיר מואב is translated τὸ τεῖχος τῆς Μωαβίτιδος, and in 16:11 לקיר חרש is represented by ὡσεὶ τεῖχος ὃ ἐνεκαίνισας (the ר of חרש read as ד).

[79] "Transliteration" refers to Greek words whose characters correspond recognizably to the Hebrew characters, whether the word has been adapted to Greek declension (e.g., Ἀσσύριος) or has been preserved indeclinable (e.g., Ασσουρ [Isa 31:8]). I include in the list of place names words that, in Isaiah's vocabulary, also designate the country's people, such as ישראל and יהודה.

[80] Seeligmann, *Septuagint Version*, 77.

[81] ירושלם is not represented in 4:4 and 36:7 (part of a large minus).

[82] For details of usage see BDAG, s.v.

only in 10:29, where it is transliterated Γαλλιμ.[83] מדמנה occurs in the Bible only in Isa 10:31, where the LXX gives Μαδεβηνα, (apparently reading מדבנה). חורנים is rendered Αρωνιιμ in 15:5, but Ωρωναιμ in Jer 31[48]:3, 5, and 34, its only other occurrences in the Bible. LXX-Isaiah represents לוחית with Λουιθ in 15:5, whereas Jer 31[48]:5 gives Αλαωθ, parallel to the MT's הלחות (Qere הלוחית).

On the other hand, of the 538 Hebrew toponyms represented, for only 86 (16%) does the translator use Hellenistic equivalents. Setting aside the ubiquitous rendering of מצרים by Αἴγυπτον (34x) or Αἰγύπτιον (16x),[84] the 36 remaining instances are distributed among 16 words. For example, the eight appearances of כוש are rendered by either Αἰθιοπία (3x) or Αἰθίοψ (5x), equivalents found throughout the LXX. צר appears six times, always rendered by Τύρος, its most common equivalent in the LXX.[85] אדום is thrice rendered Ἰδουμαία, a common LXX equivalent (but Εδωμ in 63:1, which is also found elsewhere in the LXX). In each of its three appearances, צען is rendered by Τάνις, a stock LXX equivalent. Both occurrences of אשדוד are rendered by Ἄζωτος, a common LXX equivalent. As for words appearing just once, נף is rendered by Μεμφις (19:13), as it is throughout the LXX, while יון is rendered with Ἑλλάς (66:19), an equivalent appearing elsewhere in the LXX.

In Isa 27:12 נחל מצרים is translated by Ῥινοκορούρων to mark the southern boundary of the territory the Kyrios will one day enclose within walls. Even though this translation stands within a utopian scene fashioned by the translator, the specification of the boundary by a Hellenistic toponym is no more remarkable than the previous examples.[86] As Ottley comments, "the Alexandrian translator *naturally* gives the Greek name for the 'brook of Egypt.'"[87]

This pattern of using standard Hellenistic equivalents makes the occasional deviation noteworthy. Most remarkable are the equivalents found in 9:11[10]–12[11]:

---

[83] In the word's only other appearance (1 Kgdms 25:44) the LXX reads τῷ ἐκ Ρομμα for the MT's אשר מגלים.

[84] The only variation from this is Ῥινοκορούρων || נחל מצרים in 27:12.

[85] While a linguistic relationship between צר and τύρος is apparent, it is not the degree of transliteration we find nine times in Ezekiel: Σορ (cf. the characteristic Σιδων for צידון).

[86] Ziegler reports that "Rinokorura ist die Grenzstadt zwischen Ägypten under Syrien" (*Untersuchungen*, 203).

[87] Ottley, *The Book of Isaiah*, 2:236, italics mine. Cf. Seeligmann, *Septuagint Version*, 80.

(10)וישֹׂנב יהוה את צרי	(11)καὶ ῥάξει ὁ θεὸς τοὺς ἐπανιστανο-
	μένους
רצין עליו	ἐπ' ὄρος Σιων ἐπ' αὐτοὺς
ואת איביו יסכסך	καὶ τοὺς ἐχθροὺς αὐτῶν διασκεδάσει
(11)ארם מקדם	(12)Συρίαν ἀφ' ἡλίου ἀνατολῶν
ופלשׁתים מאחור	καὶ τοὺς Ἕλληνας ἀφ' ἡλίου δυσμῶν
ויאכלו את ישׂראל בכל פה	τοὺς κατεσθίοντας τὸν Ισραηλ ὅλῳ τῷ
	στόματι

Immediately arresting is τοὺς ἐπανιστανομένους ἐπ' ὄρος Σιων for
MT's את צרי רצין, since elsewhere רצין is transliterated Ῥαασσων, both
inside Isaiah (7:1, 8:6) and out (e.g., 4 Kgdms 15:37; 16:5, 6, 9).[88] While
Seeligmann posited that the translator merely took advantage of the
orthography to find a reference to Zion,[89] the occurrence of ציון as
a gloss in the *Vorlage* at 1:21 and of הציון in place of חזיון in 22:1, 5
favors concluding that the LXX's *Vorlage* read את צרי הר ציון, as Duhm
posited.[90]

More striking is τοὺς Ἕλληνας || פלשׁתים, the singular occurrence
of this equivalence in the LXX and the only place Ἕλλην appears
in LXX-Isaiah, which otherwise translates פלשׁתים by ἀλλόφυλοι (2:6,
11:14), its most common equivalent throughout the LXX and the one
it uses for פלשׁת in 14:29, 31.[91] Ἕλλην occurs five other times in the
LXX, each corresponding to יון in the MT (Joel 4:6; Zech 9:13; Dan 8:21;
10:20; 11:2), a Hebrew toponym that appears in Isa 66:19, where it is
translated by Ἑλλάς. While a graphically anomalous substitution of
ויין for ופלשׁתים in the *Vorlage* cannot be ruled out, we should at least
note that S, T, and V attest ופלשׁתים, while the initial ופל and part of
the final שׁ are visible in 1QIsaᵃ.[92] Given the fact that this is a singular

---

[88] N.B. רצין is translated by ἰάσομαι in Isa 7:4, on which see Troxel, "Isaiah 7,14–16
through the Eyes of the Septuagint," 13 n. 63.

[89] Seeligmann, *Septuagint Version*, 81. 1QIsaᵃ, 4QIsaᵇ, S, and V = MT; T: סנאיה דישׂראל
רצין (in a lacuna in 4QIsaᶜ).

[90] Cited by George Buchanan Gray, *A Critical and Exegetical Commentary on the Book of
Isaiah I–XXVII* (ICC; Edinburgh: T&T Clark, 1912) 185.

[91] Redpath infers that "the translators of these books had some notion that the
Philistines were not of the same blood, i.e., Semite, as the other inhabitants of Canaan,
but of an origin akin to the Hellenic race" ("The Geography of the Septuagint,"
295). He adds that the use of ἀλλοφυλεῖν and ἀλλοφυλισμός "in 4 and 2 Maccabees
respectively, also points toward the Greek world, for they are used of the Hellenizing
party" (ibid., 295 n. 16).

[92] S reads ܐܪܡ for ארם, a common equivalence in the Peshiṭta (Michael Weitzman,
The Syriac Version of the Old Testament [Cambridge, New York, Melbourne: Cambridge,
1999] 49).

equivalence within the book (like 'Ρινοκορούρων in 27:12), it is likely the translator's interpretation of פְּלִשְׁתִּים with an eye to the Hellenized coastal cities, which lay ἀφ' ἡλίου δυσμῶν (מֵאָחוֹר).[93]

The surmise that the translator equated the פְּלִשְׁתִּים with the Hellenistic costal cities of his day finds support from another toponym in this passage, Συρίαν. At first blush this rendering of אֲרָם seems unremarkable, since it is a stock equivalence throughout the lxx (134x).[94] And yet, 9:12 is the only appearance of Συρία in lxx-Isaiah, although we find Σύρος for אֲרָם in 17:3.[95] On the other hand, אֲרָם is transliterated Αραμ in 7:1, 2, 5, and 8,[96] an equivalence found elsewhere in the lxx only in Gen 10:22, 23; 36:28 (mt אֲרָן), and 1 Chr 2:10, 23; 7:34. While in each of those cases Αραμ refers to a person who became the progenitor of a nation,[97] in Isaiah 7 Αραμ designates the nation, as is evident from the rendering of מֶלֶךְ אֲרָם by βασιλεὺς 'Αραμ (7:1). Wevers's speculation that "Αραμ was used to parallel the proper names Ισραήλ and Ιουδά of v. 1 and Εφράιμ of vv. 2, 8 and 9" does not account for why the more frequently occurring Συρία was not used.[98]

Notably, the translator renders another toponym distinctively in chapter 7. Rather than translating שֹׁמְרוֹן by Σαμαρεία, as elsewhere in lxx-Isaiah (8:4; 9:8; 10:9, 10, 11; 36:19) and throughout the lxx, he chose Σομορων, found elsewhere only in 2 Chr 13:4, Ezra 4:10, and Neh 3:34. Taken alongside Αραμ, this suggests that the translator *archaized* the names to lend an air of antiquity to a narrative expressly set in the time of Isaiah.

In contrast to that, and alongside τοὺς ῞Ελληνας, the translator's use of Συρίαν in 9:12 evidently had in view the Syrians of his day, the Seleucids.[99] However, this example proves the rule: the translator did not, by-and-large, treat Isaianic toponyms as surrogates waiting to be unmasked; but when he regarded a place name as relevant to events in his day, he was not shy about substituting a Hellenistic toponym,

---

[93] As Seeligmann summarizes, in these verses "we are directly and unmistakably transported into the historical atmosphere of Palestine in Hellenistic times" (*Septuagint Version*, 81).

[94] For an overview of the lxx's translation of אֲרָם see John Wevers, "Aram and Aramaean in the Septuagint," in *The World of the Aramaeans I*, ed. P. M. Michèle Daviau, John Wevers, Michael Weigl, vol. 1 (JSOTSup 324; Sheffield: Sheffield Press, 2001).

[95] Not surprisingly, Σύρος translates אֲרַמִּי 8x, although 15x it corresponds to אֲרָם.

[96] The lxx lacks a clear equivalent for רְצִין וּבֶן רְמַלְיָהוּ וַאֲרָם in v. 4.

[97] Cf. the conclusion drawn by Wevers, "Aram and Aramaean," 250.

[98] Ibid., 245.

[99] So also Seeligmann, *Septuagint Version*, 81.

even if it was at variance with the Hebrew toponym. As a result, there is no *prima facie* case for taking a commonly occurring equivalent as a cipher for a political entity in the translator's day.

This conclusion applies to two instances noted in the survey of scholars' discussions of place names. While van der Kooij finds significance in the fact that the LXX translated אַשּׁוּר in 10:5 not as the name of a country but a people, he notes that this equivalence is typical for LXX-Isaiah (42x).[100] Moreover, Ἀσσύριοι is the most common equivalent for אַשּׁוּר throughout the LXX (138x). This undercuts the inference that Ἀσσύριοι is, itself, noteworthy. While we will have to await examination of 10:5–14 to see whether the context signals that the translator perceived a Seleucid ruler behind the Assyrian king, that argument cannot rest on his choice of Ἀσσυρίοις. Equally, in 10:24 Ἀσσυρίων, by itself, cannot be used to assert that the translator had in mind Seleucid action against Judea, as Seeligmann proposed.

On the other hand, as noted earlier, van der Kooij has argued that the translation of תַּרְשִׁישׁ by Καρχηδών in 23:1, 6, 10, and 14 is proof the translator engaged in mantological exegesis, inasmuch as it reflects the Roman destruction of Carthage in 146 B.C.E.[101] He bases this identification, first, on the (initially ambiguous) subjects of ἀπώλετο, ἔρχονται, and ἧκται in v. 1:

הֵילִילוּ אֲנִיּוֹת תַּרְשִׁישׁ כִּי שֻׁדַּד	ὀλολύζετε πλοῖα Καρχηδόνος ὅτι ἀπώλετο
מִבַּיִת מִבּוֹא מֵאֶרֶץ כִּתִּים נִגְלָה	καὶ οὐκέτι ἔρχονται ἐκ γῆς Κιτιαίων
	ἧκται αἰχμάλωτος

He points out that v. 14 stands parallel to the first line:

הֵילִילוּ אֲנִיּוֹת תַּרְשִׁישׁ	ὀλολύζετε πλοῖα Καρχηδόνος
כִּי שֻׁדַּד מָעֻזְּכֶן	ὅτι ἀπώλετο τὸ ὀχύρωμα ὑμῶν

Accordingly, "it stands to reason that this fortress is also the implied subject of the last part of vs 1 ('it is led captive'), because both verbs of vs 1 are in the singular."[102] Given that in v. 14 this fortress is Carthage itself, the demise referred to in v. 1 is of that city, the home port of the ships.

---

[100] Van der Kooij, *Die alten Textzeugen*, 35–36.

[101] Idem, *The Oracle of Tyre*, 96–98. This is the only time in Isaiah that Καρχηδών translates תַּרְשִׁישׁ, which is transliterated Θαρσις in 60:9 and 66:19, while in 2:16 כָּל אֲנִיּוֹת תַּרְשִׁישׁ is translated by πᾶν πλοῖον θαλάσσης. LXX-Ezekiel renders תַּרְשִׁישׁ by Καρχηδόνιοι in Ezek 27:12, 25, another oracle about Tyre.

[102] Ibid., 76.

In similar fashion, the subject of ἔρχονται in v. 1 is clarified by the rendering of v. 10:

עברי ארצך	ἐργάζου τὴν γῆν σου
כיאר בת־תרשיש אין מזח עוד	καὶ γὰρ πλοῖα οὐκέτι ἔρχεται ἐκ Καρχηδόνος

If v. 1b is interpreted in the light of this fuller statement, then "the subject of ἔρχονται appears to be '(the) ships'.... That is to say, ships no longer come 'from the land of Kittim', apparently because 'their fortress' has been destroyed."[103]

Vv. 2–3 are equally important to van der Kooij's reading of the LXX's rendition of chapter 23:

למו דמו ישבי אי	[2]τίνι ὅμοιοι γεγόνασιν οἱ ἐνοικοῦντες ἐν τῇ νήσῳ
סחר צידון עבר ים מלאוך	μετάβολοι Φοινίκης διαπερῶντες τὴν θάλασσαν
ובמים רבים זרע שחר	[3]ἐν ὕδατι πολλῷ σπέρμα μεταβόλων
קציר יאור תבואתה	ὡς ἀμητοῦ εἰσφερομένου
ותהי סחר גוים	οἱ μετάβολοι τῶν ἐθνῶν

As van der Kooij notes, μετάβολος, which "refers to the retailer, i.e. the small business man," appears only in these verses in the LXX, whose regular equivalent for סחר is ἔμπορος, "the 'wholesaler', the merchant, the big business man."[104] In fact, ἔμπορος appears in v. 8:

מי יעץ זאת על צר	τίς ταῦτα ἐβούλευσεν ἐπὶ Τύρον
המעטירה אשר סחריה	μὴ ἥσσων ἐστὶν ἢ οὐκ ἰσχύει
סחריה שרים כנעניה נכבדי ארץ	οἱ ἔμποροι αὐτῆς ἔνδοξοι ἄρχοντες τῆς γῆς

Invoking the distinction between the μετάβολοι and the ἔμποροι and recalling that, according to v. 2, "'the retailers of Phoenicia' are supposed to live in Tyre," van der Kooij asks "where the 'wholesalers', 'the merchants', are thought to live."[105] His answer is that they live in Carthage, arguing that "the merchants of Carthage could be regarded as the merchants of Tyre because of the fact that Tyre was the mother-city of Carthage."[106]

---

[103] Ibid., 77.
[104] Ibid., 52.
[105] Ibid., 60.
[106] Ibid., 81.

Also significant for this picture, in van der Kooij's explanation, is the comparison of the μεταβόλοι to activity during harvest: ὡς ἀμητοῦ εἰσφερομένου οἱ μεταβόλοι τῶν ἐθνῶν. He asserts that the meaning of this simile "is not difficult to guess: Instead of 'crossing the sea' as 'the retailers of the nations' 'the retailers of Phoenicia' have become 'as when a harvest is gathered in', that is to say, they have to stay at home."[107] Accordingly, "when the ships no longer come from Carthage…the retailers of Phoenicia, being dependent on the merchants (of Carthage), can no longer do their job."[108]

Parts of van der Kooij's analysis are convincing, such as his argument that v. 1 and v. 10 have been translated synthetically, as evidenced by elements of each verse that derive from the other. Thus, in the case of ἔρχονται (v. 1), he aptly compares the translation of מבוא by τοῦ μὴ εἰσελθεῖν in 24:10 and concludes that, because the translator construed מבוא with the words that follow rather than those that precede it (as does the MT), he rendered it so as to introduce "an independent verbal clause."[109] Because there is no Hebrew construction in v. 10 to warrant ἔρχεται, the translator must have supplied it based on v. 1.

Conversely, οὐκέτι (rather than a simple negative) has been introduced into v. 1 based on οὐκέτι in v. 10, where it translates אֵין...עוֹד. In this light, van der Kooij convincingly argues that καὶ οὐκέτι ἔρχονται "is best understood as part of a strategy of producing a coherent Greek version of ch. 23."[110] Likewise, while πλοῖα in v. 1 is recognizable as a translation of אֳנִיּוֹת, πλοῖα in v. 10 lacks a Hebrew equivalent, suggesting that it has been injected from v. 1.

However, although the translation of v. 1 and v. 10 undeniably entails a type of "cross-fertilization," the question is whether this cross-fertilization runs deep enough to conclude that v. 10 can fill out for us the meaning of v. 1, or if the relationship between them lies more on the level of sharing words and images, without those assuming the same referents in each verse.

For example, while πλοῖα is undoubtedly the subject of ἔρχεται in v. 10, van der Kooij's claim that πλοῖα is the subject of ἔρχονται in v. 1 overlooks the fact that, while the grammatically singular ἔρχεται is what one expects with the neuter plural πλοῖα, the grammatically

---

[107] Ibid., 54.
[108] Ibid., 81.
[109] Ibid., 49.
[110] Ibid., 125.

plural ἔρχονται in v. 1 is peculiar if its subject is πλοῖα. The only plural neuter noun that uses a grammatically plural verb in LXX-Isaiah is
ἔθνος (11:10; 42:4; 43:9; 51:5). While one might argue that ἔρχονται is
a *constructio ad sensum*, the problem for this is καί, which leads the reader
to read this clause consecutively with the preceding one. Given that the
verse begins by exhorting the ships to bewail someone or something
that has perished, the most natural construal of καὶ οὐκέτι ἔρχονται is
as a further reason for doing so. If, as van der Kooij claims, "this part
of the verse has been rendered more freely by creating an independent
clause,"[111] it is curious that the translator did not take measures to disjoin
it from the first half of the verse, such as by inserting anaphoric ταῦτα
or αὐτά. The supposition that he expected the reader to recognize
καὶ οὐκέτι ἔρχονται as introducing a statement independent of what
preceded is strained, and the fact that the translator *chose* to introduce
this clause with simple καί hobbles this argument.[112] Therefore, despite
the clear cross-fertilization between v. 1 and v. 10b, πλοῖα is not likely
the subject of ἔρχονται.

A second problem with van der Kooij's reading of this passage is his
assumption of the perspicuity of the simile, ὡς ἀμητοῦ εἰσφερομένου οἱ
μεταβόλοι τῶν ἐθνῶν. For van der Kooij, the evident meaning is that
the retailers "have to stay at home"; but this is hardly the only possibility. For example, the image of a harvest being brought in could signify
hard work, or it could have in view the surfeit of goods the harvest
supplies. Either of these (which are but two alternatives) seems more
likely than a parallel between a circumstance incidental to the harvest
itself and the circumstances of the retailers.

Moreover, given van der Kooij's explanation of v. 1 as urging the
"ships of Carthage" to lament their fallen port, his explanation of this
simile as requiring the μεταβόλοι of Phoenicia to stay home proves
tortuous, as is apparent from his later exposition of the simile's import:
"when the ships no longer come from Carthage...the retailers of
Phoenicia, being dependent on the merchants (of Carthage), can no
longer do their job."[113] While this is consistent with the initial image

---

[111] Ibid., 124.
[112] This is a good example of why the questions of translation style and of *Vorlage*
cannot be severed; they affect one another.
[113] Van der Kooij, *The Oracle of Tyre*, 81. Cf. his summary of vv. 2–3 conjointly with
v. 10: "Tyre is called to change to agriculture, because there is no longer work for the
retailers, since ships with merchandise no longer come from Carthage" (ibid., 79).

of the "ships of Carthage" (presumably carrying merchandise), it collides with the simile if that implies that "instead of 'crossing the sea' as 'the retailers of the nations' 'the retailers of Phoenicia'...have to stay at home."[114] Who, after all, is traveling in this passage: the ships bringing merchandise to Tyre or the retailers voyaging to Carthage? The confusion this reading introduces into the passage as a unit in Greek invalidates it.

Finally, while the translator's choice of μεταβόλοι in 23:2–3 is striking, it is not as significant as van der Kooij suggests, especially in terms of a contrast with the ἔμποροι in v. 8. On the one hand, while μεταβόλος appears only here in the LXX, we must note that μεταβολή occurs elsewhere, including Isa 47:15:

| כן היו לך אשר | οὗτοι ἔσονταί σοι βοήθεια |
| יגעת סחריך מנעוריך | ἐκοπίασας ἐν τῇ μεταβολῇ σου ἐκ νεότητος |

It is difficult to see any difference in this use of μεταβολή from his use of ἐμπορία in 23:18, where it likewise (and twice) translates סחר:

והיה סחרה ואתננה	καὶ ἔσται αὐτῆς ἡ ἐμπορία καὶ ὁ μισθὸς
קדש ליהוה	ἅγιον τῷ κυρίῳ
לא יאצר ולא יחסן	οὐκ αὐτοῖς συναχθήσεται
כי לישבים לפני יהוה	ἀλλὰ τοῖς κατοικοῦσιν ἔναντι κυρίου
יהיה סחרה לאכל לשבעה	πᾶσα ἡ ἐμπορία αὐτῆς φαγεῖν καὶ πιεῖν καὶ ἐμπλησθῆναι
ולמכסה עתיק	εἰς συμβολὴν μνημόσυνον ἔναντι κυρίου

The fact that the translator can use μεταβολή and ἐμπορία synonymously raises the question of whether μεταβόλος and ἔμποροι were semantically distinct for him. Assuming that they were compels van der Kooij to identify them as different groups. However, he also assumes that this entails a *geographic* distinction: "Since 'the retailers of Phoenicia' are supposed to live in Tyre (cf. vs 2), then the question arises where the 'wholesellers', the 'merchants', are thought of to live."[115] He posits that these "wholesellers of Tyre" are Carthaginians whose title is attributable to the fact that "Tyre was the mother-city of Carthage."[116] And yet, why assume that the μεταβόλοι and ἔμποροι hail from different cities, even if it could be shown that the translator assumed they held

---

[114] Ibid., 54.
[115] Ibid., 60.
[116] Ibid., 81.

the roles van der Kooij distinguishes? The only reason to posit this is the *a priori* that the translator finds forecast in chapter 23 the loss of Tyre's trading partner in 146 B.C.E.

Each of these criticisms undermines van der Kooij's claim that the translator presents an "updated prophecy" that finds presaged in the oracle against Tyre the fall of Carthage to the Romans. There is no indication that Καρχηδών was chosen due to contemporaneous political circumstances. More likely, the translator wanted to identify תרשיש in chapter 23 with a city allied economically with Tyre in his day, just as he used the Hellenistic Ῥινοκορούρων for נחל מצרים in 27:12, and just as Gen 23:2 equates קרית ארבע with חברון for its readers.

In sum, the translator's choice of Greek equivalents for Hebrew toponyms is, in general, too unremarkable to assume that he character-istically perceived Hebrew names as ciphers for political entities of his day. While he sometimes reflects his milieu through use of Hellenistic toponyms, and occasionally those might reflect the political map of his day (as is surely the case with τοὺς Ἕλληνας || פלשתים in 9:12[11]), that is merely one of the influences on his rendering of Isaiah. Each case must be taken on its own, but the evidence presented here argues against the sort of rampant "contemporization" of toponyms in the light of political circumstances often posited for this translator, even as his non-specialized use of ἔσχατος undercuts the portrayal of him as an eschatological enthusiast.

Of course, we have yet to study passages where Seeligmann and van der Kooij (in particular) have perceived the translator treating Ἀσσύριοι as a cipher for Antiochus IV and the Seleucids. Because those passages are crucial to estimating to what degree he "contemporized" the text, we must turn to how LXX-Isaiah portrays rulers and the question of whether he identified his era and its rulers as the ultimate referents of Isaiah's oracles.

CHAPTER SEVEN

ISRAEL'S OPPRESSORS IN LXX-ISAIAH

The general critique of "contemporization" given in chapter six must yield to exploration of whether the translator infused Isaiah's images of a tyrant afflicting Israel with allusions to Antiochus IV and prohibition of Torah study and practice during Jerusalem's Hellenistic crisis of the early second century B.C.E. As a first step, we must note that the translation does reflect the practice, common among Hellenistic rulers, of heavily taxing subjected peoples.

Fiscal oppression

This leitmotif, indebted to ideas extrinsic to the translator's source text, is noticeable in three passages,[1] the first of which is 3:12–15:

עמי נגשׂיו מעולל[2]	[12]λαός μου οἱ πράκτορες ὑμῶν καλαμῶνται ὑμᾶς
ונשׁים משׁלו בו	καὶ οἱ ἀπαιτοῦντες κυριεύουσιν ὑμῶν
עמי מאשׁריך מתעים	λαός μου οἱ μακαρίζοντες ὑμᾶς πλανῶσιν ὑμᾶς
ודרך ארחתיך בלעו	καὶ τὴν τρίβον τῶν ποδῶν ὑμῶν ταράσσουσιν
נצב לריב יהוה[3]	[13]ἀλλὰ νῦν καταστήσεται εἰς κρίσιν κύριος
ועמד לדין עמים	καὶ στήσει εἰς κρίσιν τὸν λαὸν αὐτοῦ
יהוה במשׁפט יבוא[4]	[14]αὐτὸς κύριος εἰς κρίσιν ἥξει

---

[1] For the theme of financial plunder in 5:5–7, 16–17; 6:11–13, where it is not explicitly bound with the malfeasance of rulers, see Ronald L. Troxel, "Economic Plunder as a Leitmotif in LXX-Isaiah," *Bib* 83 (2002) 375–91.

[2] V. 12–1QIsaᵃ reads נגשׂו for נגשׂיו, משׂריו for מאשׁריך, and has a *yôd* written above the *kāp* of ודרך, while בלעו is obscured by a tear, although the top of a *lāmed* is visible, as is a final *wāw*. S reformulates עמי נגשׂיו מעולל as ܐܠܦܗ̈ܝܢ, ܕܚܪ ܐܬܬܠܘ; it reads ܐܠܦܗ̈ܝܢ for מתעים, likely attributable to the translator supplying a pronoun parallel to ܟܘܢ (cf. LXX, V, T); its translation of בלעו by ܕܠܘ parallels ταράσσουσιν (cf. its rendering of תטחנו in v. 15). V reads *ipsi te decipiunt* || מתעים (cf. LXX & S). T's expansion of מעולל into אכרם into כמעללי בזוזה parallels καλαμῶνται; its rendering of נשׁים by חובא כמרי is inscrutable; like LXX, S, and V, it provides a pronoun in its rendering of מתעים (אטעיוך).

[3] V. 13–1QIsaᵃ does not attest the initial *wāw* of ועמד (it reads a *wāw* mater after ע). S reads ܠܚܡܡ for עמים. V presupposes a *Vorlage* = MT, as does T's expansive rendering.

[4] V. 14–1QIsaᵃ = MT. 4QIsaᵇ preserves only עם זקני עם and יבא and [בבתי]כם, although many letters are indistinct. S accords with the MT. V reads *in domo vestra* (singular) for בבתיכם. T generalizes the sense of בערהם, translating it with אנסתון, but concretizes הכרם עמי with עמי.

עם זקני עמו   μετὰ τῶν πρεσβυτέρων τοῦ λαοῦ
ושריו   καὶ μετὰ τῶν ἀρχόντων αὐτοῦ
ואתם בערתם הכרם   Ὑμεῖς δὲ τί ἐνεπυρίσατε τὸν ἀμπελῶνά μου
גזלת העני בבתיכם   καὶ ἡ ἁρπαγὴ τοῦ πτωχοῦ ἐν τοῖς οἴκοις ὑμῶν
מלכם תדכאו עמי[5]   [15]τί ὑμεῖς ἀδικεῖτε τὸν λαόν μου
ופני עניים תטחנו   καὶ τὸ πρόσωπον τῶν πτωχῶν καταισχύνετε[6]

Especially revealing is the translation of נגשיו by οἱ πράκτορες ὑμῶν,[7] the sole occurrence of this noun in the LXX.[8] BDAG (s.v.) defines πράκτωρ as a technical term "designating certain officials, esp. tax-collectors and other finance officials," while Moulton and Milligan report that "the πράκτωρ in Ptolemaic times was specially concerned with the exaction of fines or payments."[9]

The reasoning behind the translator's use of πράκτωρ is disclosed by his choice of καὶ οἱ ἀπαιτοῦντες ('and those who demand payment'), a verb frequently used in the papyri for the collection of taxes.[10] The translator evidently construed נשים as a participle from נשה (= נשא), helping him also arrive at οἱ πράκτορες ὑμῶν for נגשיו, for which he later

---

[5] V. 15–1QIsaᵃ = MT in 15a–b, while אדני is written superlinearly over יהוה in 15c (not attested in the LXX). 4QIsaᵇ preserves only מלכם תדכאו עמי, although several letters are indistinct. S reads ܐܬܡܟܟܘ for תטחנו, like καταισχύνετε (cf. its rendering of בלעו in v. 12); whether its ܣܠܒܐ ܐܡܪ ܬܒ ܡܪܝܐ || נאם אדני יהוה צבאות attests the absence of אדני [cf. 1QIsaᵃ] or simply a collapsing of אדני יהוה is uncertain. V accords with the MT. T gives the obscure equivalent דאתון ממסכנין for תדכאו, while its equivalent for ופני עניים תטחנו is expansive and oblique: מובלין אתון ומיתן בדיניהון (ואפי חשיכיא).

[6] The LXX lacks the phrase אדני יהוה צבאות in v. 15c.

[7] While ὑμῶν might reflect נגשיך (rather than נגשיו) in the *Vorlage* (with ὑμῶν expressing the collective 2ms suffix—cf. οἱ μακαρίζοντες ὑμᾶς || מאשריך, τῶν ποδῶν ὑμῶν || ארחתיך), it is also possible that the translator adjusted the pronoun under influence of עמי (understood as a vocative), since elsewhere he altered pronouns to produce homogeneity (cf. 3:7, where ἔσομαι ἀρχηγός || תשימני קצין is likely due to the parallelism with οὐκ ἔσομαί σου ἀρχηγός || לא תשב אהיה earlier in the verse). Similarly, while (κυριεύουσιν) ὑμῶν might reflect בך for בו, and πλανῶσιν ὑμᾶς might attest מתעיך instead of מתעים (kāp/mēm confusion in paleo-Hebrew?), the translator's tailoring of pronouns elsewhere suggests he likely created these differences. He was certainly responsible for supplying ὑμᾶς as the direct object of καλαμῶνται.

[8] נגש is rendered variously in LXX-Isaiah. In 14:2 נגשיהם is translated with οἱ κυριεύσαντες αὐτῶν, while in 60:17 נגשיך is translated τοὺς ἄρχοντάς σου (the *Vorlage* suffered transposition of ונגשיך and פקדתך). On the other hand, in 9:4 (3) הנגש בו is represented by τῶν ἀπαιτούντων (see below), while in 14:4 נגש is represented by ὁ ἀπαιτῶν.

[9] James H. Moulton and George Milligan, *The Vocabulary of the Greek Testament Illustrated from the Papyri and other Non-Literary Sources* (Grand Rapids: Eerdmans, 1930) 533.

[10] Ibid., 52. Ziegler reports that ἀπαιτητής in the papyri designates a tax collector (*Untersuchungen*, 200). Cf. Ottley's translation of οἱ ἀπαιτοῦντες κυριεύουσιν ὑμῶν: 'the tax gatherers shall lord it over you' (*The Book of Isaiah*, 1:73).

also used ἀπαιτεῖν (9:4[3]; 14:4). The translation of נגשיו by πράκτορες (parallel to οἱ ἀπαιτοῦντες for נשׁים) suggests the Hellenistic system of tax collection, showing that the translator cast these abusive rulers as "tax farmers."[11]

While καλαμῶνται reflects the translator's association of מעולל with עוללות, 'gleanings' (cf. 24:13), that choice was equally studied, given the variety of equivalents for עלל√ earlier in the chapter (καὶ ἐμπαῖκται for ותעלולים in v. 4 [cf. 66:4]; μετὰ ἀνομίας for ומעלליהם in v. 8;[12] τῶν ἔργων for מעלליהם in v. 10). This translation, no doubt encouraged by the mention of the vineyard in v. 14, creates a striking metaphor in which (as Ottley observed) καλαμῶνται approaches "the sense of English 'fleece.'"[13]

Thus, while v. 12 in the MT demeans Judah's officials for childish behavior and ridicules as "women" those misleading the people, the LXX depicts leaders who are guilty of imposing onerous taxes, behavior also referred to as "troubling the paths of this people."[14] Clearly the translator lived in an age when rulers severely taxed their population.[15]

That milieu is equally reflected in the rendering of the lament for the מלך בבל in 14:4:

איך שׁבת נגשׂ   πῶς ἀναπέπαυται ὁ ἀπαιτῶν
שׁבתה מדהבה   καὶ ἀναπέπαυται ὁ ἐπισπουδαστής

Ὁ ἀπαιτῶν || נגשׂ is revealing, since in v. 2 ורדו בנגשׂיהם is rendered as καὶ κυριευθήσονται οἱ κυριεύσαντες αὐτῶν. Moreover, parallel to ὁ ἀπαιτῶν is ὁ ἐπισπουδαστής,[16] which appears only here in the LXX and,

---

[11] See Hengel, *Judaism and Hellenism*, 1:18–23.

[12] As Seeligmann suggested, this is likely based on מעל, as in 1 Chr 9:1; 10:13 (*Septuagint Version*, 54).

[13] Ottley, *The Book of Isaiah*, 2:118.

[14] The translator characteristically renders בלע with καταπίνειν (9:16; 16:8; 25:8; 28:4; 49:19), while he employs ταράσσειν erratically, using it 12x, but never more than once for any Hebrew word and sometimes with an opaque relationship to the word in the MT (e.g. for צהלי in 24:14; התרעעה in 24:19; להנפה in 30:28). Accordingly, it is likely that he chose ταράσσουσιν for בלעו in 3:12 to resolve the oblique metaphor of "*devouring* the way of your paths."

[15] Raurell sees this verse, which he calls "the most targumic or midrashic of the whole chapter," as defining ἐμπαῖκται, the epithet applied to these rulers in v. 4, in as much as they fail to show correct esteem for the Lord and his people ("«Archontes»," 346, translation by Prof. Mary Lou Daniels). Das Neves likewise perceives here a characterization of the rulers as seeking "to pervert the faithful class who follow the paths of justice" (*A Teologia*, 76, translation mine).

[16] The LXX's *Vorlage* may well have read מרהבה, as Ottley (*The Book of Isaiah*, 2:176) and Ziegler (*Untersuchungen*, 200) argued and as 1QIsaᵃ now attests (cf. S's ܡܣܬ,

like πράκτωρ, is a *Beamtenbezeichnung* from the Ptolemaic administrative system, in which it designated a tax agent.[17] By pairing ὁ ἀπαιτῶν and ὁ ἐπισπουδαστής, the translator ascribes to the Babylonian king a prime attribute of rulers in his own day. This does not necessarily mean that he considered the מלך בבל a surrogate for a particular Hellenistic ruler. It need mean no more than that he assumed this behavior of rulers in his era would have been followed by the despised Babylonian king; it is just what rulers do.

3:13 describes the reign of such rulers coming to a dramatic end. While the MT simply juxtaposes its descriptions of inept rulers and judgment,[18] the LXX subjoins the judgment scene in a more nuanced way by means of ἀλλὰ νῦν. Even if this phrase should reflect a ו prefixed to נצב in the *Vorlage*, the translator's choice of ἀλλὰ νῦν strikingly introduces the reversal of conditions in the judgment of the rulers.[19]

Whereas in the MT the LORD stands to judge peoples (עמים), in the LXX the Kyrios appoints (καταστήσεται) and stations (στήσει)[20] τὸν λαὸν αὐτοῦ for judgment (probably reflecting עמו in the *Vorlage*; cf. S).[21] Although εἰς κρίσιν (for both לריב and לדין) might suggest that the Kyrios marshals his people in preparation for passing judgment on them, v. 14 takes us in a different direction.

The representation of יהוה במשפט יבוא עם by κύριος εἰς κρίσιν ἥξει μετά shows that the translator constructed a coherent representation of the action in these verses. While the translation of every other occurrence of this idiom in the LXX connotes entering into litigation,[22]

'he who incites'). The only other appearance of רהב in Isaiah is in 3:5, where the LXX translates ירהבו הנער הנקלה בנכבד והנקלה בזקן with προσκόψει τὸ παιδίον πρὸς τὸν πρεσβύτην ὁ ἄτιμος πρὸς τὸν ἔντιμον.

[17] Ziegler, *Untersuchungen*, 200.

[18] Indeed, in the MT judgment is not even directed against the rulers of v. 12, but against עמים. Even if we were to adopt עמו instead (based on the LXX and S), it is not clear that the judgment of v. 13 is to be associated with v. 12.

[19] Cf. διότι νῦν in 3:8; διὰ τοῦτο in 8:15; καὶ νῦν in 2:5 and 26:11. Note especially νῦν δέ in 14:15; 33:4; 47:9, where in each case it has been supplied by the translator to signal a reversal of conditions.

[20] Given the awkwardness of the transitive verbs καταστήσεται and στήσει in the LXX's scene, it seems likely that its *Vorlage* read יצב for נצב and ויעמד for יעמד; it seems unlikely the translator would have concocted this awkward element in the action.

[21] As Gray suggested, the MT's עמים has "arisen from the desire to turn the particular judgment of Israel into a world judgment" (*Isaiah I–XXVII*, 69). The likelihood that LXX's *Vorlage* read עמו rather than עמים finds support in S's ܥܡܗ, especially since S does not follow the LXX's rendering of these verses in other respects.

[22] Elsewhere this phrase is translated: μὴ εἰσέλθῃς εἰς κρίσιν μετά (Ps 142[143]:2), εἰσελθεῖν ἐν κρίματι ἐνώπιόν (Job 14:3), καὶ συνεισελεύσεταί σοι εἰς κρίσιν (Job 22:4), ἄξει ὁ θεός ἐν κρίσει (Qoh 11:9), ἄξει ἐν κρίσει (Qoh 12:14).

this phrase means something different.[23] First, since both occurrences of εἰς κρίσιν in v. 13 mean *"for* judgment," εἰς κρίσιν here most likely carries the same meaning.[24] Second, the translation of יבוא with ἥξει (rather than εἰσέρχεσθαι or the like [cf. n. 22]) connotes the *arrival* of the Kyrios to execute judgment. Consequently, αὐτὸς κύριος εἰς κρίσιν ἥξει signals a judgment theophany: 'the Kyrios himself shall come for judgment'.[25] While αὐτός might reflect הוא in the translator's *Vorlage*, more likely he supplied it. Just as he marked the reversal of affairs with ἀλλὰ νῦν at the beginning of v. 13, his interpolation of αὐτός spotlights the arrival of the Kyrios to effect a reversal by judging the rulers.

The representation of the suffix of ושריו with αὐτοῦ indicates the translator perceived its antecedent as עמו rather than יהוה (for which ἑαυτοῦ would be expected). Thus, τῶν πρεσβυτέρων τοῦ λαοῦ and τῶν ἀρχόντων αὐτοῦ are those the Kyrios judges rather than those accompanying him;[26] they are the rulers who "fleece" the people.

While τὸν ἀμπελῶνά μου might reflect כרמי for הכרם in the *Vorlage*, the translator's accent on the indictment of the wicked rulers could just as easily have prompted him to insert the possessive pronoun,[27] opposite ὑμεῖς at the start of the accusation.[28] Similarly, while τί before ἐνεπυρίσατε could reflect למה after ואתם, the translator might well have supplied it himself to correspond to τί in v. 15 (מלכם).[29]

Moreover, while ἁρπαγή at first blush seems a suitable match for גזלת, it is noteworthy that everywhere else גזלה appears in the Bible, the LXX renders it with ἅρπαγμα (Lev 5:23; Ezek 18:7, 12, 16; 33:15), a word LXX-Isaiah uses to render גזל in 61:8.[30] By contrast, the translator uses ἁρπαγή in the sense of 'the act of plunder' in 10:2, the only other occurrence of ἁρπαγή in LXX-Isaiah, where εἰς ἁρπαγήν

---

[23] As Aejmelaeus reasons, it is in the use of non-standard equivalents that the intention of a translator becomes evident ("Translation Technique," 28–30).

[24] It is impossible to determine whether the translator's *Vorlage* read למשפט for במשפט.

[25] Cf. the theophany of 4:5 (καὶ ἥξει || ובא), although it is likely due to a *Vorlage* that read ובוא (cf. one de Rossi manuscript: יבוא) or ויבוא (cf. 1QIsa: ויברא).

[26] Μετά before τῶν ἀρχόντων αὐτοῦ might reflect a second עם in the *Vorlage*, inserted to enhance the parallelism, although it is also possible the translator supplied it for the same reason.

[27] Cf. T's concretization of the image with עמי.

[28] Cf. v. 6, where the opposition τὸ ὑπὸ σὲ ἔστω led the translator to render הזאת with τὸ ἐμόν.

[29] No interrogative pronoun or particle is found in 1QIsa³, S, or T, while V translates ואתם with *vos enim*.

[30] The translator also uses ἅρπαγμα in 42:22: ὁ ἐξαιρούμενος ἅρπαγμα || מציל משסה.

translates שׁללם and stands parallel to εἰς προνομήν (|| יבזו). These data hint that the translator chose ἁρπαγή in 3:14 with a view to the *act* of plundering rather than the goods taken, which suggests that the translator understood the metaphor of the burned vineyard in light of the description of the people as economically plundered by οἱ πράκτορες/οἱ ἀπαιτοῦντες.

Because in v. 13 the Kyrios stations the people for judgment, and yet those arraigned are the rulers, the stationing of the people is but a prelude to the rulers' arraignment,[31] meaning that the people fill the role of victims rather than malfeasants. It is, then, towards the abusive rulers that the questions of v. 15 are directed.

In continuing the charges against those who have mistreated the people, the translator represented תדכאו by ἀδικεῖτε, the lone occurrence of this equivalence in the LXX. While דכא ('crush') was probably unfamiliar to him,[32] his choice of ἀδικεῖν for תדכאו is likely more than arbitrary, since (as Seeligmann observed) for LXX-Isaiah ἀδικεῖν is a "special wellnigh [sic] technical term, to express, without any direct sanction from the Hebrew text, the violence from which Israel was made to suffer by other peoples."[33] Even if those taken to task here are native rulers, this use of ἀδικεῖν fits the pattern Seeligmann noted, inasmuch as this is a case of violence against Israel.[34]

The other noteworthy element is the translation of תטחנו by καταισχύνετε. In 47:2 the translator renders וטחני קמח with ἄλεσον ἄλευρον ('grind meal'), comporting with equivalents for טחן elsewhere in the LXX.[35] Ziegler justifiably concludes that the translator chose

---

[31] Raurell overlooks these signals and thus constructs an artificial scheme in which τὸν λαὸν αὐτοῦ of v. 13 designates "the powerful ones of the people," while τοῦ λαοῦ in vv. 14 designates the poor ("<<Archontes>>," 350).

[32] In 53:10 he connects דכאו with Aramaic דכא (καθαρίσαι αὐτόν), as does T. And while the LXX translates ולהחיות לב נדכאים with καὶ διδοὺς ζωὴν τοῖς συντετριμμένοις τὴν καρδίαν in 57:15, the translation of ואת דכא ושפל רוח as καὶ ὀλιγοψύχοις διδοὺς μακροθυμίαν earlier in the verse raises questions about the translator's knowledge of דכא, 'to crush'. A perusal of equivalents elsewhere suggests דכא posed problems for all LXX translators.

[33] Seeligmann, *Septuagint Version*, 42. Cf. Raurell, "<<Archontes>>," 342. Cf. T's generalizing דאתון ממסכנין for תדכאו.

[34] Cf. Coste, who notes that "la version grecque d'Isaïe connaît les ἀδικήσαντες, c'est-à-dire les ennemies du peuple saint pris comme un tout," citing 20:20, 51:23, and 65:25, and directing the reader to compare 3:15 ("Le texte Grec," 53).

[35] ἀλεῖν is an Attic form of ἀλήθειν, which is used for טחן in Num 11:8; Judg 16:21; Qoh 12:3, and for טחנה in Qoh 12:4. The compound καταλεῖν appears in Exod 32:20 and Deut 9:21.

καταισχύνειν (as well as ἀδικεῖν) because "die Bilder sind wohl... dem griech. Übersetzer zu real und derb vorgekommen."[36] Given his selection of ἀδικεῖν for the unfamiliar דכא, the translator settled on καταισχύνειν as a comparable action.[37]

The cumulative effect of the translator's maneuvers in 3:12–15 is to describe Israel's rulers as "fleecing" the people through heavy taxation, metaphorically depicted as "burning my vineyard," but also described concretely as ἁρπαγή. Such oppressors will be judged, via a theophany, for doing violence to the people of he Kyrios.

Isa 9:4(3)–5(4) reprises the theme of the people wrongly deprived of goods by tax collectors who will, in turn, incur punishment:

כי את על סבלו[38]	[4)]διότι ἀφαιρεθήσεται ὁ ζυγὸς ὁ ἐπ' αὐτῶν κείμενος
ואת מטה שכמו	καὶ ἡ ῥάβδος ἡ ἐπὶ τοῦ τραχήλου αὐτῶν
שבט הנגש בו	τὴν γὰρ ῥάβδον τῶν ἀπαιτούντων
החתת כיום מדין	διεσκέδασεν κύριος ὡς τῇ ἡμέρᾳ τῇ ἐπὶ Μαδιαμ
כי כל סאון סאן ברעש[39]	5)ὅτι πᾶσαν στολὴν ἐπισυνηγμένην δόλῳ
ושמלה מגוללה בדמים	καὶ ἱμάτιον μετὰ καταλλαγῆς ἀποτείσουσι
והיתה לשרפה מאכלת אש	καὶ θελήσουσιν εἰ ἐγενήθησαν πυρίκαυστοι

The translator's path from his *Vorlage* to his rendering can be reconstructed with reasonable certainty. On the one hand, his translation of [ואת מטה] שכמו by [καὶ ἡ ῥάβδος] ἡ ἐπὶ τοῦ τραχήλου αὐτῶν[40] suggests that [ὁ

---

[36] Ziegler, *Untersuchungen*, 81. Cf. S's ܡܣܚܒܝܢ and T's מובלין אתון ומיתן בדינהון.

[37] On at least two other occasions the translator appealed to forms of αἰσχύνη when faced with difficulties. In 28:16 the LXX translates המאמין לא יחיש with καὶ ὁ πιστεύων ἐπ' αὐτῷ οὐ μὴ καταισχυνθῇ, while in 47:10 the translation of שובבתך by σοι αἰσχύνη (cf. its difficulty with שוב in 49:5; 57:17) evinces how close to hand the notion of shame was for the translator.

[38] V. 4–1QIsaᵃ reads והחתת (plus initial *wāw*) and מדים for מדין. 4QIsaᶜ reads only [הח]תותי כ[יום], although both the initial ת and the כ are indistinct. S translates סבלו with ܣܘܒܠܗ (cf. its ܬܒܪ || הנגש) and renders the 3ms suffix of שכמו as 3mp (ܣܘܒܠܗܘܢ), as it does the suffix of בו (ܒܗ). V's *exactoris eius* || הנגש בו shows the influence of the LXX's τῶν ἀπαιτούντων. T's rendering is expansive (including insertion of the verb אעדיתא at the outset) but appears to presuppose a *Vorlage* = MT.

[39] V. 5–1QIsaᵃ = MT. 4QIsaᶜ preserves only [בדמ]ין והיתה לש[רפה]. S appears stumped by סאון סאן, which it renders with ܠܐ ܐܝܟܐ, probably comparing it to שאון. V seems equally at a loss, rendering כי כל סאון סאן ברעש with *quia omnis violenta praedatio cum tumultu*; it does not represent the initial *wāw* of והיתה. T also seems to have had difficulty with כי כל סאון סאן ברעש, rendering it by ארי כל מיסבהון ומיתנהו, ברשע אתנעלו בחובין while the remainder of its verse is strongly periphrastic.

[40] For τραχήλου αὐτῶν || שכמו cf. 10:27. The representation of the 3ms suffix by αὐτῶν was determined by εὐφρανθήσονται, v. 2.

ζυγὸς] ὁ ἐπ᾽ αὐτῶν κείμενος is his guess for סבלו [את על], a noun apparently unfamiliar to him.[41] On the other hand, he probably supplied ἀφῄρηται in light of the like phrases in 10:27 and 14:25.

His insertion of γάρ shows that he saw the second half of the verse explaining the first: the yoke and the rod lying on the people has been removed, inasmuch as τὴν... ῥάβδον τῶν ἀπαιτούντων has been shattered.[42]

The rendering of הנגש בו by τῶν ἀπαιτούντων is striking, given what we witnessed in 3:12–15. While the *Vorlage* likely read הנגשם (i.e., בו ligated into ם), the choice of ἀπαιτεῖν recalls his rendering of ונשים by καὶ οἱ ἀπαιτοῦντες in 3:12, parallel to his translation of נגשיו with οἱ πράκτορες. Given the talk of these ἀπαιτούντων 'repaying' (ἀποτείσουσιν) garments gained 'deceitfully' (δόλῳ)[43] and of exacting an 'exorbitant fee' (μετὰ καταλλαγῆς),[44] τῶν ἀπαιτούντων denotes the same sort of tax agents described as the people's oppressors in chapter 3.

The "rod" of these tax collectors is said already to have been broken by the Kyrios. While one can perceive the translator's path from החתת to διεσκέδασεν, his interpolation of κύριος as its subject is noteworthy, not simply because it requires a different grammatical person for החתת (unless his *Vorlage* had suffered haplography of the final *tāw*) but also because the assertion that the κύριος has acted against this group echoes the insistence of chapter 3 that the κύριος himself would judge the rulers who had "gleaned" the people.

Accordingly, 9:3–4 provides further evidence that the motif of the people's economic plunder by their rulers superintended the translator's interpretation of some passages. Again it is not clear that the translator had in view a specific ruler. He simply describes rulers according to the behaviors with which he is familiar.

Having seen evidence of the translator insinuating behavior commonplace among rulers in his day, we must investigate whether his renderings were driven by more than just subliminal influences: whether

---

[41] As indicated by his rendering of סבלו with ὁ φόβος αὐτοῦ in 10:27 and τὸ κῦδος αὐτῶν in 14:25.

[42] Cf. Johan Lust, "Messianism in the Septuagint: Isaiah 8:23b–9:6 (9:1–7)," in *The Interpretation of the Bible*, ed. Jože Krašovec (Sheffield: Sheffield University Press, 1998) 159.

[43] The choice of δόλῳ for ברעש (read as ברשע, as also in T) is revealing, since it specifies the kind of "wickedness" he saw at work in these dealings.

[44] As Ziegler suggests, the translation of בדמים by μετὰ καταλλαγῆς may be based on the late Hebrew use of דמים to denote a purchase price (Ziegler, *Untersuchungen*, 195).

he deliberately molded the depiction of Israel's oppressor in Isaiah to the image of Antiochus IV Epiphanes.

Antiochus IV

Chief among the translator's reflections of his political environment that Seeligmann detected was the refashioning of Isaiah's "figure of the great king...threatening Israel...into a Hellenistic ruler of the translator's own period."[45] Comparing the cryptic allusions to Antiochus in the book of Daniel and the explicit images in 1 & 2 Maccabees, Seeligmann concluded that "popular imagination endowed Antiochus Epiphanes with all the features of the Oppressor described by Isaiah" and that the translator of Isaiah wove those popular images into his "midrashic" renderings of 8:8, 14:18–20, and 10:5–6, 24.[46]

Van der Kooij has endorsed Seeligmann's judgment on most of these passages. He concludes for 14:19–20 that "mit einem König von Babylon, der das Volk Gottes getötet hat, dürfte der seleukidische König Antiochus IV. gemeint sein."[47] Equally in accord with Seeligmann, he judges that "der Übersetzer in LXX Jes 8,8ª die Absetzung Onias' III. durch Antiochus IV. anvisiert."[48] He also affirms Seeligmann's perception that behind the 'Ασσύριοι in 10:5 lurk the Seleucids,[49] although he disputes Seeligmann's conclusion that talk of seizing τὴν χώραν τὴν ἐπάνω Βαβυλῶνος καὶ Χαλαννη οὗ ὁ πύργος ᾠκοδομήθη (v. 9) is an exegetical reflex of Gen 11:2,[50] considering it, instead, to reflect Antiochus III's recapture of territory north of Babylon in 222 B.C.E., with Χαλαννη serving as a cipher for "der Hauptstadt der seleukidischen Reiches."[51] He differs with Seeligmann even more markedly regarding 10:24, contending that "ist aufgrund von LXX Jes 22,1–11...unwahrscheinlich, dass der Übersetzer πληγή auf eine religiöse Verfolgung durch Antiochus IV. bezog," thinking it more likely that "viel eher verband er damit das Unheil, das das Gottesvolk in Jerusalem vor allem 167 v.Chr. getroffen hat, und dieses Unheil scheint eine Flucht nach Ägypten

---

45 Seeligmann, *Septuagint Version*, 82.
46 Ibid., 83.
47 Van der Kooij, *Die alten Textzeugen*, 41.
48 Ibid., 52.
49 Seeligmann, *Septuagint Version*, 88.
50 Ibid., 78.
51 Van der Kooij, *Die alten Textzeugen*, 37.

ausgelöst zu haben."[52] Thus, even though van der Kooij does not find an allusion to Antiochus IV in 10:24, he still divines there a reflection of Jerusalem's Hellenistic crisis during Antiochus's rule.

Koenig, likewise, supposes that the translator deliberately wove references to Antiochus IV into his rendering. Although he makes only a brief comment on this issue, he concludes that Sennacherib, in Isaiah 37, serves as "une «figure» d'Antiochus Epiphane," while the ruler of Isaiah 14 "a également été influencée par l'allusion au roi séleucide."[53]

Das Neves, on the other hand, disputes Seeligmann's interpretation of chapter 14, arguing that the LXX's talk of one who has bloodied himself beyond purification (vv. 19–20) does not refer to Antiochus IV or any other foreign leader, but to "the person or persons who lead the Israelite people in the time of the translator."[54]

Similarly, in discussing the LXX's referents in chapter 10, das Neves concludes that ἔθνος ἄνομον of v. 6 designates Israel, while Assyria, as the divinely appointed chastiser, is accorded the distinguished epithet τῷ ἐμῷ λαῷ.[55] In keeping with this, he finds the translator focused on the impiety of Israel rather than the deeds of a foreign ruler in this chapter.[56] He regards 10:24 as anticipating salvation for Israel.[57]

This does not mean, however, that das Neves finds no allusion to Antiochus IV in the translator's contemporizations. He considers ἐξέλιπεν ἄνομος καὶ ἀπώλετο ὑπερήφανος (|| אפס עריץ וכלה לץ) in 29:20 a reference to the death of the Seleucid, particularly since it echoes the application of ὑπερήφανος (and its nominal forms) to Antiochus IV in 1 & 2 Maccabees.[58]

If one starts from the conviction that the translator deliberately reflected conditions during Jerusalem's Hellenistic crisis of the early second century B.C.E., discovering Antiochus IV in these texts is plausible, since some passages in the LXX can be read as mirroring actions of the Seleucid ruler, if one is so inclined. However, I will argue that

---

[52] Ibid., 39.

[53] Koenig, *L'Herméneutique*, 45 n. 35.

[54] Das Neves, *A Teologia*, 78, translation mine.

[55] Ibid., 201.

[56] Ibid., 202.

[57] Ibid., 69. Das Neves asserts that the translator, working during Jerusalem's Hellenistic crisis, found in Isaiah a forecast that those faithful to the Torah—the group to which he himself belonged—would be "les fondateurs d'un Israël nouveau, d'un Israël spirtuel" (ibid., 283).

[58] Ibid., 175.

none of these texts supports the supposition that the translator *intended* their figures to serve as ciphers for Antiochus IV or any other particular Hellenistic ruler.

The anchor passage for this discussion is Isaiah 14, especially vv. 18–21:

כל מלכי גוים[59]	[18]πάντες οἱ βασιλεῖς τῶν ἐθνῶν
כלם שכבו בכבוד	ἐκοιμήθησαν ἐν τιμῇ
איש בביתו	ἄνθρωπος ἐν τῷ οἴκῳ αὐτοῦ
ואתה השלכת מקברך[60]	[19]σὺ δὲ ῥιφήσῃ ἐν τοῖς ὄρεσιν
כנצר נתעב	ὡς νεκρὸς ἐβδελυγμένος
לבוש הרגים	μετὰ πολλῶν τεθνηκότων
מטעני חרב	ἐκκεκεντημένων μαχαίραις
יורדי אל אבני בור	καταβαινόντων εἰς ᾅδου
כפגר מובס	ὃν τρόπον ἱμάτιον ἐν αἵματι πεφυρμένον
	οὐκ ἔσται καθαρόν
לא תחד[61]	[20]οὕτως οὐδὲ σὺ ἔσῃ καθαρός
אתם בקבורה	
כי ארצך שחת	διότι τὴν γῆν μου ἀπώλεσας
עמך הרגת	καὶ τὸν λαόν μου ἀπέκτεινας
לא יקרא לעולם	οὐ μὴ μείνῃς εἰς τὸν αἰῶνα χρόνον
זרע מרעים	σπέρμα πονηρόν
הכינו לבניו מטבח[62]	[21]ἑτοίμασον τὰ τέκνα σου σφαγῆναι

---

[59] V. 18–1QIsaᵃ lacks כלם, while the תו of בביתו has been marred by a tear and the stitching that was used to fix it. S lacks a representation of כלם, either because it was absent from its *Vorlage* (cf. 1QIsaᵃ) or because the translator considered it redundant after حلم. || כל. V comports with the мт. T translates בביתו with בבית עלמיה.

[60] V. 19–1QIsaᵃreads לבש for לבוש, has *wāw mater* in הרוגים, and reads יורדו for יורדי; the א at the start of אל is clear, but the *lāmed* is lost in the tear; אבני is written superlinearly (and in a different hand) above בור. S's rendering of מטעני חרב with ܕܡܦܩܠ (following ܕܡܦܩܠ || ܠܒܘܫ ܗܪܢܝܡ) is likely a guess for מטעני (cf. LXX & V). V's *inutilis* gives an extended meaning to נתעב (cf. S's ܠܡܣܒ), while *pollutus et obvolutus* || לבוש הרגים, *qui interfecti sunt* || מטעני (cf. LXX & S), and *putridum* || מובס seem periphrastic. T translates כנצר נתעב with כיחט טמיר (likely with an eye to כנפל טמון in Job 3:16) and renders אבני בור expansively with לגוב בית אבדנא.

[61] V. 20–1QIsaᵃ reads תחת for мт's תחד; it reads superlinear ה (*mater*) at the end of שחת (one already stands on הרגתה); the *lāmed* of לא falls in the tear, but א is apparent; it reads יקראו for the мт's יקרא. It appears that 4QIsaᵉ reads the כ of כי, but this is uncertain. S reads ܝܣܡܦ for יקרא (cf. LXX & T) and ܘܐܝܐ ܕܒܣ for זרע מרעים. V renders לא תחד periphrastically (*non habebis consortium*) and inserts a conjunction before its equivalent to אתם: *neque cum eis*. T paraphrases לא תחד אתם with לא תהי כחד מינהון; it reads לא יתקיים for לא יקרא (cf. LXX & S).

[62] V. 21–1QIsaᵃ reads יקומ, although the far left hand side of the *mêm* (and any evidence of a final *wāw*) fall in the tear; it reads ומלו for the мт's ומלאו (א problem). 4QIsaᵉ preserves only בל יק[מו]. S reads the grammatically singular ܠܒ for мт's הכינו, and reads ܡܘܬ for ערים. For мт's ערים, T has בעלי דבב, 'men of evil speech' or 'opponents', perhaps reading רעים (?).

בעון אבותם   ταῖς ἁμαρτίαις τοῦ πατρός σου
בל יקמו וירשו ארץ   ἵνα μὴ ἀναστῶσι καὶ τὴν γῆν κληρονομήσωσι
ומלאו פני תבל ערים   καὶ ἐμπλήσωσι τὴν γῆν πολέμων

While v. 18 shows a high proportion of agreements between the LXX and the MT,[63] and vv. 19–21 contain a number of equivalents transparent to MT,[64] numerous differences also appear: ἐν τοῖς ὄρεσιν || מקברך, ὡς νεκρός || כנצר, μετὰ πολλῶν τεθνηκότων || לבוש הרנים, ὃν τρόπον ἱμάτιον ἐν αἵματι πεφυρμένον || כפגר מובס (all in v. 19), οὐκ ἔσται καθαρόν οὕτως οὐδὲ σὺ ἔσῃ καθαρός || לא תחד אתם בקבורה, the lack of an equivalent for אתם בקבורה, τὴν γῆν μου || ארצך, τὸν λαόν μου || עמך, μείνῃς || יקרא, σπέρμα πονηρόν || זרע מרעים[65] (v. 20), ἑτοίμασον τὰ τέκνα σου || הכינו לבניו, τοῦ πατρός σου || אבותם, and πολέμων || ערים (v. 21).

The crux of the debate over whether the translator alludes to Antiochus IV is the rendering of מקברך by ἐν τοῖς ὄρεσιν, in which Seeligmann found a transparent allusion to Antiochus's death. Noting that 2 Macc 9:28 uses similar language to describe the tyrant's death (ὁ μὲν οὖν ἀνδροφόνος καὶ βλάσφημος τὰ χείριστα παθὼν ὡς ἑτέρους διέθηκεν ἐπὶ ξένης ἐν τοῖς ὄρεσιν οἰκτίστῳ μόρῳ κατέστρεψεν τὸν βίον), Seeligmann judged that "the death ἐν τοῖς ὄρεσιν was a constant *motif* in the paraenetic meditations upon the ultimate end of this ἀνδροφόνος and βλάσφημος Antiochus Epiphanes."[66]

Van der Kooij has taken a more cautious approach, noting that because 2 Maccabees is younger than LXX-Isaiah, its author may have simply adopted the phrase from Isaiah 14.[67] He provides a substantive foundation for that scenario based on a phrase that appears earlier in 2 Maccabees 9. According to vv. 2–4, after being repelled in his attempt to plunder temples in Persepolis, and having received bad news about the campaigns of his generals, Antiochus mounted his chariot, ordering his

---

[63] While the lack of an equivalent for כלם in v. 18 might indicate that it was absent from the *Vorlage* (as in 1QIsaᵃ), the translator may have considered it redundant after כל מלכי גוים (cf. S, n. 59).

[64] The rendering of אל אבני בור with εἰς ᾅδου in v. 19 is one of only two times ᾅδης translates בור in the LXX, the other being in Isa 38:18, where οἱ ἐν ᾅδου translates יורדי בור, parallel to οἱ ἐν ᾅδου as the equivalent for שאול, although this stands outside the chapters attributable to the translator of chapters 1–35 and 40–66. His choice of εἰς ᾅδου here was likely influenced by εἰς ᾅδου || אל שאול in v. 16.

[65] σπέρμα πονηρόν does not reflect a variant, given σπέρμα πονηρόν || זרע מרעים in 1:4.

[66] Seeligmann, *Septuagint Version*, 84, italics his.

[67] Van der Kooij, *Die alten Textzeugen*, 40 and n. 111.

driver to take him, non-stop, to Judea to vent his anger on the Jews. V. 5 reports, ὁ δὲ παντεπόπτης κύριος ὁ θεὸς τοῦ Ισραηλ ἐπάταξεν αὐτὸν ἀνιάτῳ καὶ ἀοράτῳ πληγῇ. Noteworthy are three words crucial in the final clause—ἐπάταξεν...ἀνιάτῳ...πληγῇ—precisely the words used in Isa 14:6 to describe a divine attack on an unnamed ἔθνος. Given that this cluster of words appears nowhere else in the LXX and nowhere in the Pseudepigrapha, 2 Maccabees appropriation of it from LXX-Isaiah 14:6 is unmistakable.[68]

Looking at the context of the phrase in LXX-Isaiah 14, v. 6 is syntactically dependent on v. 5, which (as part of a mock lament) asserts, συνέτριψεν ὁ θεὸς τὸν ζυγὸν τῶν ἁμαρτωλῶν τὸν ζυγὸν τῶν ἀρχόντων. That theme continues in v. 6, with God inflicting an incurable blow on an unnamed nation. To posit, as Das Neves does, that this ἔθνος must be Israel, since (in his assessment) ἁμαρτωλός is consistently reserved for Israel,[69] creates a Procrustean bed that leads us away from the more natural inference that τὸν ζυγόν in v. 5 belongs to the oppressor of v. 4, the one whose fall occasions the earth's celebration. And that oppressor, in v. 4, is designated τὸν βασιλέα Βαβυλῶνος.[70] Consistent with that, the ἔθνος of v. 6 that bear the incurable blows of the Kyrios's wrath are most likely the people allied with that tyrant.

Accordingly, 2 Maccabees 9 has appropriated language LXX-Isaiah 14 uses to describe punishment the Kyrios inflicts on the king of Babylon to describe punishment inflicted on Antiochus IV. However, the application of such language to the death of Antiochus tells us nothing of whether the translator of Isaiah 14 had a covert identity in mind for "the king of Babylon," anymore than the book of Daniel's appropriation of phrases from Isaiah tells us what meaning the prophet invested in them. Whether the translator perceives this figure as a cipher for a ruler of his own day must be determined on other grounds.

The same conclusion can be drawn for 2 Maccabees's appropriation of the phrase ἐν τοῖς ὄρεσιν from Isaiah 14:19. First, we must recognize the different functions of this phrase in 2 Maccabees and LXX-Isaiah. 2 Maccabees 9 has Antiochus, struck with illness, falling from his chariot as he rushes to inflict more suffering on the Judeans. In summarizing

---

[68] Ibid.

[69] Das Neves, A Teologia, 284 (cf. ibid., 88).

[70] This observation equally refutes van der Kooij's assertion that by reading this verse in the light of v. 20, one can conclude that "der Übersetzer dabei an τὸ ἔθνος τῶν Ἰουδαίων denkt" (Die alten Textzeugen, 41).

the tyrant's death, v. 28 places ἐν τοῖς ὄρεσιν in emphatic position (just before the predicate) in the company of two others: ἐπὶ ξένης ('in a foreign land') and οἰκτίστῳ μόρῳ ('in a most lamentable doom') thereby clarifying the prior generalization, τὰ χείριστα παθών ('having suffered the worst [of fates]'). V. 28 stresses that the tyrant's suffering was an appropriate measure of divine justice, even as vv. 5–12 highlight the correspondence between Antiochus's death pangs and his affliction of others.[71] Thus, for example,v. 6 insists that the pains and torments of the tyrant were "wholly justified" (πάνυ δικαίως) in light of the tortures he had inflicted on others. Similarly, his death "in a foreign land, in the mountains, and by the most lamentable doom" describes his *experience* of death as a fitting retribution.

In LXX-Isa 14:19, on the other hand, ἐν τοῖς ὄρεσιν designates the ruler's resting place, shared with other warriors slain by the sword. It is as a warrior that he dies, while his corpse is just another "tossed aside" (ῥιφήσῃ) and regarded as "reproachful" (ἐβδελυγμένος). Thus, his death ἐν τοῖς ὄρεσιν accents not the pathos of his demise but his commonplace fate: he dies in the company of his soldiers and just like them. We cannot simply note the common phrase, ἐν τοῖς ὄρεσιν, in these passages; we must note how it contributes to different portrayals of the ruler's demise in each passage.

Equally noteworthy is how the role this phrase plays in these passages compares with the role of mountains in reports of warfare among Greek historians. Polybius reports that the Celts fled to the mountains to escape Roman forces under the command of Marcus Claudius (*Histories* 2.34); Xenophon reports that the Thynians fled their homes on the plain and took refuge in the mountains, in the face of the approach of Seuthes and the Greeks (*Anabasis* 7.4.2); Appian reports Hannibal's forces using the ruse of flight to the mountains to entrap the Romans (*Foreign Wars* Hann. 4.22); and Josephus reports that following Mattathias's instigation of revolt, εἰς τὰ ὄρη καταφεύγει (*B.J.* 1.36). While flight to the mountains accords with the refuge mountain terrain could afford, the stock nature of this trope becomes evident from Xeonophon's report

---

[71] Accenting the appropriateness of punishment for the crime is a leitmotif in 2 Maccabees, as noted by Jonathan A. Goldstein, *II Maccabees* (AB 41A; New York: Doubleday, 1983) 256, 354. For the distinctiveness of 2 Macc 9 in Jewish literature before the turn of the era, see Jörg-Dieter Gauger, "Der 'Tod des Verfolgers': Überlegungen zur historizität eines Topos," *JSJ* 33 (2002) 42–64.

that the Carduchians, whom he has already described as living in the mountains (*Anabasis* 3.5.16), abandoned their houses and ἔφευγον ἐπὶ τὰ ὄρη (*Anabasis* 4.1.8).

Mountains are also frequently depicted as a place of hardship and barbarity endured by an army on military campaign. Polybius reports that Hannibal's army endured starvation and a significant loss of pack animals in the mountains (*Histories* 3.60). Similarly, Xenophon has Seuthes admonish his weary troops, trudging through the snowy mountains, to take courage, because once they surmount them, ἥξομεν εἰς κώμας πολλάς τε καὶ εὐδαίμονας (*Anabasis* 7.3.43). As elsewhere in *Anabasis*, mountains are the obstacles or strategic means to capturing the cities of the plains and what must be endured to attain them (cf. *Anabasis* 3.5.18).

Intelligible, in this light, is the role mountains play throughout 2 Maccabees. 2 Macc 5:27 reports that, upon Antiochus's arrival in Jerusalem, Judas Maccabeus ἀναχωρήσας εἰς τὴν ἔρημον θηρίων τρόπον ἐν τοῖς ὄρεσιν διέζη σὺν τοῖς μετ' αὐτοῦ; life in the wilderness is compared to the manner of life of beasts in the mountains. In accord with this, 2 Maccabees 10 reports the cleansing of the temple by Judas and his allies after defeating the Greeks, noting that their celebration matched the exuberance of the feast of booths, whose observance they had missed while ἐν τοῖς ὄρεσιν καὶ ἐν τοῖς σπηλαίοις θηρίων τρόπον ἦσαν νεμόμενοι (2 Macc 10:6). Here again ἐν τοῖς ὄρεσιν is a place of flight and hardship.

2 Maccabees's depiction of mountains becomes more striking when we note the references to mountains in 1 Maccabees. The latter reports the flight of Mattathias and his sons εἰς τὰ ὄρη after Mattathias killed the official overseeing the mandated sacrifices. 1 Maccabees also reports the maneuvers of troops in the mountains, undoubtedly reflecting the strategies of the combatants. However, 1 Maccabees's use of the mountain motif is restricted to simple reports of location, whereas 2 Maccabees alone utilizes the trope of mountains as places of hardship in a military campaign.

Of course, 2 Maccabees makes much hay out of pathos in all sorts of events, such as the Jerusalemites' overwrought response to Heliodorus's assault on the temple. But this is precisely the point: highlighting the sufferings of Judas and his band in the mountains is of a piece with highlighting the pathos of Antiochus's experience of death in 9:28. The fanciful depiction of Antiochus meeting his fate ἐν τοῖς ὄρεσιν cannot be separated from ἐπὶ ξένης and οἰκτίστῳ μόρῳ as part of the author's description of a leader suffering death made bitter by being on campaign in the mountains.

Thus, not only is ἐν τοῖς ὄρεσιν one of two phrases 2 Maccabees borrowed from LXX-Isaiah 14, but it has been melded into the larger issue of Antiochus's fate as just comeuppance, with an accent on the pathos of his death. Whatever role death in the mountains plays in LXX-Isaiah 14, its application to Antiochus in 2 Maccabees 9 is part of Jason of Cyrene's larger concerns.

By contrast, we can account for the translator's rendering of מקברך by ἐν τοῖς ὄρεσιν in light of the motif of battle in the mountains in a way distinct from its use in 2 Maccabees. We must first note the translator's penchant for rendering phrases periphrastically in this chapter. Thus, in v. 12 we find בן שׁחר translated with ὁ πρωὶ ἀνατέλλων. While πρωί translates שׁחר in Gen 32:25 and Judg[B] 19:25 (ὄρθρος is more common, used in 14 out of 24 instances), this is the lone occurrence of the periphrastic phrase ὁ πρωὶ ἀνατέλλων.

His periphrastic style is evident again in v. 13, with καθιῶ ἐν ὄρει ὑψηλῷ ἐπὶ τὰ ὄρη τὰ ὑψηλὰ τὰ πρὸς βορρᾶν for ואשׁב בהר מועד בירכתי צפון.[72] Emphasis on the mountains' height is likely due to the foregoing εἰς τὸν οὐρανὸν ἀναβήσομαι ἐπάνω τῶν ἄστρων τοῦ οὐρανοῦ θήσω τὸν θρόνον μου and invokes the motif of height that goes unexpressed in the translation of כסאי ארים by θήσω τὸν θρόνον μου. While the translator gives an apt equivalent for ומועדיכם in 1:14 (καὶ τὰς ἑορτὰς ὑμῶν), he stops short of rendering it in 14:31 (ὅτι καπνὸς ἀπὸ βορρᾶ ἔρχεται καὶ οὐκ ἔστιν τοῦ εἶναι || כי מצפון עשׁן בא ואין בודד במועדיו)[73] and, as discussed in chapter four, renders קרית מועדנו with ἡ πόλις τὸ σωτήριον ἡμῶν in 33:20. As for his rendering of בירכתי, we can compare his translation of ירכתי בור אל in v. 15 with (εἰς) τὰ θεμέλια τῆς γῆς, a phrase that everywhere else renders a locution involving מוסד, except in Isa 44:23, where it translates תחתיות ארץ. We are justified, then, in

---

[72] The א and the ב of ואשׁב are apparent in 1QIsaᵃ, but שׁ stands in a tear, while there is clearly no initial wāw (N.B. MT's preceding כסאי, which is also read in 1QIsaᵃ). 4QIsaᶜ attests only the sequence [ב]הר מו[עד], although the wāw is uncertain. 4QIsaᵉ has a lacuna in the place this phrase would stand. S reads ܒܪ ܛܘܪ for בהר מועד, perhaps following a logic similar to that of the LXX. V & T accord with the MT.

[73] 1QIsaᵃ reads מודד for בודד. 4QIsaᵒ preserves only the final two words and reads בסועדיו for במועדיו. S accords with MT. V's et non est qui effugiat agment eius ('and there is not one who escapes his troop') seems a guess. T's דמאחר for בודד appears interpretative. In sum, no other textual witness lacks ואין בודד במועדיו, although V and T finesse it in different ways.

concluding that he rendered בירכתי בהר מועד periphrastically, based on the preceding context.[74]

In keeping with this, μετὰ πολλῶν τεθνηκότων is likely a paraphrase of לבוש הרגים, as Seeligmann recognized.[75] We might well describe it as *concretizing* the image, something we find the translator doing elsewhere, such as in 5:8, where the accusation that the wealthy add property to property עד אפס מקום becomes a charge that they have accumulated property ἵνα τοῦ πλησίον ἀφέλωνταί τι.

In fact, ἐν τοῖς ὄρεσιν || מקברך likewise concretizes the fate of this ruler by locating where he met his end rather than describing something he lacked. The translator rightly understood the addressee as a king fallen in battle whose body lies exposed. Given that mountains are frequently designated as the scene of battle, the use of ἐν τοῖς ὄρεσιν for a location where a warrior would lie unburied is intelligible, as is the fact that his body would lie μετὰ πολλῶν τεθνηκότων ἐκκεκεντημένων μαχαίραις. And it was likely to further depict the ruler as a slain warrior that the translator rendered כנצר נתעב with ὡς νεκρὸς ἐβδελυγμένος.[76] The translator's rendering of this unit is guided by the image of this ruler as a warrior-king who shares the ignominious fate of warriors.

This may also explain his rendering of ומלאו פני תבל ערים by καὶ ἐμπλήσωσι τὴν γῆν πολέμων in v. 21 (cf. S's ܘܢܡܠܘܢ ܐܪܥܐ ܩܪ̈ܒܐ).[77] This ruler's death, together with that of his sons, will bring his legacy of warfare to an end. Underscoring this is the rendering of בל יקמו וירשו ארץ ומלאו with a purpose clause: ἵνα μὴ ἀναστῶσι καὶ τὴν γῆν

---

[74] We might legitimately speak of ἐν ὄρει and ἐπὶ τὰ ὄρη as a double rendering of בהר, but this seems to have been prompted by a (curious) impulse to provide an equivalent for בירכתי as well as מועד.

[75] Seeligmann, *Septuagint Version*, 84.

[76] Seeligmann posited that νεκρός arose from a transliteration of נצר as νεσρ (ibid., 30). However, the similarity of νεκρός to νεσρ is so oblique as to beg the question of why the translator chose νεκρός rather than (say) νέρτος, and that can be answered only by speculating about how the translator reasoned from context. It is less complicated to consider how he sought a lexical equivalent for נצר based on the context. While νεκρός might anticipate פגר at the end of the verse (cf. καὶ οἱ νεκροί || ופגריהם in 34:3), his *Vorlage* likely read כבנד for כפגר (see below, p. 218).

[77] This reading is attested by all mss, except *V-oII* (along with σ', α', θ'), which read πολέων, in agreement with the мт. Seeligmann declares πολέων to be among Origenic variants which, while secondary, "borrow authentic material from older sources or must be regarded in the light of a fortunate conjecture and, therefore, actually re-establish an older textual form" (*Septuagint Version*, 14). However, never does the proliferation of cities figure in descriptions of the tyrant's activities, while the tyrant's execution of warfare does, as in the description of the tyrant's resolve to conduct military campaigns in 10:5–14 (see below). πολέμων is likely the original reading.

κληρονομήσωσιν καὶ ἐμπλήσωσι. The translator's deliberateness in this rendering is demonstrated by his more common translation (17x) of בל by οὐ/οὐκ/οὐχ, οὐδὲ μή, and οὐ μή (ἀλλά occurs twice in 26:18), while he uses ἵνα μή for בל again only in 26:10.[78] His use of this construction in 14:21 clearly means to emphasize that the tyrant's ability to wage warfare will come to an end with his death and that of his sons in battle.

This reconstruction of how the translator arrived at ἐν τοῖς ὄρεσιν for מקברך, based on contextual inferences that the tyrant's death took place in battle, elucidates the phrase ὃν τρόπον ἱμάτιον ἐν αἵματι πεφυρμένον. On the one hand, ὃν τρόπον ἱμάτιον likely reflects כבגד instead of כפגר in the translator's *Vorlage*, as Ottley suggested.[79] On the other hand, the identification of blood as the substance in which the garment was drenched is a logical inference from the talk of slain soldiers. Ziegler pointed out that ἐν αἵματι conjoined with φύρεσθαι appears often in the LXX,[80] so that the phrase was likely ready to hand.

Others, however, have identified this rendering as a case of actualization. Seeligmann concluded that the simile is "a paraenetic meditation upon לבוש הרגים, in which לבוש is seen as the construct case of the noun לְבֻשׁ = garment, and the whole phrase as a metaphor for the hated tyrant."[81] It is not clear, however, why should we posit "paraenetic meditation" as the source when the context provides sufficient motivation for this rendering.

Van der Kooij speculates that the translator's development of the simile is an allusion to the amount of blood shed by Antiochus IV and that ἐν αἵματι πεφυρμένον is based on ושמלה מגוללה בדמים in 9:5(4).[82] However, the quite different translation of the phrase there (καὶ ἱμάτιον μετὰ καταλλαγῆς)[83] makes this unlikely. Moreover, the suggestion that this rendering alludes to blood shed by Antiochus IV begs the question of what indicates that the translator meant to allude to that ruler.[84] It

---

[78] This equivalence appears again only in the Psalter (9:39 [10:18]; 15(16):8; 16[17]:5), along with ὅπως (ἂν) μή (16:3 [17:4]; 77[78]:44) and τοῦ μή + infinitive (9:32 [10:11]).

[79] Ottley, *The Book of Isaiah*, 2:180. Cf. Ziegler, who posits that the translator "hat an בֶּגֶד 'Kleid' gedacht" (*Untersuchungen*, 94). As Ziegler notes, בוס is translated by φύρεσθαι again in Ezek 16:6, 22 (ibid.).

[80] Ziegler, *Untersuchungen*, 94.

[81] Seeligmann, *Septuagint Version*, 83.

[82] Van der Kooij, *Die alten Textzeugen*, 41.

[83] Cf., however, Aquila's ἱματισμὸς πεφυρμένος ἐν αἵμασιν.

[84] Cf. his judgment that while v. 13 patently agrees with the MT, "kann dieser

seems preferable to conclude that he lighted on ἐν αἵματι πεφυρμένον as a familiar phrase that befit his understanding of the passage.

As Ottley concludes, οὐδὲ σὺ ἔσῃ καθαρός || לֹא תֵחַד likely attests טָהֵר.[85] Based on the signal that the sentence entails a comparison (כָּבֶגֶד) and construing לֹא טהר as the predicate of the clause, the translator filled out the comparison by analogy. Most likely, he construed אֹתָם as אַתֶּם, as Ottley suggested, and then conformed the number of the pronoun to the divine address of the tyrant already underway. There is no reason to suppose that he labored to find some empirical grounds to derive καθαρός from בִּקְבוּרָה.[86] Having seen the sentence as a comparison controlled by לֹא טהר, he supplied a fitting conclusion. As Ziegler concluded, "die Wiedergabe zeigt deutlich, wie der Übers. seine Vorlage umgebogen, ausgedeutet und aus eigenem hinzugefügt hat, um einen Sinn zu gewinnen."[87]

These inferences elucidate the differences in pronoun of τὴν γῆν μου || אַרְצֶךָ and, parallel to that, τὸν λαόν μου || עַמֶּךָ. These transform a charge that the tyrant harmed his *own* people into an accusation that he mistreated the people of the Kyrios. While τὴν γῆν μου and τὸν λαόν μου might point to a *Vorlage* that read אַרְצִי and עַמִּי, other changes in pronouns in this context suggest that they are attributable to the translator. I have already concurred with Ottley that in v. 20 the translator read אֹתָם as אַתֶּם and then conformed the number to the second person *singular* form of the verb that preceded it. The latter

---

greichische Text dennoch auf Antiochus IV. anspielen; denn er trifft sich mit Dan 8,10 und 2 Makk 9,10 in der Deutung des Verhaltens dieses Königs" (van der Kooij, *Die alten Textzeugen*, 42). However, lacking any evidence in this chapter that Antiochus IV stands behind the translator's rendition, the similarity between 14:21 and those other passages is moot.

[85] Ottley, *The Book of Isaiah*, 2:180.

[86] *Pace* Ottley's suggestion that "καθαρός, if not added to complete the sense, would seem to be מכבב, 'cleansed,' for בִּקְבוּרָה, perhaps with some confusion with מוּבָס" (ibid.).

[87] Ziegler, *Untersuchungen*, 94. The translator followed a similar line of reasoning in v. 6:

מַכֵּה עַמִּים בְּעֶבְרָה מַכַּת בִּלְתִּי סָרָה   πατάξας ἔθνος θυμῷ πληγῇ ἀνιάτῳ

רֹדֶה בָאַף גּוֹיִם מֻרְדָּף בְּלִי חָשָׂךְ   παίων ἔθνος πληγὴν θυμοῦ ἣ οὐκ ἐφείσατο

(1QIsaᵃ = MT. 4QIsaᵉ reads only מַכֵּה עַמִּים בַּ]עֶבְרָה] (= MT). S = MT. V translates בְּלִי חָשָׂךְ idiomatically with *crudeliter*, while T renders both בְּעֶבְרָה and בָאַף with בְּתַקּוֹף.) The translator allowed the initial words of this verse to guide him, with πατάξας providing the template for his choice of παίων for רֹדֶה (which he translated with κυριεύειν in v. 2) while the position of ἔθνος in the clause matches the position of ἔθνος in the preceding line. In that light, it seems likely that πληγήν is attributable to the translator overriding מֻרְדָּף, based on the foregoing πληγῇ and the semantic parallel between בְּלִי חָשָׂךְ and בִּלְתִּי סָרָה.

part of v. 20 exhibits a similar adjustment of a pronoun, with μείνῃς translating יקרא. However, that difference in pronoun accompanies a semantic difference that must be discussed first.

Neither μένειν nor its compounds are used for קרא elsewhere in the LXX, but μένειν does translate קום elsewhere (14:24; 27:9; 32:8; 40:8). Since S reads ܢܩܘܡ and T reads יתקיים, there is little doubt that the LXX's *Vorlage* read יקום. This still leaves us in need of an explanation for the 2nd person form μείνῃς.

This issue must be viewed in the light of how thoroughly the second person singular reigns in the next verse (21), where the rendering is again guided by a perception of the overarching message. The translator contents himself with translating מטבח by the aorist passive infinitive σφαγῆναι—not unreasonable given the *mêm*-prefixed infinitives in Aramaic. It was likely his perception of the whole passage as an address to the tyrant that spurred him to conform the pronouns to the second person singular ones that dominate in v. 21.

What makes τὴν γῆν μου and τὸν λαόν μου of v. 20 remarkable, then, is that at the very point the MT has second person singular pronouns the translator uses *first* person singular pronouns. On the face of it, this would seem a good argument that his *Vorlage* read ארצי and עמי; why else would he deviate from the second person singular pronouns he imposed elsewhere? On the other hand, if his *Vorlage* did read ארצי and עמי, why did he not conform those pronouns, also, to the second person?

To answer these questions, we need to notice a feature of the introduction to this passage in v. 4, where we find two differences between the LXX and the MT:

ונשאת המשל הזה על מלך בבל	καὶ λήμψῃ τὸν θρῆνον τοῦτον ἐπὶ τὸν βασιλέα Βαβυλῶνος
ואמרת	καὶ ἐρεῖς ἐν τῇ ἡμέρᾳ ἐκείνῃ
איך שבת נגש שבתה מדהבה	πῶς ἀναπέπαυται ὁ ἀπαιτῶν
שבתה מדהבה	καὶ ἀναπέπαυται ὁ ἐπισπουδαστής

θρῆνος translates משל nowhere else in the LXX,[88] and this is the only occurrence of משל in Isaiah. θρῆνος was likely chosen due to the tenor of the following words.

---

[88] משל is most often translated by παραβολή, while θρῆνος renders קינה 18x and נהי 4x.

The plus ἐν τῇ ἡμέρᾳ ἐκείνῃ[89] must be considered in association with v. 3:[90]

והיה ביום הניח יהוה לך	καὶ ἔσται ἐν τῇ ἡμέρᾳ ἐκείνῃ ἀναπαύσει σε ὁ θεὸς
מעצבך ומרגזך	ἐκ τῆς ὀδύνης καὶ τοῦ θυμοῦ σου
ומן העבדה הקשה אשר עבד בך	καὶ τῆς δουλείας τῆς σκληρᾶς ἧς ἐδούλευσας αὐτοῖς

Whereas in the MT v. 3 is a temporal phrase that specifies when the addressee will take up the lament that begins in v. 4, in the LXX these verses form distinct clauses. V. 3, with its ἐν τῇ ἡμέρᾳ ἐκείνῃ, is closely bound with the description of the reversal of fortunes for Israel and its foes just announced in vv. 1–2. By means of the anaphoric ἐν τῇ ἡμέρᾳ ἐκείνῃ, v. 3 summarizes those reversals of fortunes as the Kyrios giving them rest from all their travails.

Correspondingly, καὶ ἔσται ἐν τῇ ἡμέρᾳ ἐκείνῃ at the head of v. 4 introduces a distinct action (lament of Babylon) that the people will commence in the same time frame. The quandary is whether this difference and its companion in v. 3 are attributable to the translator or go back to his *Vorlage*. On the one hand, the translator shows himself adept at handling temporal phrases introduced by ביום (e.g., 11:16; 30:26). On the other, ἐν τῇ ἡμέρᾳ ἐκείνῃ corresponds to ביום ההוא twenty-two times in the MT of Isaiah. In only two others of the twenty-seven cases where this Greek phrase appears is ההוא lacking in the MT (and most likely the *Vorlage* read ביום ההוא in those cases),[91] while of the 14 other times ביום appears without ההוא in Isaiah, none are translated

---

[89] This phrase is not attested in 1QIsaᵃ, S, V, or T. It would fall within the lacuna in 4QIsaᶜ that consumes everything in this verse after [מרת]וא.

[90] 1QIsaᵃ reads עבדו for MT's עבד. 4QIsaᶜ attests [ה]יהוה הניח [ביו]ם, although the *mêm* is uncertain (the Tetragrammaton is in Paleo-Hebrew script), while 4QIsaᵉ preserves the first five letters, [ביום]ב והיה (although the *bêt* is uncertain) and the concluding בך עבדו אשר (N.B. עבדו = 1QIsaᵃ), with the א uncertain. V reads *et erit in die illa cum requiem dederit* || הניח ביום והיה. As a translation for בך עבד אשר, S reads ܕܫܥܒܕܬ, V reads *qua ante servisti*, and T reads בך אתפלח די.

[91] In 10:17 καὶ φάγεται ὡσεὶ χόρτον τὴν ὕλην τῇ ἡμέρᾳ ἐκείνῃ is the equivalent for the MT's אחד ביום ושמירו שיתו ואכלה (1QIsaᵃ, 1QIsaᵇ, S, V, and T accord with the MT), while the LXX translates אחד ביום with ἐν μιᾷ ἡμέρᾳ in 47:9 and 66:8. Likely the *Vorlage* read ההוא ביום. In 30:25, where the LXX translates מגדלים בנפל רב הרן ביום with ἐν τῇ ἡμέρᾳ ἐκείνῃ ὅταν ἀπόλωνται πολλοὶ καὶ ὅταν πέσωσιν πύργοι (1QIsaᵃ and 1QIsaᵇ = MT, while S, V, and T presuppose a *Vorlage* = MT), the translator seems to have been impelled to include the first ὅταν due to the parallel with the second, but that would not require the inclusion of the demonstrative pronoun. Accordingly, his *Vorlage* likely already read ההוא ביום.

with ἡμέρᾳ ἐκείνῃ. Accordingly, it seems likely that ἐν τῇ ἡμέρᾳ ἐκείνῃ attests ביום ההוא in the LXX's *Vorlage* also in 14:3, 4.

As noted earlier, Ottley's and Ziegler's surmise that ὁ ἐπισπουδαστής reflects מרהבה in the *Vorlage* is likely,[92] and 1QIsaᵃ now offers this reading in a Hebrew ms. As previously noted, the pairing of this official term for a tax agent with the synonymous ὁ ἀπαιτῶν figures in the translator's evident interest in portraying rulers as guilty of financially plundering Israel, a motif to which he has given voice in several other passages, especially 3:12–15, where he constructs a scene in which such rulers are brought to task by the Kyrios.[93]

It seems hardly coincidental, then, that in this fourteenth chapter, where the translator chooses a distinctive Ptolemaic *Beamtenbezeichnung* to accuse the ruler harming the people of the Kyrios of financial plunder, that he switches the pronouns to the first person in v. 20, as he depicts the Kyrios confronting his people's foe, in a way reminiscent of 3:12–15. While the characterization of this tyrant as a tax farmer reflects a Hellenistic milieu, it overreaches the evidence to suggest that the translator shaped the image of the tyrant to reflect a specific ruler. He gives the tyrant of Isaiah 14 characteristics of tyrants in his day, but none that are distinctive to a particular ruler.

More momentous is his creation of an address in place of the MT's 3mp forms (ἑτοίμασον || הכינו; τοῦ πατρός σου || אבותם).[94] Even if הכינו can be construed as an imperative, the representation of it as grammatically singular (ἑτοίμασον) accords with the translator's willingness to modify number and person to suit his perception of context. This directive to prepare the ruler's sons to die sheds light on οὐ μὴ μείνῃς εἰς τὸν αἰῶνα χρόνον σπέρμα πονηρόν, in v. 20. The use of the epithet σπέρμα πονηρόν (|| זרע מרעים) for the addressee explains why his sons must die for his *father's* sins, even though the addressee himself is the one accused of destroying the land of the Kyrios and killing his people. The translator's perception of the annihilation of a royal line in vv. 19–20 explicates his translation of יקום (לא) in his *Vorlage* by the second person singular grammatical form (οὐ μὴ) μείνῃς.

---

[92] Ottley, *The Book of Isaiah*, 2:176; Ziegler, *Untersuchungen*, 200. Cf. S: ܡܣܬܘܕܐ, 'he who incites'.

[93] See above, pp. 201–07.

[94] While S accords with the LXX in rendering הכינו as a second person singular imperative (ܛܝܒ), it reflects the 3ms suffix of לבניו and the 3mp suffix of אבותם, so that it commands preparing death "for *his* sons due to the sins of *their* father."

His translation of 14:20b–21 anticipates the demise of this ruler and the elimination of any threat that his offspring might perpetuate his hegemony. However, this undercuts the perception that the translator had Antiochus IV in view as the addressee. Even though Antiochus V was assassinated after less than two years on the throne, the usurper was his brother, Demetrius I, who was succeeded by his son, Demetrius II, who was, in turn, succeeded by his brother, Antiochus VII, in 139 B.C.E.[95] If the translator, working in the latter half of the second century, meant to tailor this passage to reflect the fate of Antiochus, his choices in v. 21 undercut his intent, since the notion that the annihilation of the tyrant's line would halt "filling the land with wars" does not accord with what happened.

The evidence suggests, therefore, that he did not intend to depict the demise of a particular ruler, but built a picture based on the Hebrew, read in light of his familiarity with the behavior of rulers in his day. Accordingly, these verses of chapter 14 lack any signal that the translator had in mind Antiochus IV.

The second passage in which Seeligmann detected a covert reference to Antiochus IV—or at least his actions—is Isa 8:8:[96]

וחלף ביהודה	καὶ ἀφελεῖ ἀπὸ τῆς Ιουδαίας
שטף ועבר עד צואר יגיע	
	ἄνθρωπον ὃς δυνήσεται κεφαλὴν ἆραι
	ἢ δυνατὸν συντελέσασθαί τι
והיה מטות כנפיו	καὶ ἔσται ἡ παρεμβολὴ αὐτοῦ
מלא רחב ארצך	ὥστε πληρῶσαι τὸ πλάτος τῆς χώρας σου
עמנו אל	μεθ' ἡμῶν ὁ θεός

The prime divergence from the MT is the talk of removing 'a man who will be able to lift a head or able to complete anything', whereas the MT describes the Assyrian army (under the figure of an overflowing river) 'pass[ing] through Judah, overflowing and moving on' until it 'reaches to the neck'. Seeligmann found that "the Hebrew text is here given greater concreteness in the translation by being made to allude to a definite contemporaneous historical event," although he conceded that

[95] Peters, *The Harvest of Hellenism*, 264–75.
[96] 1QIsaᵃ = MT. 4QIsaᵉ preserves the final four words, whose sole difference with the MT is צער || צואר. 4QIsaᶠ is even more fragmentary, but it attests no differences with MT (including that it reads צואר). The lemma in 4QpIsaᶜ preserves only [וה]יו מטות כנפו מלא רחב ארצכ[ה], with the *pesher* providing no further evidence. S and V accord with MT. T is expansive, but appears to presuppose a *Vorlage* = MT.

the allusion is oblique.[97] Obscurity notwithstanding, he judged it likely that the translator "was thinking of the deposition of Onias III as High Priest."[98] Not only does the suggestion that this alludes to the deposition of Onias III lack a firm base in this verse, but it is uncertain that this translation betrays a desire to reflect contemporaneous circumstances.

Above all, we must notice how the translator arrived at his rendering, especially in light of vv. 6–7, beginning with the assertion that the people demanded foreign rule:[99]

יַעַן כִּי מָאַס הָעָם הַזֶּה	[6]διὰ τὸ μὴ βούλεσθαι τὸν λαὸν τοῦτον
אֵת מֵי הַשִּׁלֹחַ הַהֹלְכִים לְאַט	τὸ ὕδωρ τοῦ Σιλωαμ τὸ πορευόμενον ἡσυχῇ
וּמְשׂוֹשׂ אֶת רְצִין	ἀλλὰ βούλεσθαι ἔχειν τὸν Ρααςςων
וּבֶן רְמַלְיָהוּ	καὶ τὸν υἱὸν Ρομελιου βασιλέα ἐφ' ὑμῶν

The LXX's ἀλλὰ βούλεσθαι seems to have been chosen as an apt contrast to μὴ βούλεσθαι || מָאַס at the outset. On the other hand, the translator may have added βασιλέα ἐφ' ὑμῶν to complete the thought, although an analogous Hebrew phrase (לְמֶלֶךְ עֲלֵיהֶם ?) may already have stood as a gloss in the *Vorlage*. In any case, the charge is the demand for foreign rule.

The consequence of this desire is the imposition of a foreign army, under the Assyrian king, much as in the MT. However, after the metaphor of "the mighty and abundant water" has been decoded as אֶת מֶלֶךְ אַשּׁוּר in v. 7, the LXX concretizes the imagery:[100]

וְעָלָה עַל כָּל אֲפִיקָיו	[7]καὶ ἀναβήσεται ἐπὶ πᾶσαν φάραγα ὑμῶν
וְהָלַךְ עַל כָּל גְּדוֹתָיו	καὶ περιπατήσει ἐπὶ πᾶν τεῖχος ὑμῶν

Ἀναβαίνειν is a typical equivalent for עלה throughout LXX-Isa, while φάραξ for אפיק (which appears only here in Isaiah) is an equivalence

[97] Seeligmann, *Septuagint Version*, 84.
[98] Ibid.
[99] In 1QIsaᵃ, the initial *hê* of הזה is marred by a crease; it reads השולח; an את precedes בן; and רמליהו is obscured by a horizontal tear, although the top of a *lāmed* is visible. While 4QIsaᵉ is fragmentary in this verse, none of its readings conflict with the MT; it reads השלח, although the *yôd* is uncertain. S accords with the MT; it reads ܪܗܛܝܐ for השלח. V's *et adsumpsit magis* || ומשוש is chosen on the basis of context; it reads *Siloae* for השלח. T's expansive rendering reflects a *Vorlage* = MT; it reads שילוהא for השלח.
[100] 1QIsaᵃ preserves only ועלה and נדותיו; the remainder stands in a lacuna. 4QIsaᵉ attests no variants from MT, as is true of 4QpIsaᶜ, which preserves all but ועלה and the final consonants of נדותיו. 1QIsaᶠ preserves only ועלה על כל and, *possibly*, the ל of והלך, but also attests no variants. S, V, and T presuppose *Vorlagen* = MT (S ܣܘܡܝܐ || נדותיו is likely a guess for this *hapax* in the book).

found in LXX-Ezekiel (6:3; 32:6; 34:13; 36:4, 6).[101] On the other hand, הלך
is translated by περιπατεῖν only here in LXX-Isaiah, its regular equivalent
being πορεύεσθαι (39x; להלכים is rendered τοῖς πατοῦσιν in 42:5). More
strikingly, the translator renders נדותיו 'its banks' (a *hapax legomenon* in
Isaiah) with τεῖχος ὑμῶν, while each of the other four occurrences of
נדיה elsewhere in the Bible is translated by κρηπίς, 'foundation' (Josh
3:15; 4:18; 1 Chr 12:16). These two distinctive equivalents indicate that
the translator has concretized the imagery, so that even the preceding
καὶ ἀναβήσεται ἐπὶ πᾶσαν φάραγα must be understood as describing
no longer a flood of water, but the maneuvers of the Assyrian king and
his army.

This concretizing becomes most explicit in v. 8, where the translator
renders וחלף with καὶ ἀφελεῖ, the only place in the LXX this equivalence
occurs. While he might have been influenced by his knowledge that
חלף in the Hiphil means 'to change'—for which reason he translated
חלפו with ἤλλαξαν in 24:5 (cf. 40:31; 41:1)—it is noteworthy that καὶ
ἀφελεῖ ἀπὸ τῆς Ιουδαίας parallels 3:1, while the plus of 8:8, ἄνθρωπον
ὃς δυνήσεται κεφαλὴν ἆραι ἢ δυνατὸν συντελέσασθαί τι, is also
reminiscent of 3:1:

3:1		8:8
כי הנה האדון	ἰδοὺ δὴ ὁ δεσπότης	
יהוה צבאות	κύριος σαβαωθ	
מסיר מירושלם	ἀφελεῖ ἀπὸ τῆς Ιουδαίας	καὶ ἀφελεῖ ἀπὸ τῆς Ιουδαίας
ומיהודה	καὶ ἀπὸ Ιερουσαλημ	
משען ומשענה	ἰσχύοντα καὶ ἰσχύουσαν	ἄνθρωπον ὃς δυνήσεται κεφαλὴν ἆραι
כל משען לחם	ἰσχὺν ἄρτου	ἢ δυνατὸν συντελέσασθαί τι
וכל משען מים	καὶ ἰσχὺν ὕδατος	

As Ottley observed, 8:8 "almost summarises iii.1."[102] While κεφαλὴν
ἆραι is a Hebraism that we can retrovert as לשׂאת ראשׁ,[103] the word order
accords with Greek style,[104] favoring the conclusion that the translator
supplied it, since his default mode is to follow the word order of his
Hebrew *Vorlage*. However, determining what led to this plus and whether

---

[101] Outside of Isaiah and Ezekiel, אפיק is translated with χειμάρους (Ps 125[126]:4;
Job 6:15) and πηγή (Ps 17(18):16; 41[42]:2). For evidence that LXX-Isaiah knew LXX-
Ezekiel, see Seeligmann, *Septuagint Version*, 74.

[102] Ottley, *The Book of Isaiah*, 2:148.

[103] As noted in van der Kooij, *Die alten Textzeugen*, 50.

[104] In no other rendering of נשׂא + ראשׁ in the LXX is the word order transposed.

the translator's *Vorlage* read something other than שֶׁטֶף וְעָבַר עַד צַוָּאר יַגִּיעַ is made problematic by the lack of any perceptible relationship to the Hebrew phrases and a lack of variant readings in the other textual witnesses. Given the meager data available, the best surmise is that the plus appropriates phrases from 3:1, explicating the meaning of ἰσχύοντα καὶ ἰσχύουσαν in terms of abilities to fulfill social leadership functions.

Even adopting the tentative suggestion that this plus was supplied by the translator does not lead inevitably to the conclusion that the translator meant to bespeak Antiochus's deposition of Onias III. In order to draw that inference, one would need to conclude that the translator ignored the preceding context, which sets this statement within an ancient political milieu: the people's choice of τὸν Ῥααασσων καὶ τὸν υἱὸν Ῥομελιου to be their king, in recompense for which the Kyrios will bring upon them τὸν βασιλέα τῶν Ἀσσυρίων καὶ τὴν δόξαν αὐτοῦ. In order to make the case that the translator finds here an allusion to Antiochus's removal of Onias it would be necessary to assert that, despite the semantic and syntactic clarity he provides in describing this as a past event, he was thinking primarily of his own day.

Note especially his affirmation that vv. 7–8 result from the people's choice in v. 6 by translating וְלָכֵן with διὰ τοῦτο. Those who wish to say that the translator freely supplied the plus of v. 8 in order to allude to Onias's removal must explain why the translator did not sever the connection of vv. 7–8 with v. 6 so as to separate the allusion to Antiochus from the eighth century political environment. Lacking that, there is no hint that the translator intended such an allusion. The reference to the removal of an effective bureaucrat is hardly specific enough to support this.[105]

As noted earlier, while van der Kooij affirms Seeligmann's perception that behind the Ἀσσύριοι in 10:5 lurk the Seleucids,[106] he asserts, against Seeligmann, that the toponyms of 10:9 can be identified with lands conquered by Seleucid rulers:[107]

---

[105] The fact that it stands in the vicinity of a text that, according to Seeligmann, Koenig, and van der Kooij, bespeaks Antiochus's prevention of Torah study (8:11–16)—even if that point were granted—cannot be used to support this interpretation, since it does not address the problem raised above.

[106] Seeligmann, *Septuagint Version*, 88.

[107] For חֲמָת 1QIsaᵃ has a large gap after כְאַרְפָּד, followed by מת (it also reads כדרמשק for כְדַמֶּשֶׂק). 4QIsaᵉ preserves only a ל (likely belonging to לֹא) and the final three letters of שֹׁמְרוֹן. S renders הֲלֹא with ܐܢ and omits an equivalent for both instances of לֹא אִם, substituting for it simple *wāw*. It reads ܒܠܘ ('they became worn out') for כְּלָנוֹ,

הלא ככרכמיש   οὐκ ἔλαβον τὴν χώραν τὴν ἐπάνω βαβυλῶνος
כלנו   καὶ Χαλαννη οὗ ὁ πύργος ᾠκοδομήθη
אם לא כארפד חמת   καὶ ἔλαβον Ἀραβίαν
אם לא כדמשׂק שמרון   καὶ Δαμασκὸν καὶ Σαμάρειαν

Rejecting Seeligmann's assertion that the translator rendered כלנו in the light of the story of the tower, on the grounds that "in Gen 11 aber nicht von einem Turmbau in <u>Chalanee</u> die Rede ist," he notes that "in der etwas jüngeren jüdischen Exegese zu Kalne in Gen 10,10 wird diese Stadt in Babylonien ist."[108] Citing also Jerome's comment on כלנו in Gen 10:10 (*postea verso nomine a Seleuco rege est dicta Seleucia*), he concludes that by using Χαλαννη the translator possibly "mit dem Turmbau in Chalanne auf den Bau der Stadt Seleucia...der Hauptstadt der seleukidischen Reiches, anspielt."[109]

Having posited this, van der Kooij equates the ruler's boast of having captured τὴν χώραν τὴν ἐπάνω βαβυλῶνος with Seleucus III's recapture of the upper regions of the Seleucid empire, while noting Polybius's report that in 218 B.C.E. "haben sich die Araber gemeinsam Antiochus III. unterworfen (Polybios, *Historiae* V. 71)."[110] Moreover, he asserts that οὐκ ἔλαβον τὴν χώραν τὴν ἐπάνω βαβυλῶνος implies "dass Babylon zum Reich der 'Assyrer' gehörte," since the oracle is directed against the Assyrians (v. 5).[111] Comparing a passage from the third Sibylline Oracle that equates the Seleucids with the Babylonians, he concludes that "der Verfasser der LXX Jes in Jes 10,9...mit dem assyrischen König auf einen seleukidischen Herrscher anspielt."[112] Thus, van der Kooij explains the toponyms of 10:9 as the translator's infusion of the text not just with Hellenistic toponyms, but also with allusions to the political realities of his day.

There are problems with this explanation, however. First, the assertion by the ἄρχων that he has taken τὴν χώραν τὴν ἐπάνω βαβυλῶνος does not necessarily imply that the ἄρχων himself was in Babylon, nor does it imply anything about the status of Babylon itself.

Second, van der Kooij's objection to Seeligmann's perception that the translator chose Χαλαννη for כלנו with an eye to Genesis 11 overlooks

---

and reads ובא ותארא for כארפד. For אם לא כארפד V reads simply *et ut Arfad*. T is expansionistic, but reflects a *Vorlage* = MT.

[108] Van der Kooij, *Die alten Textzeugen*, 37.
[109] Ibid.
[110] Ibid., 38.
[111] Ibid., 36.
[112] Ibid.

the way Seeligmann builds his argument not simply on Gen 11:2, but also by linking it to the mention of Χαλαννη in Gen 10:10, which places it ἐν τῇ γῇ Σενναρ, the same location given for the tower in Gen 11:2.

Of course, van der Kooij's identification of these toponyms with Seleucid conquests is bound up with his assertion that the translator equated the Assyrian king of chapter 10 with a Seleucid ruler.[113] However, this contention is difficult to support in the light of the translator's handling of vv. 5–14, which the translator construed as an address of a ruler preoccupied with conquest. As Ziegler asserted, the translator twice supplied ἔλαβον in v. 9, as well as λήμψομαι in v. 10, because "er an die Eroberung der genannten Länder durch den König von Assur dachte," which Ziegler concluded was an expedient forced on him "weil ihm der Satzbau von V. 9 nicht recht klar war."[114] More likely, however, this translation is the product of a reasoned interpretation of vv. 5–14.[115]

Whereas the MT of v. 5 defines Asshur as אֲפִי שֵׁבֶט and asserts that it wields the staff of the LORD's wrath, the LXX follows the announcement of woe to the Assyrians with:

שֵׁבֶט אַפִּי[116]   ἡ ῥάβδος τοῦ θυμοῦ μου

וּמַטֶּה הוּא בְיָדָם   καὶ ὀργῆς ἐστιν ἐν ταῖς χερσὶν αὐτῶν

The translation of וּמַטֶּה by καὶ ὀργῆς creates an extended phrase modifying ἡ ῥάβδος, rather than introducing a phrase defining Asshur's role, as is the structure in the MT.[117] While this restructured syntax keeps the "rod of wrath" in Assyrian hands, a change introduced in v. 6 gives that assertion a different meaning. Rather than the LORD sending the Assyrian(s) (presumed as subject from the preceding verse) against an "impious nation" (בְּגוֹי חָנֵף), the Kyrios sends τὴν ὀργήν μου εἰς ἔθνος

---

[113] Ibid., 35–36.

[114] Ziegler, *Untersuchungen*, 63–64.

[115] It is doubtful that the translator failed to understand the syntax. Compare his adept translation of וְהָיָה כָעָם כַּכֹּהֵן by καὶ ἔσται ὁ λαὸς ὡς ὁ ἱερεύς in 24:2.

[116] 1QIsaᵃ = MT. 4QIsaᶜ is fragmentary, but attests no variance with MT. S construes שֵׁבֶט אַפִּי as a predication rather than an appositive: ﺍﻟ ﺍﻟ; V accords with MT. T's paraphrase suggests no variant vis-à-vis the MT.

[117] The probability that καὶ ὀργῆς is the translator's equivalent for וּמַטֶּה is strong, given his rendering of וּמַטֵּהוּ by καὶ ὁ θυμὸς αὐτοῦ in 10:26, as well as his use of ὀργή for atypical equivalents elsewhere (καὶ ὀργῆς || וְנָאצָה in 37:3; ἡ ὀργὴ παρὰ κυρίου || רוּחַ יְהוָה in 59:19).

ἄνομον.[118] Still more striking is the translator's rendering of the next clause:

ועל עם עברתי אצונו[119]   καὶ τῷ ἐμῷ λαῷ συντάξω

While the first person singular suffix of עברתי is recognizable in ἐμῷ, the lack of an equivalent for the noun is perplexing, until we compare how other versions finessed עם עברתי: S translates it with ܥܡܐ ܪܓܙܐ, 'a wrathful people', while T expands it into עמא דעברו על אוריתי, 'the people who transgressed my instruction'. In this light, the LXX seems to have adopted an equally interpretive rendering. Given that the first half of the verse speaks of the Kyrios's intent to send his wrath on a "lawless nation," the translator evidently perceived in עם עברתי 'the people who execute my wrath' and collapsed it into 'my people'.

As a result of these interpretive ploys, the assertion that "the rod of my anger and wrath" is in the hands of the Assyrians does not mean that they wield the Kyrios's wrath, but rather that his wrath is directed against them and executed by Israel.[120] As Seeligmann summarizes, with ἔθνος ἄνομον "the translator apparently had in mind not Israel, but hostile Assyria…and he regarded it as a duty with which God had charged the Jewish people, to plunder towns and trample them under foot."[121]

As in the MT, v. 7 focuses on the ruminations of this bellicose ruler. However, whereas in the MT the ruler is ill disposed to acknowledge that he is merely a vehicle of the LORD's wrath against Israel, in the LXX he fails to consider that the Kyrios's anger is poised against him and his cities. Rather, he is intent on a course of destruction that will engulf numerous nations.

Noteworthy is the choice of ὁ νοῦς αὐτοῦ to translate בלבבו, since the more typical equivalents for לבב in LXX-Isa are καρδία (25x) and ψυχή

---

[118] The translator read זעמי with (our) v. 6 and took the 3rd masc. sing. object suffix of אשלחנו as resumptive.

[119] 1QIsaᵃ = MT. 4QIsaᵉ preserves only ועל עם and may read the initial ע of עברתי. S & V accord with MT, while T's expansive rendering presupposes a *Vorlage* = MT.

[120] This is preferable to das Neves's conclusion that τῷ ἐμῷ λαῷ refers to the "Assyrians," while ἔθνος ἄνομον designates Israel (*A Teologia*, 202). Even if ἔθνος ἄνομον denotes Israel elsewhere, the characterization of the subsequent Assyrian ruler as haughty (vv. 7–11) and the Kyrios's resolve to judge his haughty mind (v. 12) make it difficult to imagine the translator entertaining the idea that the Assyrians were the people of the Kyrios.

[121] Seeligmann, *Septuagint Version*, 88.

(6x), as in the preceding clause: καὶ τῇ ψυχῇ || ‏ולבבו‎.[122] Because νοῦς appears for ‏לבב‎ outside this passage only in 41:22 (although διανοία translates it in 14:13[123] and 35:4), its reappearance in v. 12 (ἐπὶ τὸν νοῦν τὸν μέγαν || ‏על פרי גדל לבב‎)[124] makes this the only double occurrence of this atypical equivalent within a single passage.

Having detailed the bent of this νοῦς in vv. 7–11, v. 12b announces judgment as follows:[125]

‏אפקד על פרי גדל לבב‎   ἐπάξει ἐπὶ τὸν νοῦν τὸν μέγαν

‏מלך אשור‎   τὸν ἄρχοντα τῶν ᾿Ασσυρίων

Rather than judgment befalling 'the fruit of the haughtiness of the heart the king of Assyria' (MT), it falls on 'the ruler of the Assyrians', designated in advance by the epithet 'the great mind', the same νοῦς that refused to consider what the Kyrios was plotting for him. While the use οἱοἰκουμένη in v. 14 to describe the extent of his intended conquests might support the hypothesis that the translator had in mind Seleucid rulers—inasmuch as it transposes the passage "from the atmosphere surrounding the Assyrian claims to world sovereignty into the Hellenistic period"[126]—the designation of this figure as an ἄρχων opposes this.

Raurell ("<<Archontes>>") has drawn attention to the importance of ἄρχων for the translator, who used it as an equivalent for seventeen Hebrew words.[127] The use of ἄρχων for ‏מלך‎ in 10:12 is especially striking, since each of the other 25 occurrences of ‏מלך אשור‎ in Isaiah is translated βασιλεύς ᾿Ασσυρίων. Moreover, for each of the 80 occurrences of ‏מלך‎ in the book the translator uses βασιλεύς (72x) or βασιλεύειν (3x), except in 10:12 and in 8:21,[128] the latter of which reads,[129]

---

[122] While the LXX's *Vorlage* may have read ‏ובלבבו‎, it is equally possible that τῇ ψυχῇ is the translator's reformulation. We encounter the same quandary with the Targum's ‏ובלביה‎.

[123] Van der Kooij argues that 14:13, even though translated literally, can refer to Antiochus IV, "denn er trifft sich mit Dan 8,10 und 2 Makk 9,10 in der Deutung des Verhaltens dieses Königs" (*Die alten Textzeugen*, 42). This, on its own, is a weak argument and certainly could not be the basis for positing an association with 10:12 as a reference to Antiochus IV (and van der Kooij posits no such connection).

[124] Undoubtedly finding ‏על פני‎ for ‏על פרי‎ in its *Vorlage*.

[125] 1QIsaᵃ = MT. S, V, and T presuppose *Vorlagen* = MT.

[126] Seeligmann, *Septuagint Version*, 81.

[127] The majority of Hebrew lexemes for which it is used share its semantic range. Most frequent is ‏שר‎, which is rendered by ἄρχων in 13 of 18 occurrences.

[128] The LXX gives no equivalent in the four other instances.

[129] 1QIsaᵃ reads ‏ונקשה‎ (+ *wāw*), but then reads ‏יתקצף‎ instead of ‏והתקצף‎.

וְעָבַר בָּהּ נִקְשֶׁה וְרָעֵב   καὶ ἥξει ἐφ᾽ ὑμᾶς σκληρὰ λιμός
וְהָיָה כִי יִרְעַב וְהִתְקַצֵּף   καὶ ἔσται ὡς ἂν πεινάσητε λυπηθήσεσθε
וְקִלֵּל בְּמַלְכּוֹ וּבֵאלֹהָיו   καὶ κακῶς ἐρεῖτε τὸν ἄρχοντα καὶ τὰ παταχρα.

As Seeligmann notes, παταχρα is a transliteration of Aramaic פַּתְכְרָא,
'idol' (which happens to appear in T's rendering of this verse).[130]
Evidently, then, the translator perceived the deities of 8:21 as foreign,
suggesting he regarded this ἄρχων as also foreign.

The address of these words to a group (ἐρεῖτε) is attributable to the
translator's tendency to conform the grammatical person and number
of pronouns to other pronouns in the context. In this case, the second
person plural resumes advice addressed to those who have been urged
by others to avail themselves of necromancy (v. 19). Those propounding such advice are described as inexcusably violating the Torah
(v. 20):[131]

לַתּוֹרָה וְלַתְעוּדָה   νόμον γὰρ εἰς βοήθειαν ἔδωκεν
אִם לֹא יֹאמְרוּ כַּדָּבָר הַזֶּה   ἵνα εἴπωσιν οὐχ ὡς τὸ ῥῆμα τοῦτο
אֲשֶׁר אֵין לוֹ שָׁחַר   περὶ οὗ οὐκ ἔστι δῶρα δοῦναι περὶ αὐτοῦ

With this rendering the translator prolongs a theme he divined just
prior to this, in vv. 14–15.[132] After admonishing addressees to trust in
the Kyrios so as not to confront him in judgment, the LXX speaks of
the house of Israel falling into a snare and troubles (vv. 14–15) and
concludes with the statement (v. 16),[133]

(צוּר) תְּעוּדָה   τότε φανεροὶ ἔσονται
חֲתוֹם תּוֹרָה בְּלִמֻּדָי   οἱ σφραγιζόμενοι τὸν νόμον τοῦ μὴ μαθεῖν

---

[130] Seeligmann, *Septuagint Version*, 9 and 50. παταχρον is used again in 37:38, its only
other appearance in the LXX (even if it is to be attributed to a different translator) in
speaking of the Assyrian king worshipping his god.

[131] 1QIsaᵃ = MT. S reads ܪ݂ܠܐ || אִם לֹא, while its ܐܡ̇ܪܝܢ ܠܗܘܢ ܐܝܠܝܢ ܕܠܐ || אֲשֶׁר
אֵין לוֹ שָׁחַר indicates that it (like the LXX) read שַׁחַד in its *Vorlage*, which occasioned
the insertion of ܡܬܠ / לַתֵּת. V supplies *magis* with *ad legem* for the sake of the target
language; its *quod si non* suggests it likely read כִּי אִם לֹא; its lack of an equivalent for
אֲשֶׁר is probably due to the target language. T's expansive rendering presupposes a
Vorlage = MT.

[132] The middle phrase of this verse shows the closest correspondence to the MT,
although the choice of εἰς βοήθειαν for וְלַתְעוּדָה might well derive from relating the
word to עֹז, just as the translation of שַׁחַר with δῶρα reflects a reading of it as שַׁחַד
(so Ottley, *The Book of Isaiah*, 2:150); cf. S. In each case the translator filled out the
sense by supplying what he considered an appropriate verb.

[133] 1QIsaᵃ reads וחתום. Similarly, S reads ܘܚܬܘܡ. V reflects a *Vorlage* = MT. T's
expansive rendering presupposes a *Vorlage* = MT.

The translator's concern for a group opposing the Torah is again clear.[134] Indeed, he seems to have been guided in the latter half of chapter 8 by his concern for the Torah and his conviction that Israel's leaders were disloyal to it. However, it is important to note the distinction between a group of people said to inhibit Torah study (οἱ σφραγιζόμενοι τὸν νόμον τοῦ μὴ μαθεῖν, v. 16)[135] or to encourage necromancy (καὶ ἐὰν εἴπωσι πρὸς ὑμᾶς, v. 19) and the solitary ruler of v. 21.

This description's point of contact with 10:12, once again, is that in it, as in 10:12, the translator deviated from his typical equivalents for מלך by using ἄρχων. And yet, aside from the possible assumption that the ἄρχων of 8:21 is a foreign ruler, 10:12 shows no similarity to the description of the ἄρχων in chapter 10. Nor does the translator take the opportunity in 8:21 to construct a fuller picture of this ἄρχων or to link him with the violations of the Torah just described. That ἄρχων is incidental to the problems affecting Jerusalem; he merely bears the brunt of popular displeasure. Thus, it is doubtful that the translator chose to deviate from his typical equivalent for מלך in 8:21 in order to identify this ruler with a specific Hellenistic overlord. This, in turn, diminishes the likelihood that in using ἄρχων in 10:12 the translator had in mind a specific Seleucid ruler or line of rulers.

We should also note that 10:12 is not the first occurrence of ἄρχων within 10:5–14. Talk of a solitary ἄρχων appeared already in 10:8:[136]

---

[134] The relationship of the second clause to the MT is discernable, even amidst enigmas, the most vexing of which is τότε φανεροὶ ἔσονται || תעודה (the formal equivalent for צור, ἄνθρωποι ἐν ἀσφαλείᾳ ὄντες stands in v. 15 and will be dealt with in addressing 8:11–16, below, p. 245). Ottley reasonably suggests that the LXX's *Vorlage* may have read מלמדי for בלמדי (*The Book of Isaiah*, 2:150), although it is also possible that the translator construed בלמדי as crasis of בל למדי (cf. his translation of בל in 14:21, ἵνα μὴ ἀναστῶσιν || בל יקמו, and in 26:10, ἵνα μὴ ἴδῃ || ובל יראה) (cf. Koenig, *L' Herméneutique*, 132–33). In the light of his perception of the second phrase, the translator may have read תעודה as תעורה and related it to ערה, even as he renders יערה with ἀποκαλύψει in 3:17 and ונער with φανερὰ ἔσται in 33:9 (cf. ibid., 2:271). While this still leaves oblique τότε || צור, the translator interjects temporal conjunctions frequently enough that its presence here is best attributed to him (cf. τότε σπείρει || והפיץ in 28:25: τότε ἔσται || ונתן in 30:23; καὶ νῦν ὁ οἶκος Ιακωβ || בית יעקב in 2:5; νῦν δὲ εἰς ᾅδου || אך אל שאל in 14:15).

[135] It is not clear, however, whether this is to be taken literally (and related to prohibitions during the Hellenistic reforms of the second century) or figuratively, as a characterization of "false teaching" of the Torah (so Seeligmann, *Septuagint Version*, 105–06).

[136] 1QIsaᵃ = MT. 1QIsaᵉ preserves only [יא]מר הלום. S presupposes a *Vorlage* = MT. V reads *simul reges* and T reads כמלכין, each perhaps reading כמלכים. T has כל שלטוני, perhaps reading כל שרי, given that כ was often mechanically inserted by scribes.

כִּי יֹאמַר הֲלֹא שָׂרַי יַחְדָּו מְלָכִים   καὶ ἐὰν εἴπωσιν αὐτῷ σὺ μόνος εἶ
ἄρχων

Even though ἄρχων renders שָׂרַי (for which reason מְלָכִים was perhaps
passed over as redundant), the translator has overridden the plural
form, against his pattern of rendering שָׂרִי with ἄρχοντες elsewhere.[137]
Moreover, the sentence has been reformulated as a question addressed
to the ruler.[138]

Most striking is μόνος || יַחְדָּו. Apparently the translator, construing vv.
9–11 as stating an intent to build a far-flung empire (cf. τὴν οἰκουμένην
ὅλην καταλήψομαι, v. 14), perceived this question pertaining to the
extent of the ruler's sovereignty.[139] This is the hubris that gives meaning
to the epithet τὸν νοῦν τὸν μέγαν in v. 12.

While this aspiration to sole mastery of the world might be well-
suited to a Seleucid ruler, the title ἄρχων ill-fits that hypothesis. In
the contemporaneous works of 1 and 2 Maccabees, the title applied
to Seleucid rulers is βασιλεύς. Moreover, although ἄρχων does not
appear in 2 Maccabees, it occurs twenty-two times in 1 Maccabees,
where ἄρχοντες ten times designates military commanders and six
times unspecified officials. The noun appears six times in the singular
number: three times to designate the commander of an army, once
for a representative sent by Antiochus to collect taxes, and twice to
designate, generically, the role of a leader (2:17, 12:53). The fact that
1 Maccabees never applies ἄρχων to a Seleucid ruler is relevant to Isaiah
10.[140] If that translator consistently used βασιλεύς for Seleucid rulers
and never applied ἄρχων to them, it becomes difficult to imagine that
our translator, who everywhere else renders מֶלֶךְ אַשּׁוּר with ὁ βασιλεύς

---

[137] Each of the four remaining occurrences of שָׂרִי is translated by ἄρχοντες, while
the other eleven occurrences of שַׂר in a plural formation are translated by plural forms
in Greek. Even the lone singular form (שַׂר) is translated τοὺς ἄρχοντας in 9:5.

[138] While Ottley implies that the translator's *Vorlage* might have read הֲלוֹ for הֲלֹא (*The
Book of Isaiah*, 2:160), it seems more likely that הֲלֹא is expressed via the question that
expects an affirmative response, while the translator supplied the pronoun as indirect
object. Cf. v. 11, where the translator omits an explicit translation of הֲלֹא, casting the
verse as an assertion.

[139] The translator may have related יַחְדָּו to אֶחָד, even as in 65:25 כְּאֶחָד זְאֵב וְטָלֶה יִרְעוּ
is rendered τότε λύκοι καὶ ἄρνες βοσκηθήσονται ἅμα, the characteristic equivalent for
יַחְדָּו in LXX-Isa. Cf. κατὰ μόνας for יַחַד in Ps 32(33):15; 140(141):10.

[140] Harold Attridge, "Historiography," in *Jewish Writings of the Second Temple Period:
Apocrypha, Pseudepigrapha, Qumran, Sectarian Writings, Philo, Josephus*, ed. Michael Stone
(Minneapolis: Fortress, 1984) 171.

τῶν Ἀσσυρίων, chose ἄρχων in a text where he perceived the Assyrian king as cipher for a Seleucid ruler.

Consequently, it seems fruitless to attempt to identify this ἄρχων with a Seleucid or to correlate Seleucid conquests with the LXX's toponyms, especially since the latter seem determined more by intertextual associations with Genesis 10 and 11.

While the infusion of passages with the theme of rulers' financial plunder of the people shows that the translator was influenced by the practices of Hellenistic rulers, the hypothesis that he wrapped Antiochus IV in the garb of Isaiah's great tyrant lacks explicit references to substantiate that.

The ΝΟΜΟΣ

We have already witnessed part of chapter eight's attack on those who oppose study of Torah. Because that theme has been identified as a reflection of events in the translator's day, we must explore it as a final test of whether the translator engaged in *Erfüllungsinterpretation*. The question is whether the translator has molded his rendering of passages speaking of the νόμος to reflect events in Jerusalem's Hellenistic crisis of the early second century B.C.E.

Given that the book of Isaiah distinctively uses תורה to designate the prophetic word as "instruction" (e.g., 1:10; 5:24; 8:16, 20; 30:9), it is unremarkable that the translator construed such passages as having to do with the νόμος, even though that gives to תורה a different meaning than it held for Isaiah of Jerusalem. More significant are passages where the translator produces a distinctive statement about the νόμος.

We have already noticed his translation of חתום תורה בלמדי by οἱ σφραγιζόμενοι τὸν νόμον τοῦ μὴ μαθεῖν in 8:16, showing that he found in this passage the theme of opposition to study of the Torah. His concern about opposition to the Torah is evident again in his rendering of 24:16, as Seeligmann noted:[141]

מכנף הארץ זמרת שמענו[142]	¹⁶)ἀπὸ τῶν πτερύγων τῆς γῆς τέρατα ἠκούσαμεν
צבי לצדיק	ἐλπὶς τῷ εὐσεβεῖ

[141] Seeligmann, *Septuagint Version*, 105.
[142] V. 16–1QIsaᵃ = MT. S & V accord with the MT. T is expansive, but seems to presuppose a *Vorlage* = MT. Note, however, its וי לאנוסיא ('woe to the violent ones'), comparable to the LXX's οὐαὶ τοῖς ἀθετοῦσιν.

וַאמַר רזי לי רזי לי אוי לי בנדים בנדו   καὶ ἐροῦσιν οὐαὶ τοῖς ἀθετοῦσιν

ובנד בונדים בנדו   οἱ ἀθετοῦντες τὸν νόμον

פחד ופחת ופח עליך[143]   [17]φόβος καὶ βόθυνος καὶ παγὶς ἐφ' ὑμᾶς

יושב הארץ   τοὺς ἐνοικοῦντας ἐπὶ τῆς γῆς

The translator's path in the first half of v. 16 is traceable from the MT,[144] but he seems to have been at a loss for what to do with the second half, particularly רזי לי רזי לי, which he omits, perhaps reckoning it "implied in the interjection," as Ottley inferred.[145] His translation of בנד by ἀθετεῖν entails the same equivalence he uses in 21:2, 33:1, and 48:8, while his translation of לי בנדים with οὐαὶ τοῖς ἀθετοῦσιν is paralleled in T's וי לאנוסיא. While this might point to a *Vorlage* reading לבנדים, both the LXX and T are so periphrastic in this verse that it is more likely they happened upon the same solution regarding how to handle this phrase.

More notable is the translator's choice to identify the νόμος as what is rejected, especially since he did not do so in 21:2, where he renders הבונד בונד והשודד שודד with ὁ ἀθετῶν ἀθετεῖ ὁ ἀνομῶν ἀνομεῖ. In fact, by inserting νόμον as the direct object, he creates an address to the impious that warns them of their fate (v. 17). This maneuver demonstrates that the translator had a special concern for the Torah and its abrogation. The question is whether this concern was due to a pressing threat in his day.

The pivotal passage for this discussion is 8:11–16. Seeligmann pointed especially to vv. 15–16,[146] the latter of which we examined earlier:

וכשלו בם רבים[147]   [15]διὰ τοῦτο ἀδυνατήσουσιν ἐν αὐτοῖς πολλοὶ

ונפלו ונשברו ונוקשו   καὶ πεσοῦνται καὶ συντριβήσονται καὶ ἐγγιοῦσι

ונלכדו[16] צור   καὶ ἁλώσονται ἄνθρωποι ἐν ἀσφαλείᾳ ὄντες

---

[143] V. 17–1QIsaᵃ = MT. S, V, and T accord with the MT.

[144] The translator rendered זמרה with αἴνεσις in 12:2 and 51:3, while he used τέρας for מופת in 8:18 and 20:3, which Ottley suggests stood in the *Vorlage* here (*The Book of Isaiah*, 2:222). While this is tenable, his choice of τέρατα was more likely influenced by his handling of צבי לצדיק. Translating זמרת שמענו with αἰνέσεις ἠκούσαμεν, while possible, would have made for an awkward fit with ἐλπὶς τῷ εὐσεβεῖ as the import of what was heard.

[145] Ibid., 2:223. The translator was probably perplexed by רזי, judging from his rendering of ישלח האדון יהוה צבאות במשמניו רזון by ἀποστελεῖ κύριος σαβαωθ εἰς τὴν σὴν τιμὴν ἀτιμίαν in 10:16 and of ומשמן בשרו ירזה by καὶ τὰ πίονα τῆς δόξης αὐτοῦ σεισθήσεται in 17:4.

[146] Seeligmann, *Septuagint Version*, 105.

[147] V. 15–1QIsaᵃ = MT. S, V, and T accord with the MT.

תְּעוּדָה[148] ¹⁶⁾τότε φανεροὶ ἔσονται

חָתוּם תּוֹרָה בְּלִמֻּדָי οἱ σφραγιζόμενοι τὸν νόμον τοῦ μὴ μαθεῖν

Seeligmann points to the translator's insertion of τότε as establishing a connection between these verses, so that v. 16 identifies those under punishment in v. 15 as "those who decline to make the law an object of their constant care and study."[149] Accordingly, he perceives the translator "polemizing [sic] against a certain group of people who fail to recognize the binding force of the law, or refuse to see in it more than the face-value of the words."[150]

Noting also that the translator supplied διὰ τοῦτο at the head of v. 15 to provide a link to the preceding verses, he explores vv. 11–14 to "discover something of the programme and the slogans put forward by the movement which is supposed to have existed at this period":[151]

כִּי כֹה אָמַר יְהוָה אֵלַי[152] ¹¹⁾οὕτως λέγει κύριος

כְּחֶזְקַת הַיָּד וְיִסְּרֵנִי מִלֶּכֶת τῇ ἰσχυρᾷ χειρὶ ἀπειθοῦσι τῇ πορείᾳ

בְּדֶרֶךְ הָעָם הַזֶּה לֵאמֹר τῆς ὁδοῦ τοῦ λαοῦ τούτου λέγοντες

לֹא תֹאמְרוּן קֶשֶׁר[153] ¹²⁾μήποτε εἴπητε σκληρόν

לְכֹל אֲשֶׁר יֹאמַר הָעָם הַזֶּה קֶשֶׁר πᾶν γὰρ ὃ ἐὰν εἴπῃ ὁ λαὸς οὗτος σκληρόν ἐστι

וְאֶת מוֹרָאוֹ לֹא תִירְאוּ τὸν δὲ φόβον αὐτοῦ οὐ μὴ φοβηθῆτε

וְלֹא תַעֲרִיצוּ οὐδὲ μὴ ταραχθῆτε

---

[148] V. 16–1QIsaᵃ reads וְחָתוּם. Similarly, S reads ܚܬܘܡܐ. V reflects a *Vorlage* = MT. T's expansive rendering presupposes a *Vorlage* = MT.

[149] Seeligmann, *Septuagint Version*, 105.

[150] Ibid., 105–06.

[151] Ibid., 106.

[152] V. 11–1QIsaᵃ reads simple יד rather than היד and reads ויסירנו for ויסרני. 4QIsaᵉ preserves only [כי כה אמר יהו]ה, while 4QIsaᶠ has only [כה אמר יהו]ה (at the start of a line). 4QIsaˡ preserves only לוא [הזה לאמ]ר (at the start of a line). S has ܡܣܒܠ || ויסרני, whether it actually read ויסירני or simply inferred that ויסרני is from סור; it renders מלכת with ܐܘܪܚܐ ܓܝ, similar to V (*ne irem*), V's only difference from the MT. T presupposes a *Vorlage* = MT.

[153] V. 12–1QIsaᵃ = MT. 1QIsaᵉ preserves only [תאמ]רון קשר לכל [א]שר [י]אמר העם, although the initial ד and all six of the final letters are uncertain. 4QIsaˡ preserves ואת מוראו לוא תיראו ו (at the start of a line; the final *wāw* is uncertain). S has ܐܟ ܡ ܕܐܟ for לכל אשר יאמר, either reflecting כאשר יאמר or it is a simplification; it reads ܘܡܢ ܕܚܠܬܗ for ואת מוראו, probably an adjustment of the pronoun in light of the context; while its reading of ܬܬܙܝܥܘܢ || תעריצו might reflect תערוצו in its *Vorlage*, more likely it is contextually chosen (cf. V and cf. S's rendering of מערצכם in v. 13). V renders לכל with *omnia enim*, which likely does not reflect כל כי in its *Vorlage*; its rendering of תעריצו with *paveatis* ('you will [not] be terrified') is probably contextual, although it could reflect a reading תערוצו (cf. S, above). For ולא תעריצו T reads וְעַל תּוּקְפֵיהּ לָא תֵימְרוּן תְּקִיף, an expansion formed parallel to the initial clause of the verse; for תוקפיה || תעריצו cf. תקפכון || מערצכם in v. 13.

אֶת יְהוָה צְבָאוֹת אֹתוֹ תַקְדִּישׁוּ[154]	[13]κύριον αὐτὸν ἁγιάσατε
וְהוּא מוֹרַאֲכֶם	καὶ αὐτὸς ἔσται σου φόβος
וְהוּא מַעֲרִצְכֶם	[14]καὶ ἐὰν ἐπ' αὐτῷ πεποιθὼς ἦς
וְהָיָה לְמִקְדָּשׁ[155]	ἔσται σοι εἰς ἁγίασμα
וּלְאֶבֶן נֶגֶף	καὶ οὐχ ὡς λίθου προσκόμματι συνα-
	ντήσεσθε αὐτῷ
וּלְצוּר מִכְשׁוֹל	οὐδὲ ὡς πέτρας πτώματι
לִשְׁנֵי בָתֵּי יִשְׂרָאֵל	ὁ δὲ οἶκος Ιακωβ
לְפַח וּלְמוֹקֵשׁ	ἐν παγίδι καὶ ἐν κοιλάσματι
לְיוֹשֵׁב יְרוּשָׁלָםִ	ἐγκαθήμενοι ἐν Ιερουσαλημ

Finding justification for detecting the opponents' program in a translation that "deviates considerably from the Hebrew original," Seeligmann regarded v. 11 as referring to group that characterized "the precepts of orthodox Judaism as hard and oppressive" and regarded those who clung to such practices as "caught in a snare," finding that God had "become a stone of offence, a stumbling-block."[156] Their alternative counsel (which the translator opposed) was not to get caught up in "superstitious fear (of all these precepts and laws), but only worship God in His holiness, and place one's trust in Him."[157] Seeligmann did not attempt to identify this "anti-dogmatic movement" with any movement we know from the second century B.C.E.[158]

Das Neves notes Seeligmann's treatment of this passage, but sets it aside, saying that he prefers "to interpret this context according to our thesis of two classes [viz., the pious and the impious] among the

---

[154] V. 13–1QIsaᵃ leaves a pronounced space after צְבָאוֹת. 4QIsaᵉ preserves only [צְבָאוֹ]ת אֹתוֹ תַקְדִּישׁוּ, of which the initial ת and final ו are uncertain. 4QIsaˡ preserves תַקְדִּ[ישׁו]מוֹרַאֲכֶם וְהוּא מַעֲרִצְכֶם. S lacks an equivalent for אֹתוֹ (likely due to the target language) and renders תַקְדִּישׁוּ with an imperative, ܩܕܫܘ (cf. LXX & V), perhaps reading הַקְדִּישׁוּ; its rendering of מַעֲרִצְכֶם by ܡܣܒܪܝܢ is likely based on context. V's *sanctificate* may reflect הַקְדִּישׁוּ (cf. LXX & S). T presupposes a *Vorlage* = MT.

[155] V. 14–1QIsaᵃ reads וְהוּא for וְהָיָה and וּלְצֹר for וּלְצוּר. The few remains of this verse in 4QIsaᵉ are too uncertain to be of use, while 4QIsaˡ preserves only וְהָיָה. S accords with the MT. V reads *et erit vobis* for וְהָיָה, likely adding the pronoun for the target language; its *et in ruinam* || וּלְמוֹקֵשׁ should be compared to its *et inretientur* || וּנוֹקֵשׁ in v. 15, which suggests both are likely contextually chosen equivalents. T's rendering is expansive, but most of it seems to presuppose a *Vorlage* = MT; however, we must note its initial plus, וְאִם לָא תְקַבְּלוּן וִיהֵי מֵימְרֵיהּ בְּכוֹן, which bears a similarity to the LXX's plus, καὶ ἐὰν ἐπ' αὐτῷ πεποιθὼς ἦς.

[156] Seeligmann, *Septuagint Version*, 106.

[157] Ibid.

[158] Ibid.

people" rather than finding in it the translator's assault on "slogans" used by an antidogmatic group.[159]

Although Lust conceded that the LXX "changed the text of Is. 8,11–14 considerably," he rejected Seeligmann's reading on the grounds that, while there is evidence of groups devoted to study of the Torah, "nothing is known of an anti-Law movement in this period, not even in Qumran."[160] Moreover, he finds that "when we consider v. 14 for itself we see no great difference between the TM and the LXX as far as content is concerned."[161]

Koenig, however, revived Seeligmann's reading with vigor, claiming, in fact, that Seeligmann had been too timid, for "en effet, tout d'abord G a retrouvé dans le texte prophétique les termes memes du programme religieux de ce parti, ce qui suppose que, pour lui, le passage d'Is avait *une valeur oraculaire*."[162] For Koenig, this case validates his belief that the translator used "une méthode herméneutique d'analogie verbale," for without it the translator would have lacked sufficient grounds to censure his antilegalist contemporaries.[163] In his detailed exposition of the translator's rendering of these verses, Koenig does not, however, try to identify more precisely the offending group.

Van der Kooij's first comment on this passage appeared in his review of Koenig's book, where he opined that "the treatment of Koenig (and also of Seeligmann) is too fragmentary to be conclusive" and, therefore, called for

> closer study of the question of the Vorlage, of the word-word relations, and of the meaning and content of the Greek text as a whole...including proper attention to passages which are related to that of 8,11–16 (comp. LXX Is 28; 30,9–11).[164]

He subsequently published two studies of these verses, describing them as reflecting "a creative approach on the part of the translator."[165]

In his first study, van der Kooij explored how the translator arrived at his rendering and concluded that answering that question must rec-

---

[159] Das Neves, *A Teologia*, 132 n. 220, translation mine.
[160] Lust, "The Demonic Character," 9–10.
[161] Ibid.
[162] Koenig, *L' Herméneutique*, 121, emphasis his.
[163] Ibid., 122.
[164] Van der Kooij, "Accident or Method?" 371.
[165] Idem, *The Oracle of Tyre*, 14–15, quotation from p. 15.

ognize "the matter of actualization."[166] His second study expanded on
that observation, arguing that the passage must be studied not only in
relationship to the MT and in terms of its literary coherence, but also
"from the point of view of *genre* ('updated' prophecy)."[167] In seeking to
identify "to which events at the time of the translator LXX Isa 8:11–16
as a prophecy (of doom) might refer," he discounted Seeligmann's view
that the translator was concerned with a movement in Alexandria, arguing that "since the passage speaks about 'the house of Jacob' and 'the
inhabitants of Jerusalem' it seems more likely to think of Jerusalem and
Judah as the scene of particular tensions within Judaism."[168] Having
argued previously that the translation was executed by refugees who
accompanied Onias III in his flight from Jerusalem, he concludes that
the LXX's rendition "makes perfect sense if understood as a prophecy
that could (and should) be read as predicting the policy of Hellenistic
leaders in Jerusalem, in the first half of the second century BCE, and
its failure."[169]

The issue before us, then, is two-fold: are Seeligmann, Koenig and
van der Kooij justified in finding in the LXX's translation of this passage
an allusion to a struggle in the translator's own day, and has van der
Kooij legitimately identified this with the antilegalists in Jerusalem of
the early second century B.C.E.?

Consistent with van der Kooij's method reviewed in chapter one, he
urges avoiding "an atomistic, or an *ad hoc* treatment of (single) words or
verses" by contemplating "whether specific readings in the Greek text
cohere with each other" to form a literary whole.[170] If this proves to be
the case, then "one may assume that the differences are the result of a
deliberate translation-process."[171] Consequently, it is not surprising that
he entertains the possibility of only a few variants in the LXX's *Vorlage*.
He rejects suggestions that ἀπειθοῦσι is based on deriving ויסרני from
סור, conceding that Fischer may be correct in finding this translation
to rest on סרר, although he is not explicit about what form may have

---

[166] Idem, "The Septuagint of Isaiah: Translation and Interpretation," in *Book of Isaiah—Le livre d'Isaie* (Louvain: Leuven, 1989) 133.
[167] Van der Kooij, "Isaiah in the Septuagint," 519.
[168] Ibid., 528.
[169] Ibid., 529.
[170] Ibid., 519–20.
[171] Van der Kooij, "Septuagint of Isaiah," 128.

stood in the *Vorlage*.[172] As for σκληρόν || קָשֶׁר, he finds it difficult to
know whether "the LXX presuppose[s]…קָשֶׁה, or is…based on an
interpretation via קָרֹם (so Koenig, *L'herméneutique analogique*, 131), or via
קָשַׁר read as a passive participle."[173] The rendering καὶ ἐγγιοῦσιν, on
the other hand, was "probably realized by associating Hebrew נוּקְשׁוּ
with the root נגשׁ," while "the expression φανεροὶ ἔσονται may reflect
the Hiphil of Hebrew ידע,"[174] although he does not specify whether
this goes back to a variant in the *Vorlage* or to etymological reasoning
by the translator.[175] The remainder of this passage that "differs greatly
from MT (and 1QIsaᵃ as well)"[176] he ascribes to the translator's desire
to present a coherent unit.

Van der Kooij's demarcation of the passage is compelling. That v.
11 begins a new unit is evident not just from its introduction of an
oracle (οὕτως λέγει κύριος) but also from the fact that the final phrase
of v. 10 creates an inclusio with the final phrase of v. 8: μεθ' ἡμῶν ὁ
θεός…ὅτι μεθ' ἡμῶν κύριος ὁ θεός.[177] He follows Seeligmann's judgment that the translator's insertion of τότε binds v. 16 to 15 and cogently
argues that καὶ ἐρεῖ "mark[s] the beginning of a new section."[178] He

---

[172] Idem, "Isaiah in the Septuagint," 524. Fischer proposed that the translator
(mis)read his *Vorlage* as לסררים (*In welcher Schrift*, 22–23), on which see below.

[173] Van der Kooij, "Isaiah in the Septuagint," 524 n. 38.

[174] Ibid., 527.

[175] Similarly, while he suggests that "the phrase τοῦ μὴ μαθεῖν seems to be based on
Hebrew למד + בל," he does not say whether he thinks the *Vorlage* contained these two
words or if the translator merely construed בלמדי this way, although the latter is likely
what he intends, since he cites Koenig's discussion (*L' Herméneutique*, 133) in support of
this surmise (van der Kooij, "Isaiah in the Septuagint," 527).

[176] Van der Kooij, "Isaiah in the Septuagint," 522.

[177] This use of these phrases to bound a unit is different than in the MT, where עמנו
אל in v. 8 constitutes an interjection, while כי עמנו אל in v. 10 explains the inevitability
of the nations' failure announced in vv. 9–10. Instrumental in this difference is the fact
that the LXX reads דעו (γνῶτε) rather than רעו, so that μεθ' ἡμῶν ὁ θεός is what they are
to take into consideration in hearing that their best schemes will come to naught.

[178] Van der Kooij, "Isaiah in the Septuagint," 523. Wagner argues that vv. 17–22
must be included in the unit, since it constitutes "the prophet's response to the oracle"
(J. Ross Wagner, "Identifying 'Updated' Prophecies in OG Isaiah: Isaiah 8:11–16 as a
Test Case," *JBL* 126 [2007] 259). While I agree with him that the translator inserted
καὶ ἐρεῖ (see below), it seems unlikely that he meant it to mark the prophet's response,
since in the light of vv. 1 (καὶ εἶπεν κύριος πρός με), 3 (καὶ εἶπεν κύριός μοι), and 5
(καὶ προσέθετο κύριος λαλῆσαί μοι ἔτι) we might reasonably expect that the translator
would have 1) placed the prophet's words in the first person (ἐρῶ), since the following
speech adopts the first person, 2) used the past tense (εἶπον) in response to the report
of what the Kyrios said (οὕτως λέγει κύριος) (even if this goes back to a *Vorlage* that
read ואמר, either ἐρῶ or εἶπον would have been possible). Accordingly, his choice of
καὶ ἐρεῖ actually imposes a disjunction between vv. 17–22 and 11–16.

also highlights διὰ τοῦτο (v. 15) as a significant marker in the logical progression of the unit.[179] Thus he securely establishes 8:11–16 as a literary unit. The problems with his reading arise from how he construes the components of that unit.

Wagner accurately observes that the key to van der Kooij's reading is his interpretation of the group's rejection of τῇ πορείᾳ τῆς ὁδοῦ τοῦ λαοῦ τούτου in v. 11 in light of v. 16.[180] For van der Kooij, because οἱ σφραγιζόμενοι τὸν νόμον τοῦ μὴ μαθεῖν "are the same as the men of power who 'disobey the course of the way of this people' (v. 11), it becomes clear that 'the course of the way of this people' is related to 'the law.'"[181] This association is linked to his inference that the antecedent of (ἐν) αὐτοῖς in v. 15 is the subject of ἀπειθοῦσι in v. 11,[182] which, in turn, rests on his deduction that διὰ τοῦτο (v. 15) introduces the punishment imposed on the speakers of vv. 11–14.[183] He finds confirmation of this in the unique rendering of כשלו by ἀδυνατήσουσιν,[184] which substantiates the perception that the group's opposition τῇ ἰσχυρᾷ χειρί "points to a position of power and might of those who 'disobey.'"[185]

Four observations are pertinent. First, as Wagner observes, van der Kooij's assumption that v. 15 begins a divine speech is arbitrary, since it could just as easily commence with ὁ δὲ οἶκος Ιακωβ in 14b, in contrast to the speakers of vv. 11–14a.[186] In that case, ἀδυνατήσουσιν ἐν αὐτοῖς πολλοί in v. 15 finds its referent in ἐγκαθήμενοι ἐν Ιερουσαλημ, providing a more proximate (and less strained) antecedent for (ἐν) αὐτοῖς than reaching back to v. 11. In this construal, the announcement of the Kyrios in 14b–16 *concurs* with the statements by the speakers in vv. 11–14a by acknowledging that "the way of this people" has led them

---

[179] Van der Kooij, "Isaiah in the Septuagint," 523.

[180] Wagner, "Identifying 'Updated' Prophecies," 257. Lust made the same observation about Seeligmann's reading (Lust, "The Demonic Character," 9–10).

[181] Van der Kooij, "Isaiah in the Septuagint," 527.

[182] Ibid., 526.

[183] Ibid., 523.

[184] Ibid., 526.

[185] Ibid., 523.

[186] Wagner, "Identifying 'Updated' Prophecies," 260. One could, of course, argue that the Kyrios need not respond at all—that vv. 11–16 are entirely a report of the words of others—but this seems unlikely for an oracle (even one translated), since sensitivity to the pattern of judgment speeches, shown by διὰ τοῦτο, suggests the translator found a divine response here.

into a snare and a trap, for they have not feared, treated as holy, and trusted in the Kyrios in the manner urged by the speakers.[187]

Second, van der Kooij's identification of the speakers in vv. 11–14 depends heavily on his perception that ἀπειθοῦσι "clearly implies that 'the course of the way of this people' is meant in a positive sense," since ἀπειθεῖν bears the meaning 'disobey'.[188] However, as Wagner points out, the translator's rendering of מאס ברע by ἀπειθεῖ πονηρίᾳ in 7:16 shows that this verb does not, itself, bear the sinister tones van der Kooij ascribes to it.[189] ἀπειθοῦσι τῇ πορείᾳ means simply "they reject the way."[190] And similarly, while τῇ ἰσχυρᾷ χειρὶ ἀπειθοῦσι suggests strong opposition, this does not validate van der Kooij's conclusion that this has to do with "leaders of the people."[191] On the one hand, there is no reason to conclude that this designates the use of force rather than serves as a metaphor equivalent to "insistently." On the other, since this is a reasonable translation of כחזקת היד, we cannot deduce from it the translator's *exegesis* of the phrase, and ἀδυνατήσουσιν || כשלו in v. 15 cannot be adduced as support, since we cannot take for granted that its subject is the speakers in vv. 11–14, especially in light of the fragile basis for identifying those speakers as opposing right behavior.

Third, van der Kooij's description of the flow of this passage, based on his construal of its components, is confused. Having heard the people's lament of the "hard and severe way of life" (σκληρόν) that strict Torah observance has brought upon them,[192] a life full of fear and dismay (τὸν δὲ φόβον αὐτοῦ οὐ μὴ φοβηθῆτε οὐδὲ μὴ ταραχθῆτε),[193] the speakers advocate a way to fear God that will bring relief: just "appear before God in his Temple . . . sanctif[y] Him by honouring Him there . . . [and] trust in Him."[194] One need not be scrupulous about "the ethical demands of the law," for "the only condition to live in security and safety is to honour God in his temple."[195]

---

[187] Ibid.

[188] Van der Kooij, "Isaiah in the Septuagint," 523.

[189] Wagner, "Identifying 'Updated' Prophecies," 262–63.

[190] I concur with van der Kooij's judgment that πορεία is used metaphorically here ("Septuagint of Isaiah," 130).

[191] Ibid.

[192] One might ask why σκληρόν is used for this purpose, when σκληρά would create a more direct (i.e., gender-matched) referent to τῇ πορείᾳ τῆς ὁδοῦ, although conceivably, σκληρόν could designate "this whole matter" in a general way.

[193] Van der Kooij, "Isaiah in the Septuagint," 524.

[194] Ibid., 526.

[195] Idem, "Septuagint of Isaiah," 133.

This summary poses two problems. First, if the speakers agree with the people's assessment that their way of life (= Torah observance) is "hard," then it makes little sense for them to exhort the people *not* to call it σκληρόν, for that is an appropriate verdict. That is why this group has "disobeyed the behavior of the way of this people." Second, to conclude that the speakers' proposal is to worship at the temple while treating the Torah's ethical demands cavalierly, and to suggest that this program is perceived as a forecast of the struggle within Jerusalem of the early second century, disregards what that struggle was about. While undoubtedly those opposed to Menelaus and his compatriots viewed their behavior as immoral, the issue that spurred Mattathias and his sons to act, according to 1 Maccabees, and what constituted the "abomination that desolates" in Daniel, was precisely the question of what constituted appropriate worship. Exhortation to merely honor the Kyrios at the temple hardly represents the program of the Hellenists in Jerusalem, at least once Antiochus IV lent aid to their cause.

A final observation that raises problems for van der Kooij's account of this passage is the fact that one can explain the translator's rendering of these verses by considering variants in his *Vorlage* and his construal of the immediate literary context.

As for variants in his *Vorlage*:

V. 11's lack of an equivalent for כי may be due to its absence from the *Vorlage* through parablepsis or because it is a secondary insertion in Hebrew, albeit one that had already made its way into all our other textual witnesses.[196] Given 1:23 (ἀπειθοῦσιν || סוררים), Fischer rightly suspected that behind ἀπειθοῦσι || ויסרני lay a form of סרר, although he posited that this variant lay only in the mind of the translator, who read ו (and possibly וי) as ל, נ as ר, and joined the initial *mêm* of מלכת to the end so as to read לסררים לכת.[197] We need not go to such extremes, nor need we posit merely a variant in the translator's mind; his *Vorlage* read either וסרנו, which he derived from סרר (cf. the discussion of קשר, below), or סררו. Either of these helps explain the third person plural form of the verb.

V. 13's ἁγιάσατε || תקדישו likely reflects הקדישו in the LXX's *Vorlage* (cf. S & V).

---

[196] Certainly a translator as creative with conjunctions as this one could have found some way to represent כי (cf. e.g., ἰδοὺ δὴ || כי הנה in 3:1).

[197] Fischer, *In welcher Schrift*, 23.

V. 14's ὁ δὲ οἶκος Ιακωβ || לשׁני בתי ישׂראל should be compared to τὸν οἶκον τοῦ Ισραηλ || בית יעקב in 2:6, which shows the reverse interchange. Moreover, the appearance of מבית יעקב in v. 18 may have influenced a scribe. Quite likely, the LXX's *Vorlage* read ובית יעקב.

V. 16's φανεροὶ ἔσονται || תעודה either presupposes a *Vorlage* that read תעורה or the ambiguity of ד/ר allowed the translator to relate this form to ערה, as discussed in chapter four.

More extensive is the list of differences with the MT that are attributable to the translator:[198]

V. 12's double occurrence of σκληρόν || קשׁר does not likely reflect קשׁה in its *Vorlage*. This is the only occurrence of קשׁר ('conspiracy') in Isaiah, and only one instance of קשׁר in the Torah, Jeremiah, Ezekiel, and the Twelve recognizes this meaning.[199] More frequently קשׁר is translated by equivalents that mean 'tie' or 'bind'.[200] Stumped by קשׁר, the translator resorted to identifying the form with קשׁה, for which he regularly uses σκληρός (14:3; 19:4; 21:2; 27:8; 48:4). Additionally, ταραχθῆτε || תעריצו is, as van der Kooij opines, simply the translator's choice of an equivalent suited to the context.[201] In fact, S & V adopt a similar tack (ܬܕܚܠܘܢ, *paveatis*). It may be that they read תעריצו as תערוצו.

V. 14's initial καὶ ἐὰν ἐπ' αὐτῷ πεποιθὼς ᾖς is the formal equivalent of והוא מערצכם, but the relationship is oblique, at best. Van der Kooij's statement that the LXX's phrase "is typical of LXX Isaiah," while "elsewhere in the LXX it occurs in a few places only," is an observation rather than an explanation.[202] S's translation of this phrase, ܘܗܘܝܘ ܡܥܕܪܢܟ ('and he is your help'), was likely chosen based on the context. The LXX translator may have taken a similar tack, and Wagner has astutely identified his source for this equivalent: καὶ πεποιθὼς ἔσομαι ἐπ' αὐτῷ in v. 17 (|| וקויתי לו).[203] In light of this substitution he inserted σοι to accompany ἔσται.

---

[198] I will pass over his handling of particles. I take for granted that the translator treated such details freely and that, in any case, it is impossible to be certain what he read in such instances.

[199] Amos 7:10 alleges, קשׁר עליך עמוס, and the translator renders this well with συστροφὰς ποιεῖται κατὰ σοῦ Αμως.

[200] This illuminates the translation of the only other occurrence of קשׁר in Isaiah: πάντας αὐτοὺς ἐνδύσῃ καὶ περιθήσῃ αὐτοὺς ὡς κόσμον νύμφης || כלם כעדי תלבשׁ ותקשׁרים ככלה (49:18).

[201] Van der Kooij, "Septuagint of Isaiah," 130.

[202] Idem, "Isaiah in the Septuagint," 525.

[203] Wagner, "Identifying 'Updated' Prophecies," 260.

His καὶ <u>οὐχ</u> ὡς λίθου || ולאבן parallels his derivation of τοῦ <u>μὴ</u> μαθεῖν from בלמדי in v. 16. The creation of a comparison saved him from directly asserting that the Kyrios would be a "stone," consistent with his aversion to translating צור as an epithet for the Kyrios (N.B. ὡς πέτρας || לצור) as epitomized in his rendering of וצור מעזך לא זכרת by καὶ κυρίου τοῦ βοηθοῦ σου οὐκ ἐμνήσθης in 17:10 and of צור יהוה עולמים by ὁ θεὸς ὁ μέγας ὁ αἰώνιος in 26:4.[204] This modification, however, barred following the syntax of ἔσται σοι εἰς ἁγίασμα and made it necessary for him to supply a predicate: συναντήσεσθε αὐτῷ.

V. 15's initial plus, διὰ τοῦτο, is unremarkable for a translator who supplies conjunctions with ease. His translation of כשלו by ἀδυνατήσουσιν is explicable by comparison with 3:8, where he reserves a form of πίπτειν for נפל and so lights on another equivalent for the preceding כשלה: ὅτι ἀνεῖται Ιερουσαλημ καὶ ἡ Ιουδαία συμπέπτωκεν || כי כשלה ירושלם ויהודה נפל ||.[205] As for καὶ ἐγγιοῦσιν || ונוקשו, his familiarity with √יקש is made suspect not only by his apparent guess for ולמוקש in v. 14 (καὶ ἐν κοιλάσματι, 'and in a hollow', a hapax in the LXX), but also by his rendering of ונוקשו by καὶ κινδυνεύσουσιν ('and they will be in danger') in 28:13. If he resorted to καὶ ἐγγιοῦσιν due to the aural similarity to נגש, as van der Kooij suggests,[206] it was because his lack of familiarity with √יקש put him in straits.

The formal equivalent for צור is ἄνθρωποι ἐν ἀσφαλείᾳ ὄντες, which Ottley explains from the use of צור as a metaphor for a place of safety.[207] The suggestion that the translator rendered צור metaphorically is made plausible by his translation of בצלה with μετὰ ἀσφαλείας in 34:15, although that occurs in a largely periphrastic rendering: καὶ ἔσωσεν ἡ γῆ τὰ παιδία αὐτῆς μετὰ ἀσφαλείας ἐκεῖ || ותמלט ובקעה ודגרה בצלה אך שם. At the least, we can say that the translator sought to find in צור a meaning befitting the context. The fact that ἄνθρωποι ἐν ἀσφαλείᾳ ὄντες follows Greek word order rather than Hebrew suggests that this is his own formulation.

As noted earlier, whether תעורה stood in the Vorlage or is due to ד/ר ambiguity, φανεροὶ ἔσονται derives from his deriving the form from √ערה.

---

[204] Cf. Lust, "The Demonic Character," 9–10.
[205] Cf. his translation of ובחורים כשול יכשלו by καὶ ἐκλεκτοὶ ἀνίσχυες ἔσονται in 40:30.
[206] Van der Kooij, "Isaiah in the Septuagint," 527.
[207] Ottley, The Book of Isaiah, 2:149.

Needless to say, this detailed alignment of equivalents and accounting for their origins is a textbook example of "an atomistic, or an
ad hoc treatment of (single) words or verses" that van der Kooij pro-
tests.[208] However, not only has his interpretation under a "contextual"
approach failed to explain how the translator arrived at his rendering,
but if attending to the details in order to recover the translator's *Übersetzsungsweise* in this passage produces the better explanation, then it is
to be preferred.

Summary

The analyses of chapters six and seven subvert the claim that the
translator interpreted the book of Isaiah as presaging events in his day,
under the belief that his era was witnessing the fulfillment of Isaiah's
oracles. The evidence from his use of ἔσχατος denies that he was an
enthusiast of eschatology, while his translation of toponyms shows no
dominating concern to detect the geopolitical realia of his own day
in Isaiah's oracles. Although his translation reflects fiscal policies of
Hellenistic rulers, it reveals no explicit alignment of Isaiah's tyrants
with Antiochus IV. Similarly, although his translation reflects pervasive
concern for the Torah, the argument that he read Isa 8:11–16 as
condemnation of an antilegalist group in his day is based on little
more than serendipitous associations in modern readers' minds. There
is, therefore, no foundation to liken the translator to the authors of
the *pesharim*. We are, in fact, on firmer ground exploring the sorts of
philological and exegetical solutions described in chapters four and five
and illustrated in the alternative explanations offered in this chapter.
It remains to see how such explanations illuminate the translator's
Übersetzsungsweise in a large span of text. Chapter eight offers as a test
case an examination of Isaiah 28.

---

[208] Van der Kooij, "Isaiah in the Septuagint," 519–20.

TRANSLATION AND INTERPRETATION IN LXX-ISAIAH

To this point I have focused on isolated verses or short units to establish elements of the translator's *Übersetzungsweise* and to reveal the weakness in pillars of one common conception of it. However, because I wish to provide an alternative view of the translator's work, I want to explore the translator's *Übersetzungsweise* in a lengthy unit, Isaiah 28. Although there is not space to address each and every feature of the chapter, this reading will suffice to demonstrate how the translator went about forming it into a literary unit.

On first glance, this chapter might seem a loose collection of ad hoc renderings. However, a closer reading provides *prima facie* evidence that the translator produced a coherent unit. Evidence of that appears already in the first verse:[1]

הוי עטרת גאות	[1]οὐαὶ τῷ στεφάνῳ τῆς ὕβρεως
שכרי אפרים	οἱ μισθωτοὶ Εφραιμ
וציץ נבל צבי תפארתו	τὸ ἄνθος τὸ ἐκπεσὸν ἐκ τῆς δόξης
אשר על ראש גיא שמנים	ἐπὶ τῆς κορυφῆς τοῦ ὄρους τοῦ παχέος
הלומי יין	οἱ μεθύοντες ἄνευ οἴνου

The most striking equivalence is οἱ μεθύοντες ἄνευ οἴνου ('those drunk without wine') for הלומי יין ('struck with wine'),[2] an equivalence the translator produced, according to Seeligmann, under the impress of 51:21:[3]

לכן שמעי נא זאת עניה	διὰ τοῦτο ἄκουε τεταπεινωμένη
ושכרת ולא מיין	καὶ μεθύουσα οὐκ ἀπὸ οἴνου

---

[1] Because citing all witnesses to every verse of chapter 28 would lengthen this chapter unreasonably, differences between the MT, the DSS, and the versions will be noted only when deemed pertinent.

[2] 1QIsaᵃ = MT. S's ܣܓܝܐܝܢ ܒܚܡܪܐ, 'who are dazed by wine', and V's *errantes a vino*, 'wandering from wine', are likely guesses, while T's כתישי חמר, 'beaten by wine', is more precise.

[3] Seeligmann, *Septuagint Version*, 71. This conception finds a parallel even closer at hand, in 29:9:

התמהמהו ותמהו השתעשעו ושעו	ἐκλύθητε καὶ ἔκστητε
שכרו ולא יין נעו ולא שכר	καὶ κραιπαλήσατε οὐκ ἀπὸ σικερα οὐδὲ ἀπὸ οἴνου

Even in this case, the point remains that the final clause of 28:1 is rendered in the light of other passages that use drunkenness metaphorically.

Spurring him to perceive a link between 51:21 and 28:1 (besides the similar phrases about being "drunk without wine") might have been the forms שׁכרי in 28:1 and ושׁכרת in 51:21. While the translator interpreted the sibilant of שׁכרי as a *śîn* in 28:1 (οἱ μισθωτοί)[4] but the sibilant of ושׁכרת as a *śîn* in 51:21 (καὶ μεθύουσα),[5] the formal similarity may have attracted the comparison. And even though he chose to render שׁכרי as שׁכרי in 28:1, his rendering of הלומי יין by οἱ μεθύοντες ἄνευ οἴνου makes οἱ μισθωτοὶ Εφραιμ the topic of the text, which affects interpretation of שׁכר in v. 7:

וגם אלה ביין שׁנו	[7]οὗτοι γὰρ οἴνῳ πεπλανημένοι εἰσίν
ובשׁכר תעו כהן ונביא	ἐπλανήθησαν διὰ τὸ σικερα ἱερεὺς καὶ προφήτης
שׁנו בשׁכר נבלעו	ἐξέστησαν διὰ τὸν οἶνον ἐσείσθησαν
מן היין תעו מן השׁכר שׁנו	ἀπὸ τῆς μέθης τοῦ σικερα ἐπλανήθησαν
בראה פקו פליליה	τοῦτ' ἔστι φάσμα

Representation of *wāw* by γάρ is common in LXX-Isaiah (e.g., 2:7; 5:12; 7:25; 10:1, 3, 24; 15:7; 16:2; 24:20; 25:7), while the translation of וגם with a single equivalent (καί) is the norm (5:2; 7:20; 21:12; 30:5; 31:2; 45:16; 66:21). Although the translation of both שׁנה and תעה by πλανᾶν is attested elsewhere in the LXX, ἐξιστάναι || שׁנה and σείειν || בלע are unparalleled.[6] Most likely the translator chose these equivalents based on the context.[7]

The most significant difference arises in the final clause, whose relationship to the MT is more oblique than the remainder of the verse. φάσμα occurs elsewhere only in Num 16:30 and Job 20:8. In the latter passage, ὥσπερ φάσμα νυκτερινόν is a sensible equivalent for כחזיון לילה. However, Num 16:30 presents a unique case. In the contest over whether Moses' authority is genuine, Moses announces that if the deaths of the

---

[4] Cf. v. 3: οἱ μισθωτοὶ τοῦ Εφραιμ || שׁכורי אפרים. As might be expected, μισθωτός aligns with equivalents for √שׁכר throughout the LXX.

[5] Cf. his rendering of כשׁכור by ὡς ὁ μεθύων in 24:20, while in 19:10 he translates כל עשׂי שׁכר with οἱ τὸν ζῦθον ποιοῦντες.

[6] καταπίνειν is the standard equivalent for בלע throughout the LXX and is used in v. 4: αὐτὸ καταπιεῖν || יבלענה.

[7] Within the LXX, σείειν most frequently translates רעש (21 out of 35 occurrences of σείειν) as it does in Isa 13:13; 14:16; 24:18. However, in 10:14 καὶ σείσω πόλεις κατοικουμένας parallels the MT's כאביר יושׁבים, in 17:4 ואוריד ואוריד, in 17:4 καὶ τὰ πίονα τῆς δόξης αὐτοῦ σεισθήσεται translates ומשׁמן בשׂרו ירזה (the translator probably chose σεισθήσεται as a contextually fitting equivalent due to his unfamiliarity with רזה, 'to dwindle'), and in 33:20 σκηναὶ αἵ οὐ μὴ σεισθῶσιν renders אהל בל יצען (σεισθῶσιν was likely chosen for the *hapax legomenon* by dint of the juxtaposed οὐδὲ μὴ κινηθῶσιν οἱ πάσσαλοι τῆς σκηνῆς αὐτῆς || בל יסע יתדתיו). Thus, the translator of Isaiah apparently sometimes used σείειν as a slot-word.

rebels (Korah, Dathan and Abiram) are not unusual, then the LORD has not sent him (v. 29). He then asserts that the LORD's creation of such a novel phenomenon (בריאה יברא יהוה) to slay the rebels certifies his own authority. The LXX casts this certification as embodied in a φάσμα:

ואם בריאה יברא יהוה	ἀλλ᾽ ἢ ἐν φάσματι δείξει κύριος
ופצתה האדמה את פיה	καὶ ἀνοίξασα ἡ γῆ τὸ στόμα αὐτῆς
ובלעה אתם	καταπίεται αὐτούς

The translation of בריאה with ἐν φάσματι there elucidates the translator's rendering of ברא with φάσμα in Isa 28:7.

On the other hand, τοῦτ᾽ ἔστι finds no support in any textual witness and is most likely the translator's paraphrase, based on his conviction that the theme of drunkenness is to be considered a metaphor, as indicated by his translation of הלומי יין with οἱ μεθύοντες ἄνευ οἴνου in v. 1. This image becomes a key element in his portrayal of rulers in this chapter, especially over against a group not drawn into the leaders' delusions.[8]

In fact, integral to the portrayal of rulers is a contrast between the delusional hopes they offer and the trustworthy hope the Kyrios affords.[9] Throughout the chapter ἐλπίς appears in striking associations that indicate a unified train of thought,[10] beginning in v. 4:

ציצת נבל צבי תפארתו	τὸ ἄνθος τὸ ἐκπεσὸν τῆς ἐλπίδος τῆς δόξης

The rendering of צבי by τῆς ἐλπίδος in v. 4 is echoed in v. 5, where ὁ στέφανος τῆς ἐλπίδος corresponds to לעטרת צבי.[11] For das Neves, ἐλπίς

---

[8] As das Neves detected, the contrast between the delusional rulers and the pious of the people is one of several antitheses unifying the chapter (A Teologia, 74; cf. 143–44). This contrast concerns "an impious class (rulers and counselors of the people) versus a faithful class (the 'remnant') (v. 8, 14, καὶ ἄρχοντες τοῦ λαοῦ τούτου; vv. 16, 29 concern an impious class, and vv. 5, 6, 14, ἄνδρες τεθλιμμένοι concerns a faithful class)" (ibid., 74, translation mine). Other antitheses he identifies include: human glory (vv. 1, 3, 4) vs. divine glory (v. 5); a human crown (vv. 1, 3) vs. a divine crown (v. 5); a divine curse versus human counsel (v. 8) (ibid.).

[9] Das Neves also identifies the theme of "hope" as central to the chapter, but without showing its connection to the delusion of the rulers, describing it only as a contrast of "divine aid versus human hope (v. 4: τῆς ἐλπίδος τῆς δόξης is a rereading of the original H[ebrew]; v. 10, 15, 17, 19 are equally a rereading of the original H[ebrew]" (ibid., translation mine).

[10] Ibid., 292.

[11] The translation of צבי by ἐλπίς occurs just once more in the LXX, in Isa 24:16 (ἐλπὶς τῷ εὐσεβεῖ || צבי לצדיק). Moreover, צבי is translated with other equivalents in LXX-Isa: βουλῇ in 4:2, δορκάδιον in 13:14 (cf. Deut 12:15, 22; 14:5; 15:22), and ἔνδοξος in 13:19 and 23:9.

"continent l'idée *d'actualisation*,"[12] insofar as it is used for "the proud self-sufficiency or false hope which the counselors, false prophets and rulers of the people place in themselves."[13] Consequently, in das Neves's view, ἐλπίς is part of the translator's vocabulary to describe the rulers of his day as impious tyrants.

Although das Neves is correct to spotlight such lexical relationships as evidence that the translator conceived of this chapter as a literary unit, he treats the terms and phrases artificially by arranging them within polarities rather than exploring them first within their own syntactic, semantic, and literary settings. By contrast, I propose to uncover the translator's synthetic understanding of the chapter by exploring how he achieved his rendering. Before doing so, however, it is important to comprehend the literary structure of this passage in the LXX without reference to its *Vorlage*.[14]

Chapter 28 as a Literary Unit

The chapter opens with a woe pronounced against "the crown of insolence," defined as a metaphor for "the hirelings of Ephraim," further described as "the blossom which has fallen from its splendor" and then as "those drunk without wine." The fate of this group is developed in vv. 2–4. V. 2 anticipates the "strong and harsh" wrath of the Kyrios, initially likened to violent, inescapable hail and then to a deluge that sweeps away the countryside. Such violent wrath has the salutary effect of giving rest to the earth. V. 3 speaks again of "the crown of insolence, the hirelings of Ephraim," against whom, by implication, the wrath described in v. 2 is brought to bear, so that they are trampled by "the hands and feet," which evidently belong to the one whose wrath descends so violently.[15] V. 4 resumes the other metaphor applied by v. 1 to "the hirelings of Ephraim," that of the "failed blossom," but elaborates its failure not simply as a loss of glory, but as the loss of the

---

[12] Das Neves, *A Teologia*, 292.

[13] Ibid., 73, translation mine.

[14] This differs from van der Kooij's comparison of the LXX to the MT as the first step of his method, insofar as I am not concerned with comparing the LXX to any possible Hebrew source.

[15] The definite articles have the force of possessive pronouns, whose antecedent is κυρίου in v. 2. While ταῖς χερσίν corresponds to ביד at the end of v. 2 in the MT, it stands parallel to τοῖς ποσίν and should be taken with v. 3.

hope of splendor. This blossom is described as attractive, since the one who spies it will desire it, just as one might the precursor of figs.[16]

The onset of a distinct section is marked in v. 5 both by the formula τῇ ἡμέρᾳ ἐκείνῃ and a switch in subjects to κύριος σαβαωθ. Here the Kyrios serves as the antithesis to the castigated rulers, under an image of him as "a crown of the hope of splendor" for "my people who are left." Given that "crown" imagery is a natural metonymy for rulers, the earlier application of it to "Ephraim's hirelings" suggests that they represent the people's rulers, even as v. 14 explicitly addresses the ἄρχοντες τοῦ λαοῦ τούτου ἐν Ιερουσαλημ, castigating them for their self-confidence in the face of disaster. Accordingly, whereas "Ephraim's hirelings" have constituted insolent overlords who have fallen short of the hope of splendor and are now vulnerable to divine wrath, the Kyrios offers his remaining people the hope of splendor.

V. 6 transitions from speaking of the benefit the Kyrios will prove to his people to a statement about the fate of the people themselves, using a lexical bond between καταλειφθήσονται (v. 6) and καταλειφθέντι (v. 5). In an attempt to define in what sense they are "my remaining people," they are said to be "left for harsh judgment,"[17] although their destruction is prohibited. They (οὗτοι) have been led astray "by wine," with priest and prophet wandering due to strong drink (v. 7). By verse's end the translator makes clear that talk of the people's inebriation is metaphorical: τοῦτ᾽ ἔστι φάσμα. The tenor of the metaphor is left unspecified, and v. 8 moves on to an assertion that "a curse will eat this counsel." That counsel is said to be due to greed (ἕνεκεν πλεονεξίας), but there is no further identification of which counsel is in view. The most likely referent of αὕτη ἡ βουλή is whatever lies behind the figure of wine and strong drink that leads the people astray in v. 7.

In vv. 6–8, then, the translator finds a description of the people of the Kyrios left vulnerable to judgment by virtue of having been subjected to a seduction rooted in greed. However, the Kyrios will spare the people full destruction and will obliterate the source of seduction that has set them in a stupor.

---

[16] πρὶν ἢ εἰς τὴν χεῖρα αὐτοῦ λαβεῖν is ambivalent, since it could imply either that further examination would dispirit that impulse, or that the desire to eat it is so strong as to override the precaution of inspecting it first.

[17] Taking ἐπὶ κρίσιν καὶ ἰσχὺν as hendiadys: 'for harsh judgment'. The subject of κωλύων is unclear, since this masculine singular form agrees with no noun in this sentence. Most likely the Kyrios is its subject, since he is implicitly the one who 'leaves' his people for judgment.

V. 9 introduces a set of speakers who reflect on their mission and role, first asking to whom they have announced calamities (κακά) and then identifying themselves as those who have been weaned from milk and the breast. V. 10 details the calamities they announce (N.B. the second person singular imperative προσδέχου, corresponding to τίνι in v. 9), although the list is highly cryptic: "affliction upon affliction; hope upon hope; yet a little, yet a little."

While it is initially appealing to regard διὰ φαυλισμὸν χειλέων at the head of v. 11 as modifying ἔτι μικρὸν ἔτι μικρόν at the end of v. 10 (i.e., "yet a little, yet a little, due to the detestability of lips through another tongue"), two considerations suggest that this phrase modifies προσδέχου (i.e., "accept affliction after affliction...on account of the detestability of lips through another tongue"). On the one hand, in v. 13 ἔτι μικρὸν ἔτι μικρόν is the final component of the tripartite oracle whose purpose is stated immediately afterwards: ἵνα πορευθῶσιν κτλ. The lack of any qualification for ἔτι μικρὸν ἔτι μικρόν there suggests that διὰ φαυλισμὸν χειλέων does not qualify that phrase in v. 10. At the same time, it seems that ὅτι λαλήσουσιν τῷ λαῷ τούτῳ means to define the contemptuous speech "through another tongue," so that διὰ φαυλισμὸν χειλέων seems closely associated with the phrases of v. 11. Moreover, the use of the aorist in the phrase καὶ οὐκ ἠθέλησαν ἀκούειν in v. 12 is not the people's response to the immediately preceding words, since they have yet to be spoken (λαλήσουσιν). Rather, καὶ οὐκ ἠθέλησαν ἀκούειν is in the same time frame as τίνι ἀνηγγείλαμεν κακὰ καὶ τίνι ἀνηγγείλαμεν ἀγγελίαν in v. 9 and is, in fact, its apodosis: "to whom have we announced calamities and to whom have we announced a message...and they were not willing to hear?" Vv. 10–12c is the content of the message this group has announced: "accept affliction upon affliction, hope upon hope, and little upon a little, due to the baseness of lips through another tongue, namely that they will speak to this people, saying to it, 'This is the rest for the hungry and this is the shattering.'" Following on this, v. 13 insists that the oracle of the Kyrios they refuse to hear will apply to them, leading them to falter, to fall prey to danger, to be shattered and captured.

Whereas in vv. 9–13 a group contemplates the rejection of their message but insists that their words will, nevertheless, afflict even those who have refused to hear them, vv. 14–15 address a group designated "afflicted men" and "rulers of this people," chastising them for supposing that they can negotiate their own contract with death so as to avoid its onslaught on the day of peril. Such confidence is mocked as hoping in a lie and looking to it for shelter.

Vv. 16–17b introduce a change of speakers, with the Kyrios rebuking the rulers' confidence in their own devices. His first response is a pledge to place "in the foundations of Zion an expensive, chosen stone, a valuable cornerstone" that will vindicate the one who has faith in it. While the meaning of this imagery for the translator is oblique, it is clear that confidence in this "stone" placed in Jerusalem's foundations will accomplish what the rulers' confidence in their "covenants" with Hades and death cannot. Indeed, the Kyrios promises to transform judgment into hope, while his mercy will become "stones."[18]

The contrast between the effectiveness of confidence in these two objects of hope becomes more explicit in vv. 17c–22, in which a voice directly addresses the rulers.[19] Whether this voice is that of the Kyrios himself is less clear, since the first person singular pronouns of vv. 16–17b disappear, and in v. 22 the speaker refers to things ἤκουσα παρὰ κυρίου σαβαωθ. (Of course, unmarked shifts between the deity's voice and that of the prophet are common in the prophetic books.) Unifying this set of verses is its continuous address of those whose object of confidence will fail them, coupled with a demand that they recognize that their fate in the coming troubles will be different than they expect. That demand is sealed with a validation of the forecast as constituting decrees the speaker has heard of what the Kyrios will do "upon the earth."

While v. 23's fresh, passionate call to attend to the speakers' words might conceivably be addressed to the rulers of vv. 17c–22, the likelihood that they address different hearers is confirmed by the return of the voice of the Kyrios in v. 28, promising the addresses that he will not be angry with them forever and, even more strikingly, that the sound of his πικρία will not trample them. This is noticeably different than the warnings issued in vv. 17c–22.

Central to the assurance given this group in vv. 23–28 is an analogy with a farmer who does not ceaselessly plow the earth, but even prior to plowing prepares seed for planting, with an eye to the growth of crops. The meaning of this analogy is unveiled in an address that uses the second person singular, beginning with the final phrase of v. 25 and concluding with v. 26.[20] It proffers assurance that the Kyrios's wrath

---

[18] On the meaning of this term, see below, p. 276.

[19] Καὶ οἱ πεποιθότες μάτην ψεύδει becomes a sentence fragment unless we construe οἱ πεποιθότες as vocative and ὅτι as recitative: 'And you who trust vainly in falsehood, [know] that the tempest will not pass you by'.

[20] The second person singular possessive pronoun suggests that ἐν τοῖς ὁρίοις σου (|| נבלתו) should be construed with καὶ παιδευθήσῃ κρίματι θεοῦ σου rather than the preceding report of the farmer sowing grain.

will be (similarly) disciplinary and lead to joy. Not since the demand to "receive (προσδέχου) affliction upon affliction, hope upon hope" (v. 10) has anyone been addressed via a second person *singular* pronoun. If we look in the passage for a candidate for such an address, the only one credible is ὁ λαός (vv. 5, 11, 14).[21] And just as ὁ στέφανος serves as a unifying figure for the group identified as οἱ μισθωτοὶ Εφραιμ, so here those called ὁ λαός can also be addressed via second person plural pronouns: ἐνωτίζεσθε καὶ ἀκούετε... προσέχετε καὶ ἀκούετε (v. 23), ὑμῖν...ὑμᾶς (v. 28). Parallel to the solemn certification of the calamities to come as divinely planned (vv. 17c–22), this section concludes with a guarantee of the promises delivered through the agrarian analogy in a statement that "these things have come forth from the Kyrios Sabaoth."

The chapter concludes with the exhortation, "plan wonders, exalt vain encouragement," a statement whose relationship to themes earlier in the chapter is clear, even if its role in the passage is oblique.

Chapter 28 and Übersetzungsweise

Within the literary structure of the passage one can see elements of the antitheses das Neves adumbrates. Above all, there is a prominent contrast between two types of hope: one which proves trustworthy and another that does not. Also evident is a contrast between a type of δόξα that has failed for "the hirelings of Ephraim" and one that is embodied in the Kyrios under the image of a competing "crown" available to "the people who remain." The antithesis between a divine curse and human counsel appears in v. 8, but only there, so that it does not belong to the larger contrasts that unify the passage. And while there is certainly a contrast between rulers who trust in what will prove illusory and people who place their trust in the resources the Kyrios provides, it is not clear that this contrast can be characterized as "a classe impio... contra a classe fiel," especially if that "classe fiel" is said to be coterminous with τῷ καταλειφθέντι μου λαῷ (v. 5), understood as some type of faithful "remnant."[22] As alleged earlier, the major flaw in das Neves's reading is

---

[21] Such a reassuring interpretation would not be addressed to the 'hirelings of Ephraim', under the guise of ὁ στέφανος ὕβρεως or τὸ ἄνθος τὸ ἐκπεσὸν ἐκ τῆς δόξης, since they have been rejected for placing their hope in falsehood and have been warned of the impending failure of their expectations.

[22] Das Neves, *A Teologia*, 74.

his identification of these antitheses outside a careful reading of their roles in their literary contexts.

A prime example of this is das Neves's assessment of the emphasis on "hope" in these verses. He categorizes the types of hope as "a esperança humana," on the one hand, and "a esperança divina," on the other.[23] For das Neves, "a esperança humana" proves false because it is rooted in human δόξα, which he considers equivalent to pride, so that "human hope is pride and human self-sufficiency in contemporary political affairs (na própria política)."[24] The only entity that can be called "a esperança divina" is divine aid ("o auxílio divino"), the prime term das Neves opposes to "a esperança humana."[25]

Das Neves rightly detects a contrast between two types of hope. Hope based in the rulers' claim to have made "a covenant with Hades and agreements with death" (v. 15) is disparaged.[26] This imagery is rendered more tangible in the words that follow, even though they employ another metaphor, καταιγὶς φερομένη, connoting a traumatic attack.[27] In a sentence patently based on a text like the MT, the substance of their "accord with death" is said to be that such an attack would leave them unscathed. Such confidence is said to be lodged in "falsehood," and the LXX places an ironic recognition of that in the mouths of exponents of this confidence:

כי שׂמנו כזב מחסנו   15)ἐθήκαμεν ψεῦδος τὴν ἐλπίδα ἡμῶν
ובשׁקר נסתרנו   καὶ τῷ ψεύδει σκεπασθησόμεθα

The translation of מחסנו by τὴν ἐλπίδα ἡμῶν echoes the translation of מחסהו with ἐλπὶς αὐτοῦ in Ps 13(14):6, of מחסה with ἐλπίς in Ps

---

[23] Ibid., 74 n. 60.

[24] Ibid., translation mine. Das Neves expresses dismay that Gerhard Kittel's study of δόξα (TWNT II, 245–48) fails to note "the range of meanings of human δόξα with a depreciative sense (pride)" (ibid., translation mine; cf. ibid., 70 n. 48).

[25] Ibid., 74 and 143.

[26] The LXX is largely transparent to the MT. Curiously, μετὰ τοῦ ᾅδου καὶ μετὰ τοῦ θανάτου appears to reflect a *Vorlage* in which מות and שׁאול were transposed (cf. v. 18, where ὑμῶν τὴν διαθήκην τοῦ θανάτου is the equivalent for the MT's בריתכם את מות). More troubling is συνθήκας corresponding to the MT's עשׂינו חזה. On the one hand, the lack of an equivalent for עשׂינו is explicable given the generic equivalence ἐποιήσαμεν || כרתנו, which verb could again be assumed with συνθήκας. The only other occurrence of συνθήκη in LXX-Isaiah is enlightening: ἐποιήσατε βουλὴν οὐ δἰ ἐμοῦ καὶ συνθήκας οὐ διὰ τοῦ πνεύματός μου || לעשׂות עצה ולא מני ולנסך מסכה ולא רוחי (30:1). Just as here, the translator omitted an equivalent for the second verb (לנסך), allowing a form of ποιεῖν to govern both objects, and his choice of an equivalent for מסכה was guided by the parallel with the preceding noun, βουλήν. In both 30:1 and 28:15, then, he chose συνθήκη as an equivalent based on a parallel noun.

[27] Καταιγὶς φερομένη translates the parallel phrase שׁוט שׁוטף in v. 18.

60(61):4, and of מחסי by ἡ ἐλπίς μου in Ps 62(61):8; 72(73):28; 90(91):9; 93(94):22; 141(142):6, although this equivalence occurs nowhere else in lxx-Isaiah (see καὶ ἐν σκέπῃ || ולמחסה, 4:6; σκέπη || מחסה, 25:4).[28] On the other hand, the translator renders מחסה with οἱ πεποιθότες in v. 17,[29] where such people trust in "falsehood" (ψεύδει), in contrast to the one who (according to v. 16) "trusts in the stone" (ὁ πιστεύων ἐπ' αὐτῷ) the Kyrios has placed in Jerusalem's foundation, so that they are spared shame (οὐ μὴ καταισχυνθῇ || לא יחיש). The antithesis between the objects of trust is part of the contrast of *types* of hope in this chapter.

The unreliability of this hope in a "pact with death" is made clear in vv. 17d–18, where those espousing such confidence are told that this pact will be removed and that their "hope directed towards Hades will not remain." The path the translator followed from the Hebrew of his *Vorlage* to this statement shows the degree to which a synthetic understanding of the whole passage guided his rendering:

ויעה ברד מחסה כזב	καὶ οἱ πεποιθότες μάτην ψεύδει
וסתר מים ישטפו	ὅτι οὐ μὴ παρέλθῃ ὑμᾶς καταιγίς
וכפר בריתכם את מות	[18]μὴ καὶ ἀφέλῃ ὑμῶν τὴν διαθήκην τοῦ θανάτου
וחזותכם את שאול לא תקום	καὶ ἡ ἐλπὶς ὑμῶν ἡ πρὸς τὸν ἅδην οὐ μὴ ἐμμείνῃ

The clause ὅτι οὐ μὴ παρέλθῃ ὑμᾶς καταιγίς rebuffs the claim, καταιγὶς φερομένη ἐὰν παρέλθῃ οὐ μὴ ἔλθῃ ἐφ' ἡμᾶς in v. 15, but is hard to align semantically with the mt. The most apparent equivalence is καταιγίς || מים,[30] although even this would be singular, since elsewhere in the book καταιγίς renders סופה (5:28; 17:13; 21:1; 29:6; 66:15) or סערה (40:24;

---

[28] Whether the lack of an equivalent for כי attests its absence in the *Vorlage* is uncertain. כי is rendered variously in lxx-Isaiah (δή, 3:1; τοίνυν, 3:10; κατά, 3:11; ἀλλά, 7:8, 23:18, 28:27 [כי²], 29:23, 30:5, 16, and 37:19; καὶ πῶς, 7:13; δέ, 15:5, 9), suggesting the possibility that the translator might also have simply omitted it on occasion (כי lacks an equivalent also in 2:22; 4:5; 7:22; 8:11; 15:5 [כי²]; 15:6 [כי¹]; 16:8; 18:5; 23:4; 26:4; et passim). Notice that an equivalent for כי in the mt is lacking again in vv. 10, 15 (כי³), 19, 20, and 21.

[29] Πείθειν is used as the equivalent for חסה in Deut 32:37; Judg 9:15 (A); 2 Sam 22:3, 31; Ps 2:12; 10(11):1; 56(57):2; 117(118):8; Prov 14:32; Ruth 2:12. These parallels controvert das Neves' judgment that οἱ πεποιθότες || מחסה involves a "rereading of the original H[ebrew]" (*A Teologia*, 74, translation mine).

[30] This alignment seems more likely than Ottley's perception that καταιγίς renders ישטפו "read as a noun, or confused with שיש, ver. 15" (*The Book of Isaiah*, 2:242). The lxx translates √שטף with σῦρον in v. 2 (cf. 30:28) and with φερομένη in vv. 15 and 18. Cf. 8:8, where the translator effectively overrides שטף (see above, p. 226).

41:16), equivalents found elsewhere in the LXX. While the equally distinctive καταιγίς || הבל appears in 57:13 (parallel to ἄνεμος || רוח), chapter 28 contains the greatest number of anomalous equivalences, with καταιγὶς φερομένη || שׁוטך [שׁוט ק'] שׁיט in vv. 15 and 18 and ὅτι οὐ μὴ παρέλθῃ ὑμᾶς καταιγίς || וסתר מים ישׁטפו in v. 17. In the latter instance, the fact that nearly everywhere else מים is translated by ὕδωρ (and never καταιγίς)[31] points to an effort to proffer a cohesive image. At the same time, the translator's choice of καταιγίς in v. 17 may well have been encouraged by ישׁטפו, which figures in καταιγὶς φερομένη || שׁוט שׁוטך in vv. 15 and 18.

Ottley aligns ὅτι οὐ μὴ παρέλθῃ with וסתר, but offers no explanation of how the translator arrived at his rendering.[32] In nine of its ten occurrences in LXX-Isaiah, παρέρχεσθαι translates √עבר.[33] Although the lack of attestation of a variant for סתר in any other textual witness does not preclude a form of עבר in the LXX's *Vorlage*,[34] the repeated use of καταιγίς in these verses suggests that the translator divined a rebuff to the boast of shelter from any καταιγὶς φερομένη that passes by (v. 15),[35] so that οὐ μὴ παρέλθῃ ὑμᾶς (v. 17) is part of that interpretation: the καταιγίς will indeed *not* pass you by.

Before considering why the translator chose μὴ καὶ ἀφέλῃ for וכפר at the start of v. 18, we must consider the syntactic conundrum the Greek text presents: how are we to understand μὴ καί sandwiched between οὐ μὴ παρέλθῃ in v. 17 and οὐ μὴ ἐμμείνῃ later in v. 18?[36] Ottley suggests

---

[31] The only exceptions to this are either when the translator took the construct form מי as an interrogative pronoun in 40:12 (rendering it with τίς) or מים appears in a phrase, as in 41:18, where מים לאגם is rendered εἰς ἕλη ('into marshes') and למוצאי מים is translated ἐν ὑδραγωγοῖς ('in[to] aqueducts').

[32] Ottley, *The Book of Isaiah*, 2:242. He points to an interesting analogy in the translation of ופסחתי by καὶ σκεπάσω (the same verb that translates נסתרנו [σκεπασθησόμεθα] in 28:15) in Exod 12:13, while ופסח is rendered καὶ παρελεύσεται in v. 23 of the same chapter.

[33] The exception is 34:16 (ἀριθμῷ παρῆλθον || מעל ספר), which Ziegler attributes to the influence of another passage: "Der Übers. hat that die nämliche Vorstellung wie Jer 40 (33), 13 im Auge: ἔτι παρελεύσεται πρόβατα ἐπὶ χεῖρα ἀριθμοῦντος. Die Tiere werden gezählt, indem man sie unter der Hand vorbeigehen läßt. Dieses Bild veranlaßte den Js-Übers., seine hebr. Vorlage so zu deuten" (Ziegler, *Untersuchungen*, 122–23).

[34] 1QIsaᵃ reads וסתר (it stands in a lacuna in 1QIsaᵇ), while S reads ܘܣܬܪ, T translates with ועל דאיטמרתון, and V offers *et protectionem*.

[35] Cf. the echo of ἔλθῃ ἡμῖν || יבואנו (v. 15) by ἐπέλθῃ || יעבר in v. 18, as discussed below, p. 263.

[36] As Ottley reports, in place of οὐ μὴ παρέλθῃ, B reads simply μὴ παρέλθῃ, providing a better parallel to μὴ καὶ ἀφέλῃ. Nevertheless, he wisely opts for the pervasively attested οὐ μὴ παρέλθῃ, noting the interpretive problems the alternative reading would

it must be construed to mean, "see lest it take away," either with ὅτι οὐ μὴ παρέλθῃ introducing the content of their trust in falsehood and μὴ καὶ ἀφέλῃ warning against the threat that event will bring ("you who trust vainly in the false belief that the tempest will not pass over you, see that it not take away your covenant with death") or taking μὴ καὶ ἀφέλῃ parenthetical to a statement introduced by ὅτι ("for the tempest will not pass you by—take heed lest it even take away your covenant with death!—and your hope directed towards Hades will not remain").[37] The problem with the first option, as Ottley notes, is that it "involves taking παρέλθῃ as practically equivalent to ἐπέλθῃ,"[38] while the second option's warning seems senseless, since the pact with Hades is precisely what was to ward off the tempest, and taking that parenthetical statement as sarcasm seems not the most elegant solution.

A better solution is to adopt Ottley's perception of μὴ καὶ ἀφέλῃ expressing an unwanted consequence ('lest'), in this case a consequence that is unavoidable, although I would not adopt his inference that this implies an admonition (viz., "take heed lest…").[39] The translator's meaning seems to be, "know that the tempest will not pass by you without [lest it] removing your covenant with death, and your hope directed towards Hades will not endure." The translator's insertion of μή before καὶ ἀφέλῃ is a minor modification of a sort we have seen him employ elsewhere.[40]

But again, to what do we attribute the translator's use of ἀφέλῃ for וכפר? Intriguingly, while the MT vocalizes the form as a Pual, in 1QIsaᵃ וכפר is followed by את, attesting a reading of the verb as transitive (1QIsaᵇ = MT). Even though the other versions render וכפר as passive, they agree with the LXX's construal of the semantics: S, ܡܬܚܒܠ ('will be annulled'); T, ויבטל ('will cease'); V, et delebitur ('will be annulled'). And in fact, these translations accord with evidence that כפר could be used of the dissolution of a covenant, justifying the LXX's choice of ἀφέλῃ.[41]

---

create and observing that "the scribe of B or B's predecessor might have dropped the οὐ, under the influence of the following clause" (Ottley, *The Book of Isaiah*, 2:241).

[37] Ibid.

[38] Ibid.

[39] E.g., 48:5 (πρὶν ἐλθεῖν ἐπὶ σὲ ἀκουστόν σοι ἐποίησα μὴ εἴπῃς ὅτι τὰ εἴδωλά μου ἐποίησαν) and 48:7 (οὐ προτέραις ἡμέραις ἤκουσας αὐτά μὴ εἴπῃς ὅτι ναί γινώσκω αὐτά). Cf. μήποτε ἴδωσιν τοῖς ὀφθαλμοῖς || פן יראה בעיניו in 6:10.

[40] For the translator's penchant of inserting negatives, see above, chapter four. Also relevant, given the motif of "hope," is the LXX's translation of נוי קו קו by ἔθνος ἀνέλπιστον in 18:2 in contrast to ἔθνος ἐλπίζον || נוי קו קו in 18:7.

[41] See KB, s.v. כפר.

The translation of וחזותכם by καὶ ἡ ἐλπὶς ὑμῶν is remarkable,[42] inasmuch as nowhere else in Isaiah—or the rest of the LXX—does ἐλπίς (or any of its synonyms) translate √חזה. Indeed, in Isa 21:2 חזות is translated τὸ ὅραμα. While his *Vorlage* might have read חסות (cf. καὶ τοῖς πεποιθόσιν || והחסות in 30:3),[43] καὶ ἡ ἐλπὶς ὑμῶν likely evinces the same impulse towards providing literary cohesion that led him to render מים ישטפו with καταιγίς in v. 17 (perhaps with the partial similarity to חסות in mind)[44] and, more important, impelled him to use ἐλπίς for צבי in vv. 4 and 5, as well as ἐλπὶς πονηρά for רק זועה in v. 19 (see below, p. 263).

While the path to the translator's rendering of מחסה כזב by οἱ πεποιθότες μάτην ψεύδει[45] in v. 17 is allied with his rendering of כזב מחסנו by ψεῦδος τὴν ἐλπίδα ἡμῶν in v. 15—insofar as the ψεῦδος in which they "believe" in v. 17 is the same ψεῦδος they have made "our hope" (τὴν ἐλπίδα ἡμῶν) in v. 15—his rendering of מחסה by οἱ πεποιθότες seems specially influenced by ὁ πιστεύων || המאמין in v. 16, an inference made indisputable by his use of πείθειν rather than ἐλπίζειν.[46] His choice of the plural form, in spite of the singular number of ὁ πιστεύων, substantiates that οἱ πεποιθότες should be taken as a vocative (to which the successive first person plural pronouns are anaphoric) and the succeeding ὅτι as recitative.[47]

In making this contrast with the assurance given "the one who believes in the stone" the Kyrios places in Jerusalem's foundation, the translator passed over ויעה ברד.[48] While יעה ('sweep away') is a hapax,

---

[42] Cf. T, ושלמכון; V, *et pactum vestrum*; S, ‿ܩܘܠܣܘ.

[43] Cf. Fischer, *In welcher Schrift*, 44.

[44] 1QIsaᵃ attests וחזותכם; it falls within a lacuna in 1QIsaᵇ. If fragment 28 of 4QIsaᶠ has been rightly identified as 28:18 (sub "?" in Ulrich et al., eds., *Qumran Cave 4 X*), then it likely preserves the initial ח, while it may also attest the following ז, although only the bottom half of those letters survive. S accords with the MT, but V renders *et pactum vestrum cum inferno* and T reads (similarly) ושלמכון דעם מחבלא; V and T likely give similar, contextually chosen equivalents rather than attest variants in their *Vorlagen*.

[45] Μάτην ψεύδει seems to be a double rendering of כזב, with μάτην underscoring the theme of the futility of such trust. Cf. the translator's supplement of κεραυνώσει with βιαίως in 30:30, discussed below, p. 260.

[46] Intriguingly, ἐλπίζειν is also a common equivalent for חסה (Ps 5:12; 7:2; 16[17]:7; 17[18]:3, 31; 24[25]:20; 30[31]:2, 20; 33[34]:9, 23; 36[37]:40; 56[57]:2; 63[64]:11; 70[71]:1; 90[91]:4; 117[118]:9; 140[141]:8; 143[144]:2). Although this equivalence does not occur in LXX-Isaiah, the use of both πείθειν and ἐλπίζειν for מחסה reinforces the perception that the contrast of the fate of those exhibiting trust in different objects in 28:16–17 is germane to the topic of "hope."

[47] See above, n. 19.

[48] Attested by 1QIsaᵃ (in a lacuna in 1QIsaᵇ), and S, which translates ויעה with ‿ܘܢܡܚܐ, 'and [hail] will beat'. V renders ויעה ברד מחסה כזב interpretatively: *et subvertet*

it is unlikely that the translator was completely bemused by וייעה ברד, given that he renders ברד with χάλαζα in 30:30. In fact, the image of χάλαζα ('hail') falling on the impious appears first in v. 2, where it receives special heightening:[49]

כזרם ברד שער קטב   ὡς χάλαζα καταφερομένη οὐκ ἔχουσα σκέπην
                                  βίᾳ καταφερομένη
כזרם מים   ὡς ὕδατος πολύ

While קטב is a hapax in Isaiah, the translator has handled שער well previously (καὶ τὰς τρίχας || ושער, 7:20). Although the absence of a diacritical mark left open the possibility of rendering it with πύλη (cf. 14:13; 22:7; 26:2; 29:21),[50] οὐκ ἔχουσα σκέπην is hardly based in such a reading and offers a conundrum that must be considered in conjunction with βίᾳ καταφερομένη.[51]

The translator inserts βίᾳ καταφερομένη in tandem with water imagery in two other passages in LXX-Isaiah, the first of which is 17:13:

לאמים כשאון מים   ὡς ὕδωρ πολὺ ἔθνη πολλά
רבים ישאון   ὡς ὕδατος πολλοῦ βίᾳ καταφερομένου

The combination of καταφέρειν with βίᾳ and its collocation with ὡς, ὕδωρ, and πολύς reveal the similarity between 17:13 and 28:2, and we can bring 30:30 alongside:

ולהב אש אוכלה נפץ   καὶ φλογὸς κατεσθιούσης κεραυνώσει
                                  βιαίως
וזרם ואבן ברד   καὶ ὡς ὕδωρ καὶ χάλαζα
                                  συγκαταφερομένη βίᾳ

The choice of κεραυνώσει ('will strike [with a thunderbolt]') for נפץ is based on the storm imagery in the context.[52] καὶ ὡς ὕδωρ || וזרם is

---

grando sepm mendacii, 'and hail will subvert the hope of liars'. T is periphrastic: וידלק רוגזי ברוחצן כדביכון,'and my anger will burn against the safety of your lies'.

[49] LXX-Isa offers diverse equivalents for זרם elsewhere: σκληρότης in 4:6; ὕδωρ in 28:2 (זרם²) and 30:30. 'Από ἀνθρώπων πονηρῶν || מזרם in 25:4 is likely due to the translator reading זרם as זר(י)ם (see above, p. 125).

[50] It is noteworthy, however, that his rendering of משיבי מלחמה שערה in 28:6 is κωλύων ἀνελεῖν. While κωλύων is intelligibly rooted in משיבי, ἀνελεῖν is (at best) a periphrastic rendering of מלחמה שערה.

[51] 1QIsaᵃ = MT. S and V accord with the MT, while T gives בעלעול רוח ('in a whirlwind of wind').

[52] Κεραυνοῦν occurs only here in LXX-Isaiah, while the noun κεραυνός does not

reminiscent of ὡς ὕδατος || כזרם in 28:2, while the collapsing of ואבן ברד into καὶ χάλαζα (parallel to the collapsing of להב אש into φλογός) is readily intelligible.[53] Unattested by Hebrew equivalents in the MT, 1QIsaᵃ, S, V, or T are βιαίως and συγκαταφερομένη βίᾳ, the latter of which once more evinces the phrase καταφερομένη βίᾳ inserted into a context suited to it, with σύν likely prefixed to καταφέρειν in light of the compound ὕδωρ καὶ χάλαζα. This evidence of the translator's insertion of phrases combining καταφέρειν and βία suggests that he also supplied the modification of κεραυνώσει with βιαίως.[54]

These parallels, then, enhance the likelihood that the translator supplied βίᾳ καταφερομένη in 28:2,[55] so that the imagery of a fierce storm has been intensified in describing the punishment awaiting the impious. Moreover, because of the collocation of καταφέρειν, βία, ὡς, and ὕδωρ in these three passages, we should probably associate βίᾳ καταφερομένη with ὡς ὕδατος πολύ ('forcefully falling like much water') and take ὡς χάλαζα καταφερομένη οὐκ ἔχουσα σκέπην as a single locution ('like hail falling without any covering [for those in its path]').

This, of course, begs the question of how the translator arrived at οὐκ ἔχουσα σκέπην. Ziegler rejects Ottley's surmise that this is a paraphrase of שׁער קטב ('a tempest of destruction')[56] and Fischer's attempt "sie aus der hebr. Vorlage zu erklären," suggesting instead that "stand eine Glosse oder Variante zur Erklärung des schwierigen Textes in der LXX-Vorlage: (מ)בְּלִי מַחְסֶה), die aus Job 24,8 stammt (|| זֶרֶם!)."[57] However, given what we have witnessed of the translator's willingness to intensify storm imagery, one must suspect that οὐκ ἔχουσα σκέπην attests a similar impulse, since it describes the χάλαζα καταφερομένη as inescapable.

---

appear in the book. While this is the only occurrence of the noun נפץ in the Bible, ונפצות is translated διεσπαρμένους in 12:12 and ונפצו is translated διεσπάρησαν in 33:3. As Ziegler perceived, the translation of בשׂומו מנפצות כל אבני מזבח כאבני גר by ὅταν θῶσι πάντας τοὺς λίθους τῶν βωμῶν κατακεκομμένους ὡς κονίαν λεπτήν in 27:9 is a rendering according to the general sense of the context (Ziegler, *Untersuchungen*, 101).

[53] The phrase אבן ברד appears elsewhere only in Josh 10:11 (אבני הברד), although there the LXX renders it literally: λίθους χαλάζης.

[54] Cf. Ziegler's comments on the translator's insertion of βία (*Untersuchungen*, 143).

[55] *Pace* Ziegler, who suggests that perhaps the LXX's *Vorlage* read מנגרם for זרם, comparing Mic 1:4 (ὡς ὕδωρ καταφερόμενον || כמים מנרים) and 2 Kgdms 14:14 (καὶ ὥσπερ τὸ ὕδωρ τὸ καταφερόμενον ἐπὶ τῆς γῆς || וכמים הנגרים ארצה) (ibid., 143). Given the translator's varied equivalents for זרם and his proclivity to introduce καταφέρειν, it seems pedantic to posit a variant to clear him of a lexical lapse.

[56] Ottley, *The Book of Isaiah*, 2:237.

[57] Ziegler, *Untersuchungen*, 119.

Even though grammatically οὐκ ἔχουσα σκέπην modifies χάλαζα καταφερομένη, it is effectively a statement about those who might seek shelter from the deluge: the storm will be so strong as to obliterate such shelter. This theme resonates with the denial of hope for those who suppose they have made arrangements to escape the destructive καταιγὶς φερομένη, according to vv. 17c–18, and who articulate their expectation that they will be spared in terms of having a σκέπη: καὶ τῷ ψεύδει σκεπασθησόμεθα | | ובשקר נסתרנו (v. 15).

There is one more parallel to be considered that strengthens the perception that the translator was guided by the idea of the severity of divine wrath, the plus in the first clause of v. 2:

הנה חזק ואמץ לאדני   ἰδοὺ ἰσχυρὸν καὶ σκληρὸν ὁ θυμὸς κυρίου

Whereas the MT speaks of the LORD having at his disposal an agent (whose function is defined by comparison to a storm), the LXX offers an independent assertion: "Behold, the wrath of the Kyrios is something mighty and harsh." To make this predication, however, required the noun ὁ θυμός, which is without a semantic equivalent in the MT or any other textual witness.[58] In fact, whereas the MT's comparisons to a storm illustrate the might of the LORD's agent, culminating in the assertion that "he will cast (the drunkards of Ephraim) to the ground" (הניח לארץ), in the LXX the subject is ὁ θυμὸς κυρίου, which will finally "give rest to the land" (τῇ γῇ ποιήσει ἀνάπαυσιν).[59] From here through the end of the chapter in the LXX, the topic is the wrath of the Kyrios and how it intersects with the plots of "the hirelings of Ephraim."

Thus, arrayed against those who place their hope in falsehood is the storm metaphor v. 2 has already used as a figure for divine wrath. Reprising the καταιγὶς φερομένη to represent the danger the impious hope to thwart, the final clauses of v. 18—mirroring the word order of the MT—assert that rather than the surging flood passing them by, it will leave them καταπάτημα.

While on first blush the translation of these clauses follows the MT exactly, the choice of ἐπέλθῃ for יעבר is remarkable. Whereas the translator used παρέρχεσθαι for עבר in vv. 15 and 19 (bis), his use of

---

[58] 1QIsaᵃ = MT, save for a superlinear bêt at the start of חזק, suggesting that it read בחזק and אמץ as nouns, as do S (ܘܒܐܝܕܐ ܥܫܝܢܐ ܘܚܣܝܢܐ ܗܘ ܡܪܝܐ) and V (ecce validus et fortis Domini). T is expansive and differs substantially from the LXX: הא מחן תקיפן וחסינן אתין מן קדם יוי.

[59] Cf. καὶ ὁ θυμὸς αὐτοῦ | | ומטהו in 10:26, μετὰ θυμοῦ | | ירנו in 28:21, and καὶ τοῦ θυμοῦ σου | | ומרגזך in 14:3.

ἐπέλθῃ here echoes the boast of those placing confidence in a pact with death in v. 15:

שׁיט [ק׳ שׁוט] שׁוֹטֵף‎   καταιγὶς φερομένη
כִּי עָבַר [ק׳ יַעֲבֹר] לֹא יְבוֹאֵנוּ‎   ἐὰν παρέλθῃ οὐ μὴ ἔλθῃ ἡμῖν

The inference that the translator decided to translate יעבר‎ with ἐπέλθῃ in v. 18 in order to echo this denial gains force from the observation that, while ἐπέρχεσθαι translates עבר‎ elsewhere in the LXX, v. 18 is the only time this equivalence appears in LXX-Isaiah. Once again the translator's lexical choices show that he was guided by his sense of the passage as a unit.

Given the many ways the translator accommodated features of his *Vorlage* to his construal of the entire passage, one must conclude that he found the motif of a tempest an important figure for divine wrath and useful in denying the confidence of those who thought they had negotiated protection from trouble. V. 19 again emphasizes the futility of such thinking:

מִדֵּי עָבְרוֹ יִקַּח אֶתְכֶם‎   ὅταν παρέλθῃ λήμψεται ὑμᾶς
כִּי בַבֹּקֶר בַּבֹּקֶר יַעֲבֹר בַּיּוֹם‎   πρωὶ πρωὶ παρελεύσεται ἡμέρας

כי‎ may have been absent from the LXX's *Vorlage*, although it is attested by all other extant witnesses.[60] In every other respect the LXX reflects a *Vorlage* identical to the MT. However, a significant variation appears in the next clause:

וּבַלַּיְלָה וְהָיָה רַק זְוָעָה‎   καὶ ἐν νυκτὶ ἔσται ἐλπὶς πονηρά[61]

1QIsaᵃ, S, and V attest the same text as the MT.[62] Ottley suggests that ἐλπὶς πονηρά indicates that the translator "read קוּ רָעָה‎, or the like."[63]

---

[60] However, see the discussion in n. 28 about the problems כי‎ presents.

[61] Whereas ביום ובלילה‎ are paired in the MT (as indicated by והיה‎), further stressing the persistent vulnerability to the scourge, ἐν νυκτί seems parallel to ἡμέρας as divisions of the day when the actions of the preceding ὅταν παρέλθῃ λήμψεται ὑμᾶς are realized: it is each morning—i.e., during the day—that the tempest will pass by, and in the night that it will seize them, so that their hope proves "evil.' The translator's construal of the syntax this way was likely encouraged by a *Vorlage* that read יהיה‎ for והיה‎ (cf. καὶ ἔσται || יהיֶה‎ [→ והיֶה‎] in v. 21). While πονηρά could be parsed as a neuter accusative plural adjective, used substantivally as the direct object of ἀκούειν, that would leave ἐλπίς without a predicate.

[62] T's לוּטָא‎ ('curse') likely also presupposes זועה‎. In any case, T's path does not resemble the one the LXX takes. 1QIsaᵇ preserves only רק זוֹ[עה]‎.

[63] Ottley, *The Book of Isaiah*, 2:243.

The appeal of this hypothesis is that it elegantly accounts for the LXX through a "scrabblesque" rearrangement of letters, leaving only *zayin* unaccounted for.[64] However, two questions are important. First, under what circumstances would scribal misreading of רק זועה lead to קו רעה? Certainly קו is a common noun in the chapter, so that a scribe might have been induced to perceive it here. And yet, רק is common enough (πλήν || רק in 4:1; ἐμπτυσμάτων || רק in 50:6) that this word sequence should no more have triggered קו in a scribe's mind than ובשקר נסתרנו in v. 15 should have inspired a reading יבש קרן סתרנו, even though that is theoretically possible (if not more so, since it involves only a *wāw/yôd* interchange and different word division). The fact that Ottley's suggestion relies on an assumption of graphic dislocation makes it necessary to find a reasonable hypothesis to explain how this occurred, and none seems at hand.

The other question is, how would this variant fit within its literary context? This question is especially pertinent because, given the inability to explain the origins of the variant through what we know about graphic confusion, this retroversion presumes that some scribe regarded קו רעה as better fitting the context than רק זועה. Since wherever קו is the subject of a clause, its verb is in the masculine gender (יצא, Ps 19:5; נטה, Zech 1:16), רעה would likely be the noun ('a line of evil').[65] In the preceding context in the MT (vv. 10, 13), the cryptic message (שמועה) designated דבר יהוה is said to be צו לצו צו לצו קו לקו קו לקו זעיר שם זעיר שם. There קו designates a (measuring) line which, along with the preceding צו, precedes perdition (v. 13). This measuring line is reprised in v. 17, where the LORD vows to make משפט לקו, parallel to making צדקה למשקלת. This amounts to the declaration of the standard by which the LORD will apply judgment to the renegades among his people.

In what sense, then, might the reading קו רעה in v. 19 be considered contextually suitable? Even granting that it is always possible that someone, somewhere could make sense of such a reading, it seems unlikely that קו, which was used earlier for the standard of evaluation, would now convey judgment ("the line [which brings] calamity"), while

---

[64] Cf. his translation of קו by ἐλπίς in vv. 10, 13, and 17, an equivalence found in the LXX only in these verses and 18:7 (cf. ἀνέλπιστον || קו קו in 18:2).

[65] While it is possible that a random scribal error might produce a solecism like קו רעה (with רעה as an adjective), it is unlikely that this variant would have arisen in that way, so that the retroversion, in that case, would have to be קו רע. However, this implies omission of both *zayin* and *hê*, lessening its likelihood.

the idea that the line is somehow tantamount to "calamity" (least of all, "evil") seems far-fetched.

Tov reports that זועה proved difficult for all LXX translators, so that ἐλπὶς πονηρά is more likely a guess based on the context.[66] This seems the soundest judgment. Given that ἐλπίς has been used for various words prior to this (including חזות), it seems more likely that ἐλπὶς πονηρά is a phrase the translator offered in lieu of רק זועה (i.e., it is a non-translation). The designation of ἐλπίς as proving to be πονηρά must be understood in light of how confidence of preservation from calamity is decried as fruitless in v. 18. Just as there the καταιγίς, failing to bypass them (v. 17), will annul their covenant with death, so here its failure to bypass them shows their ἐλπίς to be πονηρά (cf. v. 15, where their hope is characterized as a ψεῦδος).

Equally attributable to the translator is the masculine plural imperative, μάθετε (|| הבין), which is part of his attempt to unify this passage. He has not needed to modify other pronouns to this point, due to the predominance of second person plural pronouns in Hebrew.[67] Notice, however, that the rendering of הבין שמועה by μάθετε ἀκούειν introduces a statement whose pronouns and semantic equivalents are difficult to align with the MT (v. 20):

כי קצר המצע מהשתרע   στενοχωρούμενοι οὐ δυνάμεθα μάχεσθαι
והמסכה צרה כהתכנס   αὐτοὶ δὲ ἀσθενοῦμεν τοῦ ἡμᾶς συναχθῆναι

The only clear semantic associations are στενοχωρούμενοι || קצר and συναχθῆναι || כהתכנס.[68] מצע is a *hapax legomenon* in the Bible and so

---

[66] Tov, "Did the Septuagint Translators," 59.

[67] Ἀκούσατε || שמעו, v. 14; εἴπατε || אמרתם, v. 15; ὑμῶν τὴν διαθήκην || בריתכם, καὶ ἡ ἐλπὶς ὑμῶν || וחזותכם, ἔσεσθε || והייתם, v. 18; ὑμᾶς || אתכם, v. 19. The only second person plural pronoun without a corresponding pronoun in the MT to this point was ὅτι οὐ μὴ παρέλθῃ ὑμᾶς καταιγίς || ישטפו מים וסתר in v. 17, although that stands amidst differences between the LXX and the MT that are attributable to the translator. Vv. 22–23 contain seven more second person plural pronouns that correspond to second person plural pronouns in the MT, while καὶ ὑμεῖς (v. 22) probably attests ואתה in the *Vorlage* in place of the MT's ועתה.

In fact, agreement of person and number is one of the more regular correlations between the LXX and the MT in this chapter, making the deviations intriguing, especially when they form a coherent sentence showing other features at variance with the MT, as in v. 20 and the final phrase of v. 25 through v. 26 (ἐν τοῖς ὁρίοις σουκαὶ παιδευθήσῃ κρίματι θεοῦ σου καὶ εὐφρανθήσῃ || נבלתו ויסרו למשפט אלהיו יורנו), which figures prominently in the translator's interpretation of the agrarian imagery as revealing the Kyrios's salutary use of judgment (see below, pp. 276–78).

[68] On the absence of an equivalent for כי (attested by 1QIsaᵃ, 1QIsaᵇ, S , T, and V), see n. 28.

may reasonably have afforded the translator difficulty. What is more, its formal equivalent, οὐ δυνάμεθα μάχεσθαι, must be considered in light of the whole verse as anticipating the distress of those who boast that they will escape calamity.[69] Indeed, the passage offers evidence that the translator relied on his own construal of what might appropriately be said in this situation rather than on a precise knowledge of the Hebrew lexemes. Thus, to his translation of (צרה) והמסכה by αὐτοὶ δὲ ἀσθενοῦμεν we can compare his rendering of והמסך הנסוכה על כל הגוים by ἡ γὰρ βουλὴ αὕτη ἐπὶ πάντα τὰ ἔθνη in 25:7, and of ולנסך מסכה by καὶ συνθήκας (parallel to ἐποιήσατε βουλήν || לעשׂות עצה) in 30:1, both of which suggest that he may have had some difficulty with והמסכה and so provided what he considered a contextually fitting equivalent.

More important, the plus αὐτοί, coupled with the conjunction δέ, establishes a contrast that reflects the translator's construal of the sense. The equivalent ἀσθενοῦμεν probably interprets צרה in the light of στενοχωρούμενοι,[70] extrapolating from the confession of their inability to wage war to the idea of being too weak to array themselves for battle.[71] Building on קצר and כהתכנס,[72] the translator fashioned a confession of abject weakness in the face of adversity. Apparently, these words are meant as a confession they are to embrace (μάθετε ἀκούειν) when their ἐλπίς proves πονηρά. In this light, it is more likely that the translator conformed the number of the person in μάθετε to the plural number of the pronouns in the address leading up to this than that his *Vorlage* read הבינו.

As previously noted, at the heart of the LXX's chapter is condemnation of leaders who presume that they have acquired protection from any threat. Their confidence is delusional, as the words given them in v. 15 admit: ἐθήκαμεν ψεῦδος τὴν ἐλπίδα ἡμῶν καὶ τῷ ψεύδει σκεπασθησόμεθα. It is this deluded spirit that likely lies behind the

---

[69] Ottley attempts valiantly to reconstruct the translator's path philologically, suggesting that for המצע "LXX may have…misread צבא" and attributing οὐ to "מ at the beginning of the next word," but finds himself forced to admit that "δυνάμεθα is difficult, nothing at all resembling the Heb. letters having this meaning" (Ottley, *The Book of Isaiah*, 2:242). After offering that "ἀσθενοῦμεν may suggest that מסוו from מסס, 'faint,' was read for ההכנס," he wisely concludes that "this is too remote to be satisfactory" (ibid.).

[70] Cf. στενοχωρήσει || הצרי in 49:19.

[71] Cf. 29:4, where the translator renders אמרתך תצפצף אמרתך ומעפר with καὶ πρὸς τὸ ἔδαφος ἡ φωνή σου ἀσθενήσει (possibly reading ובעפר; cf. εἰς τὴν γῆν || ומעפר in the preceding clause), evidently reasoning that to have one's voice sink to the ground (N.B. καὶ ταπεινωθήσονται οἱ λόγοι σου εἰς τὴν γῆν || ושפלת מארץ תדברי earlier in the verse) is to have it weakened.

[72] 1QIsaᵃ reads בהתכנס.

translator's οἱ μεθύοντες ἄνευ οἴνου in v. 1 and his qualification of verse 7's imagery of men seduced by wine with τοῦτ' ἔστι φάσμα. The rulers' placing confidence in deceit is what makes them deluded and behaving as though they were under the influence of alcohol.

In this context we must note the contrast between a "curse" and "this counsel" in v. 8:[73]

| כי כל שלחנות מלאו קיא | ἀρὰ ἔδεται ταύτην τὴν βουλήν |
| צאה בלי מקום | αὕτη γὰρ ἡ βουλὴ ἕνεκεν πλεονεξίας |

As Ziegler recognizes, "es ist sehr schwer zu sagen, wie die LXX zu ihrem Texte... gekomment ist."[74] Ottley suggests that ἀρά aligns with פליליה at the end of v. 7, which "the LXX, if they did not mistake the meaning, perhaps read קללה," while "כי כל might have been read as יאכל."[75] Ziegler, however, notes the similarity to 24:6 (ἀρὰ ἔδεται τὴν γῆν || אלה אכלה ארץ) and suggests, "es ist möglich, daß von hier aus die Wiedergabe 28,8 beeinflußt ist."[76] This seems the more likely explanation.

In fact, the bulk of the translator's rendering of v. 8 seems dependent on other passages in LXX-Isaiah, since the topic of βουλή appears often in the book and frequently without a discernable equivalent in the MT:[77]

3:9	כי נמלו להם רעה	διότι βεβούλευνται βουλὴν πονηρὰν καθ' ἑαυτῶν
10:25	ואפי על תבליתם	ὁ δὲ θυμός μου ἐπὶ τὴν βουλὴν αὐτῶν
25:7	והמסכה הנסוכה על כל הגוים	ἡ γὰρ βουλὴ αὕτη ἐπὶ πάντα τὰ ἔθνη
31:6	שובו לאשר העמיקו סרה בני ישראל	ἐπιστράφητε οἱ τὴν βαθεῖαν βουλὴν βουλευόμενοι καὶ ἄνομον
32:7	וכלי כליו רעים הוא זמות יעץ	ἡ γὰρ βουλὴ τῶν πονηρῶν ἄνομα βουλεύσεται
32:8	ונדיב נדיבות יעץ והוא על נדיבות יקום	οἱ δὲ εὐσεβεῖς συνετὰ ἐβουλεύσαντο καὶ αὕτη ἡ βουλὴ μενεῖ

---

[73] 1QIsaᵃ = MT. 4QIsaᶜ preserves only the final ם and (possibly) the left stroke of the ρ. S, V, and T presuppose *Vorlagen* = MT.

[74] Ziegler, *Untersuchungen*, 146. 1QIsaᵃ = MT, while the literal translation by S attests a *Vorlage* identical to the MT, as does V's slightly less literal rendering, which joins צאה with קיא (*vomitu sordiumque*), while its rendering of בלי מקום forms a result clause (*ita ut non esset ultra locus*). Even T's slightly expansive rendering appears to reflect a *Vorlage* = MT.

[75] Ottley, *The Book of Isaiah*, 2:239. Cf. Fischer, who attributes this reading directly to the translator (*In welcher Schrift*, 44).

[76] Ziegler, *Untersuchungen*, 146.

[77] I list here only the most striking cases in which βουλή appears without a discernable equivalence in the MT. βουλή often translates עצה (5:19; 8:10; 11:2; 14:26; 19:3, 11, 17; 25:1; 29:15; 30:1; 36:5; 44:26; 46:10; 47:13) and thrice it serves as an equivalent for מחשב (55:7–8).

Even a cursory read of these passages suggests that βουλή was a term that came readily to the translator's mind without any necessary foundation in his *Vorlage*.[78] In this passage, where the leaders' schemes to protect themselves from calamity are the issue, the threat that a curse will devour "this counsel" was likely supplied by the translator. And the same is, then, true of his diagnosis of what lies behind it—ἕνεκεν πλεονεξίας—which is equally impossible to align with an equivalent in the MT.[79] And because this word occurs only here in LXX-Isaiah (neither πλεονεκτεῖν or πλεονέκτης appear in the book), it is not easy to discern what πλεονεξία is the root of this βουλή. Indeed, this is one of several assertions in this text that remain impenetrable, including the language of a "covenant with death" and "pact with Hades," as well as the image of the καταιγίς; they are too oblique to align with any known referent. And yet, it is clear that the translator considers the anticipated calamity a figure for divine wrath from which these rulers cannot protect themselves by their devices.

Standing immediately after the characterization of the rulers as seduced by strong drink (which the translator marks as a metaphor), ταύτην τὴν βουλήν refers to the course of behavior just described as delusional. Even if at this point the content of this βουλή is not detailed, it is clear that the leaders' determined course is destined for failure, even as their ἐλπίς is said to be later in the chapter. And while v. 8 is not explicit about what will thwart the rulers' plan, the earlier description of the θυμὸς κυρίου as a threat to them implies that the ἀρά that will devour their scheme is sent by the Kyrios.

At the same time, as das Neves detected, there is a type of ἐλπίς endorsed in this chapter, most expressly in v. 16, which makes the following promise regarding the "stone" the Kyrios will place "in the foundation of Zion":

המאמין לא יחיש   καὶ ὁ πιστεύων ἐπ' αὐτῷ οὐ μὴ καταισχυνθῇ

---

[78] Also striking, although more readily explicable, is the translator's insertion of βουλή in 7:5 (ἐβουλεύσαντο βουλὴν πονηρὰν περὶ σοῦ || יעץ עליך ארם רעה), paralleled by his supply of it as the subject of קום in 7:7 (οὐ μὴ ἐμμείνῃ ἡ βουλὴ αὕτη οὐδὲ ἔσται || לא תקום ולא תהיה). More familiar is the translation of צמח יהוה לצבי by ἐπιλάμψει ὁ θεὸς ἐν βουλῇ in 4:2, discussed above, p. 77.

[79] Ottley wisely rejects his own speculation that πλεονεξίας "may be due to a confusion of צאה 'filth' with ץב 'mire' and בצע 'greed,'" concluding that "this is hardly traceable" (*The Book of Isaiah*, 2:239).

While we might posit that the *Vorlage* read בו following הַמַּאֲמִין,[80] it is more likely that translator supplied ἐπ' αὐτῷ, based on comparison with other places where LXX-Isaiah has ἐπί + pronoun as a plus with πείθειν: ἰδοὺ ὁ θεός μου σωτήρ μου κύριος πεποιθὼς ἔσομαι ἐπ' αὐτῷ || הנה אל ישועתי אבטח (12:2); ἐφ' οἷς ἦσαν πεποιθότες || מבטם (20:5). Equally noteworthy are assimilations to this formula, such as 30:3 (καὶ τοῖς πεποιθόσιν ἐπ' Αἴγυπτον ὄνειδος || והחסות בצל מצרים לכלמה) and 32:3 (καὶ οὐκέτι ἔσονται πεποιθότες ἐπ' ἀνθρώποις ἀλλὰ τὰ ὦτα δώσουσιν ἀκούειν|| ולא תשעינה עיני ראים ואזני שמעים תקשבנה).[81] We can reasonably conclude, therefore, that ἐπ' αὐτῷ was supplied by the translator.

The simplest explanation of καταισχυνθῇ || יחיש is that the LXX's *Vorlage* read יבוש,[82] which it may have. However, LXX-Isaiah gives unusual equivalences for חוש in its other appearances:

5:19	האמרים ימהר יחישה מעשהו	οἱ λέγοντες τὸ τάχος[83] ἐγγισάτω ἃ ποιήσει
60:22	אני יהוה בעתה אחישנה	ἐγὼ κύριος κατὰ καιρὸν συνάξω αὐτούς

Because these translations indicate that the translator did not understand the meaning of יחיש, it is at least as possible that καταισχυνθῇ is an equivalent he considered contextually appropriate as it is that his *Vorlage* read יבוש. Indeed, while κατῃσχύνθης translates תבוש in 54:4, in 3:15 καταισχύνετε aligns with תטחנו in the MT, and there is good reason to think that LXX's rendering in that case is part of its exegesis of that passage (cf. ἡ αἰσχύνη || הכרת in 3:9).[84]

As noted earlier, the assurance to those who trust in the "stone" the Kyrios has placed in Zion's foundation contrasts with those who place confidence in falsehood. Hope is available for those who do not adopt such delusional confidence. And this contrast of types of hope is

---

[80] 1QIsaᵃ, S, and V have no preposition after הַמַּאֲמִין; T's באלין (וצדיקיא דהימינו באלין) is a product of its exegesis.

[81] Cf. 17:7: τῇ ἡμέρᾳ ἐκείνῃ πεποιθὼς ἔσται ἄνθρωπος ἐπὶ τῷ ποιήσαντι αὐτόν οἱ δὲ ὀφθαλμοὶ αὐτοῦ εἰς τὸν ἅγιον τοῦ Ισραηλ ἐμβλέψονται || ביום ההוא האדם ישעה על עשהו ועיניו אל קדוש ישראל תראינה.

[82] So Ottley, *The Book of Isaiah*, 2:241; Fischer, *In welcher Schrift*, 44. 1QIsaᵃ, S, T, and V all reflect יחיש (1QIsaᵇ preserves only the final ש).

[83] Based on position and on other passages where מהר, conjoined with another verb, is translated adverbially (e.g., 8:3; 32:4; 49:17), τὸ τάχος renders ימהר.

[84] See above, pp. 206–07.

apparent in the antithesis das Neves speaks of as "a divine crown versus a human crown,"[85] with the latter featured in vv. 1 and 3:

v. 1	הוי עטרת גאות	οὐαὶ τῷ στεφάνῳ τῆς ὕβρεως
v. 3	תרמסנה עטרת גאות	καταπατηθήσεται ὁ στέφανος τῆς ὕβρεως

The correspondences between LXX and MT are patent.[86] ὁ στέφανος τῆς ὕβρεως is one of two metaphors for a group designated more directly as οἱ μισθωτοὶ Εφραιμ. The second metaphor describes them as a withered blossom:

v. 1	וציץ נבל צבי תפארתו	τὸ ἄνθος τὸ ἐκπεσὸν ἐκ τῆς δόξης
v. 4	ציצת נבל צבי תפארתו	τὸ ἄνθος τὸ ἐκπεσὸν τῆς ἐλπίδος τῆς δόξης

As previously noted, ἐλπίς || צבי occurs elsewhere in LXX-Isaiah. While the absence of a distinct representation for צבי in v. 1 might, at first blush, suggest that it was lacking in the *Vorlage*, it is also possible that the translator collapsed צבי תפארתו into the simpler ἐκ τῆς δόξης. Lending credence to that suggestion is the way he collapsed צבי and תפארתו in reformulating 13:19a:

והיתה בבל צבי	καὶ ἔσται Βαβυλὼν ἣ καλεῖται ἔνδοξος
ממלכות תפארת גאון כשדים	ὑπὸ βασιλέως Χαλδαίων

His consolidation of צבי, תפארת, and גאון into ἔνδοξος stands in contrast to his translation of each of these nouns distinctly in 4:2 (ἐν βουλῇ μετὰ δόξης ἐπὶ τῆς γῆς τοῦ ὑψῶσαι καὶ δοξάσαι || לצבי ולכבוד ופרי הארץ לגאון ולתפארת), even as he translates each noun of צבי תפארתו distinctly in 28:4, after consolidating them in 28:1.[87] However, if the translator varied his equivalents for צבי תפארתו within three verses *and* in a chapter where he otherwise rendered repeated phrases with the same equivalents,[88] we are forced to consider whether his variation in renderings here signals a nuance in his interpretation.[89]

---

[85] Das Neves, *A Teologia*, 74, translation mine.

[86] στέφανος || עטרת is commonplace. ὕβρις translates גאות again in 13:11 and 25:11.

[87] While comparison to v. 4 seems to support the absence of צבי in the *Vorlage* at 28:1, the very different ways identical phrases are rendered in vv. 10 and 13 creates uncertainty about whether τῆς δόξης reflects the absence of צבי, or if it collapses צבי תפארתו into one word.

[88] E.g., הוי עטרת גאות שכרי אפרים is translated identically in v. 1 and v. 3; the only difference between the rendering of אשר על ראש גיא שמנים in vv. 1 and 4 is τῆς κορυφῆς (v. 1) versus ἄκρου (v. 4); צו לצו צו לצו קו לקו קו לקו זעיר שם זעיר שם is given the same (abbreviated) equivalents in vv. 10 and 13; שוט שוטף is rendered καταιγὶς φερομένη in vv. 15 and 18.

[89] Ἐλπίς occurs eight more times in the chapter, five of them for קו (vv. 10 [bis], 13 [bis], 17) and three times for other nouns (מחסנו, v. 15; חזות, v. 18; דך, v. 19). As observed

In all of the LXX, ἐκπίπτειν translates נבל only here, v. 4, and 40:7, and each time it is juxtaposed with ἄνθος as the translation of either ציץ or ציצה.[90] Ἐκπίπτειν occurs in a simile in 6:13, where it means something like "to be deprived of" (καὶ πάλιν ἔσται [sc. ἡ γῆ] εἰς προνομὴν ὡς τερέβινθος καὶ ὡς βάλανος ὅταν ἐκπέσῃ ἀπὸ τῆς θήκης αὐτῆς).[91] Thus, for the translator of Isaiah, ἐκπίπτειν signifies being deprived of something, whether literally or metaphorically. Accordingly, the phrase τὸ ἄνθος τὸ ἐκπεσὸν ἐκ τῆς δόξης means 'the blossom which has been deprived of its δόξα'.[92]

For das Neves, this δόξα is "human pride" that stands in antithesis to the "divine glory" spoken of in v. 5:[93]

ὁ στέφανος τῆς ἐλπίδος ὁ πλακεὶς   לעטרת צבי ולצפירת
τῆς δόξης τῷ καταλειφθέντι μου λαῷ   תפארה לשאר עמו

Standing as the counterpart to human δόξα as self-reliance, das Neves asserts, is divine δόξα that forms the substance of the divine crown: a "crown of hope, woven of glory."[94] In support of this translation for ὁ στέφανος τῆς ἐλπίδος ὁ πλακεὶς τῆς δόξης one can adduce Matt 27:29: καὶ πλέξαντες στέφανον ἐξ ἀκανθῶν. However, the fact that v. 5 reuses and rearranges imagery from vv. 1–4, which includes the phrase τῆς ἐλπίδος τῆς δόξης, makes it likely that τῆς δόξης should be associated with τῆς ἐλπίδος rather than πλακείς. Accordingly, we should probably translate v. 5, "on that day, the Kyrios Sabaoth shall be the crown of the hope of splendor, woven for that which remains of my people." As noted in chapter four, the translator sometimes allows nouns in the genitive and the nouns they qualify to be separated, in accord with high literary style.[95] Even though ὁ στέφανος τῆς ἐλπίδος ὁ πλακεὶς τῆς δόξης matches the word order of the MT (and likely that of his *Vorlage*), that may simply have serendipitously provided him with the basis for a more literary style of syntax.

---

in n. 87, v. 10 and 13 are additional evidence that the translator could render identical phrases in close proximity differently.

[90] Ἐκπίπτειν occurs with ἄνθος three times outside of Isaiah, all in the book of Job and each time representing a different verb (מלל in 14:2; סור in 15:30; and שלך in 15:33).

[91] See Troxel, "Economic Plunder," 386–87.

[92] The article here probably has the force of the possessive pronoun (|| MT's תפארתו).

[93] Das Neves, *A Teologia*, 74. Das Neves writes of the LXX's application of δόξα to humans in this passage, "G always accents the idea of 'pride' (δόξα)" (ibid., 143, translation mine).

[94] Ibid., 143, translation mine. So also Ottley, *The Book of Isaiah*, 2:165.

[95] See above, p. 90.

In this connection, ὁ πλακείς itself calls for comment. Even though it may constitute a good equivalent for צפירת, when that is compared to Arabic *tsafara*, 'to interweave',[96] and to Palestinian Aramaic צפירה ('a border made of plaited ropes'[97]), that meaning fails to explicate הצפירה in Ezek 7:7, 10,[98] where the translator seems to have been as perplexed as any modern, omitting a rendering in 7:7 (7:4 in the LXX) and translating הנה באה יצאה הצפרה הנה היום in v. 10 with ἰδοὺ τὸ πέρας ἥκει ἰδοὺ ἡμέρα κυρίου.

The other ancient translators of Isa 28:5 recognized in צפירת a garland:

S   ܘܢܗܘܐ ܡܪܝܐ ܥܙܝܙܐ ܠܟܠܝܠܐ ܕܫܘܒܚܐ ܘܠܟܠܝܠܐ ܕܬܫܒܘܚܬܐ, 'the mighty Lord will serve as a fearful crown and a glorious garland'

T   יהי משיחא דיוי צבאות לכליל דחדוא ולכתר דתשבח, 'the anointed of the Lord of hosts will be a crown of joy and a garland of praise'

V   *erit Dominus exercitum corona gloriae et sertum exultationis*, 'the Lord of hosts will be a crown of glory and a garland of joy'

Each equivalent for צפירת in S, T, and V is a noun,[99] whereas the LXX translates it with a participle. Whatever insight the translator had into צפירת as designating something twined or plaited, he chose to render it as modifying ὁ στέφανος rather than make it a topic of its own.

While the crown of v. 5 is contrasted to that in vv. 1 and 3, the nature of this relationship is more nuanced and the language less freighted than das Neves describes in his schema of "divine glory" (v. 5) opposed to "human glory" (vv. 1, 3, 4) and the "divine crown" (v. 5) to the "human crown" (vv. 1, 3).[100] This proves too simplistic a parsing, inasmuch as v. 5 conflates the images of vv. 1–4. For example, in vv. 1 and 3 ὁ στέφανος τῆς ὕβρεως is distinct from τὸ ἄνθος τὸ ἐκπεσὸν (τῆς ἐλπίδος) τῆς δόξης, so that ὁ στέφανος τῆς ἐλπίδος ὁ πλακεὶς τῆς δόξης is not in direct contrast to these different phrases. In fact, vv. 1, 3, and 4 do not speak

---

[96] Wildberger, *Isaiah 28–39*, 5.

[97] Marcus Jastrow, *Seper Millim*, 2 vols. (New York: Judaica Press, 1971) s.v. צפירה.

[98] On which see Walther Zimmerli, *Ezekiel: A Commentary on the Book of the Prophet Ezekiel*, vol. 1 (Hermeneia; Fortress Press, 1979) 195–96.

[99] ܟܠܝܠܐ designates "anything twisted or plaited," such as "wickerwork" or "a garland" (Payne Smith, s.v. ܟܠܝܠܐ). V's *sertum* designates a 'wreath', and T's כתר is regularly used for a garland or crown, as in 3:23, where it translates צניפות. Even though each of these is related to a verb meaning "to twist," they are nominal forms designating a product of such twisting.

[100] Das Neves, *A Teologia*, 74.

of "human glory" but use the figure of a flower that has been deprived of glory, so that the topic is the *lack* of glory. And it is not lack of "glória humana" in a general sense, but a denial of glory for a particular group of people. Das Neves's schema homogenizes the images, slotting them within a prearranged polarity that obfuscates their roles in the passage.

Consistent with this, we must observe that the function of these metaphors differs. In vv. 1 and 3 ὁ στέφανος τῆς ὕβρεως is an appellative that provides the initial frame for evaluating οἱ μισθωτοὶ Εφραιμ, which (in v. 1) receives further definition through the image of τὸ ἄνθος τὸ ἐκπεσὸν ἐκ τῆς δόξης. In v. 4 τὸ ἄνθος τὸ ἐκπεσὸν τῆς ἐλπίδος τῆς δόξης is surrogate for οἱ μισθωτοὶ τοῦ Εφραιμ and is used in a simile that portrays οἱ μισθωτοὶ Εφραιμ as prone to seizure by outside forces. Thus, in each case the primary designation for those decried is οἱ μισθωτοὶ τοῦ Εφραιμ, while ὁ στέφανος τῆς ὕβρεως and τὸ ἄνθος τὸ ἐκπεσὸν (τῆς ἐλπίδος) τῆς δόξης are ancillary. We must consider how each phrase functions.

In the phrase ὁ στέφανος τῆς ὕβρεως, the noun in the genitive is not a natural qualifier for στέφανος, since it attributes to "the crown" behavior appropriate for people. As such, τῆς ὕβρεως elevates the metaphor so as to ascribe a quality to οἱ μισθωτοὶ Εφραιμ.[101] That is not to suggest, however, that ὁ στέφανος is a neutral vehicle for this predication.

That the translator had in view the sort of στέφανος used in the Hellenistic era is evident from his qualification of ὁ στέφανος with ὁ πλακείς (on which see above).[102] Such wreaths, woven from foliage (or designed to resemble one so fashioned), were presented to winners of athletic contests or to those who had made "exceptional contributions to the state or groups within it," most often "public officials or civic-minded pers[ons] serving at their own expense."[103] While a στέφανος was awarded to many who achieved such distinction, it was a common appurtenance of rulers, and that is likely the metonymy at play here,

---

[101] Even if we take στέφανος as a symbol of rule, so that ὁ στέφανος τῆς ὕβρεως amounts to "proud rulers," only by resolving the metaphor does the adjective's role become intelligible.

[102] Based on descriptions within the Bible and on archaeological remains, royal עטרות appear to have been made of precious metals (see especially the description of the Ammonite crown in 2 Sam 12:30, the command to make עטרות out of silver and gold in Zech 6:11, and the mention of an עטרה as an adornment among others made of precious metals in Ezek 16:11–13). See Elizabeth E. Platt, s.v. "Jewelry," ABD 3.

[103] BDAG, s.v. στέφανος.

since this group is said to provide guidance to the people through their words (vv. 11c–12) and they are later addressed as ἄρχοντες τοῦ λαοῦ τούτου τοῦ ἐν Ιερουσαλημ.

The use of this figure for the Kyrios in v. 5, on the other hand, does not define his character. While the imagery of ὁ στέφανος τῆς ὕβρεως describes the behavior of οἱ μισθωτοὶ Εφραιμ as rulers, ὁ στέφανος τῆς ἐλπίδος ὁ πλακεὶς τῆς δόξης denotes the role the Kyrios plays for "my remaining people" (τῷ καταλειφθέντι μου λαῷ). Because στεφάνοι were awarded in recognition of extraordinary achievements, στέφανος came to be used as a figure for any sort of reward.[104] Consequently, while ὁ στέφανος in vv. 1 and 3 pertains to the role of οἱ μισθωτοὶ Εφραιμ as rulers, and τῆς ὕβρεως connotes their proud behavior, the Kyrios's salutary role as στέφανος for the people seems to draw more on the idea of a reward given to them. The most salient observation supporting that judgment is the different parts played by δόξα in these verses.

In contrast to the way τῆς ὕβρεως conflicts with the vehicle of the metaphor in v. 1, τῆς δόξης there comports with its metaphor: τὸ ἄνθος τὸ ἐκπεσὸν ἐκ τῆς δόξης. As noted above (p. 271), ἐκπίπτειν is used elsewhere for the withering of a plant.

Equally notable is that δόξα is used in LXX-Isaiah for splendor attaching to an object. Thus, 3:18 envisions a day when the Kyrios removes τὴν δόξαν (הפארת) τοῦ ἱματισμοῦ αὐτῶν καὶ τοὺς κόσμους αὐτῶν, while 3:20, similarly, speaks of an array τοῦ κόσμου τῆς δόξης (הפארים).[105] It is with this sense of "splendor" that τὸ ἄνθος τὸ ἐκπεσὸν ἐκ τῆς δόξης in v. 1 makes sense as a consistent metaphor: these rulers are blossoms that have lost their splendor. The reuse of this image in v. 4 is intensified through the translator's decision to render צבי with τῆς ἐλπίδος, deriding the people's rulers as a blossom deprived of even the *hope* of splendor.

If this reading is right, then v. 5 promises to the people that the Kyrios will be the "crown" offering the (legitimate) hope of splendor for the people. Further encouraging this interpretation is the phrase ὁ

---

[104] See ibid.

[105] For additional examples of δόξα used for "splendor" throughout the LXX, see Takamitsu Muraoka, *A Greek-English Lexicon of the Septuagint* (Louvain: Peeters, 2002) s.v. δόξα. For a discussion of τὴν δόξαν τοῦ ἱματισμοῦ αὐτῶν καὶ τοὺς κόσμους αὐτῶν in 3:20, see van der Kooij, "Interpretation of the Book of Isaiah in the Septuagint and Other Ancient Versions," in *SBLSP* 40 (Atlanta: Scholars Press, 2001) 224.

πλακείς, which brings vividly to the reader's mind precisely the sort of Hellenistic-era στέφανος bestowed as a reward.

As for the people designated by τῷ καταλειφθέντι μου λαῷ,[106] v. 6 provides clarification by reformulating the participle as a finite verb (καταλειφθήσονται) and indicating that this is a matter of leaving them "for a spirit of judgment" (ἐπὶ πνεύματι κρίσεως), further defined as "mighty judgment" (ἐπὶ κρίσιν καὶ ἰσχύν),[107] albeit with reassurance that the Kyrios will forbid their complete destruction (κωλύων ἀνελεῖν).[108]

With this assurance that judgment will not be simply destructive we should compare what follows verse sixteen's promise to the one who puts confidence in the stone the Kyrios has placed in Jerusalem:

ושמתי משפט לקו   καὶ θήσω κρίσιν εἰς ἐλπίδα
וצדקה למשקלת   ἡ δὲ ἐλεημοσύνη μου εἰς σταθμούς

All these equivalents are attested elsewhere, including ἐλεημοσύνη || צדקה, which occurs again in Isa 1:27 and 59:16. While the *Vorlage* might have read וצדקתי, more likely the translator supplied the personal pronoun to correlate with θήσω.

The stock nature of these equivalents notwithstanding, these statements serve important roles. Judgment is not an end in itself, but will be transformed into hope, while the Kyrios's mercy will serve as

---

[106] Apparently the LXX's *Vorlage* read עמי rather than עמו.

[107] Das Neves proposes distinguishing between ἐπὶ πνεύματι κρίσεως and ἐπὶ κρίσιν based on his observation that the translator "ordinarily develops his thought" through antitheses, leading to the conclusion that the first κρίσις connotes salvation, while the second designates the "punitive judgment of the impious people" (*A Teologia*, 144–45, translation mine). While there certainly are antitheses in this chapter, extrapolating from them to a "method" is tenuous, and using that "method" to distinguish two juxtaposed phrases containing κρίσις is untenable; we must reason philologically. In this case, it is questionable whether the translator intends to create a distinction in meaning by his use of ἐπί with the dative and the accusative. We only need compare vv. 10 and 13, where ἐπί has the same force in θλῖψιν ἐπὶ θλῖψιν and ἐλπίδα ἐπ᾽ ἐλπίδι. Thus, ἐπὶ κρίσιν καὶ ἰσχὺν (as a hendiadys) likely stands in apposition to ἐπὶ πνεύματι κρίσεως. In this light κωλύων ἀνελεῖν (see the next note) serves as an even more compelling qualification to the people's predicament.

[108] Ottley correctly surmises that the translator based κωλύων on משיב (*The Book of Isaiah*, 2:238). His translation of מלחמה שערה with ἀνελεῖν might be a reflex of his rendering of v. 8 in the previous chapter, where similar vocabulary appears:

בסאסאה בשלחה תריבנה   μαχόμενος καὶ ὀνειδίζων ἐξαποστελεῖ αὐτούς
הגה ברוחו הקשה   οὐ σὺ ἦσθα ὁ μελετῶν τῷ πνεύματι τῷ σκληρῷ
ביום קדים   ἀνελεῖν αὐτοὺς πνεύματι θυμοῦ

As Ottley judges, the final clause "seems a made-up attempt from the context" (ibid., 2:235).

"stones" (σταθμούς). These stones are unrelated to the λίθον of v. 16. σταθμός is frequently used for the pan weights used to measure the value of goods, even in the singular number (cf. τίς ἔστησε τὰ ὄρη σταθμῷ || ושקל בפלס הרים in Isa 40:12). Thus, the Kyrios's assertion that his mercy will serve for "weights" connotes that whatever judgment falls will be counter-balanced by mercy.

The full meaning of the reassurance that the Kyrios will prevent a full destruction and will transform judgment into hope is played out in vv. 23–28:

האזינו ושמעו קולי	²³⁾ἐνωτίζεσθε καὶ ἀκούετε τῆς φωνῆς μου
הקשיבו ושמעו אמרתי	προσέχετε καὶ ἀκούετε τοὺς λόγους μου
הכל היום יחרש החרש	²⁴⁾μὴ ὅλην τὴν ἡμέραν μέλλει ὁ ἀροτριῶν ἀροτριᾶν
לזרע יפתח וישדד אדמתו	ἢ σπόρον προετοιμάσει πρὶν ἐργάσασθαι τὴν γῆν
הלוא אם־שוה פניה	²⁵⁾οὐχ ὅταν ὁμαλίσῃ αὐτῆς τὸ πρόσωπον
והפיץ קצח וכמן	τότε σπείρει μικρὸν μελάνθιον καὶ κύμινον
יזרק ושם חטה שורה	καὶ πάλιν σπείρει πυρὸν καὶ κριθὴν καὶ ζέαν
ושערה נסמן וכסמת	
⁽²⁶⁾ויסרו למשפט אלהיו נבלתו	ἐν τοῖς ὁρίοις σου ²⁶⁾καὶ παιδευθήσῃ κρίματι θεοῦ σου
יורנו	καὶ εὐφρανθήσῃ
כי לא בחרוץ יודש קצח	²⁷⁾οὐ γὰρ μετὰ σκληρότητος καθαίρεται τὸ μελάνθιον
ואופן עגלה על־כמן יוסב	οὐδὲ τροχὸς ἁμάξης περιάξει ἐπὶ τὸ κύμινον
כי במטה יחבט קצח	ἀλλὰ ῥάβδῳ ἐκτινάσσεται τὸ μελάνθιον
וכמן בשבט ⁽²⁸⁾לחם יודק	τὸ δὲ κύμινον ²⁸⁾μετὰ ἄρτου βρωθήσεται
כי לא לנצח אדוש ידושנו	οὐ γὰρ εἰς τὸν αἰῶνα ἐγὼ ὑμῖν ὀργισθήσομαι
והמם גלגל עגלתו ופרשיו	οὐδὲ φωνὴ τῆς πικρίας μου
לא ידקנו	καταπατήσει ὑμᾶς

As understood by most modern scholars, 28:23–29 in Hebrew offers a two-stage didactic narration, introduced by a call to listen and bearing an accent on instruction.[109] The first stage spotlights the farmer's method of tilling the soil and planting crops, accenting his strategy of working the field until it is ready for planting, but then seeding it with the appropriate grains (vv. 23–25). The second stage emphasizes the care with which the harvested crop is threshed so as to retrieve the grain (vv. 26–28). The relevance of this narration to the literary context is left tacit, and the passage equally lacks any signal of the situation of the

---

[109] V. 29 in the MT is the conclusion to this didactic unit (see Wildberger, *Isaiah 28–39*, 51 and 60–61). In the LXX, however, it correlates with v. 22, on which see below, pp. 282–83.

readers.[110] Its emphasis is on the farmer's skills as originating with and taught by the LORD.

The LXX develops the contrast between the farmer's activities differently. While the MT limits the farmer's work to what is necessary to prepare the ground for planting, the LXX accentuates his *prior* preparation of the seed for sowing (ἢ σπόρον προετοιμάσει πρὶν ἐργάσασθαι τὴν γῆν, v. 24); only after the seed has been prepared does he till the ground. The LXX highlights the crucial role of the seed in its rendition of the second stage of the process, with its talk of the careful processing of the grain for a purpose. Whereas the MT leaves unstated the relevance of this narrative, the LXX makes it clear by its translation of v. 26 and v. 28b–c.

Through v. 23, the first clause of v. 24, and the bulk of v. 25, the LXX's *Vorlage* was likely identical to the MT.[111] However, vv. 24b and 26–28 demand further explanation.

V. 27 is the most easily disentangled of these verses. It bears the marks of the translator interpreting this passage so as to emphasize the salutary effects of the Kyrios's judgment. Most significant are the equivalents καθαίρεται || יוּדַשׁ and ἐκτινάσσεται || יֵחָבֵט. The translator's familiarity with דושׁ is established by 25:10, where he translates נָדושׁ with καταπατηθήσεται and כְּהַדּושׁ with ὃν τρόπον πατοῦσιν. Intriguingly, among the direct objects specified for πατοῦσιν in 25:10 is ἅλωνα ('threshing floor'), while the means of trampling is described as ἐν ἁμάξαις ('with wagons'), even though the MT compares the trampling of Moab to a trampling of "straw mixed with dung" (מַתְבֵּן בְּמִי [ק׳ בְּמוֹ] מַדְמֵנָה). The reason for that translation becomes clear when we compare 41:15:

הִנֵּה שַׂמְתִּיךְ לְמוֹרַג חָרוּץ	ἰδοὺ ἐποίησά σε ὡς τροχοὺς ἁμάξης
חָדָשׁ בַּעַל פִּיפִיּוֹת תָּדוּשׁ הָרִים	ἀλοῶντας καινοὺς πριστηροειδεῖς καὶ
	ἀλοήσεις ὄρη

---

[110] Needless to say, this has occasioned a debate over the import of the passage, a dispute addressed in Wildberger's critical review of suggested interpretations (ibid., 53–56 and 61–62).

[111] The translator likely collapsed the list of seeds at the end of v. 25, which contains two *hapax legomena* (שׂוֹרָה and נִסְמָן). πυρός || חִטָּה and κριθή || שְׂעֹרָה are equivalents elsewhere in the LXX, while ζέα || כֻּסֶּמֶת is semantically appropriate, although this is its only occurrence in the LXX (ὀλύρα translates כֻּסֶּמֶת in Exod 9:32 and Ezek 4:9). The translator inserted καὶ πάλιν before σπείρει to distinguish a second round of sowing, involving three more types of seeds.

Here the translator renders תדוש with ἀλοήσει, while ἀλοῶντας suggests that he read הדש rather than חדש, and καινούς appears to be a double rendering of חדש, read this time as חדש.[112] מורג occurs just two times outside Isaiah: 2 Sam 24:22, where מורנים is translated with τροχοί, and 1 Chr 21:23, where מורנים is rendered with ἀμάξας. In Isa 41:15, however, the phrase ὡς τροχοὺς ἀμάξης translates the phrase למורג חרוץ, suggesting that the translator associated חרוץ with the field of meaning established by מורג and that he simply provided equivalents sufficient to account for each member of the Hebrew phrase. His translation of הדש (MT: חדש) with ἀλοῶντας indicates his understanding of the type of "wagons" in view. This image is likely what spurred his concoction of πατοῦσιν ἄλωνα ἐν ἀμάξαις in 25:10 and appears to have been behind elements of his translation of 28:27, where the phrase τροχὸς ἀμάξης appears again, even if there it accords with the MT's אופן עגלה.[113]

Indeed, 28:27 also contains חרוץ, which is part of the phrase underlying ὡς τροχοὺς ἀμάξης in 41:15. However, in 28:27 the LXX translates בחרוץ with μετὰ σκληρότητος. Given that τροχὸς ἀμάξης in the next clause designates a process that damages grain, and given the translator's association of such a wagon with harsh threshing in 25:10 and 41:15, μετὰ σκληρότητος || בחרוץ is likely chosen with a view to the larger context.[114]

This, in turn, sheds light on καθαίρεται || יודש and ἐκτινάσσεται || יהבט in Isa 28:27. Both verbs concern the handling of one grain: τὸ μελάνθιον. In both clauses the method is set over against a harsher means of processing grain. Via καθαίρεται and ἐκτινάσσεται the translator attenuates the portrayal. καθαίρεται describes the salutary goal of the process (cleansing), in keeping with the translator's rendering of v. 26 to reassure readers that divine judgment would be salutary. Similarly, by choosing ἐκτινάσσεται ('is shaken off') for יודש, he specifies the purpose for using a rod on the grain as the removal of its impurities rather than the harsh action suggested by חבט.[115]

---

[112] For the distinction between "translation doublets" and "double renderings," see above, p. 120.

[113] Not surprisingly, τροχός is a common equivalent for אופן (31x in the LXX), while ἄμαξα frequently translates עגלה (22x).

[114] Cf. T, which translates בחרוץ with במורני ברזלא ('with threshing sledges of iron' [Amos 1:3]) as well as V, which uses in serris ('with saws').

[115] The only other occurrence of חבט in Isaiah is in 27:12, where יהבט is rendered with συμφράξει, although the meaning of that Greek verb in the context is so unclear as to cause Ottley, noting that א reads συνταράξει, to wonder (partly with a view to

More significant differences are found in vv. 26 and 28, since these mini-homilies are at the core of what the translator designates as the significance of the imagery, and thus they help determine how he shapes the imagery in the equally striking v. 24b.

The semantic relationships in v. 26 are transparent once we concede that the LXX's translation of יורנו with καὶ εὐφρανθήσῃ is based on reading וירנו in its *Vorlage*,[116] as also seems presupposed by S's ܘܢܚܕܐ.[117] Even at that, his use of εὐφραίνειν is striking, given that he renders וירנו by καὶ ἀναγγελεῖ ἡμῖν in 2:3 and given that the preceding ויסרו in 28:26 might reasonably have led him to construe וירנו as from ירה and employ an equivalent like διδάσκειν (cf. διδάσκοντα || מורה in 9:15[14]). Accordingly, even though the relationship between εὐφρανθήσῃ and יורנו is explicable, this lexical choice embodies interpretation.

V. 28 presents more perplexing semantic relationships. While ἄρτου is a recognizable equivalent for לחם, the LXX seems to lack an equivalent for בשבט, unless the translator took לחם (בשבט) as equivalent to the phrase מטה לחם.[118] Given his use of βρωθήσεται for יודק,[119] his streamlined rendering of בשבט לחם by μετὰ ἄρτου is intelligible. Indeed, his choice of βρωθήσεται parallels his use of καθαίρεται for יושד and ἐκτινάσσεται for יחבט: just as those choices were guided by the perception that the passage concerns treatment of seed that equips it for a task, so here the cumin is not crushed, but used as food.[120]

While οὐ γὰρ εἰς τὸν αἰῶνα transparently renders כי לא לנצח, the relationship between the clauses that follow and the MT is largely

---

[116] ἐκτινάσσεται in 28:27) whether συντινάξει ('shall shake violently') might "be the real word here" (*The Book of Isaiah*, 2:236). In Judges 6:11 (A&B) and Ruth 2:17 חבט is translated by ῥαβδίζειν, whose nominal form the translator has already used for מטה.

[116] For εὐφραίνειν as the translation equivalent for רנן, see 12:6; 16:10; 24:14; 26:19; 42:11; 44:23; 49:13; 52:8; 54:1). The translator demonstrates his familiarity with ירה in 28:9, where he renders יורה by ἀνηγγείλαμεν.

[117] 1QIsaᵃ = MT. V's *docebit eum* presupposes a *Vorlage* = MT (it supplies *illud*, 'that', as a second object for both *erudiet* and *docebit* to specify what God teaches the farmer: viz., the skills of tilling and planting). T's מחוי להון likewise reflects a *Vorlage* = MT.

[118] מטה לחם is rendered στήριγμα ἄρτου in Ezek 4:16, 5:16, 14:13, and Ps 104(105):16. Cf. ἰσχὺν ἄρτου || משען לחם in Isa 3:1.

[119] 1QIsaᵃ reads ידק, with ו written superlinearly between the *yôd* and the *dālet*; the space for this verb stands in a lacuna in 4QIsaᵏ. S translates with ܢܬܕܝܫ ('treaded'), while T uses the same verb, but in a different binyan and number: מדדרכין; V reads *comminuetur* ('is diminished').

[120] The translator's ability to handle יודק well (even if this form is derived from דוק rather than דקק) is attested by 41:15, where he renders ותדק with καὶ λεπτυνεῖς (λεπτύνειν is the common equivalent for דקק throughout the LXX; e.g., 2 Kgdms 22:43; 4 Kgdms 23:6, 15; Jer 48:12; Micah 4:13; Psalms 17[18]:43; 28[29]:6).

inscrutable, except that καταπατήσει ὑμᾶς seems a rendering of ידושנו,
just as καὶ καταπατηθήσεται translates ונדוש in 25:10. In any case,
the translator has established his familiarity with other words in v. 28,
having chosen ἁμάξης for עגלה in v. 27, οἱ τροχοὶ (τῶν ἁρμάτων αὐτῶν)
for וגלגליו in 5:28, and having used both ἱππεῖς (21:7) and ἵπποι (22:6) as
equivalents for פרש.

If we compare the other textual witnesses to v. 28, 1QIsaᵃ attests
several variants,[121] the most significant of which is the absence of לחם,
although that sheds no light on the LXX's *Vorlage*, since ἄρτου attests לחם.
1QIsaᵃ also reads הדש for the MT's אדוש and ידיקנו for the MT's
ידקנו. 4QIsaᵏ appears to have a *wāw* written superlinearly before the *lāmed* and
otherwise attests clearly only לא לנצח, although it appears that the top
of a *yôd* (from the preceding כי) is present.

As for the other versions, V's lack of an equivalent for the 3ms suffix
of עגלתו (*plaustri*) is most likely a matter of the target language, since
it renders המם with *vexabit*, making representation of the 3ms suffix
superfluous. S, trying to make sense of the verse, supplies a prepositional
phrase—ܪܝܫܐ ܡܬܕܝܫ ܡܛܠܬܢ ('food is treaded *for our sake*')—whose
meaning is illuminated by the next clause: ܠܐ ܗܘܐ ܓܝܪ ܠܡܚܣܢ ܬܕܘܫܝܗ
('for it was not to achieve victory [that] he thoroughly tread
it');[122] both are expansions rather than attestations of a different *Vorlage*.[123]
T interpretatively casts vv. 23–28 as an exposition of the role of prophets
and the potential their message has for altering the people's behavior,[124]
leaving only a sketchy relationship to the MT in vv. 23–25. However,
with vv. 27 and 28 its equivalents become suddenly more transparent,
revealing a *Vorlage* apparently identical to the MT.[125]

Consequently, none of the other textual witnesses attests the sort
of multiple variants that would explain the LXX's translation of v. 28.

---

[121] In v. 25 it reads נבולותו for the MT's נבלתו, corresponding to the LXX's plural noun,
ὁρίοις. It reads ידש for the MT's יודש in v. 27, even as it reads הדש for the MT's אדוש in
v. 28. Similarly, it reads יסוב for the MT's יוסב in v. 27 and ידיקנו for the MT's ידקנו.

[122] Noteworthy is the translation of לנצח by ܢܨܚ. For most occurrences of לנצח in
Isaiah the translator resorts to ܠܥܠܡ (13:20; 33:20; 34:10; 57:16). His only other use of
for לנצח is in 25:8, where it is paired with ܠܥܠܡ in a double rendering: ܡܒܠܥ ܡܘܬܐ
בלע המות לנצח || ܢܒܠܥ ܡܘܬܐ ܠܥܠܡ.

[123] Also notable, although hardly any more probative of a different *Vorlage*, is his translation of והמם by ܘܕܪܟ ܐܢܘܢ, probably through association of המם (a *hapax legomenon* in
Isaiah) with המון, which is translated with ܣܓܝ ܐܘ in 29:5, 7, 8; 31:4.

[124] This theme is introduced by prefixing to v. 23's call for attention the words אמר נבייא.

[125] The emphatic reassertion of the initial v. עיבורא ית after the verb (מדרכין אף יתיה)
seems in preparation for the contrastive ארי לא לעלמא אדרכא ידרכוניה: 'but not forever
will they fully (= 'brutally') tread it'.

In this light, most feasible is Ziegler's suggestion that οὐ γὰρ εἰς τὸν αἰῶνα ἐγὼ ὑμῖν ὀργισθήσομαι shows the translator working under the influence of another passage containing לֹא לָנֶצַח, such as Isa 57:16: כִּי לֹא לְעוֹלָם אָרִיב וְלֹא לָנֶצַח אֶקְצוֹף.[126] Buttressing Ziegler's argument is evidence that the translator was influenced elsewhere in the chapter by passages beyond the immediate context, such as in his translation of הַלוּמֵי יָיִן by οἱ μεθύοντες ἄνευ οἴνου under the influence of 51:21 and 29:9, discussed above (pp. 247–48).

Ziegler's perception of the translator's path to ἐγὼ ὑμῖν ὀργισθήσομαι points to a likely explanation of how the translator arrived at the parallel οὐδὲ φωνὴ τῆς πικρίας μου καταπατήσει ὑμᾶς. As already noted, the equivalence καταπατεῖν || דוֹשׁ is attested elsewhere and may lie behind καταπατήσει. While the clause φωνή...καταπατήσει ὑμᾶς is a peculiar locution, οὐδὲ φωνή is likely based on וְהָמֹם, even as כַּהֲמֹת יָם is translated with ὡς φωνὴ θαλάσσης in 5:30. There is, however, no apparent connection between τῆς πικρίας μου and נֶגֶל עֲנָלְתוֹ וּפָרָשָׁיו, lexemes that, as noted earlier, the translator renders well elsewhere.

The most striking equivalent in that phrase is πικρία, since it appears nowhere in vv. 23–27. However, πικρία did occur in v. 21:

כִּי כְהַר פְּרָצִים יָקוּם	ὥσπερ ὄρος ἀσεβῶν ἀναστήσεται
יְהוָה כְעֵמֶק בְּגִבְעוֹן יִרְגָּז	καὶ ἔσται ἐν τῇ φάραγγι Γαβαων μετὰ θυμοῦ
לַעֲשׂוֹת מַעֲשֵׂהוּ זָר מַעֲשֵׂהוּ	ποιήσει τὰ ἔργα αὐτοῦ πικρίας ἔργον
וְלַעֲבֹד עֲבֹדָתוֹ	ὁ δὲ θυμὸς αὐτοῦ ἀλλοτρίως χρήσεται
נָכְרִיָּה עֲבֹדָתוֹ	καὶ ἡ πικρία αὐτοῦ ἀλλοτρία

Three variants in the LXX's *Vorlage* seem evident: וְהָיָה rather than the Tetragrammaton, and עֲבָדָתוֹ for both instances of עֲבֹדָתוֹ,[127] each of which cases involves ambiguity of ו/י or ד/ר. The translation of עֲבָדָתוֹ by πικρία (found only here) is intelligible from the fact that while עֶבְרָה is typically translated by θυμός (9:18; 13:9, 13; 14:6), θυμός was used for יִרְגָּז earlier in v. 21, while πικραίνειν is used for רָגְזָה in 14:9. Accordingly, πικρία and θυμός likely shared semantic ground in the translator's mind and seem to be synonyms in v. 21.

More peculiar, though, is the equivalence πικρίας || זָר in the clause ποιήσει τὰ ἔργα αὐτοῦ πικρίας ἔργον. Frequently underlying πικρός,

---

[126] Ziegler, *Untersuchungen*, 120. So also Seeligmann, *Septuagint Version*, 71.

[127] The remainder of the differences, which are primarily grammatical rather than semantic, are likely due to the translator's reformulation. On the other hand, χρήσεται is probably based on reading לַעֲבֹד in the light of Aramaic עֲבַד (throughout the LXX, χρᾶσθαι frequently translates עֲשָׂה). Cf. τοὺς ἐργαζομένους || עֹבְדֵי in 19:9 and οἱ ἐργαζόμενοι || עֹבְדֵי in 30:24.

πικρῶς, or πικρία in LXX-Isaiah is מַר (5:20 [*bis*]; 22:4; 24:9; 33:7) so that one might suspect that מַר stood at this point in the LXX's *Vorlage*. However, we must note that just as in the final clause of v. 7 the translator clarified his metaphorical interpretation of the motif of drunkenness, so in the final two clauses of v. 21 he qualifies his statement that the Kyrios will make his deeds πικρίας ἔργον, asserting that his wrath behaves differently (ἀλλοτρίως) and is of a different sort (ἀλλοτρία).[128] The insinuation of this theme at the end of v. 21 shows the translator working within a conception of the entire verse, fashioning the clause ποιήσει τὰ ἔργα αὐτοῦ πικρίας ἔργον as the apodosis to ὥσπερ ὄρος ἀσεβῶν ἀναστήσεται καὶ ἔσται ἐν τῇ φάραγγι Γαβαων μετὰ θυμοῦ. Just as in v. 24 he rendered לזרע יפתח וישדד אדמתו with ἢ σπόρον προετοιμάσει πρὶν ἐργάσασθαι τὴν γῆν based on his understanding of its context, so here he chose πικρίας parallel to μετὰ θυμοῦ. He postponed rendering זָר in its location, translating it by ἀλλοτρίως slightly later (N.B. ἀλλοτρία || נכריה).[129]

Quite likely, then, in v. 28 the translator created οὐδὲ φωνὴ τῆς πικρίας μου καταπατήσει ὑμᾶς as the counterpart to οὐ γὰρ εἰς τὸν αἰῶνα ἐγὼ ὑμῖν ὀργισθήσομαι, based on his grasp of the context. Even as in 8:14 καὶ ἐὰν ἐπ' αὐτῷ πεποιθὼς ᾖς takes the place of a translation of והוא מערצכם, with the translator modeling that phrase on καὶ πεποιθὼς ἔσομαι ἐπ' αὐτῷ || וקויתי לו in 8:17,[130] so here τῆς πικρίας μου replaces a rendering of גלגל עגלתו ופרשיו by drawing on the motif of ἡ πικρία αὐτοῦ in v. 21. The translator's grasp of the context determined his rendering more than his knowledge of the individual lexemes.

As noted earlier, while in the MT v. 29 concludes the didactic unit begun in v. 23, in the LXX v. 29 forms an inclusio with v. 22 and must be considered together with it:

ועתה אל תתלוצצו	²²⁾καὶ ὑμεῖς μὴ εὐφρανθείητε
פן יחזקו מוסריכם	μηδὲ ἰσχυσάτωσαν ὑμῶν οἱ δεσμοί
כי כלה ונחרצה	διότι συντετελεσμένα καὶ συντετμημένα πράγματα
שמעתי מאת אדני יהוה צבאות	ἤκουσα παρὰ κυρίου σαβαωθ
על כל הארץ	ἃ ποιήσει ἐπὶ πᾶσαν τὴν γῆν
גם זאת מעם יהוה צבאות יצאה	²⁹⁾καὶ ταῦτα παρὰ κυρίου σαβαωθ ἐξῆλθε
הפליא עצה	τὰ τέρατα βουλεύσασθε
הגדיל תושיה	ὑψώσατε ματαίαν παράκλησιν

---

[128] This is the prelude to his use of the description of the farmer's handling of seed in vv. 24–28, which emphasizes the salutary purposes of the methods.

[129] He translates זָר by ἀλλότριος again in 1:7 (bis) and 43:12.

[130] See above, p. 244.

Both verses pose the challenge of identifying the addressees. V. 22 follows on the heels of the assertion that the Kyrios will make his deeds πικρίας ἔργον, while his wrath ἀλλοτρίως χρήσεται καὶ ἡ πικρία αὐτοῦ ἀλλοτρία. That assertion is embedded in an address (beginning with v. 19) that summons the hearers to adopt a confession acknowledging their helpless defeat. In that light, the prohibition of rejoicing (καὶ ὑμεῖς μὴ εὐφρανθείητε) makes sense as spoken to those who place confidence in falsehood.[131] The imprecation, "let not your bonds be strong" is clear enough as a locution,[132] but the referent of ὑμῶν οἱ δεσμοί seems impenetrable (are these bonds placed on others [if so, whom?] or bonds restraining them in some way?).

More significant for the frame vv. 22 and 29 give to vv. 23–28 is the reason propounded in prohibiting these actions: the speaker has heard what the Kyrios intends "to do on the earth." The translator's rendering of v. 22 provides a fitting transition to the instruction that follows about the Kyrios's practice in executing judgment (vv. 23–28). However, in fashioning this transition, the translator made some noteworthy lexical choices, such as συντετελεσμένα καὶ συντετμημένα πράγματα || כלה ונחרצה, a phrase that reprises equivalences used in 10:22, 23:

10:22	כליון חרוץ שוטף צדקה	λόγον γὰρ συντελῶν καὶ συντέμνων ἐν δικαιοσύνῃ
10:23	כי כלה ונחרצה אדני יהוה צבאות	ὅτι λόγον συντετμημένον ποιήσει ὁ θεός

Common to these verses is συντέμνειν || חרוץ/נחרצה, the latter of which we encountered in 28:27 (where it is rendered by [οὐ γὰρ] μετὰ

---

[131] The LXX's *Vorlage* evidently read ואתה for ועתה, as does 1QIsaᵃ. εὐφραίνειν occurs 31 times in Isaiah: 11 times corresponding to שׂמח/שׂמחה in the MT, 10 times רנן (including εὐφρανθήσῃ || ירנו in 28:26), 5 times שׂושׂ, and once גיל. ὑμᾶς εὐφραίνεσθαι translates השׁיר יהיה לכם in 30:29, while εὐφράνθητι ἔρημος renders ישׂאו מדבר (parallel to εὐφρανθήσονται οἱ κατοικοῦντες πέτραν || ירנו ישׁבי סלע) in 42:11. εὐφρανθήτω ὁ οὐρανὸς translates הרעיפו שׁמים in 45:8, probably due to unfamiliarity with the verb רעף, which appears only here in Isaiah. Ottley's suggestion that the LXX's *Vorlage* read תעלצו or תעלוז in 28:22 (*The Book of Isaiah*, 2:243) seems pedantic. On the one hand, תתלוצצו is attested by all textual witnesses (1QIsaᵃ = MT, ܠܐ ܬܬܪܫܥܘܢ, *nolite inludere*); on the other hand, the translator shows no more inclination to use εὐφραίνειν for עלז (καὶ οἱ λοιμοί || ועלז, 5:14; τοῦ ὑβρίζειν || לעלז, 23:12) than for ליץ (ὑπερήφανος || לץ, 29:20; καὶ οἱ ἄρχοντες αὐτῶν || ומליציך, 43:27). More important, given the translator's willingness to render his *Vorlage* with some freedom in this passage, there is a strong likelihood that his choice of εὐφρανθείητε was not determined by the word in his *Vorlage*. In this case, Fischer's suggestion that the translator read תתלוצצו as (Aramaic) תתלרועעו (*In welcher Schrift*, 45) is hardly necessary.

[132] The translator's path to his rendering is also clear: μηδὲ ἰσχυσάτωσαν ὑμῶν οἱ δεσμοί || פן יחזקו מוסריכם.

σκληρότητος) in the description of methods for threshing that serves as a ground of comparison for the Kyrios's execution of wrath.

Equally noteworthy is the similarity of συντετελεσμένα || כלה in 28:22 to λόγον…συντελῶν || כליון in 10:22, about which Fischer suggested that the translator read כליון as מליון.[133] However, we must also note that λόγον συντετμημένον || כלה ונחרצה in the next verse, 10:23, contains no apparent equivalent for כלה. Fischer suggested that, just as the translator (mis)read כליון as מליון in v. 22, so also he read כלה as מלה in v. 23.[134] Ziegler follows Fischer part way, suggesting, "bei 10,22 kann λόγον συντελῶν Doppelübers. von כליון sein" and adding that "שוטף ist vom Übers. übergangen worden."[135] Having already noted the translator's good rendition of שוטף within chapter 28 (σῦρον || שטפים, v. 2 [cf. 30:28]; καταιγὶς φερομένη || שוטף [שוט ק'] שיט, v. 15; καταιγίς || מים ישטפו, v. 17; καταιγὶς φερομένη || שוט שוטף),[136] it is likely that he would have understood שוטף, so that Ziegler's judgment seems justified.[137] However, Ziegler does not discuss the process that led to this, which must take its start in the fact that 10:22 and 23 have influenced each other, as is signaled by συντέμνων || שוטף in v. 22, an equivalence apparently chosen with an eye to συντετμημένον (|| נחרצה) in v. 23,[138] the latter being an equivalence we find again in 28:22 (καὶ συντετμημένα || ונחרצה).

Συντελεσθήσονται translates יכלו in 1:28, an equivalence found sixty-five times throughout the LXX (e.g., Gen 2:1, 2; Exod 5:13, 14).[139] While this confirms that συντελῶν translates כליון 10:22, it leaves the quandary of why כלה in v. 23 lacks a counterpart in Greek, unless Fischer is correct to perceive מלה behind λόγον.[140] In that case, however,

---

[133] Fischer, In welcher Schrift, 26–27. He insists that this is a misreading by the translator, not a variant in his Vorlage: "auch kaum von einem Tr., sondern vom Ü.r selbst herstammend" (ibid., 27). Cf. Ottley, The Book of Isaiah, 2:163.

[134] Fischer, In welcher Schrift, 26–27.

[135] Ziegler, Untersuchungen, 140.

[136] Cf. 43:2 (οὐ συγκλύσουσί σε || לא ישטפוך) and 66:12 (καὶ ὡς χειμάρρους ἐπικλύζων || וכנחל שוטף).

[137] It is also noteworthy (though coincidental) that the translator overrides שטף in 8:8 (καὶ ἀφελεῖ ἀπὸ τῆς Ιουδαίας ἄνθρωπον ὃς δυνήσεται κεφαλὴν ἆραι ἢ δυνατὸν συντελέσασθαί τι || וחלף ביהודה שטף ועבר עד צואר), on which, see above, p. 226.

[138] 1QIsaᵃ reads שוטף, while 4QpIsaᵃ (4Q161) reads ושוטף. שוטף is attested also by S (ܘܢܫܛܘܦ, 'and overwhelm'), V (inundabit), and probably T (ומידברן, 'and taken away').

[139] Elsewhere in Isaiah כלה is translated by κατεσθίειν (10:18), παύεσθαι (10:25; 24:13), ἐκλείπειν (15:6), ἀναλίσκειν (32:10), and διδόναι (εἰς οὐθὲν ἔδωκατὴν ἰσχύν μου || והבל כחי כליתי, 49:4).

[140] 1QIsaᵃ reads כי כלה ונחרצה, agreeing with the MT, while S's ܠܗܒܠ ܘܒܚܝ܂ܕܘܐ

there seems little advantage in attributing it to a "misreading" rather than a variant in the *Vorlage*, especially since graphic confusion between *kāph* and *mêm* in Paleo-Hebrew is well attested. If מלה is accepted as the reading of the LXX's *Vorlage*, then λόγον in v. 22 would simply be another evidence of mutual influence between vv. 22 and 23, similar to συντέμνων || שׁוטף in v. 22.

On the other hand, as Ziegler also suggests, λόγον in both verses may be the translator's own insertion, even as it is in 28:22.[141] In fact, the plus, πράγματα, in 28:22 finds a parallel in 25:1:

עשׂית פלא   ἐποίησας θαυμαστὰ πράγματα
עצות מרחוק אמונה   βουλὴν ἀρχαίαν ἀληθινήν

This parallel makes it likely that the translator has supplied πράγματα in both 25:1 and 28:22, leading Ziegler to wonder whether "es mag daher sein, daß 10,22f. ebenfalls λόγον Zusatz ist."[142] As he concludes, while "eine sichere Lösung ist nicht zu geben, jedenfalls gehören beide Stellen [10:22, 23 and 28:22] zusammen und haben aufeinander eingewirkt."[143] The crucial issue for 28:22 is the recognition that the συντετελεσμένα καὶ συντετμημένα πράγματα the speaker has heard are plans that will be executed.[144] In fact, the assertion that συντετελεσμένα καὶ συντετμημένα πράγματα are ἃ ποιήσει [sc. κύριος σαβαωθ] ἐπὶ πᾶσαν τὴν γῆν (|| על כל הארץ) parallels 10:23's assertion that its λόγον συντετμημένον ποιήσει ὁ θεὸς ἐν τῇ οἰκουμένῃ ὅλῃ (|| עשׂה בקרב כל הארץ), suggesting that mutual influence between these verses led to the insertion of ἃ ποιήσει in 28:22.

Corresponding to this introduction to the exposition of the Kyrios's aims in judgment is καὶ ταῦτα παρὰ κυρίου σαβαωθ ἐξῆλθεν || גם זאת מעם יהוה צבאות יצאה at the beginning of v. 29. The translation of זאת

___

בל ('because destruction and judgments the Lord has done'), T's ארי נמירא ושיצאה יוי צבאות עביד ('because a complete and finished thing the Lord of hosts is doing'), and V's *consummationem enim et adbreviationmen Dominus Deus exercituum faciet* ('for a completion and summation the Lord God of hosts will accomplish') point to the same text.

[141] Ziegler, *Untersuchungen*, 140. Cf. Ottley, *The Book of Isaiah*, 2:163.
[142] Ziegler, *Untersuchungen*, 140.
[143] Ibid.
[144] While it is true that συντέτμηται καὶ συντετέλεσται ἡ βασιλεία σου in Dan 5:27 depends on the phraseology in Isaiah (Seeligmann, *Septuagint Version*, 75), Ziegler's conclusion that "das Begriffspaar συντελεῖν—συντέμνειν bereits in der LXX einen apokalyptischen Sinn trägt" (*Untersuchungen*, 140) exceeds what can be inferred based on the terminology in these passages of LXX-Isaiah, where the phrase simply denotes events decreed for the earth.

by ταῦτα parallels πράγματα in v. 22, looking back on the events whose detailing v. 22 introduced.

On the other hand, the concluding commands, issued to groups (βουλεύσασθε ὑψώσατε ματαίαν παράκλησιν), while easy to align with the MT (הגדיל תושיה עצה), are difficult to comprehend in the context of chapter 28 and the question of their role must be left unresolved.

Summary

Even if a full treatment of each verse in this unit might identify additional nuances, the preceding analysis uncovers many of the interpretative devices exampled in isolated cases in chapters four through seven, such as: interpretations of graphically ambiguous letters that gave rise to double renderings; the resolution of conundrums by interpreting lexemes and syntax in the light of their context, even if that required substituting a phrase found elsewhere; looking beyond the immediate context for guidance from passages with similar words or motifs. We have also seen indications that his *Vorlage* at times contained variants vis-à-vis the MT. At other times, we have had to admit that the translator's path and his *Vorlage* are beyond recovery. We have not seen a reference to contemporary circumstances specific enough to support a claim that the translator pursued a program of *Erfüllungsinterpretation*.

CHAPTER NINE

CONCLUSIONS

On one level, the most significant conclusion of this study is that there is no basis to view the translator's work under the rubric of *Erfüllungs-interpretation*. The translation lacks any marked interest in eschatology, while evidence of "contemporization" in the translation—other than pedestrian matters like the use of toponyms common in the Hellenistic era or technical terms common in Ptolemaic Egypt—is virtually absent. Even the most striking case of contemporization—καὶ τοὺς Ἕλληνας || וּפלשׁתּים in 9:11(10)—is notable because it is atypical. In particular, examination of passages alleged to embody *Erfüllungsinterpretation* through covert references to Leontopolis, Antiochus IV, and Hellenistic re-forms in Jerusalem shows them unremarkable in this respect. Conse-quently, we must rely on other features to understand this translator's *Übersetzungsweise*.

The primary rubric under which to describe him is that of *transla-tor*. He regularly follows the word order of his *Vorlage*, while phrase- or sentence-structure that accords with literary Greek (e.g., genitives sepa-rated from the nouns they qualify) typically derives from the translator himself. And while he can use equivalents tailored to their context (e.g., his translation of עלל with four different words in 3:4–12) and even highly nuanced renderings (e.g., ἀπέστησαν || פחדו in 33:14), he also uses stock equivalents in a way tone-deaf to their context (e.g. καὶ παρωξύνθη τὰ ὄρη || וירגזו ההרים, 5:25).

On the other hand, the frequency of conjunctions and adverbs to nuance connections between clauses (ἀλλά, γάρ, νῦν, οὐδέ, οὔτε, τοιγαροῦν, and τοίνυν) is among the highest in the LXX and attests the translator's desire to convey the sense of the book as clearly as possible in Greek. If translation involves a continuum from precise reflection of the source language, on the one end, to concern for fluency and linguistic appropriateness in the target language, the translator stands closer to the latter end of the continuum than most other Septuagintal translators.

Equally attesting the translator's concern to convey what he considered the meaning of Isaiah's words are the times he interprets a word in

the light of one occurring later in the context (e.g., πρὶν ἢ γνῶναι
αὐτόν || לדעתו, 7:15, based on πρὶν ἢ γνῶναι || ידע בטרם in v. 16),
his supply of a phrase to complete the meaning he finds implied (e.g.,
ἀγαθὸν ἢ κακόν, 7:16), or his insertion of a word based on a parallel
expression in the nearby context (e.g., βοσκηθήσονται in 11:6, based
on βοσκηθήσονται in v. 7). Similarly, his reformulations of phrases and
sentences are meant to permit his reader to grasp the import of Isaiah's
words. Even if these can be justifiably considered interpretations of
the text's meaning, they are different from a lemmatized commentary
not only in form, but also in the transfer of meaning from Hebrew
into Greek. Even though every translation engages in such transfer
at the grammatical and semantic levels, the types of expansion and
reformulation found in LXX-Isaiah attest a translator concerned to bring
an *understanding* of Isaiah to his Greek readers, not simply a competent
representation of its sentences.

It was because of this concern that he apparently felt forced into
decisions that strike us as odd for a translator. In particular, this accounts
for his impulse to insinuate a negative particle in some passages or to
omit one in others when his perception of the meaning demanded it.
This is not a matter of the translator *changing* the meaning of the passage, as Orlinsky rightly argued,[1] but of him focusing on how well his
rendering into Greek represented what he saw as the import of the passage. Much like his expansions of phrases and insertions of words, the
insinuation of a negative appears to have been his way of conveying the
only meaning he considered permissible in the context. Such maneuvers
must be understood as ad hoc attempts to make sense of the text for
the reader, not evidence of a "method."

The same concern is evident in his choice of contextually appropriate
equivalents based on etymological interpretations that show familiarity
with morphological changes common in Hebrew (aphaeresis, syncopation, apocopation, etc.), although without an understanding of the
phonetic processes as we understand them. The frequent result is
that he associates Hebrew words with lexemes in a way that modern
grammar and lexicography would consider unschooled. The effects of
this on his translation would be wrongly cast as "manipulations" or an
"exegetical method." Rather, they are products of the translator using

---

[1] Orlinsky, "Studies in the Septuagint of the Book of Job, Chapter III," 252–53.

the state of knowledge of Hebrew of his time and place to provide a clear representation of the message of Isaiah in Greek.

We must also remember that the state of the manuscript at the translator's disposal played a role in his rendition of the book. Besides likely having to deal with places where the text was illegible, certain consonants were frequently open to more than one interpretation. Phenomena like *wāw/yôd* obscurities and the similarities between *dālet* and *rêš* opened options for meaning that were not always easy to adjudicate. Doubtless, *dālet/rêš* interchanges had often already occurred in the manuscript tradition, so that some such variants are attributable to the *Vorlage*. On yet other occasions, the translator seems to have been aware of two possible readings, as in 29:3, where he shows familiarity with both דור and דוד.

In that light, it is likely that some apparent variants are matters of the translator reading a consonant in the light of the word that best fit his understanding of the context, as in 33:14, where twice τίς ἀναγγελεῖ ὑμῖν is the counterpart to מי יגור לנו in the MT. Moreover, the translator's adjusting the pronoun of לנו in that verse in order to fit the context (ὑμῖν) suggests that he had strong inducement to convince himself that his *Vorlage* read יני because that word fit his understanding of the context. This is not evidence of manipulation, but of a concern to provide a representation of Isaiah that conveyed the sense that fit his reading of the context.

At other times his perplexity over lexemes led him to utilize stop-gap words to fill in for an unfamiliar word, selecting a word with a generalized meaning (e.g., ἡττᾶσθαι) that matched his sense of the context. At other times his willingness to plug in such words hints that he regarded the book to have recurrent themes that could be read into a context without explicit warrant from the Hebrew, without being untrue to the meaning of the book.

That intuition is confirmed more explicitly by his insinuation of themes he appears to have regarded as at the core of the book's message. Thus, his introduction of σώζειν, σωτήριον, and σωτηρία into passages that lack such terms in Hebrew, or his insertion of δοξάζειν and δόξα under similar circumstances, attest his perception that certain themes are so integral to the book that novelly weaving them into a context gives expression to what is essential in the book.

This mindset is even more evident in the translator's willingness to interpret words and phrases in light of the broader context, as well as to borrow locutions from elsewhere in the book or even from outside it. His willingness to, in effect, substitute words from another passage for those in the passage at hand attests his belief in a sort of legitimate intertextuality among the scriptures of his Jewish community. Much as Aristarchus could illuminate a difficult passage in Homer by appealing to the broader realm of myth, so the translator seems to have considered there to be a certain homogeneity to the literature revered in his circles.

More important to understanding the milieu in which such interpretative schemes make sense is the widespread belief in this era that interpretation was a divinely inspired activity. The very structure of the Museum as a religious institution, overseen by priests who inculcated religious life, is eloquent testimony to this on the Greek side. And we have equally strong evidence of this belief from Jewish Palestinian literature, inasmuch as a work like the Temple Scroll passes itself off as spoken entirely in the divine voice. Such a work can be penned only if the author regards himself inspired to present what amounts to an updated set of divine mandates.

Still more important, for this Alexandrian translator, is the tradition witnessed by *The Letter of Aristeas* about the origins of the LXX-Pentateuch in divine inspiration. Even if this motif is an element of the special role accorded the translation by Pseudo-Aristeas, the widespread evidence that literati of this period saw their work as divinely guided suggests that this motif was not especially constructed to praise this translation. In this milieu, the sorts of interpretative schemes we have seen this translator using are intelligible as means of disclosing, under the assumption of divine guidance, the "true" meaning of Isaiah.

Finally we must consider the question of how we situate this translator among the literati of the ancient world. While the primary comparison must be with the work of other translators, such as those who produced the LXX-Pentateuch, some of the exegetical tacks the Isaiah translator employs are comparable to methods used by others throughout the Mediterranean basin.

Most importantly, even though some devices (such as etymological reasoning) are attested long before the translator's era, and even though literati throughout the ancient world used these devices, we must consider it likely that he was directly influenced by the work of Aristarchus and other γραμματικοί in the Museum, since the evidence suggests that their work would have been familiar to any Alexandrian enamored of letters. Not only does this circumstance accord with the way the description of the translation of the Torah in the (roughly contemporaneous) *Letter of Aristeas* follows the model of collation of manuscripts in the Museum, but it also tallies with the esteem evident for the γραμματικοί in the lament of their disappearance in the LXX of Isaiah 33:18.[2]

The hypothesis that the translator was influenced by their work seems especially strong in the frequent instances when he rendered passages in the light of others in Isaiah and elsewhere in the Hebrew scriptures. Just as Aristarchus practiced interpretation of Homer by Homer, as well as interpreted him in light of the tropes of mythology in general, so the Isaiah translator found a sure guide to meaning by looking to other passages inside and outside Isaiah that contained similar words, phrases, or themes. Of course, we can compare this reflex to the Rewritten Scriptures genre (found in Jewish literature from Palestine), which frequently recasts a passage in the light of a similar one elsewhere. And harmonizations of one passage with another are rife within manuscripts of both the Hebrew Bible and early Christian literature. However, when looking for the most likely influences on the translator of Isaiah, we must consider first parallels within his Alexandrian milieu.

In adducing these parallels I do not assert that the translator was a γραμματικός, any more than that he saw himself fitting the mold of a סוֹפֵר. He was, above all, a translator, which means that he was intent on rendering his Hebrew *Vorlage* into Greek. While the evidence shows that his divergences from his *Vorlage* were not limited to passages where he faced *aporiai*, claims that he liberally injected his own ideas misrepresent his work. He was concerned to convey the sense of Isaiah to his readers, even if that sense was derived from within a larger notion of literary context than is permitted a modern translator.

His perplexities and ad hoc solutions sometimes created renderings that have suggested to some an exegetical method. In the end, however, he seems to have employed no method, but used whatever devices were at his disposal to deliver a translation that would make the book's sprawling networks of meaning intelligible to his Greek-reading coreligionists.

If we adopt this image in answer to the question of who the translator was, we will improve our chances of understanding what he produced.

---

[2] See above, pp. 20–24.

WORKS CITED

Aejmelaeus, Anneli. "Translation Technique and the Intention of the Translator." In *VII Congress of the International Organization for Septuagint and Cognate Studies*. 23–36. Atlanta: Scholars Press, 1991.

———. "Von Sprache zur Theologie." In *The Septuagint and Messianism*, edited by Michael A. Knibb. 21–48. Leuven, Paris, Dudley, MA: Uitgeverij Peeters, 2006.

———. "What Can We Know about the Hebrew *Vorlage* of the Septuagint?" *ZAW* 99 (1987) 58–89.

Attridge, Harold W. "Historiography." In *Jewish Writings of the Second Temple Period*, edited by Michael E. Stone. Minneapolis: Fortress, 1984.

Barr, James. "Common Sense and Biblical Language." *Bib* 49 (1968) 377–87.

———. *Comparative Philology and the Text of the Old Testament*. Oxford: Clarendon Press, 1968.

———. "'Guessing' in the Septuagint." In *Studien zur Septuaginta*, edited by Detlef Fraenkel, Udo Quast and John W. Wevers. 19–34. Göttingen: Vandenhoeck & Ruprecht, 1990.

———. *The Semantics of Biblical Language*. Oxford: Oxford University Press, 1961.

———. *The Typology of Literalism in Ancient Biblical Translations*, Mitteilungen des Septuaginta-Unternehmens 15. Göttingen: Vandenhoeck and Ruprecht, 1979.

———. "Vocalization and the Analysis of Hebrew among the Ancient Translators." In *Hebräische Wortforschung*, edited by James Barr. 1–11. Leiden: Brill, 1967.

Baumgärtel, Friedrich. "Die Septuaginta zu Jesaja das Werk zweier Übersetzer." In *Beiträge zur Entstehungsgeschichte der Septuaginta*, edited by Johannes Hermann and Friedrich Baumgärtel. 20–31. Berlin: W. Kohlhammer, 1923.

Beek, Martinus A. "Relations entre Jérusalem et la diaspora Égyptienne au 2ᵉ siècle avant J.-C." In *OtSt*, edited by P. A. H. de Boer, vol. 2. Leiden: Brill, 1943.

Beentjes, P. C. "Scripture and Scribe: Ben Sira 38:34c–39:11." In *Unless Some One Guide Me*, edited by J. W. Dyk. Maastricht: Shaker, 2001.

Bickerman, Elias. "Some Notes on the Transmission of the Septuagint." In *Studies in Jewish and Christian History*, part 1, edited by Elias Bickerman. 137–66. Leiden: Brill, 1976.

———. "The Septuagint as a Translation." In *Studies in Jewish and Christian History*, part 1, edited by Elias Bickerman. 167–200. Leiden: Brill, 1976.

———. "Zur Datierung des Pseudo-Aristeas." In *Studies in Jewish and Christian History*, part 1, edited by Elias Bickerman. 109–36. Leiden: Brill, 1976.

Black, Jeremy A., and W. J. Tait. "Archives and Libraries in the Ancient Near East." In *Civilizations of the Ancient Near East*, vol. 4, edited by Jack M. Sasson. 2197–209. New York: Scribner, 1995.

Boyd-Taylor, Cameron. "In a Mirror Dimly—Reading the Septuagint as a Document of Its Times." In *Septuagint Research: Issues and Challenges in the Study of the Greek Jewish Scriptures*, edited by Wolfgang Kraus and R. Glenn Wooden. 15–31. Atlanta: Scholars Press, 2006.

Brock, Sebastian. "Aspects of Translation Technique in Antiquity." *GRBS* 20 (1979) 69–87.

———. "The Phenomenon of the Septuagint." In *Witness of Tradition: Papers Read at the Joint British-Dutch Old Testament Conference, Woudschoten, Netherlands, 1970*, edited by Martinus A. Beek. 11–36. Leiden: Brill, 1972.

———. "To Revise or not to Revise: Attitudes to Jewish Biblical Translation." In *Septuagint, Scrolls and Cognate Writings*, edited by George J. Brook and Barnabas Lindars. Atlanta: Scholars Press, 1992.

Brockington, L. H. "The Greek Translator and His Interest in ΔΟΞΑ." *VT* 1 (1951) 23–32.

Budd, Phillip J. *Numbers*, Word Biblical Commentary 5. Waco: Word Books, 1984.

Buchanan, George Wesley. "Eschatology and the 'End of Days'." *JNES* 20 (1961) 188–93.

Cameron, Alan. *Callimachus and His Critics*. Princeton: Princeton University Press, 1995.

Carmignac, Jean. "La notion d'eschatolgie dans la Bible et a Qumrân." *RevQ* 7 (1967) 17–31.

Carr, David M. *Writing on the Tablet of the Heart*. New York: Oxford University Press, 2005.

Cicero. *De Inventione, De Optimo Genere Oratorum, Topica*. Translated by H. M. Hubbell, Loeb Classical Library. Cambridge: Harvard University Press, 1949.

Collins, Adela Yarbro. "Aristobulus." In *The Old Testament Pseudepigrapha*, edited by James H. Charlesworth, vol. 2. New York: Doubleday, 1985.

Collins, John J. "Apocalyptic Eschatology as the Transcendence of Death." *CBQ* 36 (1974) 21–43.

———. *Between Athens and Jerusalem*. Edited by Astrid B. Beck and David N. Freedman. Second ed. The Biblical Resource Series. Grand Rapids: Wm. B. Eerdmans, 2000.

———. "Eschatology." In *Encyclopedia of the Dead Sea Scrolls*, edited by Lawrence H. Schiffman and James C. VanderKam, vol. 1. Oxford and New York: Oxford University Press, 2000.

Coste, J. "La première expérience de traduction biblique: la Septante." *Maison Dieu* 14 (1958) 56–88.

———. "Le texte Grec d'Isaie xxv:1–5." *RB* 61 (1954) 36–66.

Cusset, Christophe. *La Muse dans la Bibliothèque: Réécriture et intertextualité dans la poésie alexandrine*. CNRS Littérature. Paris: CNRS Éditions, 1999.

das Neves, J. C. M. *A Teologia da Tradução Grega dos Setenta no Livro de Isaías*. Lisbon: Universidade Católica Portuguesa, 1973.

Davies, J. K. "Cultural, Social and Economic Features of the Hellenistic World." In *The Hellenistic World*, edited by F. W. Walbank, A. E. Astin, M. W. Frederiksen and R. M. Ogilvie. Cambridge: Cambridge University Press, 1984.

Davies, W. D., and Dale C. Allison. *The Gospel According to St. Matthew*, vol. 3. International Critical Commentary. Edinburgh: T & T Clark, 1997.

Dines, Jennifer M. *The Septuagint*. Understanding the Bible and its World. London and New York: T & T Clark, 2004.

Dorival, Gilles. *La Bible d'Alexandria: Les Nombers*, Bible d'Alexandrie 4. Paris: Cerf, 1994.

———. "Les phénomènes d'intertextualité dans le livre Grec des Nombres." In *KATA TOUS O'/Selon les Septante*, edited by Gilles Dorival and Olivier Munnich. Paris: Cerf, 1995.

Fischer, Johann. *In welcher Schrift lag das Buch Isaias den LXX vor?* Giessen: Alfred Töpelmann, 1930.

Fishbane, Michael. *Biblical Interpretation in Ancient Israel*. Oxford: Clarendon Press, 1985.

Flint, Peter W. "The Septuagint Version of Isaiah 23:1–14 and the Massoretic Text." *BIOSCS* 21 (1988) 35–54.

Forster, A. Haire. "The Meaning of Δόξα in the Greek Bible." *ATR* 12 (1929/30) 311–16.

Frankel, Zacharias. *Ueber den Einfluss der palästinischen Exegese auf die alexandrinische Hermeneutik*. Leipzig: J. A. Barth, 1831. Reprint, Gregg International Publishers Ltd., 1972.

Fraser, P. M. *Ptolemaic Alexandria*. 3 vols. Oxford: The Clarendon Press, 1972.

Fritsch, Charles T. "The Concept of God in the Greek Translation of Isaiah." In *Biblical Studies in Memory of H. C. Alleman*, edited by O. Reimherr, Jacob M. Myers, and H. N. Bream. Locust Valley, NY: J. J. Augustin, 1960.

Gauger, Jörg-Dieter. "Der 'Tod des Verfolgers': Überlegungen zur historizität eines Topos." *JSJ* 33 (2002) 42–64.

Goldstein, Jonathan A. *II Maccabees*, AB 41A. New York: Doubleday, 1983.

Gray, George Buchanan. *A Critical and Exegetical Commentary on the Book of Isaiah I–XXVII*, ICC. Edinburgh: T&T Clark, 1912.

———. *Numbers*, ICC. Edinburgh: T & T Clark, 1903.

———. "The Greek Version of Isaiah, Is It the Work of a Single Translator?" *JTS* 12 (1911) 286–93.

Hadas, Moses. *Aristeas to Philocrates*, Dropsie College Edition. New York: KTAV, 1973.

Hanhart, Robert. "Die Septuaginta als Interpretation und Aktualisierung." In *The Bible and the Ancient World: Isaac Leo Seeligmann Volume*, edited by Alexander Rofé and Yair Zakovitch, vol. 3, non-Hebrew Section. 331–46. Jerusalem: E. Rubinstein's Publishing, 1983.

———. "The Translation of the Septuagint in Light of Earlier Tradition and Subsequent Influences." In *Septuagint, Scrolls and Cognate Writings*, edited by George J. Brooke and Barnabas Lindars. 339–79. Atlanta: Scholars Press, 1992.

Hanhart, Robert, and Hermann Spieckermann, eds. *The Septuagint Version of Isaiah and Cognate Studies*, Forschungen zum alten Testament 40. Tübingen: Mohr Siebeck, 2004.

Hengel, Martin. *Judaism and Hellenism*. Translated by John Bowden. 2 vols. Philadelphia: Fortress Press, 1974.

Honigman, Sylvie. *The Septuagint and Homeric Scholarship in Alexandria*. London and New York: Routledge, 2003.

Howard, George. "The Letter of Aristeas and Diaspora Judaism." *JTS* 22 (1971) 337–48.

Hurwitz, Marshall S. "The Septuagint of Isaiah 36–39 in Relation to that of 1–35, 40–66." *HUCA* 28 (1957) 75–83.

Janowitz, Naomi. "The Rhetoric of Translation: Three Early Perspectives on Translating Torah." *HTR* 84 (1991) 129–40.

Jastrow, Marcus. *Seper Millim*. 2 vols. New York: Judaica Press, 1971.

Kleinknecht, Hermann. "πνεῦμα, πνευματικός." Translated by Geoffrey Bromiley, W. In *Theological Dictionary of the New Testament*, vol. 6, edited by Gerhard Friedrich and Geoffrey W. Bromiley. Grand Rapids: Wm. B. Eerdmans, 1968.

Koehler, Ludwig, Walter Baumgartner, and Johann Jakob Stamm. *The Hebrew and Aramaic Lexicon of the Old Testament*. 5 vols. Leiden: Brill, 1994–2000.

Koenig, Jean. *L' Herméneutique analogique du Judaïsme antique*, VTSup 33. Leiden: Brill, 1982.

Kosmala, Hans. "At the End of the Days." *ASTI* 2 (1963) 27–37.

Kutscher E. Y. *The Language and Linguistic Background of the Isaiah Scroll (IQIsaᵃ)*. Leiden: Brill, 1974.

Liebmann, Ernst. "Der Text zu Jesaja 24–27." *ZAW* 22 (1902) 1–56.

Liesen, Jan. *Full of Praise: An Exegetical Study of Sir 3,12–35*. JSJSup 64. Leiden: Brill, 2000.

Lindblom, J. "Gibt es eine Eschatologie bei den alttestmentlichen Propheten?" *ST* 6 (1953) 79–114.

Lloyd, G. E. R. "Hellenistic Science." In *The Hellenistic World*, edited by F. W. Walbank, A. E. Astin, M. W. Frederiksen and R. M. Ogilvie. Cambridge: Cambridge University Press, 1984.

Long, Anthony A. *Hellenistic Philosophy*. Berkeley and Los Angeles: University of California Press, 1986.

Lust, Johan. "Messianism in the Septuagint: Isaiah 8:23b–9:6 (9:1–7)." In *The Interpretation of the Bible*, edited by Jože Krašovec. Sheffield: Sheffield University Press, 1998.

———. "The Demonic Character of Jahweh and the Septuagint of Isaiah." *Bijdragen* 40 (1979) 2–14.

Luz, Ulrich. *Matthew 21–28*. Translated by James E. Crouch. Hermeneia. Minneapolis: Fortress Press, 2005.

Meecham, Henry G. *The Letter of Aristeas*. Manchester: Manchester University Press, 1935.

Meijering, Roos. *Literary and Rhetorical Theories in Greek Scholia*. Groningen: Egbert Forsten, 1987.

Mélèz-Modrzejewski, Joseph. "Law and Justice in Ptolemaic Egypt." In *Legal Documents of the Hellenistic World*, edited by Markham J. Geller and Herwig Maehler. London: The Warburg Institute, University of London, 1995.

———. "Le règle de droit dans l'Égypte ptolémaïque. État des questions et perspective de recherches." In *Essays in Honor of C. Bradford Welles*. 125–73. New Haven: American Society of Papyrologists, 1966.

Monsengwo-Pasinya, Laurent. "Isaïe 19:16–25 et universalisme dans la LXX." In *Congress Volume, Salamanca*. 192–207. Leiden: Brill, 1985.

Moulton, James H., and George Milligan. *The Vocabulary of the Greek Testament Illustrated from the Papyri and other Non-Literary Sources*. Grand Rapids: Eerdmans, 1930.

Muraoka, Takamitsu. *A Greek-English Lexicon of the Septuagint*. Louvain: Peeters, 2002.

Murray, Oswyn. "Aristeas and His Sources." *StPatr* 12 (1975) 123–28.

O'Hara, James J. *True Names: Vergil and the Alexandrian Tradition of Etymological Wordplay*. Ann Arbor: University of Michigan Press, 1996.

Olley, John W. *'Righteousness' in the Septuagint of Isaiah*, Septuagint and Cognate Studies, 8. Missoula: Scholars, 1979.

Orlinsky, Harry M. "The Septuagint as Holy Writ and the Philosophy of the Translators." *HUCA* 46 (1975) 89–114.

———. "Studies in the Septuagint of the Book of Job, Chapter II." *HUCA* 29 (1958) 229–71.

———. "Studies in the Septuagint of the Book of Job, Chapter III (Continued)." *HUCA* 32 (1961) 239–67.

———. "The Treatment of Anthropomorphisms and Anthropopathisms in the Septuagint of Isaiah." *HUCA* 27 (1956) 193–200.

Orton, David E. *The Understanding Scribe: Matthew and the Apocalyptic Ideal*. London and New York: T&T Clark, 1989.

Ottley, Richard R. *The Book of Isaiah According to the Septuagint*. 2 vols. Cambridge: Cambridge University, 1904–06.

Payne-Smith, J. *A Compendious Syriac Dictionary*. Oxford: Clarendon Press, 1903.

Pelletier, André. "Josephus, the Letter of Aristeas, and the Septuagint." In *Josephus, the Bible, and History*, edited by Louis Feldman and Gohei Hata. Detroit: Wayne State University Press, 1989.

Peters, F. E. *The Harvest of Hellenism*. New York: Barnes and Noble Books, 1970.

Pfeiffer, Rudolf. *History of Classical Scholarship from the Beginnings to the End of the Hellenistic Age*. Oxford: The Clarendon Press, 1968.

Pietersma, Albert. "A New Paradigm for Addressing Old Questions: The Relevance of the Interlinear Model for the Study of the Septuagint." In *Bible and Computer: The Stellenbosch AIBI–6 Conference*, edited by Johan Cook. Leiden: Brill, 2002.

———. "Exegesis in the Septuagint: Possibilities and Limits." In *Septuagint Research: Issues and Challenges in the Study of the Greek Jewish Scriptures*, edited by Wolfgang Kraus and R. Glenn Wooden. 33–45. Atlanta: Scholars Press, 2006.

Pietersma, Albert, and Benjamin G. Wright III. "To the Reader of NETS." In *The Psalms*. Oxford: Oxford University Press, 2000.

Porter, James I. "Hermeneutic Lines and Circles: Aristarchus and Crates on the Exegesis of Homer." In *Homer's Ancient Readers: The Hermeneutics of Greek Epics Earliest Exegetes*, edited by Robert Lamberton and John J. Keaney. 67–114. Princeton: Princeton University Press, 1992.

Rabin, Chaim. "The Translation Process and the Character of the Septuagint." *Textus* 6 (1968) 1–26.

Rad, Gerhard von. *Old Testament Theology*. Translated by D. M. G. Stalker. 2 vols. New York: Harper, 1962–1965.

Raitt, Thomas M. *A Theology of Exile*. Philadelphia: Fortress Press, 1977.

Raurell, Frederic. "«Archontes» en la interpretació midràshica d'Is-LXX." *RevCT* 1 (1976) 315–74.

———. "La «Doxa» com a Participació en la Vida Escatológica." *RevCT* 7 (1982) 57–89.

Redpath, Henry. "The Geography of the Septuagint." *AJT* 7 (1903) 289–307.

Rife, J. Merle. "The Mechanics of Translation Greek." *JBL* 52 (1933) 244–52.

Saldarini, Anthony J. *Matthew's Christian-Jewish Community*. Chicago Studies in the History of Judaism. Chicago: University of Chicago Press, 1994.

Scholz, Anton. *Die alexandrinische Übersetzung des Buches Jesaias*. Würzburg: L. Woerl, 1880.

Schürer, Emil. *The History of the Jewish People in the Age of Jesus Christ*. Edited by Geza Vermes, Fergus Millar and Martin Goodman. Vol. III, part 1. Edinburgh: T&T Clark, 1986.

Seebass, Horst. "אַחֲרִית." Translated by John T. Willis. In *Theological Dictionary of the Old Testament*, vol. 1, edited by G. Johannes Botterweck and Helmer Ringgren. Grand Rapids: Wm. B. Eerdmans, 1974.

Seeligmann, I. L. *The Septuagint Version of Isaiah*. Leuven: Brill, 1948.

———. "Problems and Perspectives in Modern Septuagint Research." Translated by Judith H. Seeligmann. *Textus* 15 (1990) 169–232.

———. "Voraussetzungen der Midraschexegese." In *Congress Volume, Copenhagen*. Leiden: Brill, 1953.

Shutt, R. J. H. "Letter of Aristeas." In *The Old Testament Pseudepigrapha*, edited by James H. Charlesworth, vol. 2. New York: Doubleday, 1985.

Simons, Jan J. *The Geographical and Topographical Texts of the Old Testament*. Leiden: Brill, 1959.

Smith, Jonathan Z. *Drudgery Divine: On the Comparison of Early Christianities and the Religions of Late Antiquity*. Chicago Studies in the History of Judaism. Chicago: University of Chicago Press, 1990.

Smyth, Herbert W. *Greek Grammar*. Cambridge: Harvard University, 1956.

Stendahl, Krister. *The School of St. Matthew*. 2nd ed. Philadelphia: Fortress Press, 1968. Reprint, Sigler Press, 1991.

Steudel, Annette. "אחרית הימים in the Texts from Qumran." *RevQ* 16 (1993) 225–46.

Swete, Henry B. *An Introduction to the Old Testament in Greek*. New York: KTAV Publishing House, 1968. Reprint, 1902 edition.

Talmon, Shemaryahu. "Aspects of the Textual Transmission of the Bible in the Light of Qumran Manuscripts." *Textus* 4 (1964) 95–132.

———. *The 'Dead Sea Scrolls' or 'The Community of the Renewed Covenant'*, The Albert T. Bilgray Lecture. Tuscon: University of Arizona, 1993.

Talshir, Zipora. "Double Translations in the Septuagint." In *Sixth Congress of the International Organization for Septuagint and Cognate Studies, Jerusalem, 1986*, edited by Claude E. Cox. 21–63. Atlanta: Scholars Press, 1987.

Tcherikover, Victor. *Hellenistic Civilization and the Jews*. Translated by S. Applebaum. Philadelphia: Jewish Publication Society of America, 1959.

———. "The Ideology of the Letter of Aristeas." *HTR* 51, no. 2 (1958) 59–86.

Thackeray, H. St. John. "The Translators of the Prophetical Book." *JTS* 4 (1903) 578–85.

Toury, Gideon. *Descriptive Translation Studies and Beyond*, Benjamins Translation Library 4. Amsterdam: John Benjamins, 1995.

Tov, Emanuel. "Compound Words in the LXX Representing Two or More Hebrew Words." *Bib* 58 (1977) 189–212.

———. "Did the Septuagint Translators Always Understand their Hebrew Text?" In *De Septuaginta*, edited by Albert Pietersma and Claude E. Cox. 53–70. Mississauga, Ontario, Canada: Benben Publications, 1984.

———. "Die Septuaginta in ihrem theologischen und traditionsgeschichtlichen

Verhältnis zur hebräischen Bibel." In *Mitte der Schrift? Ein jüdisch-christliches Gespräch*, edited by Martin Klopfenstein, Ulrich Luz, Shemaryahu Talmon and Emanuel Tov. 237–68. Bern: Peter Lang, 1987.

———. "The Impact of the LXX Translation of the Pentateuch on the Translation of the Other Books." In *Mélanges Dominique Barthélemy: Études bibliques offertes à l'occasion de son 60e anniversaire*, edited by Pierre Casetti, Othmar Keel and Adrian Schenker. 578–92. Göttingen: Vandenhoeck & Ruprecht, 1981.

———. "The Nature and Study of the Translation Technique of the LXX in the Past and Present." In *VI Congress of the International Organization for Septuagint and Cognate Studies*, edited by Claude E. Cox. 337–59. Atlanta: Scholars Press, 1987.

———. *The Text-Critical Use of the Septuagint in Biblical Research*. Second ed., Jerusalem Biblical Studies 8. Jerusalem: Simor Ltd., 1997.

———. "Theologically Motivated Exegesis Embedded in the Septuagint." In *Translation of Scripture: Proceedings of a Conference at the Annenberg Research Institute, May 15–16, 1989*. 215–33. Philadelphia: Annenberg Research Institute, 1990.

Troxel, Ronald. "Economic Plunder as a Leitmotif in LXX-Isaiah." *Bib* 83 (2002) 375–91.

———. "Ἔσχατος and Eschatology in LXX-Isa." *BIOSCS* 25 (1992) 18–27.

———. "Isaiah 7,14–16 through the Eyes of the Septuagint." *ETL* 79 (2003) 1–22.

———. "What's in a Name? Contemporization and the Rendering of Toponyms in LXX-Isa." In *Seeking Out the Wisdom of the Ancients*, edited by Ronald L Troxel, Kelvin Friebel and Dennis Magary. 327–44. Winona Lake: Eisenbrauns, 2005.

Turner, E. G. "Ptolemaic Egypt." In *The Hellenistic World*, edited by F. W. Walbank, A. E. Astin, M. W. Frederiksen and R. M. Ogilvie. Cambridge: Cambridge University Press, 1984.

Turner, Nigel. *A Grammar of New Testament Greek: Vol. III, Syntax*. Edinburgh: T & T Clark, 1963.

Ulrich, Eugene. "The Absence of 'Sectarian Variants' in the Jewish Scriptural Scrolls Found at Qumran." In *The Bible as Book: The Hebrew Bible and the Judaean Desert Discoveries*, edited by Edward D. Herbert and Emanuel Tov. 179–95. London: The British Library and Oak Knoll Press, 2002.

———. "The Developmental Composition of the Book of Isaiah: Light from 1QIsaᵃ on Additions in the MT." *DSD* 8 (2001) 288–305.

Ulrich, Eugene, Frank M. Cross, Russell E. Fuller, Judith E. Sanderson, Patrick W. Skehan, and Emanuel Tov, eds. *Qumran Cave 4 X: The Prophets*. DJD XV. Oxford: Clarendon Press, 1997.

Unnik, W. C. van. "Der Ausdruck ἙΩΣ ἘΣΧΑΤΟΥ ΤΗΣ ΓΗΣ (Apostelgeschichte 1:8) und sein alttestamentlicher Hintergrund." In *Studia Biblical et Semitica*, edited by W. C. van Unnik and A. S. van der Woude. Wageningen, the Netherlands: H. Veenman en Zonen N. V., 1966.

Vaccari, A. "ΠΟΛΙΣ ΑΣΕΔΕΚ Is. 19, 18." *Bib* 2 (1921) 353–56.

van der Kooij, Arie. "A Short Commentary on Some Verses of the Old Greek of Isaiah 23." *BIOSCS* 15 (1982) 36–50.

———. "Accident or Method? On 'Analogical' Interpretation in the Old Greek of Isa and in 1QIsaᵃ." Review of *L'Herméneutique Analogique du Judaïsme Antique. BO* 43 (1986) 366–76.

———. "'Coming' Things and 'Last' Things: Isaianic Terminology as Understood in the Wisdom of Ben Sira and in the Septuagint of Isaiah." In *The New Things: Eschatology in Old Testament Prophecy, Festschrift for Henk Leene*, edited by Ferenc Postma, Klaas Spronk and Eep Talstra. 135–40. Maastricht: Uitgeverij Shaker Pub, 2002.

———. *Die alten Textzeugen des Jesajabuches*. Orbis Biblicus et Orientalis 35. Göttingen: Vandenhoeck und Ruprecht, 1981.

———. "Die Septuaginta Jesajas als Dokument Jüdischer Exegese." In *Übersetzung und Deutung: Fs. Alexander Hulst*, edited by Dominique Barthélemy. Nijkerk: Uitgeverij G. F. Callenback, 1977.

———. "Interpretation of the Book of Isaiah in the Septuagint and Other Ancient Versions." In *SBLSP* 40. 220–39. Atlanta: Scholars Press, 2001.

———. "Isaiah in the Septuagint." In *Writing and Reading the Scroll of Isaiah*, vol. 2. 513–29. Leiden: Brill, 1997.

———. "Perspectives on the Study of the Septuagint: Who are the Translators?" In *Perspectives in the Study of the Old Testament and Early Judaism*, edited by Florentino García Martínez and Edward Noort. 214–29. Leiden: Brill, 1998.

———. "The City of Alexandria and the Ancient Versions of the Hebrew Bible." *JNSL* 25 (1999) 137–49.

———. "The Old Greek of Isaiah in Relation to the Qumran Texts of Isaiah: Some General Comments." In *Septuagint, Scrolls and Cognate Writings*, edited by George J. Brook and Barnabas Lindars. 195–213. Atlanta: Scholars Press, 1992.

———. *The Oracle of Tyre: The Septuagint of Isaiah 23 as Version and Vision*. Leiden: Brill, 1998.

———. "The Septuagint of Isaiah: Translation and Interpretation." In *Book of Isaiah— Le livre d'Isaie*. 127–33. Louvain: Leuven, 1989.

———. "Zur Theologie des Jesajabuches in der Septuaginta." In *Theologische Probleme der Septuaginta und der hellenistischen Hermeneutik*, edited by Henning Graf Reventlow. 9–25. Gütersloh: Christian Kaiser, 1997.

van der Ploeg, J. P. M. "Eschatology in the Old Testament." *OtSt* 17 (1972) 89–99.

Vermes, Geza. "Bible and Midrash. Early O.T. Exegesis." In *Cambridge History of the Bible*, edited by S. L. Greenslade, vol. 3. Cambridge: Cambridge University Press, 1970.

Waard, Jan de. "'Homophony' in the Septuagint." *Bib* 62 (1981) 551–61.

Wagner, J. Ross. "Identifying 'Updated' Prophecies in OG Isaiah: Isaiah 8:11–16 as a Test Case." *JBL* 126 (2007) 251–69.

Wasserstein, Abraham, and David J. Wasserstein. *The Legend of the Septuagint: From Classical Antiquity to Today*. Cambridge: Cambridge University Press, 2006.

Weissert, David. "Alexandrinian Analogical Word-Analysis and Septuagint Translation Techniques." *Textus* 8 (1973) 31–44.

Weitzman, Michael. *The Syriac Version of the Old Testament*. Cambridge, New York, Melbourne: Cambridge, 1999.

West, Stephanie. "The Greek Version of the Legend of Tefnut." *JEA* 55 (1969) 161–83.

Wevers, John W. "Aram and Aramaean in the Septuagint." In *The World of the Aramaeans I*, edited by P. M. Michèle Daviau, John Wevers, Michael Weigl, vol. 1. 237–51. Sheffield: Sheffield, 2001.

———. *Notes on the Greek Text of Deuteronomy*. Atlanta: Scholars Press, 1995.

———. *Notes on the Greek Text of Numbers*. Atlanta: Scholars Press, 1998.

———. "The Interpretative Character and Significance of the Septuagint Version." In *Hebrew Bible, Old Testament: The History of its Interpretation*, edited by Magne Sæbø. 84–107. Göttingen: Vandenhoeck & Ruprecht, 1996.

Wildberger, Hans. *Isaiah 28–39*. Translated by Thomas H. Trapp, Continental Commentary. Minneapolis: Fortress Press, 2002.

Williams, James M. "The Peripatetic School and Demetrius of Phalerum's Reforms in Athens." *AncW* 15 (1987) 87–97.

Wolff, Hans Walter. *Hosea*. Translated by Gary Stansell. Hermeneia. Philadelphia: Fortress, 1974.

Wright III, Benjamin G. "Access to the Source: Cicero, Ben Sira, the Septuagint and their Audiences." *JSJ* 34 (2003) 1–27.

———. "Translation as Scripture: The Septuagint in Aristeas and Philo." In *Septuagint Research: Issues and Challenges in the Study of the Greek Jewish Scriptures*, edited by Wolfgang Kraus and R. Glenn Wooden. Atlanta: Scholars Press, 2006.

———. "Why a Prologue? Ben Sira's Grandson and His Greek Translation." In *Emanuel: Studies in Hebrew Bible, Septuagint, and Dead Sea Scrolls in Honor of Emanuel Tov*, edited by Shalom M. Paul, Robert A. Kraft, Lawrence H. Schiffman and Weston W. Fields. Leiden: Brill, 2003.

Wutz, Franz. *Die Transkriptionen von der Septuaginta bis zu Hieronymus.* Texte und Untersuchungen zur vormasoretischen Grammatik des Hebräischen. Stuttgart: W. Kohlhammer, 1927.

Ziegler, Joseph. *Isaias.* Göttingen: Vandenhoeck and Ruprecht, 1983.

———. *Untersuchungen zur Septuaginta des Buches Isaias.* Münster: Aschendorffschen Verlagsbuchhandlung, 1934.

Zillessen, Alfred. "Bermerkungen zur alexandrinischen Übersetzung des Jesaja (c. 40–66)." *ZAW* 22 (1902) 238–63.

Zimmerli, Walther. *Ezekiel: A Commentary on the Book of the Prophet Ezekiel,* vol. 1. Translated by Ronald E. Clements. Hermeneia. Philadelphia: Fortress Press, 1979.

Zuntz, G. "Aristeas Studies II: Aristeas on the Translation of the Torah." In *Studies in the Septuagint: Origins, Recensions, and Interpretations,* edited by Sidney Jellicoe. New York: KTAV Publishing House, 1974.

INDEX OF REFERENCES*

HEBREW BIBLE

* (treatments of verses that span multiple pages are marked by a hyphen)

INDEX OF AUTHORS

SUBJECT INDEX